To Oliver,
This is also the story of Isabel, 'a grand wee wife', I hope you like it. Best Wishes,
August 2008 Barbara

A Remarkable Man

LETTERS FROM A DOCTOR/MISSIONARY IN THE SOUTH SEAS TO HIS MOTHER

C1

Barbara Mayne

TRAFFORD
USA • Canada • UK • Ireland

Note for Librarians: A cataloguing record for this book is available from Library and Archives Canada at www.collectionscanada.ca/amicus/index-e.html
ISBN 1-4120-9976-5

Printed in Victoria, BC, Canada. Printed on paper with minimum 30% recycled fibre.
Trafford's print shop runs on "green energy" from solar, wind and other environmentally-friendly power sources.

Offices in Canada, USA, Ireland and UK

Book sales for North America and international:
Trafford Publishing, 6E–2333 Government St.,
Victoria, BC V8T 4P4 CANADA
phone 250 383 6864 (toll-free 1 888 232 4444)
fax 250 383 6804; email to orders@trafford.com
Book sales in Europe:
Trafford Publishing (UK) Limited, 9 Park End Street, 2nd Floor
Oxford, UK OX1 1HH UNITED KINGDOM
phone 44 (0)1865 722 113 (local rate 0845 230 9601)
facsimile 44 (0)1865 722 868; info.uk@trafford.com
Order online at:
trafford.com/06-1733

10 9 8 7 6 5 4 3

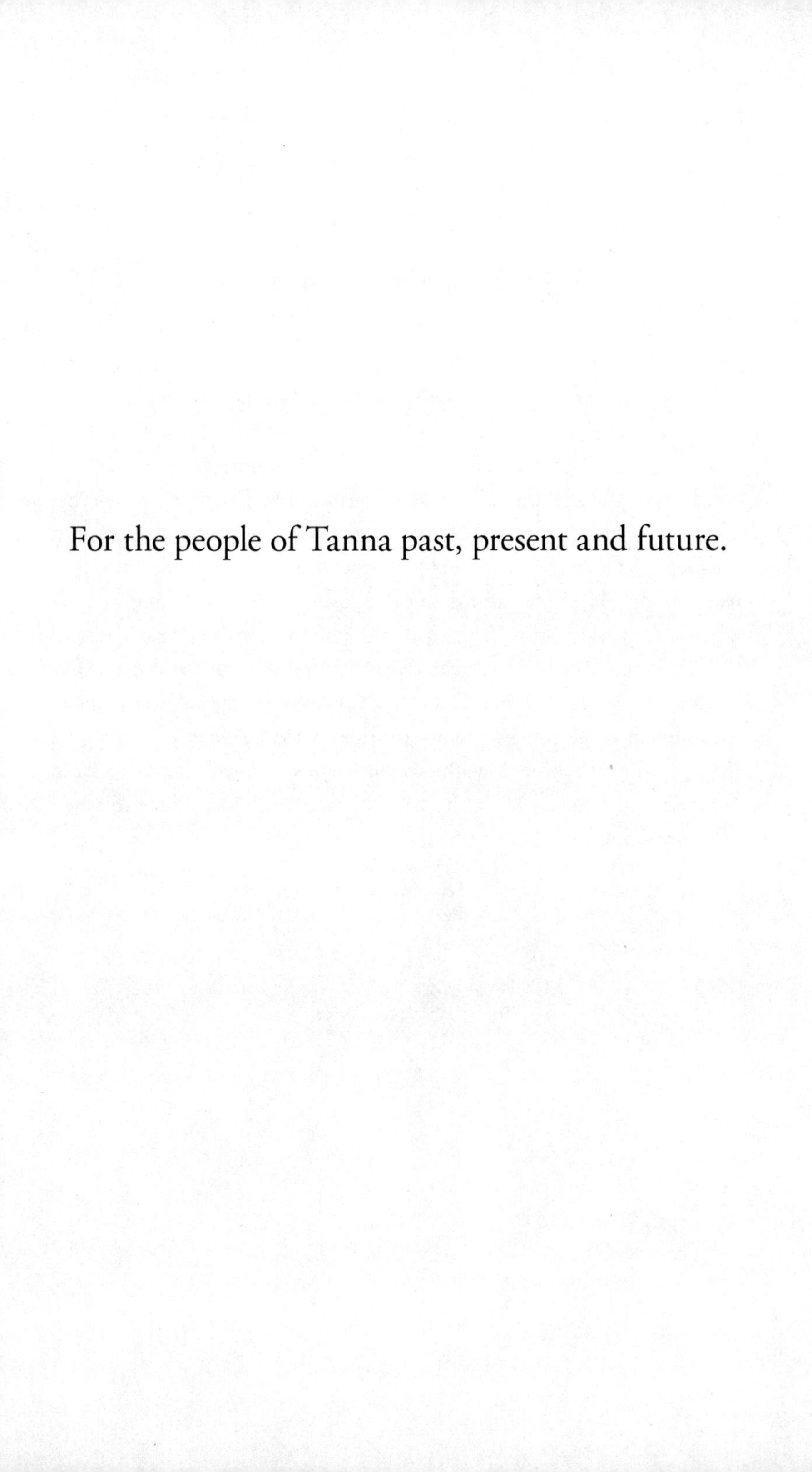
For the people of Tanna past, present and future.

Acknowledgements

I t was not my intention to write this book, I simply wanted to publish my grandfather's letters and write a bit of a foreward. But my husband, Eric, suggested I do a bit more. It turned out to be a journey of great interest and I am very glad I did it. My grateful thanks Eric. There are many other people who helped along the way, Professor Bill Addeley of the Belfast Theological College, our friends John and Angela Ley; Mark Lomas for resurrecting old photos and doing the cover; Reverend Graham Miller who was a missionary in Vanuatua for 40 years and lives in Australia with his wife in retirement. To the Co. Down Spectator for the wealth of information I found in their archives in the Carnegie Library. Also thanks to the ladies at the Carnegie Library for their patience when I couldn't get the microfilm machine to work! To our friends in Australia, Port Vila in Vanuatu and Lenakel in Tanna, and many friends back home for their help, my gratitude.

Contents

Introduction

A book containing letters written by a missionary to his mother sounds like a bit of a dull read, but you may be surprised: adventure, tribal warfare, hurricanes and volcanoes, they all play their part and through it all runs the strong, steady thread of love. The following letter was written by my grandfather to his mother in April, 1910:

Dear Mother,

Seven years ago this Easter time we landed on Tanna and since then have seen many changes, but Easter Sunday morning showed us a change we did not think probable, our station was simply a wreck. If two Dreadnoughts had bombarded us all night they could not have done much more harm. We knew we were in for a blow and spent Saturday getting things ready and snug for it. I did not go to bed as the glass was fast falling and the roar of the wind terrific from ten p.m. to three a.m. I fought single- handed keeping doors and ventilators closed. Our doors are double, the outside ones are venetian doors and open out, the inner doors open in. The tremendous pressure of the wind suddenly relaxed would make the outer doors spring their bolts and bang outwards like the report of a rifle, the inner doors would then bend inwards and I had to crawl out on the lee side and get round and close the outer doors to prevent the inner ones from being burst. Isabel could not sleep much but the children slept well, I got drenched repeatedly. At 3 a.m. the glass was down to 27.76 and the needle waving about wildly. A ventilator burst open and the inside doors of the house between the rooms began to go. I was trying to hold the one upon which most depended and getting the worst of it. When the surveyors came out of their room with their help we nailed up and stayed the doors all round leaving one sheltered one to let us out in case we had to run. Natives began to arrive in a pitiful condition. Their house had been blown down and I found out that the hospital was gone and crawled across to look for the patients. 10 ft. sheets of galvanised iron were flying about like paper, wood, branches of trees, filled the air. Sometimes one had to lie down and hold on. I found one poor fellow stripped naked by the wind and wailing but could not lift him so wrapt him in a blanket lying handy and went back for help.

A Missionary's life could never be described as a dull one and certainly for my Grandfather, the Easter Sunday of 1910 proved to be the case. As a child I was not aware of what my Grandparents had accomplished and it was only in my teens that I discovered what the contents of my Grandmother's boxroom really meant

James Campbell Nicholson was born in Bangor on 26th July,1872, the son and grandson of a sea captain, which could have had a strong influence on him. Raised in Bangor and living in Ellenville on the Princetown Road at first, he went with his parents to Conway in Wales where his father was overseeing the building of a ship. He went to school there and when the family returned from Wales, he attended the Model School in Belfast, before joining the firm of Messrs.Thomas McMullan & Sons. Leaving there, he went to the United States for a short time, but returned after contracting rheumatic fever.

Nobody knows when he decided to become a missionary, but in the latter years of the nineteenth century, evangelical meetings were a regular event in Northern Ireland and one of the most well-known evangelists in those days to visit the Province was Dr.John G Paton, who was himself a missionary. His autobiography had just been published and was extremely popular and I am sure had been avidly read by many of the family. It is likely that my grandfather attended meetings, maybe accompanied by his mother, who by all accounts was rather devout. The John G. Paton Mission liked their missionaries to have a medical knowledge and because of this, my Grandfather decided to study medicine before going overseas. He studied at Queens University from 1896-98, finishing his degree in Edinburgh where he became a Licentiate of the Royal College of Surgeons in 1902 and was elected a Fellow the following year. He was a gifted man, and would have gained a reputation as a surgeon at home but the calling was there and sixteen days after my grandparents were married on 31st December 1902, in a quiet ceremony at Ellenville, they sailed for Tanna in Vanuatu (what was then the New Hebrides). Grandfather had joined the John G.Paton Mission Fund which had its headquarters in Glasgow, and when John Paton first went to Tanna as a missionary in 1858 the New Hebrideans were a warring people, the slain of their enemies were eaten and widows of dead men strangled to accompany their husbands to the other life, even when grandfather arrived.

John G.Paton was born in Braehead near Dumfries in 1824, and was one of the first missionaries to be sent out to Vanuatu by the Reformed Presbyterian Church of Scotland in Dec.1857, to take up his post on Tanna. In those days the Tannese were cannibals, the men fierce and avaricious, the women little more than slaves. Rev.Paton had arrived on the island with his wife, but less than a year later she and her baby were dead. He was taken off the island in 1862 because of fears for his safety and returned to Australia where he worked amongst the aborigines, and went back to Scotland to raise financial support and missionaries a year or so later. Having been successful on his trip home, he returned to the New Hebrides and remained there until the early 1880s. Reverend Paton noted on visiting a kanaka hospital in the early 1860s on a plantation in Australia that was more humane than most, *'I found nothing but girls and women who had been confined or were about to be confined. An overseer, in charge of about eight hundred kanakas, said to me, – "Many children are born here by the girls and women, white children; it is a mercy that nearly all die in infancy"*. Between 10,000 and 11,000 kanakas died during those 40 odd years and that was in Queensland alone [1]

In the Nicholson family of seven children, four served in the mission field. Sarah the eldest sister, was the first female Zenana[2] missionary of the Irish Presbyterian Church to serve in Manchuria and married the Reverend Dan Robertson who also served in the same mission. Eleanor, or Nellie as she was called, served with her husband in Anand in India where he was a doctor/missionary for the Irish Presbyterian Church to the Jungle Tribes Mission; she had qualified as a midwifery nurse. William, or WP, was a well-known evangelist. In his early 20s Grandfather felt the calling to devote his life to Christianity and although rather shy by all accounts, began evangelical work.

I first became aware of my grandmother being more than the jolly little lady who gave marvellous Sunday afternoon teas, when my brother, cousins and I used to creep into the boxroom in her home in Maxwell Park in Bangor. It was full of such interesting things, like grass skirts, black boxes with large coloured slides and my favourite, a large conch shell. I was only about six or seven at the time and didn't seek to find out more and unfortunately left it until it was too late and my grandmother was dead, a year after my father. That was in 1958 when I was in my teens. The slides, the skirt and the conch shell have all gone but one precious item remained; my grandfather's letters home to his mother. Luckily, my auntie Eileen (Collier) had had the presence of mind to have a number of copies made of them and I have a copy. The letters have been read by a number of friends and family and they all said how interesting they found them and what a pity to leave them lying in some drawer, never maybe, to be seen again and to me that seems a terrible shame; he and my grandmother deserve better than that.

My grandmother was born in 1879, the daughter of James and Mary Campbell who lived in Furzefield, a large farm which is still there, situated on the Donaghadee/Newtownards Road. In 1897, on the death of his wife, James Campbell moved to Bangor where the family lived in the Princetown area. There were five children at that stage, but I discovered that in 1896, in the space of 8 weeks, three children had died aged two, four and six; Granny would have been 17 at the time and her mother died a year later, possibly never recovering from the death of her three children. Her elder sister Lizzie took over the running of the household.

It is hard to imagine the hardships and lack of everyday needs that they stoically accepted when they arrived in Tanna, to leave these shores knowing you wouldn't set eyes on your family and friends again for four years; no phone calls or telegrams, just letters three or four months old and no guarantee that they would arrive. From cannibals and volcanoes to hurricanes and drought, Tanna had it all. I visited there with my husband Eric, in 1989 and was surprised that so little seemed to have changed. People mostly live in bamboo and grass-roofed huts although there are brick buildings and there is a modern, one storied hospital. But grandfather's church is still standing, although a bit the worse for wear, and the volcano still gently bubbles away. The amazing thing was his name is still remembered by people wherever we went. When I said he was my grandfather they would say, 'oh Dr.Nicholson!' and shake my hand. We visited the church after the service one Sunday. The congregation had gathered outside for 'lap-lap' – a picnic – and the minister, when I told him who I was, kindly took us outside and introduced us to many of them, Lomai and Iavis' grandsons and one very old lady whose eyes filled with tears as she took hold of my hand when I sat down beside her and they explained who I was. When the minister translated, it was to tell me that she remembered playing as a child with my father behind the house. Needless to say I was overcome with emotion. We were there in November and the weather was beautiful, not too hot and cool in the evenings but in the hurricane season, between November and the end of March, it would be a different story.

In attempting to write about my grandfather I have come across all sorts of stumbling blocks, not least the fact that he died in 1934, so what I have gleaned about him is from his letters, and the articles that he wrote for the periodical the Jottings, a quarterly magazine issued by the John G.Paton Mission Fund, the mission society that had sent him to Tanna. What does come across is the essence of the man, passionate in his beliefs, but with a tender and human touch as well. He was devoted to his family and to have raised four children on the island who survived well into later life was an achievement in itself considering the climate; I would say due to his dedication to them. If it hadn't been for the insight I gained from two of the books written about the history of church planting on Vanuatu by the Reverend J.Graham Miller, I would have missed a lot. He was a missionary himself on the islands for forty years and he and his wife now live in Australia. I am in correspondence with him and he has been a great help. I have not edited the letters as I believe that their contents give them the right to stand on their own: I will only link them on occasions with explanations and background information.

Maybe I should explain exactly where Vanuatu is and a little of its history. It was first discovered in 1606 by Pedro Fernando de Quiros who named it Australia in honour of Philip III of Spain and Archduke of Austria who believed it was the Great Southern Continent, he promptly left and it wasn't until over a century later that Bougainville discovered more of the adjacent islands which he named the Great Cyclades, but did not stay to explore them. Then in 1777 Captain Cook sailed through the northern islands and voyaged south, eventually dropping anchor in Resolution Bay in Tanna where he replenished his water supply and wood. For many years Captain Cook's charts of Vanuatu were the only ones. There are many islands, large and small, stretching 400 miles over the sea. To the south west, 1400 miles brings you to Queensland and New Zealand lies 1000 miles to the south. It was Cook who renamed them the New Hebrides. I have mentioned where Vanuatu lies but have not explained where Tanna is in relation to the rest of the islands. It is the second most southerly island, 25 miles long by 12 miles wide, Tukosmera being the highest point at 717 metres high. The most fertile of all the islands in Vanuatu, producing copra and tea for export. The population today is 19,825, but in Grandfather's time it was greater. Vanuatu is on the Pacific Rim, lying on a fault line and like many of the Pacific islands on the Rim, is subject to volcanic activity.

Circling the Pacific Ocean on the bottom of the seabed, lies a dramatic volcanic zone called the 'ring of fire', notorious for its frequent earthquakes and volcanic eruptions. It coincides with the edge of one of the world's main tectonic plates and more than half the world's active volcanoes above sea level are found here. Mt.Yasur is an active volcano on Tanna, 361 metres high lying on the south east corner of the island, with the larger bulk of Tukosmera lying further south. Two other islands in the group have active volcanoes, Ambrym and Lopevi.

Ireland was a far cry then from what it is now. The Irish Land Purchase Act came in 1903, a major land reform that alleviated the problem of Irish farm ownership with justice to the Irish farm workers as well as the landlords. In Newtownards Market you could buy oats at 6s6p a cwt.(50 kilos for 32p), typhoid was endemic in the Stoneyford area of Belfast, a single passage to Australia cost £19 or you could take an excursion ticket to Edinburgh for 19s (about 80p) return, three different shipping lines were sailing twice a month to America – £10 first class, £4 single – travel sounds cheap, but in relation to earnings probably similar with today's prices. The King, Edward VII, was crowned in 1902 and attended a magnificent Durbar in Delhi and visited Malta, Italy, Portugal and France in 1903. So it was from this world that they left Gravesend in London to sail to a far different one 10,000 miles away.[3] There was trouble all round the world in 1903 when my grandparents left: skirmishes in Morocco, student riots in Spain, fighting in the Balkans, trouble in Manchuria. In America, President Roosevelt's favouritism of the negroes had caused violent outbreaks of anti-negro demonstrations with many negroes killed; the Boer War had finished the year before. Things haven't changed much. Mind you, the price of houses has gone up; then you could buy a detached villa in Bangor with 5 bedrooms for £750! On the sailing front the Americas Cup contestant, Shamrock III owned by Sir Thomas Lipton, was dismasted by a freak squall on the south coast with one man drowned.

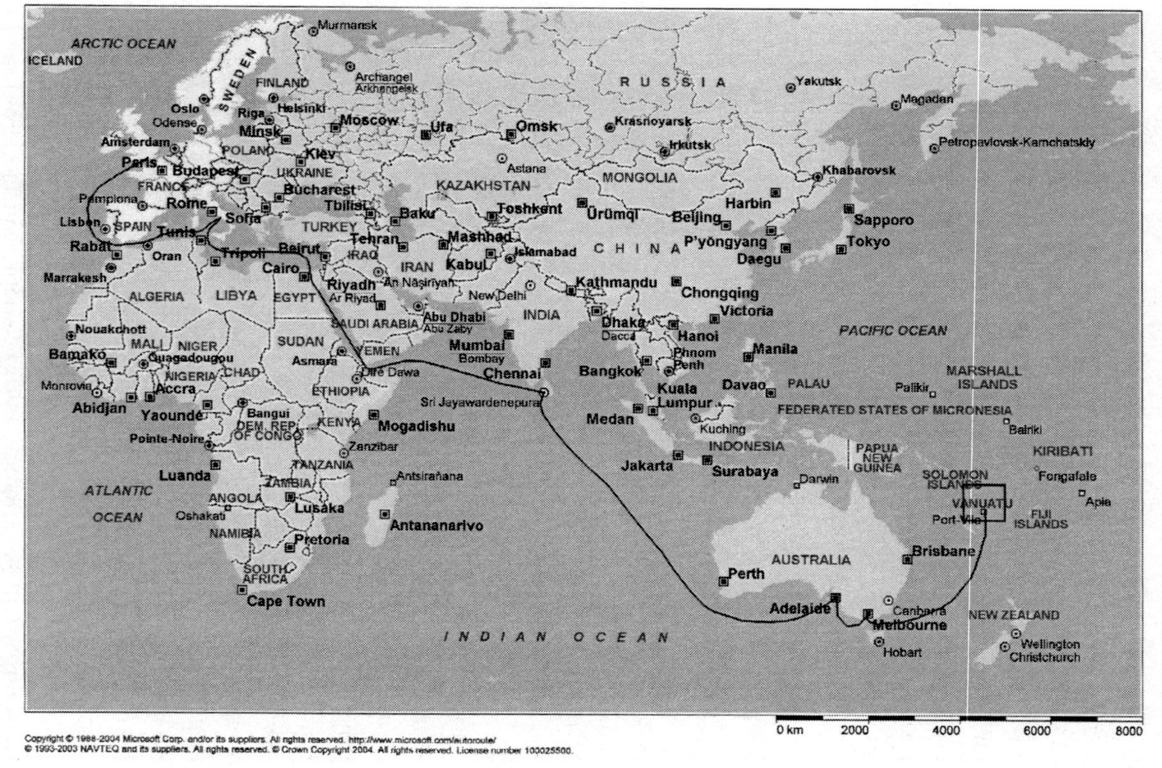

ARCTIC OCEAN
ICELAND
SWEDEN
FINLAND
RUSSIA
Murmansk
Archangel
Arkhangel'sk
Oslo
Odense
Amsterdam
Paris
FRANCE
Pamplona
SPAIN
Lisbon
Rabat
Marrakesh
Oran
Tunis
Rome
Budapest
POLAND
Riga
Helsinki
Minsk
UKRAINE
Kiev
Moscow
Bucharest
Sofia
Tripoli
Beirut
TURKEY
Tbilisi
Baku
Ufa
KAZAKHSTAN
Astana
Omsk
Toshkent
Tehran
Mashhad
IRAQ
IRAN
Kabul
Islamabad
New Delhi
Riyadh
Ar Riyad
An Nāşirīyah
SAUDI ARABIA
Abu Dhabi
Abu Zaby
YEMEN
Cairo
EGYPT
LIBYA
ALGERIA
SUDAN
Asmara
ETHIOPIA
Dire Dawa
KENYA
Mogadishu
Zanzibar
TANZANIA
Antsirañana
Antananarivo
Nouakchott
MALI
NIGER
CHAD
NIGERIA
Bamako
Ouagadougou
Monrovia
Abidjan
Accra
Yaoundé
Pointe-Noire
Bangui
DEM. REP. OF CONGO
Luanda
ANGOLA
ZAMBIA
Lusaka
NAMIBIA
Oshakati
SOUTH AFRICA
Pretoria
Cape Town
ATLANTIC OCEAN
INDIAN OCEAN
Mumbai
Bombay
INDIA
Chennai
Sri Jayawardenepura
Kathmandu
Ürümqi
MONGOLIA
CHINA
Krasnoyarsk
Irkutsk
Dhaka
Dacca
Bangkok
Hanoi
Phnom Penh
Kuala Lumpur
Medan
Jakarta
Surabaya
Kuching
INDONESIA
Chongqing
Victoria
Beijing
P'yŏngyang
Harbin
Daegu
Manila
Davao
PALAU
Yakutsk
Khabarovsk
Sapporo
Tokyo
PACIFIC OCEAN
FEDERATED STATES OF MICRONESIA
Palikir
MARSHALL ISLANDS
Bairiki
KIRIBATI
Fongafale
Apia
Magadan
Petropavlovsk-Kamchatskiy
PAPUA NEW GUINEA
Darwin
AUSTRALIA
Perth
Adelaide
Melbourne
Canberra
Brisbane
Hobart
SOLOMON ISLANDS
VANUATU
Port Vila
FIJI ISLANDS
NEW ZEALAND
Wellington
Christchurch
0 km 2000 4000 6000 8000

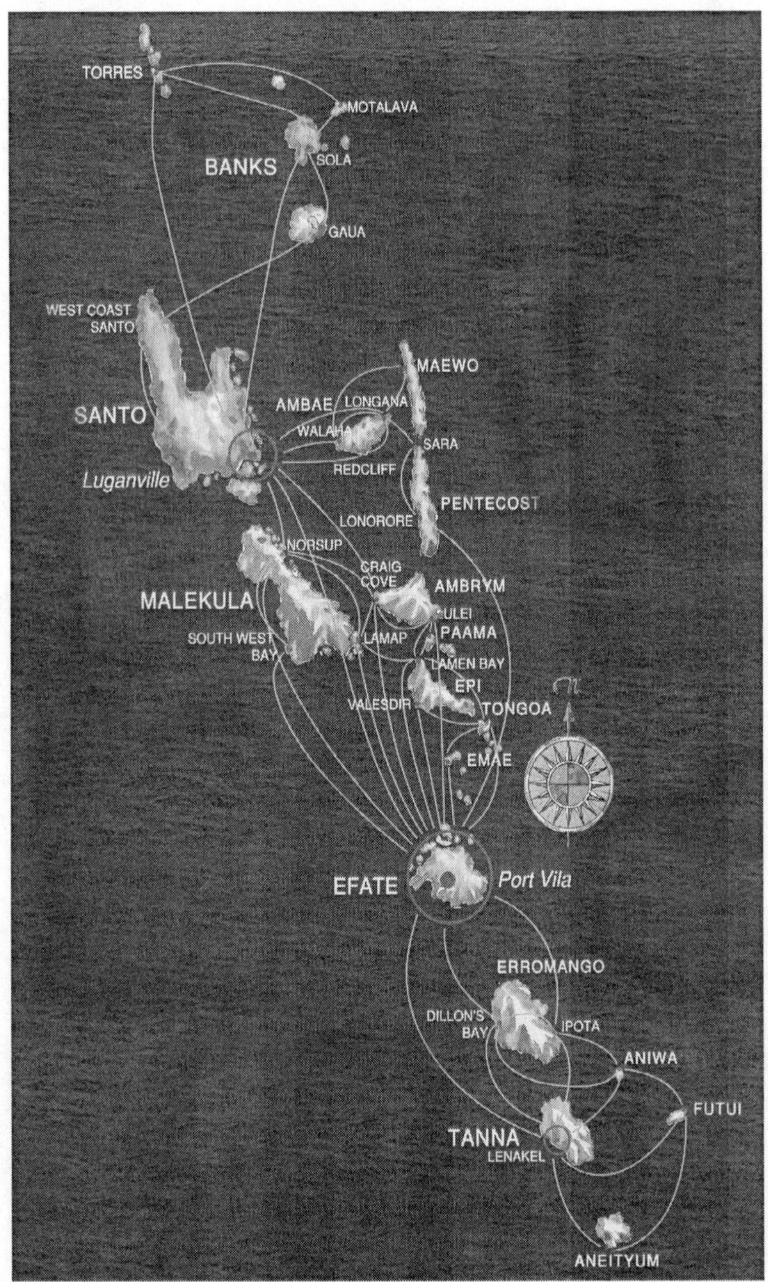
TORRES
MOTALAVA
BANKS
SOLA
GAUA
WEST COAST
SANTO
MAEWO
AMBAE
LONGANA
SANTO
WALAHA
SARA
REDCLIFF
Luganville
PENTECOST
LONORORE
NORSUP
CRAIG
COVE
AMBRYM
MALEKULA
ULEI
PAAMA
SOUTH WEST
BAY
LAMAP
LAMEN BAY
EPI
VALESDIR
TONGOA
EMAE
EFATE
Port Vila
ERROMANGO
DILLON'S
BAY
IPOTA
ANIWA
FUTUI
TANNA
LENAKEL
ANEITYUM

Chapter I

Preparation and Departure

Grandfather's name appears in the Jottings for the first time in 1901 (Jot.35) as one of the Fund's new missionaries and again in 1903 (Jot.39)

Quite by inadvertence we omitted in last Jottings to give the name of the fifth of "Our Own" Missionaries, as promised in the preceding number. We apologise to our readers and to our Missionary elect, who is J.Campbell Nicholson, L.R.C.P. & S. (Ed.), of Bangor, Ireland.

Dr.Campbell Nicholson will not be going out, as we at first anticipated, in January or February. Indeed it may be January,1903, before he sails, though a clear call from God to go sooner would we know meet with a ready response from our friend.

He has a strong impression that further study and higher professional qualifications may increase his usefulness in the Mission. He has resolved therefore, with the Committee's approval, to prosecute his studies and obtain practice and general knowledge for a time, by placing himself at our disposal for a series of visits before sailing to take up his life's work. In the meantime the Missionaries in Synod will probably be able to decide upon a suitable opening for the pioneer work which our Fifth Missionary is to undertake for Christ.

In the Jottings of October 1903:

Will friends wishing to see Dr.Nicholson, or wishing him to address meetings, kindly communicate at the earliest moment with one or other of our Hon. Secretaries.

We would remind all who are interested, that the personal element bulks largely in our work. It is a Mission carried on and supported by personal friends, in a homely way, and with only as much organization as is needed to make friendly effort businesslike. Too many missionaries, we fear, are mere counters to the supporters at home. We want to avoid this unhappy state of affairs in our little endeavour, and so friends will take the opportunity now afforded of meeting those of "Our Own" Band who are going forth; giving them a word of cheer and a handshake before they leave. Prayer and interest will assuredly be stimulated thereby on both sides.

In Jottings 39 more information appears about him:

"About eight years ago, chiefly through the influence of a godly mother, he accepted the Lord Jesus Christ to be his own Saviour.

A residence of eighteen months in the United States may, not improbably, have strengthened the characteristic 'go' of our New Missionary's nature. Having given himself to Christ, he openly confessed Him, overcoming his timidity by resolute effort, and plunging into active Evangelistic work – work which has ever since been his joy and strength all through his medical course.

At Queen's College, Dublin (should read Belfast) and afterwards at Edinburgh, Dr.Nicholson pursued his medical studies, qualifying L.R.C.P.& S., and afterwards F.R.C.S.E. His desire to go to the Mission field in no sense blunted his ambition to obtain the highest qualification in his profession – which stood him in good stead, never loosing a patient under anaesthetic when in Tanna – But side by side with his medical studies he faithfully and eagerly preached Christ, taking a special interest in, and displaying a special aptitude for, work amongst children.Dr.Nicholson is to be married on the 31st December, and he sails from London per the Orient s.s. Orizaba on the 16th January."

"ORIZABA"
8.2.03

Dear Mother,
As we are nearing Colombo and the opportunity of sending you a line, we

have roused ourselves from laziness and lethargy and in the cool of the evening on deck now write, the weather is now fairly warm, but a good breeze has been constantly with us and this with the awnings and light clothing makes us very comfortable and enables us to go in for all the different deck games but the breeze had one great disadvantage, it kept all week on our port hole side of the ship and we could not get it opened. The cabin was very stuffy at night and we sweated continuously, but one gets used to being in a constant perspiration and we do not feel so grumpy about it now. However, the wind is round to the other quarter and we have the port hole constantly open and a wind chute out as well. As regards great heat, we really have had none so far. We did not take off our heavy underclothing until we were nearly through the Red Sea and have never changed any day yet. Our date of sailing was the best in the year.

We have much to thank God for since our marriage. He has truly made all things work together for our good and has kept us in health and strength all the way, except the cold I had at Naples and it did not keep me from eating so was not very bad. I remember the mustard leaves Isabel put on till this day – we laugh at the terrible hurry I was in to get her to pull them off. We had a great tournament of deck games and Isabel has won most of the ladies prizes. I got two and we won our double together. We enjoyed them very much and are feeling stronger and harder for them. We had the Episcopal Service this morning and tonight we have an evangelistic meeting on the steerage deck. I am to help the Rev.Fleming. The people enjoy this, I think, much better than the official one. We were ashore at Port Said and had a good time. We got on donkeys and had a gallop round the town and on the sand. You would have laughed if you had seen us; Isabel was the only lady in the cavalcade but sat her beast well and kept up with the rest of us. The Arabs ran behind and whacked with sticks and kept up a constant yelling. We bought helmets (pith) at 4/- each and invested in oranges at 3d a dozen. After leaving Port Said darkness soon set in so that we saw very little of the canal, but were up in time in the morning to see the last two or three miles, Arab villages, camels and children running along the bank begging for coppers. We did not stay long at Suez so did not get on shore and soon we were passing the wilderness of the wanderings and saw the Mountains of which Sinai is a peak. The Red Sea behaved well and was only stuffy at the end. The bath is our necessity every morning now after a sweaty night but it feels luke warm. Isabel is looking well, stouter a little and the picture of health and her spirits keep up very well. Sometimes we get the doldrums and we never can speak together yet about that last night and not much about home. The queer feeling comes if we do. I hope you are all well, love to Father and Nellie, much to yourself. I enjoy that book very much – Meyers. We still keep at Abraham, it is grand, now goodnight in Christ, your affect. Son,

J.Campbell Nicholson

The Orient Pacific Line. *R.M.S."Orizaba"*

17.2.03

Dear Mother,

We expect to get into Freemantle on the 19th, the day after tomorrow, so I will send you a short letter and then write a longer one from Melbourne. We spent an evening on shore at Colombo, Ceylon, had a ride in rickshaws and looked through bazaars and bought some little things that were good value. For instance, I got nicely carved bone napkin rings at 6d.each and Isabel got a silk blouse for a few shillings; silk things are very, very cheap and things beautifully made. Isabel is an awful bargainer with the natives and if 6/- is asked and she wants the article can generally get it for half of the price asked. I'm no good, I simply can't and when Isabel talks to them I either sit on a chair and mop myself or else wait at the door. I have been done so often now in buying fruit I have given it up.

After leaving Colombo, which, by the way, we were thankful to do as they coaled there and all port holes etc. were closed so that nearly everybody was driven up on deck by the heat and in the morning, what sights. The day breaks suddenly and each laughed at the other not knowing that their face was also as black as a nigger's.

Isabel and I sleep in the saloon in a sheet and perspiration. I lay on a table and she on the couch beside me and glad we were, as it was all the clothes we had on at Colombo were soiled past wearing.

Well, after Colombo we got into hot, moist weather, the temperature in the cabin being as high as 90 deg. And this with the stuffiness made one as limp as a wet cloth. We slept fairly well at night and mighty well in the daytime, after breakfast, after dinner, after tea, sweated and slept. No games, little reading, but two days after the line was passed it gradually got cooler and today the bath had a suggestiveness of coldness and the breeze tonight makes one think of an undershirt. All round we have had a splendid trip and not till near Colombo did we feel inconvenienced by the heat. We have not changed a single day yet because of being very wet with sweat. All agree on board it has been an unexceptionally fine trip.

We had a nice service on board on Sunday again and the people attend well. We have yet another Sunday on board, between Adelaide and Melbourne. We are counting the days though. It wearies towards the end, loafing is alright but it gets very wearisome and one longs for duty of some kind or other. I am looking forward to Melbourne. After their great revival we expect to meet and enjoy fellowship with people out and out for God. There is very little Godliness on board, plenty of the opposite and to be boxed up closely with the latter is not good for one's soul.

We are still in the best of health. Our spirits sometimes droop a bit and we can never talk of the last night yet to each other, but we look forward and up. Isabel is writing beside me and looking nicer than you ever saw her. She is stouter a little and more womanly in many ways. This is her birthday,(23rd). The people on board thought her between 18 and 19 and one lady told us she could never imagine us married and that few did at first, they thought we were courting. Indeed, when I think of it we are always together sitting reading in a quiet corner at night talking away, taking our exercise together. One lady tried to separate us. She said we were far too much together and I think it was her got us separated in the games, but she gave it up, and us too and few are the minutes of the day we are away from each other and yet we always have others gathered about us for a chat. Mrs.McCausland has been so much confined to her cabin that we have scarcely got to know her yet. Mrs. Fleming is a very quiet douce woman. Dr.McCausland is in great form, just a muckle school bairn at times, but now we long for letters from home. None since Naples on the 25th of last month, and still we write in faith for the answers later.

I hope all are well at home, love to them all. We remember you all daily in our prayers. Much love to you, mother mine, to Father and Nellie.

In Christ,
Your affect.son, J.Campbell Nicholson
The Orient Pacific Line *R.M.S.Orizaba*
25.2.03

Dear Mother,
We are behind our time in reaching Melbourne and will not get in until 12 or 1a.m. tonight, so that means staying on board till the morning. We are to stay with Mr.Frank Paton just outside Melbourne –

16 High Street,
Kew,
Melbourne.

He wrote us a very nice letter, which we received at Freemantle giving us a very hearty welcome and asked us to make his home our home in Australia.

We were at Adelaide yesterday and went on shore and had a look round. It was nice to be in a British city again free from the crowd of beggars and hawkers, which we met with at other places of call. Fruit is very cheap, splendid grapes 1d.and 2d.per pound, peaches 2 and 3d.a dozen, pears big ones, 1d each.

The weather is cold and necessitates an overcoat and if sitting at night we need a rug. The country is very parched looking, it being the hinter end of a droughty summer. We shall be glad to see our green isle. Isabel is very well and keeps cheery and we are both glad to think our present voyage is soon to end. It will be nice to get room to move without bumping each other and things often much harder than ourselves. Today we will be busy packing and squaring up. We are looking forward to getting letters from you all. We have had none since Naples. A Bangor Gazette would go high.

Dr.McCausland and Mrs. McC.are well. Mr. and Mrs. Fleming ditto, the two ladies have picked up wonderfully. Our old passengers are gradually diminishing but we are fuller than ever receiving fresh batches at Freemantle and Adelaide, people mostly from the mines.

I hope you are quite well. I often wonder what you are doing. Sometimes one begins to feel queer but I think the both us try to bear up for each other's sake.

These separations do make heaven more real and near, and His promises exceeding precious.

Now Love to Father and Nellie and yourself from you affect. Daughter and Son in Christ,

J.Campbell Nicholson

The Jottings (41) of July 1904 finds my Grandparents, along with other new Missionaries, safely in Australia, with only another 1,500 miles to go:

from Dr.John G. Paton.

74, Princess Street,
Kew, MELBOURNE
26th March, 1903
Dear Friends,
The four young Missionaries and their wives reached Melbourne in health and happiness. It was a great joy to me to be here to meet them all. They have been cordially received wherever they have been, and by their preaching on Sabbaths and addresses on the week evenings they have made many friends whose sympathy and prayers will follow them.

Last Monday, numbers were at the station to bid them farewell as they left for Sydney, and I learn that they were kindly welcomed and entertained there. They sail for the Islands on Wednesday, in the steamer Tambo. Owing to the weak state of Mrs.Paton's health, I am prohibited from going with them, but if she is better I hope to follow by the next steamer, two months' hence, to help in their settlement.

As from: Lenakel,
WEST TANNA,
New Hebrides,
via Sydney.

S.S.TAMBO,
Norfolk Island.

April 7th, 1903

Dear Mother

We are thus far on our journey and expect to reach Tanna about Sunday. We have had a pretty rough time and we both succumbed to seasickness. Our steamer is a small one about twice the size of the Rosabella, 600 tons only. We have had and still have a good many passengers on board. The ladies are all packed into cabins and we men into others, but we got rid of some at Lord Howe Island and some more here. Still, we cannot get a cabin to ourselves. We have both recovered and make a good show at mealtime now. Isabel felt her seasickness a good deal. It was her first real experience of it and she did not like the retching. All the others were very bad and it was hard to get a quiet place to boke in peace. Dr.McCausland I found one day nearly lying down in it and I laughed so heartily that I could not do it myself, but all are up and looking well again. The Chief Engineer and supercargo were bad so you may guess we had excuse enough. The weather has been delightful and cool today and we need wraps for deck.

Our passengers are mostly missionaries and we had two Services last Sunday to which nearly all on board came. We did enjoy them and sang from our hearts the old hundred, containing 23rd psalm and a great many hymns. 9 of us are new missionaries, the rest are returning ones. We have a naturalist and two or three health seekers ,also some settlers for the New Hebrides. We have a regular live farmyard – 5 horses ,sheep, goats, pigs, pigeons, ducks, hens, dogs, cats, canaries. We have two pups, fox terriers, one called Jean and one Charlie. They have been ill but we gave them castor oil and they are much better. I hope they live. We have Mrs.Worthington, the trader's wife at Lenakel with us. She is a middle-aged woman and seems fairly nice, but we do not chum much. Their business and ours clash too much for that I'm afraid. We are lying at anchor here and hope to get to shore tomorrow. The Island used to be a convict settlement, but was given up and the descendants of the Mutineers of the Bounty from Pitcairn Island were brought here. There are about 800 of them, poor, and a mixture of races. The British round the World cable station is here, 3d.a word to Australia. We have been fishing all evening. I caught nothing, Isabel two, fish called Brim. It is nice on board the steamer. The Captain and Officers are very nice and do anything they can for us, rig us up fishing lines and do all manner of little things for us.

We got mails on board, the only one from Bangor being a postcard from Lizzie with a photo of Miss Brison's on it. I had one and papers from Edinburgh, no home papers, one for Isabel from Mrs.James Paton, Glasgow, our London and other accounts all found us out.

I begin to feel far away but don't say much. Isabel does too but seldom shows it. We both look forward with lively interest to our new home and what we have to do there. If it were not for Christ, I would turn back though. I have no heart for being so far away and travelling, but he has so ordered it and is with us and will teach us of all that concerns His Kingdom. If we only knew more, how much more joy we should have in His Service. We are slow scholars, but by His Grace we will go forward and remember the great time coming.

I hope all are well at home. Did you get the letter with Money Order for £8. If not, claim that amount at Bangor P.O., sent to Ellen Nicholson by J.Campbell Nicholson from Sydney and you'll get it.

Kind regards to all enquiring friends. Love to Father, Nellie, Netta and Willie, much to yourself from Isabel and

Your affect. son in Christ,
J.Campbell Nicholson

Chapter II – The First Year

Settling In

WEST TANNA
New Hebrides
Via Sydney
26.4.03

Dear Mother,

Here we are and fairly well settled and well pleased with our new home. It sits up on the hill about 250 or 300 feet above the sea and we have the constant music of the ocean breaking on the reef below us. Through a small opening in the reef we steer our boat out and in. I will try and get some photos to illustrate our home and surroundings for you. Isabel is well and is making better progress with the language than I am. She has four girls for servants and a man cook. I have a little boy as valet, called Pilot, a fine intelligent little fellow. He always goes about with me and washes up things while I am dispensing medicine.

Now would you like a walk round? But first get out of the boat. Some of the teachers lift you to shore, you must shake hands all round, you are the Doctor's mother and will be looked up to. Lomai first, a fine looking man in white suit and straw sailor hat. He lifts his hat to you. Tousi, Titonga, Javis do likewise, Lomai and Javis are Tanna's new chiefs, the other two Aniwans. Lomai and Javis used to have several wives but only one now. Javis was a great war chief. The others are assistant teachers and Christians. The women now want to shake your hand and even the youngest urchin, but see the crowd beside, naked and worse, but the native women all wear grass skirts of goodly dimensions, shake with the heathen, they put down their muskets to do so, some of their faces painted, earrings, nose sticks, hair plaited, etc. All the muskets are loaded, but they are harmless and more afraid of you than you of them. Now on through the gate, a nice avenue, some big broad fruit trees and coconut palms, but more are planted, a good well and pump at one side, the avenue about 100 yards long, then into an open field. The house used to be here, some very large trees, banyan and others and good grazing, a mare and foal[1] 12 or 13 sheep and 30 or so goats. Across the field there are the teachers' houses. Now for a climb, the road winds to the house, terraces in front, about 12 acres in Indian corn behind the house and at the side. Now what a good lookout over the ocean and country and a good breeze blowing. It is refreshing after the climb. Now through the house – no windows except one, all French doors or windows. At the right hand side is a study, next a bedroom, ours, then the sitting room, then another bedroom. All the rooms big with high ceilings with ventilators in the roof. A 7 foot veranda runs round all. The dining room is behind, biggest of all, and behind it again a harness and tool room, pantry, storeroom and out on the back veranda a stove and all that there is for a kitchen. Now underneath, a cellar the whole size of the house, plenty of head room and windows facing the sea; but no sash or glass. Here we have timber, paint, packing cases, etc.etc. It is a splendid place but needs more digging out and we will concrete the floor by and by, but everything looks unfinished, no paint inside, and only a coat or so outside 6 years ago. How many other little things are needed to make it look finished and settled. Furniture not much. I paid Mr.Paton too much for what is here. It was cheap when he bought it and is none the better of wear. We brought a hair mattress and a good thing too, as we burnt the old one on the bed after coming.

This is Mr. and Mrs. Anderson our assistants, young, and we have got on well so far and I think we will, but they have to get a house of their own as it is awkward about servants and food etc.

Mr.McCausland is staying with us. The Doctor has gone on but will be back and will stay here until June.

<u>Now a day's rounds.</u>

Breakfast, 7 o'clock a.m. Porridge, maybe an egg or a little bacon, a banana or orange.

Conch shell blows for school, Mr.A. and myself go down. The church is near the shore, a hymn, a teacher prays, men sit at one side, women the other, little classes and reading taught, then a short address or scripture lesson and writing lesson. About 10 o'clock Teachers' bible class, take a chapter out of Matthew, only part of the bible here yet, ask questions etc., all through Lomai as interpreter. Now all to work, women to weed paddocks, men to get post for the hospital or work the corn or make fences. Dinner 11.30, tinned meat or sometimes a goat or kid or fowl roasted, bananas, yams, onions, lemon drink, dessert arrowroot or rice, fruit. 1 o'clock horn blows for work till four. Five o'clock worship under a big tree, singing – some prayers. Sun sinking it will soon be black dark, tea with a lamp, sit and talk or music on the organ or read or write and 9 o'clock bed.

Sunday, breakfast at seven, service at 8 a.m. I do preaching through Lomai, about 150 present, good singing and attention. An hour loafing about and another, some of the teachers preach after noon. Visiting in the villages, worship at five.

But we have breaks in the routine. On Friday last Mr.A. and me and a double boat crew started for the most northern station about 12 or 15 miles up. Sails had not been used for a year and more or so. I got them patched and rigged up. Mr.A. and some others nervous about going, would like to pull all the way, but I am in command and Lomai a good first mate. A fair wind, but a big rolling sea; up the sails and away we go racing. Mr.A. and two others very sick, but we stand on and make the record trip, two hours and we are at the landing place for Lopelail, nasty passage through the reef. Lomai stands in the bow – indicates the way and I steer, the others pull. We pull the boat up on the shore, every man his bundle, for we are staying all night, my swag in a carryall; you gave me a splendid thing. Up the face of a cliff, holding on to coral and roots, single file through the bush on top, then down the cliff and into a native village. Here we have a little native hut built for ourselves and sling our hammocks, boil our can and make tea, natives eat rice and biscuits, etc., and camp out in the church. The teacher here went astray and was brought by Mr. A. to Lenakel. I packed him back to Aniwa the day of my arrival. It is hard for these people to see sin of immorality.

We take to the bush again and get to another station, see all the sick, plenty of malaria, bone disease and ulcers, one case of consumption near gone. They come back with us, at least as many as can walk and we have all worship at Lopelail, a feast at night, native puddings, chicken, etc., bed at nine, mosquitoes all night, long night, up at daybreak. Pilot gets our can of water to boil and we breakfast, then a service again, every man his bundle. (I pull a tooth to the delight of all, and wish I had a photo of them taking their medicine.) We reach the boat and launch her, sail up and away. Mr.A. sick again, but after rounding the point about half way we can sail no further as too big a sea to row so we get through an opening in the reef, pull up the boat and walk home, 5 miles, mostly sand. I sweat, the ladies meet us at the beach and all are glad to see us as we intended getting back sooner.

Other days I see patients after school, a good many come. Sometimes, off through the bush to see patients, it is rough riding, sometimes in cane which meets overhead, others, lying on the horse's neck to escape branches, jumping trees and native fences or crevices in the rock. I got a toss one day trying too high a one. Since coming I have broken in a young horse to the saddle and ride him every day. Isabel has been out twice with me and gets on well. We have two saddle horses, a mare and a foal. We are getting the foundations of the hospital ready. Now as the steamer does not call for two weeks more I will leave this part for additions. We got here on Easter Monday.

May 10th To finish up. Isabel is putting a note in also. This is Sunday night. We had our usual two Services here and then I was miles into the bush and had a service with the heathen. They always come and are attentive, but are so afraid of each other that they must have their muskets at hand. I like the work. It is arduous but it is grand to preach the old gospel. My old patients whom I have treated here, are glad to see me at their villages and facilitate our getting a congregation. We had a funeral here, a child of teacher's. It was the first funeral service I had ever conducted. My heart was sore for the parents, their only child. You will be getting up now to begin God's day. We have fin-

ished it and have prayed that you might have a day of blessing. Now we long for letters, but none till June. Everything going on here well. We are very busy so much to be done. Isabel has learned to work the typewriter, but it makes a long letter seem very short.

I hope all are well at home. Love to all. If I have time I will drop Father a line. Our work here would interest him. Much love to yourself from us both.

Your affect. Son in Christ,
J.Campbell Nicholson

In Jottings 42 October 1903 there appears the first news of Grandfather on Tanna:

For the first time in its history the Island of Tanna boasts the presence of a qualified doctor!

Medical aids and comforts are not unknown to the natives – much having been done in this direction by other missionaries: but the advent of professional skill and experience carries weight and inspires confidence. Even in this special work Dr.Nicholson has found a helper ready to his hand in the person of Lomai.

In Grandfather's first contribution to the Jottings he tells of the living conditions of some of the natives: *'Malarial fever abounds, none of the natives seem to escape; and all the children have protuberant abdomens from great enlargement of the spleen. Quinine, quinine, is the cry from morning to night. I thought I brought plenty, but I have not had enough to tackle the cases as they should be. Sores and skin diseases. Ugh! It takes a lot of grace and bandaging at times. But my wife, Lomai and myself sail in and get through with it. Treatment is almost hopeless under their present conditions of life. Dirty of person and dirty of house. They live in a crawling dust. The ashes of their fires accumulate in their houses and they sleep amongst them on a coconut leaf. I intend starting a crusade against dirt soon.'* Later he says: *'I wish I could bring some of the readers up to the back verandah to see the motley group awaiting treatment. The sun beats down on us, flies swarm in thousands around the patients. We call one and interrogate her through Lomai. She exposes sores on her arms, legs, everywhere. These covered with flies and emitting a loathsome smell. We look at her, then at our little stock of band-*

ages and dressing. We dress the worst. "Here, Lomai, take a turn." I go round the corner for a whiff of pure air." Further on in the same Jottings with a mixture of devotion and hard work he tells of the progress being made both spiritual and physical:

"On May 21st we laid the foundation-stone of our hospital. We gathered on the grounds and had a short service. I told them of the Great Physician, who sent out His disciples with the command to heal the sick and preach the Gospel, and of His followers at home who, in obedience to His command, had sent us and the building out; and that they themselves must do their share by helping to build it. Four of our Teachers prayed, thanking God for His goodness, and asking His help with the construction, and that the building may be a blessing to soul and body of those who may have need to come, and that He may make all our hearts warm and strong for Himself and His service. The Old Hundredth fittingly closed our service, and then the work began. Sand, lime and stone had to be carted up, the women carried up water in tubs slung on poles – not the easiest part of the work. Titonga and Tousi had charge of mixing the mortar. Iavis captains the boat, bringing the lime from our kiln, a little way round the coast. Dick, with cart and horse, ascends and descends the winding road from the beach bringing up lime, sand, stone and gravel; while Mr.Anderson and myself take measurements and find levels. All of us together, therefore, build this house for the Lord and His work.

Our medical and surgical work have already broken bounds and encroached on the time I had set apart for learning the language. On Monday, the 26th inst., we had over sixty cases. Lomai and I were done up. "Soon all Tanna he come along", said Lomai. "News gone out all the same as we read about in Matthew – your one hand he full up, your other hand he full up, me all the same, hands full, must get more hands." And so we must. I know of a pair of young Tannese hands which can be trained; they belong to my own special boy Pilot, whom I trust will yet be a "Sky Pilot". He is as sharp as a needle, and, though he does not know English, can understand me when I speak. And as I know the negative and affirmative in his language, we get on A1. Here is a sample: 'Any more sore legs, Pilot?" "O'oh" (yes). "Trot them up, then", and he does it, too, with a face as grave as a judge's.

We are making slow progress at the language, but progress all the same. It is a language as crooked as a native track.

Here is a sample: "Netakamailhiapninipus in." I twist my tongue into all shapes to try and pronounce it, when my wife breaks in, "What does that mean, Lomai?"

"They all the same think him cranky along head," says Lomai. We turn up our English version, and it reads, "They laughed him to scorn." I'm afraid I'll have to send you the Tannese Matthew, to get you to believe there is such a word in the language." Jottings 42 October 1903

Lenakel,
WEST TANNA,
New Hebrides,
Via Sydney.
June 12th, 03

Dear Mother,

Your welcome letters have been read and read pretty often. Isabel says she just reads them over when she begins to feel she should get a letter. We will get our letters this time as we go to Aneitum for Synod, which we do next Friday, 19th inst. I feel sorry to have to go, we have so much to do here, but as it is our first we must show up.

The time is passing quickly, sometimes we are a bit homesick, but still God is giving us great joy in the work here. I only wish you could come, we could make you very comfortable and the natives would adore you as our mama. We get to love the people more and more. Isabel and her girls get on splendidly. She has four and they really do their best to help her in every way. They surprise her at every turn by little attentions. Lomai was telling us they, the people, think her a piccaninny. She has been well tried this last month having the McCauslands and Andersons to cater for and having no shops at hand. She was puzzled at times but won her way through. The Macs are now with Mr.McMillan at White Sands and we have more time and freedom. We have one or two photos for you and Isabel has learnt the typewriter and has written the Jottings letter with. She is now (as I write) practising on the organ. I've got a grand wee wife, none better, people at home did not know what she was capable of doing. We were away at White Sands for Communion and stayed with the McMillans from Friday till Wednesday. It took us nearly seven hours in the saddle, but Isabel was none the worse and we were out on horseback the next day seeing the volcano and a lake beside it. We saw a lot of heathen and had a kind of chat with them.

The McMillans are a grand couple, the good real sort. He is doing a grand work. Twenty three were baptised, two of them noted old fighters and chiefs, but you will read more of this I expect in Jottings. I always get a lot of medical work to do and had to go to Port Resolution, Mr.Watts' station, to see some of his sick ones. This was the place Dr.Paton was chased from and where his first wife lies buried.

Coming back from White Sands we got an awful drenching, but we were none the worse. We had a warm bath and change as soon as we arrived. We were glad to get back, to home and our people, of course we have a bodyguard always with us, Lomai, Tousi and two others came. The road is a native track, single file, winding about, up and down steep hills, but our horses are like goats and seldom stumble. The one Isabel rides, is as wise as a human being nearly, and so nimble that the natives say 'Tom he plenty close up climb a coconut tree', i.e., that he is almost able to climb a tree.

Our work here is going on well, the services are being well attended at this Station. We intend to have Communion on the last Sunday of July, some baptisms, adult and infant, opening of the hospital, a dedicatory service setting apart three new teachers for outstations, so you see we have a big order on hand. Mr.McMillan will come over and help us, we always exchange pulpits at times like this.

There has been an awful lot of backsliding. There had been a great revival in Mr.Paton's time and then as he was so ill and ultimately had to leave and a stranger came, Mr.Anderson who is a good man but not a teacher, he was a cabinet maker by trade and had little education but he did well, but the people were not built up and became unstable. However, we are all getting stirred up to prayer and waiting on God. The teachers and native Christians say their hearts are sore, and have many meetings amongst themselves for prayer and talk. We are bound together to claim the Blessing, promised to those who agree to ask and Isa.44 and three we are asking for. I have got quite used speaking by interpretation and talk to the people just as if they understood, then Lomai drives it home. We are doing as much as we can at the Language. Isabel is ahead of me, she learns all day from her girls, who cannot speak any English but I'll get there too.

Mrs.Anderson is going home to her mother at Synod time, so we only will have Mr.Anderson. It is not easy to drop into second place after having occupied first, but we got on rightly, but we always had the feeling she felt it pretty hard. There cannot be two mistresses though and Isabel is to be mistress in my home. Mr.Anderson has commenced to study and when the hard work is over here intends to go on to the Colonies to study for ordination. At present he goes away for Friday and Saturday to Mr.McMillan who helps him, but this is inconvenient at times, but Mr.McMillan's furlough is due this autumn so that he will not be able to go then.

We have a great deal to do, after the hospital a kitchen, the house to be finished inside and painted out and in, a Church to build as soon as we can get at it, our present one is nearly done. These native ones only last about 5 or 6 years. I have had a great deal of medical work to do, 60 one morning. I am always done up by the time I get through, but God has blessed our work in this respect and the news has gone out all over the Island so that we get all kinds from north, south, east and west, some of them hopeless cases and they are disappointed when I tell them God has not committed us power to make new only to heal.

I want you to make up a small case for us and send it out in September. I need some suits, white and khaki, also some of those linen mesh undershirts without sleeves, but I'll write the order. Isabel wants some things too. Willie might get the suits in Paisleys of Glasgow and I shall instruct Dr.James Paton to send you some money to pay for them, the remainder of it for yourself to help to pay what I owe you.

What a lot of marrying is going on at home. I am sorry Willie is not going to finish his course. What about Nellie, I wish she would write to us. I hope Father is better, we never got a Herald to let us see how he is getting on. I hope the sale of work will be a great success, I wish I could drop in on you, 'but the King's business requireth haste'. I have great hopes to see the World evangelised in our generation. Keep on believing. I will write out list of goods – enclose also some photos to show you what the place is like. Love to all and yourself from us both, In Christ, your affect. son,

J.Campbell Nicholson

P.S. We have a chance of sending letters by a Man of War. The Captain is very kind and was up for tea. I will send another letter by regular mail in three weeks.

JCN

Lenakel,
WEST TANNA,
New Hebrides,
Via Sydney.
July 7th

Dear Mother,

The last letter we got a chance of posting per a man of war, the Captain kindly took my letters we had written to Nonmed, thence they would proceed by mail to Sydney.

The Captain was very nice. He came up for tea and is a good Christian man. He has service each day on board his ship. He came to Anietyum whilst we were there at Synod and took Communion with us, all us missionaries then went on board for Service on Sunday and in the evening too held an Evangelistic Service for the crew. We expect his ship back here in September, when he hopes to stay for a day or two.

We enjoyed Synod very much, though it meant sitting eight or ten hours each day on a hard seat. We have a grand set of men and it was grand and encouraging to hear the reports of each station. A letter was read from China signed by Dan and Mr.Fulton, in answer to one of sympathy sent by our Synod after the Boxer Rising.

We were five days in all at Anietyum and had to rough it. The men were all put up in an old school room each bringing his own stretcher. We had to live like soldiers. The ladies were put up two in a bed. Isabel had Mrs. McCausland for a bed mate. The mosquitoes were an awful pest. To sleep without a net (as I did one night) is not to sleep at all or very little, to get up with every exposed part covered with lumps. The strange thing is that Isabel while there did not get bit at all, nor yet in Melbourne, whilst I was eaten up in two places, whilst here I never get bit and she gets all that are going, but here we have few mosquitoes, never need a net, we are on too high ground.

Since returning we have been very busy. Mrs.Anderson has gone home to stay with her mother so we have only Mr.Anderson here now. We like to have the house to ourselves for a bit after being so crowded. Isabel is getting it into good trim and bye and bye when we get some paint on it will be very nice. Isabel got her case which had been left at Sydney by the shipping company. It was the one with the wedding cake and machine. The cake was a bit soft but the machine and other things were in good order. The shipping people are very careless about landing things. Last time they took on about a dozen cases so that we were a month late in receiving them. This time they broke our mangle and took away a big case full of stuff so that it will be about two months late in coming. I only wish they had a little opposition. These letters I will have to send by a bearer to Port Resolution (a two-day journey on foot), as they do not call here, but I hope that our postal arrangements will improve in the future. We have had the matter up in Synod and as the Company are subsidised by us pretty well they will listen, lest we try to get another company to start.

We are working hard at the hospital. A great many of the Christians from all around are helping us. We give them one good solid meal of goat, rice and yam but no pay. We have the verandahs and roof covered now and are getting the weather boards on. One night we worked by moonlight (Mr.Anderson and I and some natives). Everything is going fairly well. We have two requests for teachers from heathen tribes, and one of these is now building a house and church for teacher, whom I shall send after our Communion (26th July). The other tribe, three villages, have proposed to amalgamate and build a village on the sea shore, if I grant them a teacher. If they do this I shall be only too glad. These latter were inveterate opponents of the gospel up till now, so that we have much reason to be glad and praise our Conquering Saviour.

A new white trader has come to one of our out-stations. He has been lavish with his money and says he is going to settle, but would like boys for his plantation on another island. This is his principal business here and of course we do not like our boys taken away. I would be glad if we had plantations and work for the natives here instead of them being exported. The said trader wished to be very friendly, but I have not encouraged him as there will be war between him and our present trader at Lenakel, who cultivates a lot of ground and whilst not a professing Xtian[2] yet, does not hinder our work in any way and he does not work on Sunday and all his boys nearly, come to our services. Besides, Mrs.Worthington has been very kind and has obliged Isabel in many ways and is ever sending us up little presents of prints and giving us cuttings of plants and roses for our garden. She gave us a dog which we call Pat.

We have got our New Testament, i.e., Math., Mark, Luke, John, Acts of Apostles, Epistles of John and Revelations, also a new hymn book and shorter catechism. They are selling well, 1/-d and 6d. Isabel takes charge of them. Dr.McCausland is to go to Ambrim hospital for two years to relieve Dr.Bowie, Mr.Fleming to North Ambrim, Mr.Yates to Santo. I am sending some photos. We are in good health and enjoyed your letters so much. His Yoke is easy, His Burden Light, Love to all at home from us both, but I will add a bit to this before I send it off on Friday.

There was nothing further included – BM

Lenekal,
WEST TANNA
New Hebrides
Via Sydney
6th August 1903

Dear Mother,

We are hurrying to write a few letters as we have a chance to send them by a steamer calling at the east side of our island, from which we have just returned. Well I have a lot to write about this time. First, we are in good health and spirits and thinking of going a trip round the islands to see the Mission Stations, methods of work, churches, hospitals etc. We should have gone when we came first to the islands, but were too glad to land and get settled for a little.

We have had our half yearly Communion, on my birthday, July 26th. For a week previous we had two services a day, also classes for the candidates for baptism, the Xtian people from all the outstations came and stayed at our village. It was a grand time and a time of blessing to us all. Mr.McMillan came over for the week and dispensed the Sacrament. I did the baptising, forty adults and six infants. I had to swat up enough Tannese to do without an interpreter. 170 in all took Communion. I should say also that we had our new Hymn Book and Isabel and I taught them some of the new hymns, also polished up some of the old as they had the tunes so altered that sometimes they were unrecognisable. We have a big Estey organ but a good baby one for the open air would be handier. I think we are to get one this trip. The people and teachers have now returned to their villages and all is quietness here again.

We have had two earthquakes, the first I did not feel, I was in the Church teaching the teachers, but Isabel heard and felt it in the house, but on the 19th we had a big shake about midnight, the house shook and rattled at an awful rate, but we quietly stayed in bed till it was over. Some bottles were shifted but no damage done. Last week we had a big time all round. Tuesday we started for White Sands, to pull Mrs.McMillan's teeth out. Half way we got a message to say she was not very well and left it to my judgement as to whether it would be wise to give her chloroform. I decided not and turned and on our way back called at some (new to us) heathen villages. We were well received and all the sick brought to us. The Sunday following Mr.Anderson and three teachers went up and had a good service with them. On Thursday we started out with them to land two teachers, their wives and chattels at new stations to which they were going, to the north of us, the sea was rough, Isabel and half the crew got sick, but we got one man and his goods landed (half way) all right, the wind and sea dropped so we decided to push on, at first no wind and we had to pull, then we got some wind and got near the passage we had to go through to the landing, but a sea was rushing across its mouth and we were carried on the reef and over it into deep water. Nearly all the crew jumped, in fact all did, but two or three stuck by the boat. The teacher's wife, Isabel and myself sat still, Isabel as cool as a cucumber, so we avoided a ducking and got safely ashore. I had determined to try and get out, as we had a fair wind home and had made no preparations for staying the night. We made all preparations for *a tight ride. put out a big steer oar, we always carry, but the cross sea caught us again and carried us bang against the reef and up onto it, but I got one or two of the crew to push her off when we got a wave (again the crew jumped into the water with the exception of two men) but she had sprung a leak so we turned and beached her, the remainder of the crew had to swim ashore for themselves. Some heathen gave us great help and when we had the boat snug, I sent two away to Lenakel with a message to Mr.Anderson to borrow the trader's boat and come for us the next day. A heathen offered us his blanket, but we declined and walked a mile or two to Lopilail, the station we were bringing the teacher for. Here we have a little house, so we were not without a roof, some native Xtians brought us tea, sugar two new cotton blankets, an old hammock. They also cooked us a fowl, gave us cocoanuts, roasted yams, these with some biscuits and a tin of sardines, gave us food sufficient. We swung the hammock, lit a little fire in our native built hut and had a nice cosy evening. Then I put Isabel into the hammock and with a coconut leaf for a bed, a biscuit tin for a pillow, my mackintosh for a blanket we slept, but Isabel got tired of the hammock and we changed. I thought she only said she was tired to give me a spell, but really after an hour or two in it I was glad for a spell on the floor again, but the twelve hours of darkness soon passed and our boy was in looking for our little kettle.*

After breakfast we sent out word and gathered all the people and had a service, then Isabel and I went down to the shore to watch for the boat. We found places where we could bathe and as we had not washed since the morning before we took each our baths and used some of our under garments and the sun for towels. By this time the boat was in sight, so we returned and tried to eat the native cooked fowl. We had no plates or knives or forks but we did justice to that old rooster. Then we had a time of singing with the natives, walked back again to the passage and prepared to embark. Tausi, Titonga and Javis and a good crew had come for us and were as glad to see us as we were them, but the passage was still dangerous, to the boat and our clothes, the sea outside rough, so rough that half way they had had to land Mr.Anderson he was so bad with seasickness, but we were all anxious to get home, so we picked a good double crew. Tausi took the steer oar, Javis did pilot and the rest pulled and backed water till a good wave came, and a good strong pull and we let go a cheer. It was good work, the reef on both sides of the passage was bare a few seconds after with the back draught. In rain with a head wind and jumping sea we pulled a racing speed for over six hours and about 9 o'clock got through our passage at Lenakel to be welcomed by a big crowd, but Lomai was missing, we surmised the reason, his wife Naupum was dying, galloping consumption. I went to see her and did not think she could live the night, but she pulled through till the morning. Lomai attended her personally to the last, and bore himself through it all with a meek and Christlike spirit. Never once did I hear a murmur of complaint pass his lips. Always trustful that what God did was best. Night and day he had been beside her trying her with beef tea, milk, and all kinds of native foods, anything, if she will but take a little. On this, the last night, he refused to lie down. Naupum remained unconscious all night, but he waited patiently beside her in the hope that she might speak one last word. Towards morning she called him and told him she was going, but immediately became unconscious again. I persuaded Lomai to come up to the house with me as I might want him to take something down for Naupum, but in reality, to force him to take some nourishment.

Sitting in the study, he did so, and was most grateful, but just as he rose to go down again, Mrs.Nicholson called me out. Titonga had come to say that Naupum was dead. I went in and told him "Naupum has gone home". We remained in the room for fifteen or twenty minutes, and neither of us spoke a single word. At the end of that time Lomai said, "I will go down now, doctor." I got him some things for the burial, and asked if he would like anything else. "Will you give me a handkerchief for my tears." I did so, and this Great Heart walked calmly down to prepare his dead for burial. Our servants and the people seemed to stand in awe as he passed through them.

A little later I went down and found him wrapping the body in its winding sheet of calico. All wailing on the part of the women had ceased. It simply could not be in the presence of this outstanding man, at such a time. He quietly told me to go and take some food, and he would send me word when the grave was ready.

The funeral was to take place after dinner. Whilst at dinner, a messenger came up to say another teacher's wife had died suddenly. I had passed her door four times that morning and whilst knowing she was suffering from the effect of prolonged fever, I did not think she was so bad. She had been about all morning. We were thunderstruck that afternoon. I buried both and felt bad, but it was really grand to see the change Christ had made in these people, instead of the awful yelloing and bad talking, they sang the 23rd psalm, read Jno.14, sang "There's a land that is fairer than day", prayed and returned quietly to their homes.

On Sunday Titonga and Javis preached, as Lomai could not interpret, rather as I would not let him, I merely conducted the service, Lomai turned out in black and looked most doleful. No wonder as Lomai is head and shoulders above his fellows. Naupum was also above the women, a gentlewoman, clean, generous. When lying almost dying Isabel and I went to see her after greeting us she asked Lomai to get sugar cane for the missis. She used to send us fruit, native puddings, etc. I examined her after coming and found cavities in both lungs, so that her case was hopeless. I did not tell Lomai, but he knew all the same. Ruth, their little girl of two years is a great comfort to her father, but mother mine I must push on.

This week, on Tuesday, we crossed to White Sands and did not feel the six hour ride tiresome, but rather enjoyed it. Lomai and two others came with us. On Wednesday I gave Mrs.McMillan chloroform and extracted 18 teeth and stumps. She had done well and when we left this morning is A.1. I also pulled four more teeth for natives, so that was not so bad for one day. We had a good ride across and tonight are trying to get some letters ready for this mail, but I will stop with this one. We are still hard at work here, we have reaped our Indian corn (pulled the cobs), are trying to get the ground cleared again, have another kiln of lime now burning, the hospital nearly finished, but the grounds have to be terraced and trimmed up a bit round it. We are in good health, praising God for all His Goodness and His Service, praying and looking for Isa.44 & 3. We are getting the North Down Heralds all right, keep on sending them, we read them through and through.

We were rejoiced to hear you were all well. We open our letters with joy mixed with fearfulness. I got a letter from Willie, I hope he will do well in this new sphere he has entered on. I am so glad Nellie is going to stay until Sarah comes.

Netta should have gone as secretary to Mr.Alexander, it would have done her good getting out. We are always expecting news from Sarah. It must have been grand in Belfast. Pray for us here, we need the same. I wonder how the sale of work has done. Poor, poor Hamilton Road, but surely she shall yet be delivered, I believe God wanted the Hamilton Road Church and will see her flourish under His blessing, keep believing.

Now good night mother mine, Love to all at home, but I'll keep this open for a day and add anything which may turn up. 9th. I have little else to add, except that Isabel has an awful craze on for breeding poultry. She has them now in all stages, just set, nearly out, wee ones to wrap in flannel and put at the fire, ones able to look after themselves, etc. We have an old Muscovie duck sitting on 14 eggs. They take a week longer (Isabel says) to come out. Another duck of the same breed is setting up house with four or five eggs. How many fowls we are going to keep I know not, but I have a good big garden almost fenced and planted with bananas and pineapples and have some seeds to put in it, also am planting a field close by with Indian corn. Our hens can fly like pigeons, we never feed them, have no house for them, they all sleep up a fig tree. Our weather now is very nice, sun hot but cool otherwise, Isabel says cold. We sleep under a pair of blankets at times. We had to change the knitted one for a heavier one.

Mr.Anderson is well, he is studying hard, so that we seldom see him in the evenings.

Now goodbye again. Love to Father, Nellie and Netta, much to yourself from us both,

In Christ,
Your affectionate son,
J.Campbell Nicholson

PS. If this is in time you might send me half a dozen white cellular shirts same as I got from Sam Campbell, 17 inches round the neck or 17 and a half. They shrink but if parcel away it does not matter.

JCN

Lenakel,

WEST TANNA,
New Hebrides.
via Sydney
Sept.10th, 1903

Dear Mother,

I only wish you could come out and spend the week-end or better still dozens of them with us. You would have so much to see and so many questions to ask. We are quite well now, but were prevented from going north by being a bit off, Isabel first then I was injudicious in eating pomegranates and had a bad six or seven hours. I thought I had peritonitis for a wee bit. Isabel put on mustard, the first time was not enough so she put on more and it did good work. I couldn't wear a belt for a week, all the skin peeled off, but we missed our trip north. Mr.Anderson went north to see his wife, so we have been alone all month and in many ways like it best, but as I have a great deal of work on hand we could not get on without an assistant at present. All the work is going on well and I think the signs of a big incoming are pretty certain, last Sunday, Lomai said the devil got a sore head, an old chief with whom we have been on very friendly terms, sent me word twice to say that there was to be a big gathering of men on Sunday up in the bush, they were raking up old feuds and saying bad things about two of our teachers. I arranged to go, but after service the teachers were not for going, said it would be no use, but I determined to keep my promise with Nekat and started off. They all followed. When we reached the place I found about 150 men all with loaded rifles sitting in groups round a big square, with a silent prayer I took Lomai and the teachers into the centre and told the people I had come to speak, without so much as by your leave. We sang. My how those teachers let it out, they were a bit afraid and were glad to get an outlet. We sang "We have heard the Joyful Sound", we prayed and then I spoke on the great common enemy and the great Friend. Soon a hush fell and all listened well. After it was finished I got the ring leaders together and in a few minutes they had agreed that the bad talk was finished and that there was to be no fighting, so peace reigns all about us. There has been fighting in Mr.McMillan's and Mr.Watt's district but not much, some four or five were killed. This is the time they always begin and it all is the outcome of their fear of a sort of Witchcraft called "netik[3]". It is supposed that if an enemy can get any part of your food or clothing, even the ground on which you spit, he can by some mummery cause your death. This is so strong amongst them that men with trifling ailments will lie down, refuse to eat and make up their minds they are going to die, even our Xtians are at times under its spell and are in constant fear of leaving anything by the wayside, but this wile of the devil is fast losing its power, Christ is destroying his hold on these poor creatures. It is grand to see the works of God as manifested in changed lives here, with scarcely any knowledge the Spirit of God leads them to renounce the things of darkness and to surrender to God. Pray much for us, that we may have wisdom from above in all our dealings with these people.

Isabel has a good influence here, she goes about a great deal with me and the women crowd about her, awee missis, awee missis and are delighted when she asks them questions. She can speak better than I can. If you asked her did she do any Xtian work she would say no, yet often in the evening the scullery is full up of boys and girls and she teaches them to read and sing and they have a kind of Family Worship. Some nights I persuade her to stay with me, and those youngsters we found have worshipped by themselves before breaking up. Our goatherd is a very good boy and he always as far as we know does the praying. I have peeped in and found them all down and this boy praying very fervently with them.

Then again she has a sewing class with women on Fridays, teaching them to patch and make dresses and shirts, this takes up nearly the whole afternoon. She leads the singing, I can't start the new hymns well, so it falls to her, her voice is getting quite strong. She is a grand little housekeeper and is making this place nice and tasty.

We are still strong on chickens and ducks. I know nothing about them. I went to have a look at some eggs yesterday and found a duck trying to get out, so I pulled the shell off. It died, I got taliwhack, I'll not meddle with hatching eggs again. We had a hen, and a duck sitting on the one next and could not separate them until we got eggs for the hen and she has been contented now to let the old duck mind its own business.

We bathe together any day we have time and I am teaching her to swim. The weather has been splendid and a thick blanket at night is indispensable. Isabel says she feels the cold, but I never do. We wear now the same clothes we wear at home in the summer. I have not had a white suit on for weeks, yet somehow or other, one gets awfully easy fagged, I think the damp atmosphere causes this. Rain is very scarce, we need it badly, the grass is getting dried up, even the weeds are drooping. We are expecting quite a party of missionaries off the boat this time, about 8, Mr. A and Mrs.Watt, Dr. and Mrs.Bowie, Rev.Fred Bowie and Mr.B. The boat will be here some time, as we have 44 bags of corn to go on board, and the trader some 300, and 15-20 tons of copra.

We had hard work shelling the corn to get it ready for the market, and after all the weeks of labour, etc. £11.10 is the result to help to pay the translations. I shall not put it in again as it is hard to get the labour, the people are discouraged with this means of raising money and prices are still falling. If we had agricultural implements like the trader and went about it as a regular thing it would pay, but to do all by hand, makes it heavy, arduous work.

I have not got the hospital in order yet but soon will. The people come in good numbers and one is always in contact with most parts of our district by one or other of its members being with us, so that no matter where we go there is someone we know, and who welcomes us cordially.

How we enjoy the North Down Herald, it comes all right, the only mistake yet, is that we got two of one week instead of different weeks, but all the same from beginning to end we read it. I was so glad to hear about the great revival, God grant that it may also bear fruit in strengthening and sustaining his work at the front. I wish I had word from Sarah, I shall write again soon. Nellie might write. I hope father is well and see that he is still able for Jas.Thompson, that John is also better, we remember all daily at the Throne of Grace, God grant that not one be missing, it will be a Halleluyah reunion.

I hope you got the money from Dr.Jas.Paton all right and had not much bother with the goods, Much Love to you Mother and to Father and all the others with you, Isabel has written.

In Christ,
Your affect.son
James

Throughout the year my Grandparents were kept abreast of the news back home by the North Down Herald which was eagerly looked forward to, following his father's progress as a counsellor on Bangor Town Council.

In Jottings 44 April 1904 the October 1903 letter from Grandfather gives news of Lomai*:*

"I have married seven couples lately – three at an out-station, and four here. Readers of Mr.Frank Paton's book will be interested to hear of Lomai's marriage. The woman of his choice is a remarkable woman. Before hearing of the Gospel she was deeply impressed by a dream in which she had revelations of the other world. Her subsequent career bears out the truth of her assertion, as she at once commenced a crusade in her own and other villages against heathenism and its concomitant wickedness. Her husband resented her conduct and words, often brutally beating her, but she persevered through it all and influenced not a few. After her husband died her tribe was nearly wiped out by their enemies. The remnants were saved by Lomai and the teachers (as described in Jottings No.37, p.7, July 1902), and were brought to live near Lenakel – a village being built for them. In my last letter I told about the opening of their new church. Keai, the rescued widow, then turned into a regular Dorcas, caring for the old women and orphans. She was baptized by Mr.McMillan last Christmas.

We had a crowded house the day of the weddings. As I could hardly ask Lomai to interpret at his own wedding, we translated the marriage service. All passed off well, though one young man's heart failed him at the last minute, and we had nearly to drag him off the seat. Rings were put on the fingers of the brides, the little register signed, and then, as is the custom, we first shook hands with the interested couples and about two hundred people followed suit, marching up single file.

Lomai took his bride to his new house behind the hospital, and we congratulated ourselves on having such worthy helpers close at hand. Keai is very proud of Lomai, and insists on coming with us when itinerating. The first Sabbath after their marriage I was surprised to see her sitting on the men's side of the church with Lomai. I did not pass any comment but waited for Lomai to explain, this he soon did, as we were going through the bush, telling me Keai had said to him that as I had read "What God hath joined let no man put asunder." it was only right they should not be separated in God's house, so she continues to sit by his side. I expect some of the other women will think they should do likewise soon.

But, alas! Lomai's troubles soon commenced afresh, his little daughter Ruth was taken ill with tubercular meningitis, and, after being unconscious for nearly a fortnight, died. Before little Ruth died, Keai was stricken down with acute pneumonia, and was a source of great anxiety to us all. Lomai bore it all bravely. After burying Ruth he returned to nurse Keai, never leaving her. Keai safely passed the crisis, but is recovering very slowly. Lomai, worn out with his grief and sleepless nights, at last broke down. It came suddenly; he seemed dull and low-spirited, and I tried to cheer him. He said God had taken away all his children, and Naupum, and now was going to take Keai. He did not know what God was going to do with him, maybe take him too. We had a long chat, and he cheered up again."

Lenakel,
WEST TANNA,
New Hebrides,
Via Sydney
Nov.18th,1903

Dear Mother,

Our mails here are contrary ones. We have to write before we get our home letters, as the boat drops our letters and receives them at the same time. This letter will now go to Vila and stay there until the 12th December when the Solomon Island boat calls and takes it to Sydney, so though we are reputed to have a monthly mail the collections are not monthly but take place within a week or ten days of each other.

We are both very well in spite of the heat but all the days are not hot, so when the wind comes from the south it is delightful and one begins to feel a joy in living.

We have Mrs.Anderson back with us again and are getting on very well.

She helps Isabel a good deal. I think too she may help in the hospital as she is taking a great interest in it. We have got it all ready, but the committee have neither given us bed or bedding. I have put an old spring mattress in and made another. We have two women and a boy in, all have been operated on and are doing very well.

Isabel gave chloroform the first time, but was a little sick and had to leave the room twice. Mr.Anderson tried but was worse. Mrs.Anderson took the next and was not sick at all, so I think she may keep on at it.

It is a great comfort to have the hospital, it is so disheartening trying to help people when their methods of living nullify any good one may do them. Besides it enables us to teach them more about our Lord and Saviour. Lomai is a great help and takes on his new duties with great zest. He also reads and sings and prays each evening with the patients.

Today I had my first case of female ailment. She had been badly hurt in childbirth, examination and treatment were permitted without dissent, so that they are giving me their fullest confidence. God help me to use it for the inbringing of their souls into the fold. One yearns for these poor brothers and sisters, their deadness is awful, almost but not as dreadful as the deadness in the midst of light such as you enjoy in Ireland. The Spirit we read, brooded over chaos at the beginning, light and order resulted so here only the brooding of the same Spirit avails to the awakening of those dead in trespasses and sin. Thank God we are not without unmistakable signs of the Spirit's working and sometimes in the darkest corner one finds a man or woman groping after God and recognise him in Christ.

We are now thinking of our Communion and Christmas Seasons. You will be praying for us, but I will write you fully about them in my next.

I am longing for this mail. I received your note on the College of Surgeons' letter, after it had been a month knocking about the Islands. I am thinking of paying for a private bag at Sydney which will be sent down sealed each month, the sorting of the letters on the Island steamer is a risky affair and I am sure plenty of letters are lost.

How I wonder what you all are looking like and what you are doing. Soon it will be a year since we left you, the time flies. Now I must stop. We shall be praying much for you all especially at Christmas. Love to all and most to yourself, from us both.

Your affec. Son in Christ,
J.Campbell Nicholson

Chapter III – The Second Year

Consolidation and a New Arrival

Lenakel
WEST TANNA
New Hebrides
Via Sydney
Jan.3rd 1904

Dear Mother,

I wish you a very happy New Year – we both do, also Father, Nellie and Netta. Last Friday was the anniversary of our wedding. It has been a very happy year for us both. We were told the first year was always the hardest to agree in, after that we would know each other better. Well we were just saying today if the succeeding years are only as good as the first we could not ask for more. "Only Goodness and Mercy has followed us" and our hope of God's home is brighter than ever. One thing being a missionary does, at least I think, is to cut one loose from a good many of the things of earth which make Heaven unreal and vague. We can never feel we are at home on Tanna and yet we know that to all intents and purposes we have no other but Heaven. The thought of going home six years from now is not altogether unmixed with pleasure, the assured fact of many changes occurring by then, makes us at times dread it and then the awful ordeal of saying goodbye again, the dull pain of the last one still lingers – we seldom speak of that night. To do so is to touch a spot in our hearts still sore.

Just think I got four letters from you last time. We got the November and December mail all in the one morning. Between business and private letters we had between seventy and eighty letters. How I am to get them all answered is the question, the ones from supporters of our work here must come after the home ones and the others when time can be found. I never find writing letters to strangers an easy matter. I wish I could write them as easily as I write to you. Christmas is over, we had a great gathering but torrential rain from early morning till 1p.m. so we had a very extended service in the Church and after the rain cleared up the people set out to enjoy themselves and kept it up till late at night. One unpleasant thing occurred. A party of heathen tried to carry away a girl by force from under our very nose. Our people were paralysed, more especially as these men were all carrying their loaded rifles. When I heard the woman's cry I started off and soon caught up on them. Four men had the girl by her arms, the others formed a sort of guard round them whilst they pulled at the girl. I burst through the guard and got the girl round the waist behind and getting my heels set brought them to a stop, then by twisting and hammering their arms I got the girl free and she ran to safety. If the heathen had not had an arm each taken up with a rifle I could not have got her off so easy. I then ordered them off the grounds and looking foolish off they went, firing their rifles in volleys after they got through the gate, to let us know they were not afraid. The heathen from the other tribes merely looked on in amazement at the daring of these fellows and also at their being so easily routed. All heathen consider the mission grounds holy and sacred, and would not dare to do such a thing, but this tribe live a good way from us and were led by a fellow who has been to Queensland. I am so glad they were foiled otherwise we might be subject to many such attempts. I think we have often told you that we are so secure here that we never use a lock and key, not a drawer locked in the place, not even the money one and the house is always open, yet we never lose anything. This safety is not altogether begotten in respect for us, but is mixed with superstition. The trader close to us is robbed repeatedly and has always to be on the watch. We have great reason to thank God for this immunity.

The foiled heathen the next day tried to shoot one of our women, the bullet just missing her head. I sent off a messenger asking them to meet me on neutral ground. They did so and we had a good talk, but today we had another and their Chief representing his tribe and myself before all the people struck hands in token that all talk was finished. We had a good gospel service and I trust yet to see many of them worshipping together with us of the True God and Jesus the only Saviour.

Our people were greatly frightened and some took to carrying rifles, but I spoke out against it as showing a want of faith in God. However, mother mine, I am carnal enough to have wished once or twice I had a revolver in my pocket, one occasion my courage left me, I had got a considerable way in advance of Mr.Anderson and Lomai and two others, (all we could get to start with us), I met six of the tribe who said the remainder were waiting further on. I made them go on the track in front of me, but after a little they split, three passing to the right among the reeds. I came to a stop, went back a little and waited. I simply could not go past where those three had disappeared and yet I do not now believe there was any treachery intended. However I encouraged myself in the Lord and in the fact of my party coming up behind and was able to go on and meet the folk first. Isabel has not been in the least put out and only once asked me not to go when I felt it my duty to do so, and then did not persist. 'She is a big hearted wee soul'.

You should hear her talking away to the natives. On Christmas day she was knocking about with a big baby slung native fashion astride her haunch and enjoyed herself amongst the people right heartily. Lomai's wife is dead, only married four months, she also died of consumption, it set in after congestion of the lungs. Poor Lomai, now a trader is trying to take his land from him, but I have threatened to take it into the mission for Lomai's use so that if the trader persists, he will not have to deal with a native, who has no court of appeal at all against things like this.

Nearly three sheets and I feel I have so much yet to write. We have been busy painting, have builded a kitchen, and have built an underground water tank which should hold I think nearly 2400 gallons. It has yet to be cemented inside and I am sending for a pump. If it is a success we should have a good cool supply of water. I hope the earthquakes will not crack it. It has taken a lot of work to dig it out and build up its sides. It is right at the kitchen door. We have been given tanks already, iron ones, capable of holding 3400 gallons, but the sun warms the water in them and as we have had three months without rain already since coming, we have to be very careful of the water as the roof is the only source up here. When heavy showers come they soon fill the tanks and then we have a difficulty with the overflow. For a week we have had very heavy rain, all the ground terraces and road are cut up. 'If our tanks had only been ready', we say, twenty times a day.

A lot of painting remains to be done yet and a good deal of carpentering. You see the house was left in a very unfinished state and Mr.Anderson says he did not care to do anything till I came, but in a month or two we should have a very comfortable and complete house. In fact you would not believe there could be such a one so far from civilization. I am keeping at the house as much as possible as Mr.Anderson expects to leave about June. His furlough is then due and he intends to study.

When I get this mail off I will have to go to the other side for Communion and Baptismal Services and visit all the stations in Mr.MacMillan's and Watt's districts, so Isabel will be alone for a bit with the Andersons, as there will be too much roughing for her to do.

Now Mother mine, this is a long letter, and I feel I could go on, but must restrain myself. Nothing has arrived from home yet, but we never expect things up to time here.

One year has gone Mother, the other six will soon go in. Of course you must stay down here at least till then and pray for your children. It is grand glorious to have assured hope of the great home. We had the 21st of Revelations as our lesson today, no more sorrow, pain, crying, death, Hallelyh (a bad attempt) Hallelujah, Love from us both to you all. We have been happy today in spite of the migginess,

In Christ your affect. son,
J.Campbell Nicholson

Lenakel,
WEST TANNA,
New Hebrides,

Via Sydney.
March 3rd 1904

Dear Mother,

Your two December letters came to hand safely. We were so glad to know all were quite well at home, with the exception of Father's cold. We hope it is quite better now. We have had a hotwet season, rain nearly every day. I got soaked through so often it is a wonder I have kept so well.

You ask about our neighbours. They have all been down off and on with Fever this season. Mr.Worthington is failing fast I think and I should not be surprised if he dropped off within a year. They have no children, but have now adopted a baby boy from an orphanage in Sydney. It is doing well and they are very fond of it. They have a niece from Australia staying with them, a girl about 16 years of age. Their partner is a Mr.Newman, about 27 or so, a fine young fellow and so far has been exemplary in character, though he does not take his place as a Christian nor do I think cares much about our work, but it is good to get a man out of the ordinary run of traders here, most of them are bad and going in for selling the natives grog although it is against the law. Mr.McMillan reported all the traders on his side for it, but nothing was done. About three miles from here we have two brothers, Pearse by name. There was another man with them called Moulton from England, but he was not strong. I had him staying here for treatment a couple of weeks, but he sold out to the Pearses and has returned to the colonies.

The Pearses, we have little intimacy with. We are dubious about them. I do not think they will stay long, but will sell out to the French, whose steamer they have brought down here twice. They bought land on Efate and sold to the French. You see the French are not liked by the natives and I am doubtful if a Frenchman could get any land to buy here at present but they get in by people like the Pearses. We are going to have trouble with these French in the future[1]*. They are determined to get these Islands and I think will get them, as the English Government don't want them. Australia objects, but she is doing nothing for the Islands and has spoiled the coffee, ginger, etc., plantations by putting a very heavy duty on them so that we cannot compete with the other producers. Mr.Worthington has 2 or 3 acres of coffee lying idle here, after* *spending a great deal of money on it. The French have subsidised a company to run steamers here. The subsidy enables them to knock about without the trade making them any profits. I hear that north there are paid French agents going about buying up all the land they can get their hands on, also reasserting all old French claims on lands which have long since been forgotten about. But all is in God's hands and we must do the work of today and do it as well as we can.*

Isabel has kept in splendid health and is so active that it would make you sweat just to look at her moving about. She is as cheery as a cricket. Mrs. Anderson has been very ill. Mr.Anderson has had fever off and on all season. I had one sharp attack and was in bed for nearly a week. I got it whilst itinerating in Mr.McMillan's district, was away from home for a week or nearly so and had wet weather and mosquitoes galore, but we will send you the duplicate of Jottings' letter and you will see about it in it.

In Jottings 44 Grandfather tells of a visit he paid to Mount Yassur when over at the beginning of the year in Mr.Macmillan's district:
I paid a midnight visit to the volcano when over. It was an awful sight and sound. It is a stiff climb up and when you get to the top you find the mountain you have been climbing in is just like a high basin, the top of which is about a mile round, maybe more. I could not see very well in the dark. The bottom of the crater is more or less a molten, restless mass. Every now and then there is an explosion and boiling red hot lava is thrown right up into the air, also big pieces of rock. The shock is awful and indeed the sight and sound is beyond description. We had a splendid sight, a good wind was blowing and took the smoke all away. We stood to windward and could sit on the very edge. The wind also took the falling stones either into the crater again or to the side furtherest from us. The natives were awfully afraid and every big explosion took to their heels. After returning I was away for two days and a night visiting my own and Mr.McMillan's stations between here and the extreme north. We had wet weather again but good winds so that we had but little pulling to do. Whilst returning and about five miles from home, I got the shakes. It seemed so strange to be shivering with cold again, especially when all the others were sweating.

As we were beating and none of the natives know anything about this kind of sailing I had to hold on to the tiller and got in safely, but by the time I got to the house was delirious. Poor Isobel did not know what to make of it. Two days after, I got the second attack, but with the aid of two hot water bags, blankets, etc. I got the cold stage over quicker, although again I acted the fool in the hot stage, trying to whistle and sing, but I feel quite strong again and am about as much as ever. I do not think I would have got the fever if I had not been itinerating in the worst part of the year, but as Mr.and Mrs. Anderson leave us in April to go to Nguna to help Mr.Milne to prepare for Synod, I have to get as much done as possible as it is not easy to leave Isabel alone and the work here also.

If you look at the map, you will see I have got all done from here to Port Resolution going north and have yet to work south from here to Port Resolution, which I hope to get done by April. The most important stations are on the coast, the inland ones must be done on horse or foot.

I am glad to say that everywhere there are signs of the working of God's spirit. Our motto 'Tanna for Christ' I hope yet to see realised. In our own district things are most hopeful and the difficulty is and will be to find teachers for the different openings, but all is in the hands of the Great and Loving Father of the Tannese.

What do you think, we have ordered the frame of a good big Church for Lenakel. It will arrive by the steamer as Mr.Anderson departs. This is awkward for me, but we"ll get it up somehow. The natives now are on the strain to raise the money, £97. A party are off today to make copra on the other side. It is understood that the Church is not to be used till every penny is paid. Mr.Anderson has had most of the work to do about the station and is yet working to get the house finished. It is nearly completed now.

Isabel looked after the hospital for me. She had three patients in it. She also treated those who came for medicine. She knows a good deal about the simpler drugs already and the native think she is a good doctor. We have six in the hospital at present, all doing well. The hospital is a great comfort to us and a blessing to the people. The rules are stringent but I have seldom to find fault.

Our people are keeping fairly healthy and we have a good many people about from other parts, either for treatment or working for dresses, shirts etc.

We have great reason to Praise God for all His Goodness and I think we both try to keep close so that the fire in our own hearts may not get low.

Love to all at home. We rejoice in the though of your prayers for us and bend the knee daily in the words of Ephe.iii.14.21.

Love again from us both in Christ,,

Your affect.son,
J.Campbell Nicholson

In Jottings 46 October 1904 Grandfather writes in May of that year:

At home, it is common to speak about March "coming in like a lion and going out like a lamb." It would be hard to find so apt a saw to describe March here. It is the last month of the hot season, when natives and foreigners alike feel fagged and listless. This March we have had plenty of wind and rain, as well as fighting disease and death. However, with grateful heart, I record that the Worshipping people in this district have been most wonderfully preserved. The fighting amongst the heathen did not in the least interfere with our people here or at the out-stations.

We had less fever and fewer deaths than the heathen. It is true that many of the native dwellings were blown down during the gale, but this will prove a wise dispensation as it means many new and better houses.

At Lenakel we have been spending all our time and energy in the erection of new houses. These are built in one long street on the southern boundary of the station.

First, we cleared and levelled the ground, then divided it into spaces for the houses. Each householder, together with such friends as may gather to help him, gets the necessary wood together. To get good hard wood that will not rot in the ground, it is necessary to go long distances. When they have the wood I measure out the ground and oversee the putting in of the posts, to insure the same height and sufficient pitch in the roof to throw off the rain.

Several of our people are splendid builders. After marking out the ground and giving them a bamboo marked to the required heights these good builders may be left to themselves. Others require one working with them if things are to turn out satisfactorily. Ten houses are almost completed and five others are to be commenced soon. Each has a clay floor; the clay we get from the hill behind the hospital. The street now presents a very animated picture; several natives are occupied on the frames of the houses, others are plaiting the long reeds into fancy fronts, others thatching, while the women and children are sitting in groups making the thatch or cleaning reeds. There is plenty of talking and laughing, and one never gets tired going in and out amongst them.

Most of the houses are uniform in size and height, but if any wish for a larger and better one, we encourage them. Titonga has a splendid house. He was so particular about it that he preferred to do all the work himself. Javis has, if anything, a better, but as he is not so skilful as Titonga, he sought help, though he was careful to have the best available.

Javis, while not to be compared, from my point of view, with Titonga and Lomai as helpers, is a model man, a born chief, and a good example in our community here. At all times he is clean and well dressed. Whatever he puts on seems to suit him; whether it be a suit of fancy coloured pyjamas, or a shirt and waist cloth, he looks what he is, a native gentleman. He was telling me the other day that he helped to build a house for "Tamate"[2]*, the great New Guinea Missionary and Martyr at Port Moresby. But he did not come into personal contact with him. Javis can tell wonderful incidents of shipwreck and adventures amongst the New Guineans. He formed one of the crew of a "Beche-de-mer*[3]*" schooner and spent several years in those waters. But during the time of his absence from Tanna he does not seem to have ever come under Christian or civilizing influences. The white men he came in contact with were apparently little better, if not worse, than the heathen.*

A teacher from an out-station joined with one in training, to build a house here for them both. They came to me about it and I heartily agreed with them, as it is necessary for our out-station teachers to have some place when they come here. We have a house used solely by teachers who may be at the head station, either for their monthly visit or for communion seasons. They expressed their determination as follows:

"We want one big fellow house."

"Yes, how many rooms?"

A brief consultation and they answer:

"One fellow room for Ielep and Numanipen to sleep in, and one fellow room for me and Sarah to sleep in, and one room for we four fellows to eat in."

We may expect an order for a drawing room next. As it is, a great step forward has been made in that each house has a small cook house at the rear, so that fires are being dispensed with in the dwelling houses. Jot.46 Oct.1904

(Taken from Jottings 46 and was also in amongst the original letters)

Lenakel,
WEST TANNA,
New Hebrides,
July 1904

In my last letter I referred to our approaching communion season. It has come and gone but the memory and blessing of that season is still very real to us all.

As usual the people began coming in about the beginning of the week. Mrs. Nicholson and myself went north in the boat to bring in the usual cargo of yams, taro, coconuts and etc. We had a splendid day, a leading wind enabling us to sail both coming and going. As we sailed along the coast we could recognise group after group travelling along the sands to Lenakel. Lomai, Titonga and Javis had been through all the stations holding preparatory services and visiting all church members and candidates. On the Wednesday our services commenced and from that till the following Monday we were kept very busy. Our houses were all packed and many of the people had to camp under the banyan trees. The spirit of joy and liberty was most manifest amongst the people, indeed the most despondent and gloomiest of men could not have passed through them without being lifted. At the services we who spoke had the greatest freedom and joy in speaking for God.

The great surprise in store for me was the first united candidates class. Indeed for a little Lomai and I thought the people had not understood the intimation, but when we had looked over those present we saw that there was no mistake, many of these had come for the first time. On the Friday those desirous of baptism at this season remained behind and of these fifty three were accepted.

As usual they are not only accepted on confession of faith, but each name is submitted to a committee composed of the three head teachers and the outstation teachers and if there is any division of opinion I, as chairman, having the casting vote. As yet I have only had to give it once and that was in favour of a young man with a hasty temper. I had every sympathy with and faith in him. That was almost a year ago and he is now one of the best young men we have in the district. It took us several hours to get through the list this time. Then we have a church court to deal with those who may have fallen into sin, but our duties were light, five were punished by temporary suspension from the Lord's Table.

It often surprises me that the people submit so willingly to discipline. Since coming only one person refused to appear when called upon. We had also a teachers' conference this time to discuss our methods of work and to seek to make them more efficient and adaptable to the separate districts. It was a very helpful time and served to make us realise the better that we were, all members of one body.

The Sabbath was a day long to be remembered, not having an assistant I had to throw the whole responsibility of the services on Lomai, Titonga and Javis. When I tell you that not a thing was forgotten, not a hitch occurred, you will know how they devolved the responsibility.

I will endeavour to give you a brief word picture of the day's proceedings. As the sun rose, the bell rang for a united prayer meeting, as I was already feeling the strain of the past four days and needed time alone, the elders conducted it. About nine o'clock the elders and teachers came up for the table, wine, vessels, bread, organ, etc. Lomai and Javis allotted to each man his burden. Led by Lomai they formed a procession and walked down to the church. Indeed Mrs. Nicholson and myself were proud of our helpers, they looked splendid, there was nothing fantastic or ludicrous in their dress, all so clean and modest. After the elders had spread the table and arranged the platform, they admitted those to be baptized, their seats being at the front; then the communicants, then the adherents, not a few of the latter having to sit outside the door. The bell now rang out as a signal, all was ready and we could come. The service lasted almost three hours but seemed like three quarters. Lomai and Javis served the bread, Titonga and Neropo assisted by Tapunus and Kahwa, the wine. To see these men serving the table of the Lord was a great privilege. In all my experience I never saw men anywhere, not even in Edinburgh do it with more grace and modesty. At this service we took for our motto 'Tanna for Christ' and pledged ourselves to work for its accomplishment. We also had a special prayer of thanksgiving for the communion set which was on its way to us. After a brief pause for lunch we had our next service and to this nine infants were brought for dedication to God and baptism, by their parents. In the evening the elders conducted another service: Mrs.Nicholson and myself resting at home.

Three couples were married on the Saturday. It was a season of great joy and blessing and as He only blesses to make us a blessing, we expect great results in time to come. Indeed we have seen the beginning already. The two tribes at Lokavit on the Monday commenced to build their house and finished it in a week. It is forty feet by fifteen, has four rooms completely separated from each other, two for men and two for women. These people not to burden our people here, walked home by moonlight returning in the early morning with food for themselves. Neither did we help them in any way and they did not receive a single ounce of food from me, so they cannot be called 'Rice christians'.

The Lopilpil people are very busy with their own new village, but expect to erect the Lopilpil house here before Christmas. One interesting item about their village, which I omitted to mention in my last letter, was that not a man commenced to build his own house until they had completed the House of God. When I visited them it was the only building on the large space of ground they had cleared. This was truly an object lesson on putting 'first things first'.

Our people here, immediately after communion, commenced to prepare lime for the foundations of the church. Two large pits have been burnt. Opportune rain slaked them so that our lime is ready for boating round. Now we are preparing the site. To do this hundreds of tons of earth have to be removed, as we are going to put the church at the head of the street on the breast of the hill. I preferred this site but did not press for it as the work to prepare it would be very great, but the people would have no other, and said, never mind the work, show us where to begin. After making the necessary measurements and taking the levels, my heart failed me and I said we had better look for another site, but they would have none of it 'leave it to us we will soon shift it' they said. After a service on the ground, they started too, like ants, men with pickaxes and shovels, women and children carrying off the earth on stretchers made with sacks and pieces of wood.

I do all the hospital work so as to allow Lomai to help, and he together with Titonga and Javis have succeeded in organising the district so that in rotation our outstation people come to help. In another week we expect to have the work completed and by that time trust we may have Mr.Mackenzie with us to help with the erection of the foundations and frame. If he cannot come we will go ahead all the same.

We had the great joy of receiving a visit from Dr.J.G.Paton and a crowd of others, amongst them were Bishop Wilson, Dr.Gunn, Mr.Leggett and Mr.Frater. The remainder were tourists and planters. Dr.Paton went through the village and into several of the houses. He was greatly pleased with all he saw, and when a missionary was not exactly favourable in his criticism of the clay floors, spoke up sharply and said 'why I was reared on a clay floor like that'. Our visitors went over the hospital and mission premises, and spent the afternoon with us. All went off to the steamer before dark except Bishop Wilson, Dr.Gunn and Mr.Leggatt who stayed and spent the evening with us. How we enjoyed their conversation and company. Bishop Wilson was greatly interested in our work, especially the hospital, and told me he intended to get one something similar for his work.

The frame of our church arrived at the same time. The Captain of the steamer asked me for a good man to steer the launch which was to tow the timber. I appointed Lomai and it was almost midnight before he had finished. He was greatly disappointed, as I had told him I was going to let him take the visitors over the hospital

I was so occupied with my visitors that I forgot about the church, but the people had not. When I got down to the beach at ten o'clock, was greatly pleased to find that they had it all carried up.

The steamer brought us our communion set, we had it on exhibition for several days. The people were delighted, one sight was not sufficient many came again and again to look at it. We had to repeat Mrs.Cunningham's name to them time and again that they might be able to pronounce it. Lomai said, 'God has been very good to us and given us a good sign to be strong and build Him a good house. Mrs.Cunningham is now spoken of as 'wusicum', this is the word used to translate 'elect lady', in the second epistle of John.

During our communion season over ten pounds was contributed towards the Church. We aimed at five, some Tanna men in Queensland sent us two pounds. In all we have now sixty seven, but the money market is almost exhausted, the last three months are the slack ones for copra. However, by Christmas we expect to clear the cost of the frame and by that time believe God will send us enough for iron and timber to complete the building. A little boy in a hospital in Victoria sent us five shillings to help us with our hospital. We were greatly touched by this gift.

On Sunday, the nineteenth of June, a little son arrived (My father – BM). *The natives are delighted, he is a real Tanna man they say. He has been called all kinds of big names, his greatest being 'Ieremere keikei' (beloved chief). I also hear him referred to as 'Doketer resuse' (the little doctor). Lomai is especially delighted. He was first to get a look at him. He said, I am a strong man to work with babies, bye and bye you will let me nurse him – by strong he meant very fond. Javis after a very critical examination said, Doketer, He all them same like you.*

In spite of having to give so much time and energy to the work at Lenakel, our general work has not suffered. The outlook for our whole district is much brighter than ever it was, this is due in a great measure to the constant coming and going to and from Lenakel, coming for medicine and treatment and to help us with the new church. When the brunt of the heavy work is over, I believe we shall be able to open up at least two new stations.

In the northern part of Mr.MacMillan's district a splendid work is being done at two outstations. The people of one of these were driven out by their enemies and found a refuge at Lenakel. After two years they returned to their homes and now their enemies have become friends. They have built a church for themselves and would like me to send them a teacher. At present I am unable to comply with their request and long for the return of Mr.MacMillan. They also made a great present of taro and yams to their erstwhile enemies, these not forgetful of the kindness of our people in time past, have brought part of the yams and taro round to Lenakel in their boat.

I have promised to visit this station at the earliest opportunity to administer the sacraments of baptism and the Lord's Supper. The other station was opened just after Mr.MacMillan left. The teacher was trained here. He has already done good service. When I visited him in February, a church had just been commenced, now it is finished and a great crowd attended the opening services. I was sorry I could not get across. The latest news to hand is that the attendances at school and services are the largest in the north of Tanna, some of my teachers who were across came back bursting with the good news. Surely we have good reason to be optimistic and to give praise and glory to our All Conquering Saviour. TANNA for CHRIST we may yet live to see an accomplished fact.

We are conscious daily of prayer being answered here, which has been offered up by many in Australia and at home.

Together let us rejoice at the ingathering. With our united kind regards,

Yours sincerely, J.Campbell Nicholson

Lenakel
WEST TANNA
New Hebrides
Via Sydney
Sept.10th 1904

Dear Mother,

Your two very welcome letters to hand on the 9th August. I am glad you got the run to the Spa and the time with your sisters, our aunts. Also to hear that you were so strong and well. I only wish you could get a run out here, it would be grand, I am sure you would enjoy yourself and take a spell at nursing your grandson. He does not yell so loud nor so much and gives us no trouble at night at all, sleeping most of the time in his cot, but always awake at daybreak, crowing and laughing and if we still sleep on begins to cry until we take a little notice of him. He is still much visited and admired. The Tanna word for yes is o'oh and when he o'ohs the natives think he is answering them in the affirmative. He seems to like the black people better than the whites and always has a smile for the former

I have been trying to take a photo of him for you, but I have only old plates I brought with me, some of them I had a year before I left home and many of them are useless, but I have persevered and succeeded in getting one or two developed. John almost refuses to have his photo taken, but I must try and have one or two for you, also one of the new church which is nearing completion and one of our servants.

I am sending for new plates and am going to make a dark room so that by Christmas I may have a few pictures for you. Mr. And Mrs.McKenzie left on the 9th August so we have had the house to ourselves and likely to for some time.

We intend D.V. to go by steamer to the other side in October and stay for two or three weeks. I would like to ride across but am afraid the journey would be too much for Isabel and John. Isabel had a bad attack of influenza, pains all over, especially her back, her stomach and bowels were also affected and I had an anxious time for a day or two, but she is as strong and hearty as ever and is busy from morning to night as she could well be, but I still insist on her lying down for an hour or so after dinner each day. I am going to write a very general letter as you will get the typewritten one which will give you the principal missionary news.

Our garden is doing splendid, we have a part of it fenced off for a kitchen garden and for the last two months or more have had a constant supply of vegetables. Some times we have peas, kidney beans, turnips, as well as yam all at one meal and we feel so much better for the fresh food. Tinned meats get tiresome but we could not well do without them just yet. However, we often have a kid killed and every week a fowl. The kid with mint sauce is not bad, but when I kill a lamb, we find there is a great difference.

We have now eighteen sheep and lambs, seven new lambs this year. Last year we were unfortunate and lost three or four sheep by poisoning and accident, otherwise we could have mutton oftener. The goats number about 40 all told and keep us well supplied in milk. The cow is dry and her calf is a good sized bull now. I wish I could sell him to get money for the new church.

The horses still number four but we should have an addition I think about Christmas. I have broken in the colt to the saddle but only ride him occasionally, he is going to be very big, is already bigger than the others, he is good in the bush and follows me along the tracks where I have to walk, without being led. I hope to get a market for him also to get money for the new church, but I must have a good price for him as he is a splendid looking beast.

The turkeys' eggs were not fertile so that we have no young ones and out of about 50 duck eggs we have only 15 or so ducks, the rest were rotten, one old duck ate hers off. We are going to eat her off next.

Chickens are by the dozen running about, nearly hundred, but the wet weather killed some off. I must get a hen house. We have neither run or house, just a tree for them. We do not bother much about feeding the hens, they get so much about that they would not take the trouble to come for any we might give them.

We shot Pat. I think I told you Jean has had a single pup, we will keep it and call it Pat.

Now that is all about the beasts.

We have nothing much new in the garden except ginger and must wait till next spring for new things. Potatoes we set seem to be doing well, we ate four little ones and they tasted very good. We should have some good ones in a week or so. Turnips and carrots did well, grubs ate the cabbages and the parsnips did not do so well. Tomatoes have done well, we have plenty and to spare, such big ones. Parsley and mint grow quickly.

I have been kept busy in the hospital but have two off my hands now. 4 remain, one man had a tremendous abscess deep in his armpit and burrowing down his arm. He was nearly gone. I made a couple of good openings and would be afraid to tell you how much pus came out. I have drainage tubes in, but will have to open the armpit up and scrape away the diseased glands, otherwise he would have running sores for life. All goes quietly here except that some of the traders are selling drink, not the Worthingtons. I will have to report them to the Commissioner. A French recruiter is lying in our bay also selling grog, but I think I have succeeded in keeping any natives from going as recruits, they could not even get boys to pull their boats and I see tonight that they have lifted their boat so that the morning may find us minus their company. They had some of the traders out for drink and cards and had a big night. Since coming here, two of the recruiters I had to do with have come to violent deaths, one abused a woman and I had to threaten him to keep him off the grounds. He was going to do all kinds of things to me, but 2 months ago was trying to shoot fish with dynamite and blew his hand and head almost to pieces. Another knocked about here and ill-treated some of the boys whom he got to pull in his boat. One in revenge tried to shoot him, but he sailed off and now I hear that people in a northern island in revenge for his having stolen two women, killed and ate him and all his crew except one half-caste who was swimming about for 24 hours and got on board the recruiting schooner again after the natives had plundered her. He hoisted a jib and cut the cable and sailed off and was picked up some days after, 16 years man-stealing, but they had an awful revenge. A native who sailed with him says this man often seized men, boys and women and carried them off. Truly we white people need well to try and make up a little for what these poor people have suffered at the hands of our brethren at least in colour.

We are hurrying to get the Church opened now. I am so sorry we had not money enough to get iron and timber and seats. We have had an awful amount of work getting thatch reeds, plaiting coconut leaves, we had had to tie bamboos all over the frame to attach the thatch to, but it is better than debt and I have greater belief in and admiration for the people since I have witnessed their zeal for God in building this house. The rain beating in has spoiled the finish of our lime floor, we must cement it next time.

All our people are well, we number now 110 at Lenakel village.

I have been reading Dr.Whyte of Edinburgh on 'Paul'. A friend in Aberfoyle sent it to me. It is a soul searching book, especially for Ministers and Missionaries. One <u>*must*</u> *pray as one reads. I can say no more nor can I speak higher about it. Pray for our reviving here, we need it.*

I was very sorry to hear about Louie, the Lord save him. We were speaking about 'all things being possible with God' we forget this so often.

I hope Sarah and Dan are better and enjoying themselves. I have written to Dan this time and Sarah with D.V. get one next mail.

We like the new paper but feel sorry for Mrs.Lyttle, send us whatever one you think right but send some one, we would miss it so much.

Your parcel has never turned up. Isabel has been awfully disappointed about it, but I am sure it will come yet. Next time just send it to Mr.Langridge for enclosure and we will be surer to get it.

Isabel has made short clothes for John but is often puzzled about what he should have. I am not up in dressing infants. The Worthingtons are well and their adopted child is a fine little fellow but cannot speak yet. He must be about 16 months or more. I believe he has an influence for good on them.

Willie has not been writing lately. Netta has forgotten us. We are wondering if Nellie has gone to India or not and look forward for the next mail as you may have had time to write about your grandson by that time. I hope Father is well. He did not acknowledge my letter. I suppose the weighty affairs of Bangor monopolise all his time.

We send our love to all, Father, Nellie, Netta and any of the others who may be with you. Very much to your own self.

In Christ,
Your affectionate son,
J.Campbell Nicholson

In Jottings 47 Grandfather tells of Dr. Paton arriving by steamer and coming ashore. During that time he baptised John and in the following week Grandfather and the Tannese started erecting the church. He says: '*One very amusing incident happened by which our church fund was benefited by over £7. The Tannese are great talkers and much talk is always considered necessary before any great effort is made. One morning, whilst at work, their tongues were wagging furiously and loudly about the necessity of getting the price of the frame (for the church) paid immediately so that they could begin to collect for iron and timber. They were not always going to keep this nice frame shrouded in grass. One man whom we call 'Silent William', got very excited, threw down his spade and said he would not lift it again unless every man gave his word for it that he would do his very best. During all this talk a very quiet man, who by the way, is thought simple by many, and who seldom ever speaks unless he is spoken to, slipped away to his house unnoticed and returned with ten shillings (50p) and laying it on the top of a barrel said, 'I talk ten shillings'. Everybody was struck dumb and went on with their work, scarcely daring to look up for a time. Then one and another slipped away and brought sums varying from a threepenny bit (two and a half p.) to a sovereign. Some boys returned with pennies others said whatever ripe coconuts were on their trees they would give as they had no money. One man who is what you call a little 'near', and has always something laid away, when he began to talk about his inability, was reminded by a shrewd fellow of the fate of Ananias and Sapphira. His talk stopped and he returned with a sovereign which I believe he had saved up towards buying a decent bedstead. The expression 'I talk 10/- puzzled me, and on enquiries I found it had its origin in an illustration I had used months before. It ran something like this: Misfortune had overtaken a man and his friends meeting together were loud in their expressions of sympathy. Another friend joined them and after listening for a bit pulled out a five pound note from his pocket and said, 'I sympathise with my unfortunate friend five pounds.' The result was that some of the loudest sympathisers cleared out, but the better hearted also expressed their sympathy in the same practical notes and the unfortunate one was considerably assisted.' (Jottings 47 January 1905). You will hear more of Silent William later on.*

One reason for the lack of letters towards the end of 1904 may be explained by an extract from the Jottings (Jot.47 Jan 1905)

'The months of August and September have been the two most trying months we have experienced since coming to Tanna.

In August, just as our church was completed and ready to be opened, an epidemic of influenza swept through our village and, with the exception of three patients in the hospital, a little girl and myself, I do not know of a single other person who escaped.

It was introduced from the steamer. She remained here at anchor all night. Mr.and Mrs.Worthington and their boat's crew spent the evening on board. Dr.and Mrs.McCausland, who have had to resign Mission work here on account of the health of Mrs.McCausland, spent the night on shore with us. After the steamer left, Mr.and Mrs.Worthington and all their boys were attacked by influenza. It did not spread to our village for a week, so that we were able to get our church completed and had arranged to open it on the Sabbath.

We had decided to have a quiet and informal opening, intending to have a special service at our Christmas gathering. I think in this we had the guidance of God, for influenza broke out amongst us on the preceding Friday, and by the Sabbath at least a third of our people here were ill. On the Sabbath we had a sickly and depressed congregation, Lomai and Iavis were scarcely able to get to the church. We were all glad when the service was over and then commenced for me three of the busiest and most anxious weeks of my life. By the end of the first week I had not a man to help me. Lomai, Iavis and Titonga were seriously ill, also their wives and all the members of their households. On the Sabbath Mrs.Nicholson, our baby and some of our girls were down. I conducted a prayer meeting in the church, a mere handful being able to come. On the Thursday of the following week the first death took place, from pneumonia. I had visited the man and came up to the house to get him some beef tea, but a message followed to say the man had just died after I left him. I could not get sufficient of our own men up to bury him and was exceedingly grateful for the help of some heathen. Iavis' wife now developed pneumonia and I had her removed to the hospital. After a very anxious night she rallied and began to take nourishment. The next day Lomai's wife, a teacher called Nilua and our goatherd all had to be brought to the hospital, suffering from pneumonia. Lomai and Iavis were now able to get about a little and they helped me in the hospital, as two men were delirious and required constant attention. Mrs.Nicholson had just given Iavis's wife some nourishment and we were beginning to have a little hope for her, having Iavis to sit with her. He, however, left the ward for a few minutes, when his wife rose and followed him and was nearly out of the hospital grounds before he saw her. He tried to get her back, but she dropped dead! We had little time for mourning or consoling, three yet remained in a critical condition in the hospital and several others almost as bad in the village.'

More deaths followed but by the middle of October, the epidemic had fizzled out at Lenakel but spread to the heathen. No sooner was the epidemic over when fighting broke out between the heathen and Grandfather was kept busy trying to keep the peace. Many talks were held with him acting as mediator, one talk lasting six hours!

The year closed with Grandfather appealing for bandages from the readers of the Jottings: 'I am almost ashamed to again appeal for old linen or calico – old muslin curtains do splendidly' and an interesting mention of whales: *'We have been visited by a large number of whales this last week. Some lie like huge rocks quite close to the reef in our bay and disporting themselves afford us much amusement. Several nights we have been wakened by the whacks of their tails on the surface of the water.'*

Notes for 1904

Back home it was interesting to note in the North Down Herald that in First Bangor Presbyterian church the idea of an organ had been put forward but the congregation was not only against it but against hymns as well! (would they just have sung psalms?). The Rev.Paton mentions in his autobiography of his wife (second wife) playing the harmonium and singing a simple hymn that the natives found entrancing and that was in 1869! (John G Paton Missionary to the New Hebrides p.362).

Many of the traders on the islands sold grog or drink to the natives which in fact was prohibited by the Government, and were also instrumental in persuading them under some sham pretext to leave the islands and go and work in Australia. This labour traffic or 'blackbirding'[4], was a thinly veiled slave trade in men and women, which started with the discovery of sandalwood on the islands in 1825 by an Irishman, Peter Dillon; there followed a steady stream of get-rich-quick opportunists whose impact on the local population was devastating. Diseases new to the islanders decimated their numbers. In the 1860s sandalwood in China began to diminish and it was then that the traders turned to 'blackbirding'. It is estimated that some 40,000 natives were transported from the islands to Queensland, New South Wales, New Caledonia and Fiji to work on the sugar plantations, from the 1860s right up to the early 1900s. Seduced on board the trading ships under false pretences, not understanding the nature of their engagement, they had to work ten to fourteen hours a day for 3 years before their contract was up. It was largely due to the missionaries' dogged perseverance in petitioning the governments in both Australia and Great Britain that the trade in kanakas[5], as they were known, eventually died out, although this was to take many years.

I believe this to be a good place to say something of Lomai. Reading about him in various books and also in the letters, he seemed to stand out from the rest of the islanders. He left Tanna as a boy, travelling to other places, eventually working in Queensland on the Cairns Railway. He spoke English and was baptised a Christian in 1898 by Frank Paton, son of John G Paton and the missionary prior to my Grandfather at Lenakel. Frank Paton speaks of him in glowing terms and Grandfather says in the Jottings 'of feeling very lonely without my constant companion', Lomai being too ill to travel with him when he visited other places on Tanna. There is a section in the Jottings, May '04 which reads, *'Lomai and the hospital, the hospital and Lomai, never one without the other. To mention one is to think of the other. Sometimes the doctor or medicine may be added to these two incidentally. I am only visiting surgeon and physician, Lomai is the rest. It would be a great day for Lomai if you could come out and let him show you round. With his hat raised in his left hand he would meet you with outstretched right and a smile as congenial as a sunny spring morning. The hospital stands in its own ground; is fenced with wire netting; the posts of which are growing and either flower or have an especially pretty foliage. The grass is kept close cut and these together form a fitting setting for the white bungalow Hospital building.*

Lomai would take you to the dispensary, it is his pride and delight. Mr.Anderson made a splendid counter for it, with locker and drawers beneath and shelves above. With its rows of medicine bottles it looks good enough for a city pharmacy. The medicines are a source of wonder to Lomai. I showed him a few simple chemical experiments to increase his awe, and make him very careful about handling them.'

Interesting that the natives didn't know anything about 'beating' when sailing, only running before the wind or 'reaching', which is the wind at right angles to the boat. (letter 3rd Mar.1903) and by what grandfather says in his letter of 26th April, they hadn't sailed for some time, preferring to row, and weren't too happy about it! (3rd Mar.'04)

Chapter IV – The Third Year

A New Year and War Threatens

Lenakel,
WEST TANNA,
New Hebrides.
Via Sydney.
Jan.3rd,1905.

Dear Mother,

We were so glad to get your letters and I am especially glad that you sent one to Isabel, always do that mother mine, even should you not address one to me. Poor Isabel only got a picture postcard from home with nothing but Lizzie's initials on it. She was awfully cut up, especially as it was the Christmas mail. She says she hardly knows how to write. I tell her she will get two or three next time to make up for it, but am doubtful.

Since the baby was born Lizzie has only written once and that was some months after. If George (Granny's elder brother) had not written she would not have got a congratulations from her own folk until months had gone by. If Lizzie does not like me she should at least remember that Isabel has no mother and that she is her eldest sister. But maybe she will do better before you get this, so do not write about it or say anything at home.

We have now got Christmas over, we dreaded it because only one case came to us from the colonies and none from home. We were dreadfully short of prizes and clothes but got through with a little bit of extra work. We gave matches, tins of meat, etc. for prizes. Isabel had a good deal of sewing to do, all our teachers, their wives and children as part of their salaries receive some clothing at Christmas, so that it is not voluntary with us to give or not. If they are not sent out we would have to buy them.

But we had a grand time and indeed all looked bright and promising and does so yet. But fearful fighting broke out amongst the heathen just after Christmas and inside a week seven had been killed and several wounded. I tried at the first to get it stopped rushing about here and there, but it was useless, they seem mad and every man is against his fellow. If it had been between tribes or two sides one might have prevailed, but every man acts on his own initiative and shoots any one he has a spite against.

Some who were going to join the worship were attacked and are now compelled to act on the defensive, only one village who had at this time declared for the worship has remained firm, they put on clothes and joined us here at Christmas, and after returning they were attacked and their chief shot in the back, but not fatally. I brought him here by boat yesterday in an awful condition. Gangrene had set in, he has a hole in his back the size of your fist, where the bullet came out. But he is doing well. He exhorted his people to remain firm and not fight. It was his fault he said as he had killed the chief of their enemies some years ago and that they might be satisfied now they had shot him. We sent word to his enemies to be satisfied and leave his people alone now. I hope they do so, I am going to send (D.V.) a teacher next week. This chief says if they must fight he will go back and do it alone, that his young people must at all cost keep clear and not make new feuds, so that is encouraging, from a dark heathen willing to risk his life that his people might become worshippers of the true God.

After we get the steamer away, I will have to go through the north again and try to render permanent the peace we made some time ago. There is still a hitch about some women but so far the terms of peace have been rigidly kept by both sides.

The people near here who are fighting I trust will learn this time to think more the Gospel of Peace which has been so often preached to them. God may have permitted all this for great purposes, we are full of hope whilst yet sorrowing for their sad condition.

All goes well at Lenakel, we try to keep our peoples' thoughts clear of all the fighting talk, by engaging them in school and service more earnestly. The out-stations are all doing well and none involved.

We had Mr.Carruthers, the young Xtian trader with us for Christmas. He was coming under the influence of the other traders and had gone into a kind of partnership with one of the worst. But thank God, he went straight across and told him he must break it off, that he must obey God and not be unequally yoked with unbelievers. He got a bad time but remained firm. They said he was no man to be influenced by me or to do what I told him. But he said it was not me but one higher who had spoken the word and whom he served. I had him about with me on horseback when the fighting commenced. The excitement and fear of the natives and seeing blood and one women with her face blown to pieces got on his nerves. That night we were awakened with awful screams. I hurried out and at last traced the screams to his room. I found him screaming and clutching the pillow. I woke him up and he seemed greatly relieved, but did not tell me what he had dreamt. He said he had a bad nightmare. But Isabel and I do not get frightened. God keeps us free, though really in the bush sometimes I have felt a quiver or two, but stifle them back as any sign of being afraid on my part would react badly on those with me.

It is not very nice for Isabel when I have to be away at night, but if there was the slightest danger of anything happening at Lenakel I would not leave her. She is very brave and good and I am sure she has the hardest part as it is much easier to go about, not to stay at home and wonder how things are going.

But the day of quietness is coming. Christ will yet win. The heathen are given to Him, so with assured hope let us pray and work on.

We have some more photos for you, one of John and Isabel, will show you the sunshine I have here in my home. The boy is growing very big and we had to begin and feed him a little on the bottle. He has cut his first tooth without much trouble and can crawl about now.

I let him fall out of bed one day and it gave us a great fright, but he was not hurt. He had been awake from sunrise and I had taken him in hand to give Isabel a spell. I put him on my arm between me and the side of the bed so that he could see the light. He lay cooing and talking and I fell asleep. He must then have rolled over and out. Neno was round at the door at once and some of the others, they heard the thump, but we never told them what happened, they asked if I had jumped out of bed or what was it made the noise. Isabel just laughed at them and they think that it must have been me, as they could not see a mark on John. I don't know what they would have said if they knew.

We have got word of your parcel at last. Wilson of Melbourne found it out and says he will send it in the next case, so we are looking forward to its arrival. I am so sorry that Nellie should have married without your consent, I never wrote her anything she might have shown you. Indeed it was hard for us to know how to write about the matter as Nellie wrote blaming me for influencing you against James Hanna. I hope Netta is getting on with her music class. Her advt. looks big in the paper. She might try and write one or other of us. Now I must stop. Isabel has written to you. Don't think we are in any danger here, all the heathen are good to us and I trust the next letter may tell you they are at peace among themselves.

Love to Father and Netta. Very much to yourself,
In Christ, your affect. son,
J.Campbell Nicholson

From the Jottings (49)

Lenakel,
TANNA
March 1905

In the concluding letter of last year I told you of peace being made in the northern part of the island: peace which affected parts of Mr.MacMillan's district and our own. Also of our Christmas gathering. At that time we had good grounds to believe that the new year would begin most auspiciously and that not only in the northern part of our district but also around Lenakel there would be the breaking up of a few strongholds of heathenism. Some of those hopes have been fulfilled beyond our expectations, others have been shattered most terribly. The hopes entertained for that part of our district lying near to Lenakel centred round two chiefs called Netiang and Niblaui. These two chiefs were united with two others near to them for offensive and defensive purposes. The most powerful chief of these four was called Iaukaim. This man was not a chief by birth but merely because he was a fearless, bloodthirsty cannibal. During the year 1904, four secret murders were traced to his tribe and in one case that of a woman the body was cooked and eaten. But his secrecy was his undoing, the other three chiefs allied with him and equally blamed with him, became suspicious and afraid of him.

The last of his victims was the chief's son, Tuputum, on account of whose death the whole of the north of Tanna was engaged in war. This war terminated in the peace making mentioned in my last letter. At that gathering it was openly declared that Iaukaim had shot Tuputum. Netiang came here to learn the result of the gathering and was greatly distressed when I told him Iaukaim was blamed. He told me Tuputum and he had bound themselves together by some Tanna rite to be friends for life and that he loved Tuputum as a brother. I pressed him to tell me who had committed some of the other murders but he said he could not speak out, if he did he would have to lie to me and he did not want to do that. As we were talking Iaukaim appeared, Netiang became very uneasy and it was with difficulty I could get him to stay. I was afraid if he left without speaking to Iaukaim, the latter would become more suspicious than ever and maybe plot Netiang's death at once. Netiang, in fact, had told his people that if he was ever shot not to hesitate but to go at once and shoot Iaukiam.

At this time Netiang and the other chief Niblaui were coming daily to the hospital bringing their sons to be treated for a disfiguring skin disease, prevalent on the islands. As we had quite a number of the same cases coming, Netiang, much to our surprise, helped Lomai to rub in the remedy and he rubbed friend and foe alike. In fact, during this time we all learnt to love Netiang. He was such a bright, handsome man and a real chief, wherever he went he was held in, and listened to, with respect. We had many a serious conversation with Niblaui and him. Niblaui did not seem much affected but Netiang over and over again declared if it were not for the awkward position he was placed in by Iaukaim he would at once join the worship. But he said he hoped soon to be in a position to join, but he would not give any explanation. Would that we had known what he was basing his hope on. Now it is too late, Netiang lies in his grave the victim of his own plans. Both came to our services occasionally and were with us at Christmas. Niblaui attended all the lantern services and after the last one was much affected and openly declared that he now believed that Jesus was the son of God and had died for men. I must say I have lately become a great believer in the efficacy of the lantern slides as a means of conveying gospel truths to the minds of men, and what is more bringing them home to their hearts. God used Sternberg's picture of the Crucifixion to the conversion of Count Zinzendorf, the founder of the Moravian missionary society. The day following being Saturday, Niblaui made preparations to attend the worship here on Sunday with his wife and son. But that evening news came that Iaukaim had been shot. It was not known by whom, but my heart was heavy, I suspected Netiang and that this was the explanation of his hope to be soon in a position to join the worship.

It was too late that night to make any investigations, but after the forenoon service on the morrow I set out accompanied by our young trader friend, Mr.Carruthers who was with us for Christmas. Having to pass through Nakat's place on our way, we were stopped by his old men and the women who were in a state of terror. Nakat had gone to buy cartridges and was going to fight against a neighbouring tribe, friends of Iaukaim, that evening. They had tried to persuade him not to go, but he was keen to take advantage of the death of Iaukaim.

We retraced our steps, when we came to the track leading to the tribe Nakat was going to attack, I sent some of our people to the coast to see if he was still there and to tell him I had gone to warn the Eroo tribe of his intentions. They found him and though he declared nothing could turn him, he did not proceed to carry out his plans but returned to abuse the old men of his tribe for informing us. As some of our men had run in advance of us we found the Eroo women in a state of terror. Their men together with Niblaui and his, had gone to Iaukaim's village to see about his death. The women said that one of their number had been at Niblaui's and whilst there it had been attacked and Niblaui's little son and two women had been shot. I was fain to believe this, but pushed on, on the way we met the Eroo men returning in haste and they told us that Niblaui's son had really been shot and they had helped to bury him, but that only one woman had been shot and she was not quite dead yet.

The Eroo men now learning of Nakat's intentions were thrown into an awful panic so that I had to send Lomai and some of the others back with them in case Nakat had followed us up. The actions of the Eroo men in their fear would have been laughable in any other circumstances, at the slightest sound they jumped about dodging imaginary bullets or else lying down to escape them. It was only after Lomai and those with him had searched all about and shouted Nakat's name that they would go near the village.

Mr.Carruthers, Titonga and myself pushed on to Niblaui's village, we found it well guarded with sentinels. The blood of the little boy lay wet on the square, the woman who had been shot had crawled into a garden and presented the most awful sight I had ever seen. She was bleeding freely and the dogs lapped up her blood. One bullet had shattered her right wrist and another had carried away the whole of her upper jaw and part of her tongue, the skin of her face hung in a tattered flap on the left side, the whole of the upper jaw bone had been blown out and the huge gap between the floor of the orbits and the mouth permitted one to see the back of the naso-pharynx, pharynx and the beginning of the oesophagus. The thoughts that rose in one's mind about the sale of ammunition to these poor creatures are best left unrecorded. Mr.Carruthers said if he had ever had any doubts about the iniquity of this traffic such a sight as this absolutely removed them.

Poor Niblaui was in an awful state about his son. He could not speak and indeed none of us felt like talking much. I exhorted him to pray to the Christ whom he professed to believe in. His enemies hearing of Iaukaim's death had like Nakat, taken advantage of it to attack his village, guessing that he most probably would be at Iaukaim's.

Mr.Carruthers and I now set out in haste after the murderers, and having the horses reached their square almost as soon as themselves. They openly gloried in their day's performance, talking was useless, and after seven hours in the sad-

dle we reached home heart sick and tired. On the Monday we learnt that others had been shot here and there. Inside a week eight had been killed and three or four wounded. As the fighting was not confined to one place, every man's hand being raised against his fellow we gave up trying to prevent it and gave all our attention to the schools and services here and at the outstations. Our people did not become involved at all so that our regular work did not suffer.

But about Netiang, as we surmised he it was who planned Iaukaim's death. He invited Iaukaim and his relatives to come to his square to talk and had arranged to shoot them every one, in this way to prevent revenge being taken and to make friends of those who had become his enemies on account of Iaukaim's murders. This was the explanation of his hope that the way would soon be clear for him to join the worship. But Iaukaim came with only one attendant, and Netiang altered his plans. Iaukaim was returning to his village when Netiang's men shot him but missed the old man who was with him. Netiang rushed off to Iaukaims village and told his brothers that their enemies had shot Iaukaim and he gave them cartridges to go and shoot some of these enemies. They believed Netiang and went to their enemies' village and shot one of them that evening and another of them a day or two after. Netiang thinking that he had secured himself now waited for a chance to carry out his original intention, but as the fighting had got beyond control he became crazed with fear and acted the traitor to some of his own people. These in return betrayed him to Iaukiam's brothers. He had been sitting talking with them and invited them to come to his garden to get some young corn to roast and eat. As he led the way they shot him in the back leaving him they returned to his village and shot his brother-in-law and a friend. It being the Sabbath a teacher Moi and some of his people itinerating, heard the shots and went to investigate. They found Netiang lying on the track vomiting blood and carried him to Iaukaim's village. He thought he had been shot by one in ambush. Iaukaim's people told him why they had shot him and that they had shot his friends. Netiang was in great distress about his friends and said that he deserved what he got but they might have spared the others. He was buried that night, our school people at Lokavit carried off his son, nephew and wife otherwise they would have been killed to prevent them taking revenge when they grew up. Indeed it is only because they will be brought up as Christians that they were allowed to live at all. Nakat like the weather cock he is, turned and joined with the Eroo people and Niblaui and they succeeded in killing the chief and his son who had attacked Niblaui's village on Christmas Sunday.

At present fighting has ceased, there have been several talks which I attended but they all ended most unsatisfactorily and no man will trust another. The Christian people say that this is a new fashion in Tanna, that the heathen are getting worse. Fighting may break out at any time and at any place and I should not be surprised if Nakat is the first to be shot.

Now for the hopes realised 'exceeding abundantly'. After the peace in the north men began to speak and think about the worship. Our teachers at the outstations followed up our work and at one place a stronghold of 'netik' (witchcraft) and fighting there was serious talk about joining the worship. A Queensland labour ship landed at this time one of their boys who had become a Christian. He came to me and asked for a teacher to live with him as he was afraid he might be pulled back, he said some of the tribe would come to the worship and others might afterwards. I told him I would do my best for him and sent Iavis and Ielbow, our evangelist, to visit them. The visit was greatly blessed; I sent others and as soon as possible went myself. God's spirit was working mightily and they soon became unanimous. As many as had a little clothing came and stayed here at Christmas and went back greatly blessed. Shortly after their return the chief was shot by an enemy whilst at worship. This chief had been a noted fighter and had killed the father of the man who now shot him, and who had taken advantage of his having commenced to worship to do so. The bullet entered his side and glanced along a rib coming out close to his spine tearing the muscles of the back in a frightful manner.

I went down in the boat for him, his people bringing him to the coast. Gangrene had set in and the stench of his wound was so great we had to put him in the bow of the boat by himself. After a month in the hospital he completely recovered and has returned and is now a real leader in the worship. Before coming to the hospital he sent word to his enemy asking him to be satisfied and not to attack his people again. I also sent word to him and there has been no further attempt made on the people.

I again visited them whilst their chief was in the hospital and found a regu-

lar revival going on. It was a real pleasure to speak to and mix with them. I chose a good site for a church and new village. The same day they cleared part for the church and we staked out the ground and gave them the lengths of the posts. In two days they built a teacher's house and I sent one called Nimiling up to live with them. In a short time they had all the timber cut for the church. Titonga and I went up and in one day we almost completed the frame. Titonga remaining behind to see it finished. It was a real joy to be amongst so hearty a people, many of them still naked, but men, women and children all doing their best to get the house of God well built.

They also have commenced itinerating amongst their friends and on the Sabbaths have a good many heathen coming to their village for the worship. Soon a number are coming to Lenakel to work for clothes and we hope to get to know them better.

At the other place still further north and inland, Leten, an old square has been cleared and preparations are being made for the erection of a teacher's house and church to be followed by a new village. Some of these people have been down working for clothes and are now assisting others from the north to build a house here for their use at communion and special services.

Tonight I received word from a chief in Mr.McMillan's district who lives inland but further east from Leten, saying he had built a church and was all ready for a teacher. The teacher who is to go has been in the hospital for some time with asthma. He had been teaching at Loanbukle but it is very low lying and he never had good health there, so I asked him to go to this place away from the sea and 12 or 1300 feet above it. I am hoping that in the course of a week or two he may be able to go. This was the chief of whom I wrote some months ago as having built a church and asked for a teacher, but I had none then who could go and asked him to wait till Mr.McMillan returned. When the war broke out he was dragged in and lost his son, a boy of about 14 years. But all through this trying time he remained true and helped me in the peace-making, after which he was most urgent that a teacher should come at once. But there was a doubt about the place he had built the church, being the best one for an outstation. He came to consult with me and returned to find out the opinion of his people and some other heathen who were interested. Now he says that his people prefer the place he had settled on first.

We are praying that this revival north may spread southward and that the heathen more immediately near us may be roused to similar interest and exertion on behalf of the kingdom of the Prince of Peace

Lenakel,
WEST TANNA,
New Hebrides,
Via Sydney.

May 7th 1905

Dear Mother,

I am tired and high strung a bit after a big day, a glorious day. Jesus is the same yesterday, today and forever. This was our Communion Sabbath and one to be remembered. Our new Church was packed, floor and seats so that the people had to sit right through, I dare not ask them to stand. We commenced at daybreak with a prayer meeting, the Church full up, even at that hour people had walked several miles to be here. At ten, baptismal and communion service lasting till nearly one. At two, thanksgiving service and babies baptised, at half past five evening worship and now at eight o'clock the people are having another in the open air and a great volume of singing swells up to the house. I translated the choruses of 'Revive Thy Work' and Jesu, Jesu, Hear my Humble Cry' and they are much used in the services at night. Thirty three adults were baptised out of a large candidates class, and nine children, including Lomai's new son.

I conducted the four services myself and did all the preaching. The three Elders did well but were a bit put about getting the people into the church.

You ask do I preach in Tannese. I do but I have to prepare and write it with Lomai beforehand. I have been backward with the language because I can never get consecutive days to work at it. There is always and has been this last year so much to do and so much going about. The hospital takes up a great deal of time and indeed I am beginning to wonder if I can go on much longer without an assistant. Lomai, Iavis and Titonga are grand but much of the work cannot be done by natives yet. However, Mr.Watt is back and Mr.McMillan soon will be so I may find things work a bit easier in the future. We certainly could not spend a long life at this rate, humanly speaking. All last week people were coming in, the services and classes commence on Wednesday. Saturday we only had a daybreak meeting and short evening worship. Each night the Elders had 2 or 3 hours free and easy services for the people in the open air. The village is crowded out and we had to get some to go and stay at an outstation two or three miles down the coast and travel up and down. We have a good many from all over Mr.McMillan's district. I invited the principal men from the outstations there and they always have a few followers each. All who have come in bring good reports of the Worship itself and the attitude of the heathen. I am glad to say that the good work at White Sands goes on strongly, every teacher who returns, is in a running over condition and comes back greatly blessed. They had heard from the ones who were over with me, but they never thought it was so grand as it was. It cheers them greatly to find heathen everywhere asking them to teach them, 'sit down and talk with us' is a common cry in that district and our teachers coming from those they have preached to so often, find these eager ones very refreshing. Mr.MacMillan will have his hands full when he gets back. He needs teachers badly and I feel sure many young men there are ready to come to him for training. The Lord send him back in the fullness of the blessing of the Gospel of Christ. One month more to Synod and I have about two months work to crush into that and most of it away from home. I will have to go all round the North of Tanna and again to White Sands. So Isabel and John will have to look after one another, the worst of it is.

We came round from White Sands by Steamer. They were keen to get me on board as a sailor was very ill. I brought him on shore, it was a case of typhoid and he has given us work night and day, but is round the corner and crying out for food. He was delirious for two weeks or more, indeed he is only beginning to know where he is and to feel a bit curious about his condition. Twice he collapsed, heart failure and only under heroic measures came round. I gave him up for days and made arrangements for his death one night, but he is still here. I had several nights, but soon taught Lomai and another to attend him when unconscious and they take watch and watch about, of three hours night and day. It would be terrible if this disease spread here, the natives would go down quickly. We have to be careful about disinfecting. Isabel has charge of the feeding of him in the day time. I get up at night, as he had several internal haemorrhages; we can only give him a little fluid stuff every two hours or so. I wish he were better so that I could get away, but I trust to be able to leave him to Isabel and Lomai in a week or so.

Isabel is in grand health and is getting stout a little. Don't tell her I said that, she is afraid of following the example of not a few mission ladies and putting on large quantities of fat. She is a very capable wee wife, today had the Communion Table splendidly spread, as good as yours at home, maybe better, and then had the organ at all the services except the daybreak one. She has a big household; the cook, a big strapping fellow who always says, yes sir to her. I never try to boss this man, but my word, Isabel makes him jump. We have his wife and three other girls as well as Nano, John's nurse. There is not much work to do in the afternoons. They all get away except John's attendant and she gets three or more afternoons, one of the girls relieving her. Then again after breakfast the whole household except Isabel and John go to school for an hour or more, so the mornings are short. I expect this is why we need so many. All the washing is done by outsiders, who are paid by being allowed soap and water to wash their own clothes after ours are finished. Now that is a big order for Isabel to manage and she does it and the sewing class and the charge of all clothing for the natives as if she had been brought up to it. Indeed I am rich in my wee wife, I thank God for her every day. We have been very few days apart and we grudge even being one except on the Lord's service. John is, well I don't think much of the man who does not think he has got as good if not much better than what is going in the way of wife and child. John is the same bunch of smiles and wins all hearts. He is trying to talk and has got a few words. He calls me Tata, the native for father. (They use it also in addressing God, i.e., 'Tata le neai', Father in Heaven), and from the verandah hails me every time I appear. Mama, is his cry when in trouble only Mama will do then. He has great fun with his mother when she is feeding him. His favourite attitude then is to sit on her knees and put his feet on the table, if he does not get doing that he lies on his back and kicks at the spoon or his mother's chin or else when he is satisfied put his toe in his mouth and so prevents his mother giving him any more. He sleeps all night now. He also calls his dog Toss Toss. I don't know whether I told you about this dog. Pat was shot and Mr.Carruthers gave us this fox terrier Toss, because he was no good, not faithful, a wanderer. We took him almost without thanks, but Toss took to John and always has to see him get his bath and even sleeps under his bed till we go and put him out. At White Sands he did the same thing. When John gets on the floor Toss lies down beside him and rolls about to get John to play with him. He also goes out with him. John also knows Tom and Bruce and calls them by name. Lamp is another word of his. Now that's enough about the baby. This is an awful letter but it's for yourself and you will not call it too long.

The parcel came down last trip, <u>but was not</u> landed. We may get it tomorrow, but indeed I am doubtful. What ails that parcel? Indeed I am afraid to mention it, I dread to hear it spoken about. Isabel got some Weldon's patterns from Sydney and keeps John trim and neat. We never give Tom any food, he only grazes. Indeed he would not eat corn and hay because he does not know what they are.

The bull is still quiet, I would kill him but I don't know how to cut him up. I wish I could sell him. The pig still thrives. I don't want any more, but Isabel had so much skimmed milk, etc. she thought she should have one. Pat is his name. If Mr.McKenzie comes he may know how to cut it up and cure a bit of him, the rest we will give away. This is the last one we will keep. Isabel agrees to that at present. We are eating two or three fowls each week but no eggs just now. We have plenty of vegetables, such as pumpkins, beans, yams and seldom open a tin of meat. We have a vegetarian dinner once a week, but I am not an out and out vegetarian. Fruit such as melons, pineapples, oranges galore. Indeed I wish we could send you a few cases, we are going to give the steamer some when she comes to get rid of them. We have been planting flower seeds to try them. Pansies, wallflowers, zinnias, honesty, chrysanthemums, etc.,etc. I wish I could get a day or two in the garden. I have plenty of seeds ready for sowing and the ground in good order. We will be a month at Synod, can't be less as the steamer does not call to bring us back sooner. She will take the northern missionaries first and lift us coming back, so that it will be a month's holiday. We do not intend to go on furlough at the end of the year, but in September we may take a trip round the Islands and see the other Mission

Stations and work. I feel I have much to learn yet and as we refused to go when we came I dare say the offer is still open. Besides it will give us more interest in the work and let us know where and how our colleagues work. The Northern ones have the advantage of us here as they see all the others whenever they come or go, but we are near the last and Anietyum is the only call after Tanna. However, we will hear what is said at Synod. But really we feel the work needs us at present and that except in case of illness it would be most unwise to leave it for a year or two.

Isabel has never had fever and John and I only get mild attacks now and again, not many. I always know when they are coming by being desperately bad tempered, I try to keep out of the way till they pass.

Worthington has been at his old tricks again, grabbing land belonging to Christians, he would not dare to do it to heathen as they would put a bullet in him. He gets some scoundrel to sell him the land he wants and for three rifles has acquired acres, some of it belonging to two teachers of mine. He tried to bluff it out, saying he had nothing to do with who owned it, it had been sold and signed for, but I brought him up with a round turn and he had to leave it. This is the third time this has happened, so I have yielded to the natives and taken over about two square miles again. The natives have the use of it, but cannot sell it. The Church undertaking to protect it for them. If it was not for the traders Tanna yet might be a little paradise, but Goodnight, love to all and much to yourself, from Isabel, John and me.

Your affect.son in Christ,
J.Campbell Nicholson
P.S. Do you ever knit socks now, I cannot wear bought things and Isabel has not time just now So if you have a pair I will be thankful.

JCN

P.S.No 2. Did I tell you the linen for David Mitchell Anstruther was for a wedding present. I Hope you got it away, he was married I believe on the 12th of April, but things like These are never too late.

JCN

From the Jottings (no.50)

Lenakel,
WEST TANNA.
May 1905

We have not had the usual hot rainy season on Tanna this year, true we have had hot days and a few rainy ones, but the season has been a very healthy one and I believe that we are all strong and vigorous now as we were at the beginning of it.

There has been no renewal of the fighting; the heathen are now busy preparing for 'Sing sings'. Strange to say no less than four fighting chiefs died inside four weeks, including the chief Niblaui mentioned in my last letter. The first, whilst under the influence of kava[1] *(the native drink), was stricken with paralysis. At first he thought the kava must have been stronger than usual, but when he became sober he found that he could neither move hand nor foot. With the exception of his head, neck and shoulders he was completely paralysed. He only lived a few days.*

Another landing from a canoe trip commenced to vomit blood and died in a few hours. Niblaui died suddenly when we were at White Sands.

A terrible accident happened on the east coast near White Sands at a place called Leolakis. The trader, his wife and baby were returning home by boat from Port Resolution, the boat was capsized in the passage opposite their home and the mother and baby were drowned. The trader who was unable to swim seized an oar and was towed ashore by the native crew. One native, a member of Mr.Mr.McMillan's church made a gallant attempt to save the lady. He actually succeeded in placing her on the overturned boat, but another roller righted the boat and after that neither mother nor baby were seen again.

Our work here has progressed most encouragingly. I have told our people a little about the glorious revival in Wales and I believe many are yearning and praying for a similar visitation of the Spirit of God on Tanna. I believe we shall yet experience it.

The most notable event since last writing has been our long deferred visit to Mr.McMillan's district. It was our intention to spend two weeks there last

September but the epidemic of influenza and serious cases in the hospital prevented us. Since then I have itinerated through parts of it, but had given up the idea of taking our household across and making a stay. Fighting had been going on continuously for the past nine months in close proximity to White Sands. The church there had suffered greatly. Several assistant teachers who had been left in charge were compelled to return to their villages in other parts of the district. Three of Mr.McMillan's best teachers, placed at outstations to the north and south of White Sands, had died. The fighting prevented the Christian people from walking about and meeting with each other, so that anything short of a prolonged stay did not give hope of any good or lasting results.

A chief called Kokari who had been baptised shortly after I came to Tanna and who lived close to the mission station, had stood fast in his profession, even though his people and one of his sons were the principals in the fighting. He had got the church (a native one) rebuilt after it had been blown down in the hurricane, and had looked carefully after the mission station. When I paid a flying visit, early in March, to White Sands Kokari together with many others pressed me to bring Mrs.Nicholson and the baby across and stay with them for a few weeks. They said they believed it would help to stop the fighting and that the Christian people would soon get confidence again and gather round us. Kokari reminded me that the crop of coconuts he had promised to give towards our new church at Lenakel was lying on the ground and would soon be useless for making copra. With not a little misgiving I promised to come, as there were several patients in the hospital and there was the possibility of serious cases turning up as they did in September to prevent us getting away. However, inside a fortnight I was able to dismiss my patients and complete arrangements for crossing.

Iavis and Titonga, I left in charge of the work and station here, taking with me Lomai and nearly forty men and women from our outstations in the north. These people I had specially invited: they were either chiefs or the outstanding Christians in their villages, over and above these many others wanted to come but we did not permit them.

From the time we decided to go prayer had been made daily that God would make us a blessing to all we met and sojourned amongst. We got a splendid day for crossing and set out full of hope and joy. On the way we came upon a gathering of heathen met to talk about the sickness of some man or other and to try and find out who was causing it. Great was their surprise as the long line came into their midst one by one. A service was held and two other halts were made for refreshment and prayer. It took us the whole day to get across, but to one and all it was most enjoyable. Our baby was carried by some of the natives in turn and enjoyed himself hugely. One chief was especially attentive to him and ourselves, this was Naukaut from the new station in the extreme north. He is a big strapping highlander minus an eye, but of pleasant countenance withal. As he carried the sleeping child in his big,strong arms, shielding him with the greatest care from intrusive branch or reed we could not help praising God for the grace which had changed this man. He was one of the chiefs who had ordered the murderous attack on Mr.Paton and party when a Munian was shot. He is coming forward for baptism early this month.

We got a great welcome at White Sands and found Kokari had arranged for the housing of our people. That night the people began a series of services amongst the heathen. They had a good gathering and came back full of joy. On the morrow, after a service to which a goodly number of heathen came, we started work in Kokari's coconut plantation. The first two days were spent in building a large drying house, so that in case of rain the work could go on uninterrupted. After that the scrub was cleared away and the nuts gathered into huge heaps. Then whilst some husked others broke open the shell and cut out the kernel which was quickly spread on the drying loft and fires lighted underneath. In ten days we had finished the crop and expect when it is sold to have £10 or £11 for our new church. If we had been two months sooner for the same work we would have had double the amount of copra, many nuts were rotten and almost all were growing so that the kernel was not more than half the thickness of nuts worked at the proper time. Coconuts abound in this part of Tanna and not a hundredth part of them are utilised by the natives. The fighting almost stopped the making of copra so that for months the traders have been getting cwts. where formerly it was tons.

The morning after we arrived I noticed two men looking seedy and thought the journey had tried them but was told by another that these two, Ielbow and Tavo had spent almost the whole night in prayer for the heathen. After that I felt confident that peace would be made and blessing come. And come it did, on Sabbath morning so many heathen donned clothes and came to the service that we had to have it in the open air, the church being too small. They continued to come to the service until at last I was told that only three men out of the villages near, had not turned up. Now peace became the burden of conversation and at last I felt free to go to their enemies some miles away and try to arrange a conference. This I succeeded in doing and we agreed to meet at a square called Loanu. The village here had been partly burnt, gardens destroyed, and the people scattered. On the day appointed we had the greatest difficulty in getting the people to gather together, the chiefs came and sat in the square but their followers were scattered on either side through the scrub. The chiefs at last called their people in and we took up our position between them. The talk lasted five hours and kept up briskly all the time. At last they thought all points worthy of attention had been discussed satisfactorily and to my surprise it was proposed that the two principal chiefs should exchange coins, to be kept as tokens of good faith. This I found on inquiry to be a new thing. I happened to ask a Queenslander what it meant, he said he supposed it was a 'bet'. Rifles were now laid aside and all gathered for a short service, after which a general handshaking took place.

Before we left White Sands the news of the good time we were having spread through our district and two more bands of people came from different parts, swelling our numbers to nearly seventy. The people all about were very kind to us and almost daily brought gifts of food. Before leaving we built this chief Kokari a new house in return for his kindness to us all.

I paid a hurried visit to Port Resolution and found everything in splendid order for the return of Mr.and Mrs.Watt. We were greatly pleased to meet there quite a number who had recently joined the worship and who had come to Port Resolution to welcome back Mr.Watt. Mr.Carruthers who worked in the district while Mr.Watt was absent told me that these people had built a church and were hoping that a teacher could be procured for them. Mr.Carruthers visited them often and has his reward in seeing them now so wholehearted to learn about Christ.

Mr.and Mrs.Watt returned by the steamer which took Mrs.Nicholson and myself back to Lenakel. We were sorry we could not see them and add our welcome to that of the people, but we had the company on board of Mr.and Mrs.F.Bowie and Mr.and Mrs.Milne, junior, the latter are coming down to assist Mr.Peter Milne at Nguna.

We were glad to get back to Lenakel and found Iavis and Titonga had looked after everything well and had a good report to give. A young sailor suffering from enteric fever was carried to the hospital; he has had a very severe attack and is not yet out of danger.

We have kept in touch weekly with White Sands, as death had removed the principal teachers and people pled with me to send one of mine until Mr.McMillan returned. I, however, have arranged that a teacher and assistant teacher together with some voluntary workers shall go over weekly and trust by this arrangement to have mutual blessing. Ielbow and Titonga have each had their week and brought back good accounts of the work. Iavis and Tapunua and two others are there at present

At Le Neai one of our new outstations, the church has been opened and a great feast made. Iavis and Ielbow and a good many of our people went up and spent two nights and a day with them. I had arranged to go up, but two days before I had to cross to the other side of the island and after two days in the saddle did not feel like another so was glad when rain came to prevent me setting out. Our people returned with joy, many heathen had come to the services and a very happy day had been spent, Iavis officiating in my absence.

A son has been born to Lomai much to his joy, his four other children being dead.

We are now preparing for our communion season and expect a large gathering. Two families of four persons each, have left their heathen places, one coming to Lenakel, the other to our nearest outstation, Loanapheremere. Both families have come from the south of Lenakel where as yet we have no outstations and but few members and adherents. However, after communion and getting the north comfortably settled, we hope to concentrate our efforts on this part. Lomai and Ielbow and some others intend to make a prolonged tour through it whilst we are at Synod.

After Synod we hope to have Mr.Mackenzie with us again and get the exterior of our church finished. We have been greatly pleased to hear that so many at home have subscribed to help us, and in the name of our people and ourselves would like to express our heartfelt gratitude to one and all.

With our kind regards.
J.Campbell Nicholson

Dillons Bay,
ERROMANGA,
5th July, 1905

My Dear Aunt,

We have been here for nearly a month now, have had a very enjoyable time. The Robertsons have been so kind, have done all to make our stay as happy as possible. It was very sad about their daughter, Mrs.Paton's death just when they were expecting her down. Mrs.Robertson had not seen her for two years and was looking forward so much to this visit. She sometimes gets very depressed but all through they have kept up well. Mr.Paton was here and tried to keep as bright as possible.

There were I suppose about 60 people here the first week counting the children. The men all camped out in the school house – all bringing their own stretchers. The ladies slept in the dwelling house and some young girls had an outhouse to themselves. The first night or two I had a lively time. In the same room with me were three ladies, six children, the youngest two months and the eldest about 3 years. They were all so excited running about the room and out onto the verandah. Poor John looked at them all running about then at me as much as to say will you take me out of this. At last we had to get one lady with her two babies to another part of the house for one of the youngsters was always falling out of bed and he woke the rest. We had a performance two or three times in the night.

The ladies all help at Synod with the work. Some attend to the cooking, another does all the breadmaking, then others see that the tables are all right, laid etc. There is not much idle time with so many to attend to. The ladies with babies get off free.

After a week the steamer came and took the northern missionaries back and we have to wait three weeks behind. There are 17 of us here yet. We have had a good many picnics and we go out very often on the river in the canoe. One day a party of us went away up the hill and visited the place where Mr.and Mrs.Gordon[2] were murdered. Dr.Robertson calls it Mount Gordon.

Another day we went to see a trader's place. He has got about 200 sheep. It was a good long walk to the place but we had two horses between us. John has improved greatly by his visit here, you could see him growing and he has cut several teeth. Everyone is so fond of him. They say he is a bonny boy and is always smiling. He gives very little trouble.

Mrs.McCausland has got a little daughter. They are in Kynetown in Victoria. He has charge of a hospital there. They are all well now.

We expect the steamer in a day or two to take us home, then in a week or two after we shall have Mr.and Mrs.Mackenzie with us. They are going to Aniwa from here.

Hope you are all very well as we are here. With much love,

I am,
Your affectionate daughter
Isabel.
PS. Mr.McMillan did not get down for Synod. The South Australia Church kept Him there to do deputation work. They are expected by the August trip. They were Disappointed at not getting down for Synod. Mrs.Watt and I occupy the same room Now, her baby is 7 months older than John. She has been round the world and is a Great talker.

On S.S.Tambo

(Efate)

Lenakel,
TANNA,
New Hebrides
Nov.3rd 1905

Dear John,

My heartiest congratulations to you and Jeannie, they come late in the day but we can't help that. Often and often have we wished that we could have been at the wedding, Sarah sent us a snap shot of you coming out of the church. It was splendid and in spite of the confetti you seemed to be enjoying yourself. The marrying is a bit of an ordeal but it is the best life after all though.

I am sorry for you and Jeannie having to be separated so much, you see Isabel and I have seldom if ever been more than a day or two separated and we don't want to either. We are sitting in the smoke room of this steamer writing and your name's sake is stretched out between us. He is a big boy now, nearly ready for trousers. He can walk a rolling deck like an old salt, from the Captain down all are devoted to him and he is to be found all over the ship. He keeps in perfect health in spite of the variety of food given to him by one and another.

We have had a great trip round the group and feel much better in every way. We had a month in Ambrim with a medical colleague and another month on this old tramcar or ferry boat. They have been very good to us and we have seen all that is worth seeing. We never thought there were such beautiful islands, harbours, rivers, lagoons etc. in the group. In the south Tanna is isolated, from our place we cannot see any other island, but north they are all bunched together.

The man of war has been down punishing the people of Malekula. They killed a few and took away 60 rifles and a lot of pigs, but they never said a word to the traders who sell the rifles and ammunition. The traders bring them to punish the natives and yet they themselves contrary to British law sell rifles, ammunition and grog and the representatives of the law wink at it. But a better day is coming.

Isabel is writing to Jeannie. We long to see the photo and expect it next trip. We have a Belfast lady journalist on board and she is coming to Tanna to stay for five weeks. Her name is Miss Grimshaw and her people live now in Portrush. She is a manly big woman of about 13 or 14 stone weight and keen on yarns. She is going to write a book. At present she contributes to some of the magazines.

In three or four days we expect to be home again and after all is said and done it is the best place

Although it is on a lonely and not too good island.

I find it very hard to write, there is such a din, about twenty boys are chipping paint and rust off the outside of the vessel.

I hope that your Christmas and New Year may be the happiest yet and that things may so arrange themselves as to permit of you being in your own home at or about that time. Tell Jeannie that we look forward very much to meeting her, only four years now, they will soon go past.

We pray that God will bless you both in your new life and grant you his guidance in all things.

With our love,
Your affect. Bro., James

In the Jottings Grandfather tells of his return to Tanna:

JOTTINGS 52 APRIL 1906

Lenakel, TANNA

November, 1905

It is now almost a month since we returned to Tanna. We enjoyed the trip round the islands immensely, and had the pleasure of visiting all the Mission stations but two, these however we got a glimpse of from the deck of the steamer. On almost every island the work is progressing encouragingly.

After our bare seascape at Lenakel, without an island to break the horizon, the number and proximity of the islands north was a delightful change. How we wished we had some of the splendid land locked harbours, lagoons or rivers on our own almost passageless coast. The east coasts of Malekula and Santo were especially good, dotted as they are with a large number of small islands, between which and the mainland are the most beautiful waterways we have ever seen or can hope to see.

But after all is said and done we saw no natives we liked so much as our Tannese. Taking them all round, we think they are the finest people in the group. On board with us we had a dozen or more from the east coast. They act as boat's crew and handle the cargo, but nothing seems to come amiss to them: chipping, painting, scrubbing decks, they tackle everything with the greatest good spirits. From the Captain down, everyone spoke well of them. The second officer, who has most to do with them, told me that sometimes at night when the steamer is anchored some distance out, and they are bringing the last heavily laden boat off after a hard spell of work, instead of growling the Tannese will break into song and laughter, so that in spite of weariness, wet clothes and darkness, no one can help getting cheered up. This has been my experience often in boating here. Getting home from the north is almost always a fight against wind and tide, but whether late at night, or in the early hours of the morning after a night at sea, my Tanna boat's crew battle round the last point and swing into our passage singing.

As we approached Tanna a heavy sea was running, and it seemed probable that we would not be able to land. But on getting opposite Lenakel we could see our people getting the "Pioneer" into the water, and soon the familiar faces were alongside.

We were delighted to find all well, no deaths in our community at Lenakel, everything was in spick and span order. Day after day we were finding out things that had been done to please and welcome us. During our absence our people had had an exciting time. The fighting raged more fiercely after we left, ten people had been killed, including the chief Nakat whom I have frequently mentioned in these letters.

The Loinio people had set fire to their enemy's country to the south, and as we have had no rain since May, the fire spread rapidly back northwards over our ground and that of the Loinio tribe, destroying old gardens and the fences of the new ones. It swept all round our station, and for a time the village was in great danger. The people cleared everything out of the houses, and on the thatched roofs men stood with buckets of water quenching the sparks. The station grounds being extensive and well cleared, the Mission house and hospital were quite safe, but there was a little scrub near the Church which caused anxiety and gave work for a time. After the fight was finished here our people went across and helped the Worthingtons to save their plantation. The fire travelled northwards for miles, and was so fierce that even forty miles off the Captain of the Tambo saw the flames. Even as I write, no rain having come, fires are still raging, and the whole country is black and charred for miles around us. Our people had their hands full to save the yams which were in the ground, and all pigs had to be captured and fenced in. The people from the stations north, hearing of the plight that their Lenakel friends were in, came to their aid, and fences were thus soon renewed to preserve all that remained of their gardens. But January, February and March will be hungry months. Hundreds of coconut trees have been destroyed or so injured that it will be two or three years before they bear again. The fruit trees have also suffered greatly from drought and fire, and it is on these our people most depend for the months mentioned. We are praying daily for rain, everything is at a standstill, and in some places the seed yams have had to be lifted out of the ground to save them until rain comes.

Notes for 1905

The year 1905 got off to a shocking start: 'Bloody Sunday' it was called which to us means Derry but then it was St.Petersburg. Strikers loyal to the Czar Nicholas II marched through the city to petition him for better conditions, were shot down by the Cossacks leaving 500 dead. And far away in the Straits of Tsushima east of Korea, the Russian fleet was destroyed by the Japanese. India wasn't having it much better; in April a massive earthquake killed 10,000 people. On a happier note the Norwegian explorer, Roald Amudsan, discovered the North-West Passage and on the way, the Magnetic Pole. Aspirin appeared in the chemist's shop for the first time.

How frustrating it must have been for my grandparents! Parcels never arriving, or the steamer appearing but not landing any cargo. This problem had been with the missionary for many years and indeed the Rev. Paton had raised money to provide the funds for the Mission to build their own steamer to service the islands. However, the Victorian Foreign Missions Committee had put an embargo on it as they said the Mission didn't have the necessary £1,000 a year to maintain the steamer; that was in the late 1880s and the problem still hadn't been resolved.

Training teachers to carry Christianity to other tribes and other islands was a problem. Native teachers were used from the very beginning; the first to arrive were Samoans in 1839 (Christianity had already arrived in Polynesia) but due to sickness and death were withdrawn. However, more Polynesians arrived and taught the local people and in 1852 the first ni-Vanuatu trained as teachers. These people proved to be more success-ful as they could speak the local language and were better able to cope with the climate. In 1862 John G.Paton set up the first Teacher Training Fund. This was to provide money to pay the local teachers who, due to the invasion of western civilization, had become used to commodities like kerosene and blankets, but the idea was to eventually make them self-sufficient. It is evident in the letters that grandfather clearly saw the need for teachers, but it takes time to train them, a thing in his case, in short supply. A school was started to train local men as teachers on Tangoa, a tiny jewel of an island off the south coast of Santo which is well to the north of Tanna, and it sent out teachers to the other islands.

Chapter V – The Fourth Year

A Sad Beginning and Synod

Lenakel,
TANNA,
New Hebrides.
Jan.6th 1906

Dear Mother,

We wish you a very happy New Year. We have entered ours in good health and spirits, plentiful rain came this week and our district will soon be green again. We have been very busy getting seeds in and shall be very glad when we can get vegetables from our garden again. The last seeds we put in May perished and the garden has been barren since.

We are very busy now, everything is in full swing and the hospital crammed, almost every week we have an operation. If this keeps up we must get more accommodation. We are now collecting to get our new church enlarged. It will cost £66.

At Xmas we were packed and they were standing outside at the windows. 33 were accepted for Baptism and 18 children baptised. We had a good communion season and a great Xmas day. We are trying to get a few photos ready for you. This has been a heavy mail. Your letter is the 34th and I am still pegging away after midnight as we expect the steamer tomorrow.

Our people have given a piece of ground and are clearing it and planting coconuts for the upkeep of the church. It will be 7 or 8 years before the nuts bear, but it is well to provide for the future. We are beginning to paint and varnish the Church.

Titonga is in the hospital, I had to open a large abscess at the hip joint on Xmas day. We miss him much for he is our painter. This week I had to operate on a little girl's elbow and last week a bad case of tubercular glands in the neck. Thank God all are doing well.

John is very interesting now and a regular little parrot. He talks all the time and knows all the people about by name. We bathe very often and John enjoys it very much. I am teaching him to swim and when I hold my hand under him he strikes out very well. He does not mind going under a bit. In the afternoon he cries out "Maiuk maiuk", bathe, bathe, carries his own towel and thinks he is a great man. He calls Isabel "Missis" now, after the girls, but Mama when he wants to be very affectionate. He tries the singing and Isabel gives him a little book to take to Church. He can sing a little of "Jesus loves me" and "Jesus shall reign" in Tannese. He prays or rather bows his head and says Amen. When I was baptising the new members he called out every name after me with frequent Amens. Indeed he keeps us all in good spirits and still believes in early rising. I have to get up and take him out every morning at six and sometimes before it. He has a funny habit of being forced to suck his thumb when he touches velvet. Indeed sometimes to make him lie down we put a piece of velvet in his hand and while he holds it he must keep down. He calls your photo Granny and points to it if we ask him where Granny is.

Isabel is a great little mother and John reciprocates all her love and care. She is the only one he will ever kiss.

I am getting very sleepy and if time permits on the morrow will try and write some more. If not, we are all well and all goes well. We send our love to you and Father and Netta and any of the others who may be at home.

PS. The steamer is here and has brought Mrs.Robertson of Erromanga to stay for a week, also a young man surveying land for the Steamship Company, so we are full up. Two patients also came from Erromanga for treatment, both will need operations. We are spending the last few minutes overhauling our mail. I hope you will get the photos alright.

Kind love to all.
J.C.N.

Jottings 53 contains a number of sad paragraphs about Titonga, some of which I have included here:

The only cloud on the day's proceedings was the absence of our elder, Titonga. He had been ill for more than a week. On the Saturday amidst all the festivities, I was told he was much worse and went across to see him, finding him very ill and requiring an immediate operation. He was carried up to the hospital at once and put under chloroform. The operation relieved him greatly, and he passed a good night, giving us little anxiety about his complete recovery. On the Sabbath he received the Lord's Supper in the ward.

In spite of repeated attacks of acute malarial fever during the next few days, his thigh recovered sufficiently to permit him to move about a little, but he seemed to have some premonition that he was not long for this world. I would playfully refer to the amount of painting he had to do outside and inside the church, and he ever answered, "If it is God's will I am ready to do it."

On Saturday, the 6th January, he complained of acute abdominal pain and became very ill. I was away from home and a messenger was sent for me, but when I returned he was much better and continued so for several days, when he had another attack and collapse. Under treatment he rallied and raised our hopes for a few days, then acute peritonitis set in and on Thursday, the 18th, our great friend and staunch helper Titonga, went home. The last few days he knew he was going , and bade goodbye to his many friends who came to see him. He was very weak, but had a bright word for all, and on the evening before his death he engaged in prayer, commending us all to the grace of God. He had nothing to ask for himself, those left behind to work, the heathen unwon, the worshipping people, his wife and son, formed the burden of his prayer. I asked him if he had any doubt or fear. He answered, "My body is very tired and weak, but my heart is rejoicing." He lingered until the afternoon of the next day. Just before his death he called me and committed his son Somo to my care and keeping. He laid his hand on his wife Litsi's shoulder, and then looked at us, we knew what he meant.

We thought he was unconscious, and were seeking to find a verse in the Acts of the Apostles which he had tried to give as a last message, but we were not sure which verse he meant. He reached out his hand for the Testament and found the twentieth chapter, and pointed to the twentieth and thirty-second verses, with its farewell message, "I commend you to God and to the word of His grace." After that he lapsed into unconsciousness and soon died. Next day we buried him, all the people attended at the graveside, but weeping did not permit of much of a service.

On Saturday the young teachers in training built a coral and lime tombstone to his memory.

Titonga was one of Grandfathers ablest helpers who had come over from Aniwa with Frank Paton and his wife in 1896. As grandfather said, *'we have lost our best all round man, one of the best and most devoted of friends'.* It was Titonga's dying wish that his young son be committed to my grandfather's care, his wife Litsi didn't want to leave and go back to her native Aniwa an island close by. With local custom, by committing his son to my grandfather's care Titonga's wish was secure.

From Port Resolution

Lenakel
TANNA,
New Hebrides.
5th May, 1906

Dear Mother,

Your two letters arrived safely. Isabel took hers with her on the steamer so that I did not get reading it till I crossed over. I had a taste of single life again, but as I commenced it with a mail and was very busy the time passed quickly. The house seemed very queer without Isabel and John. I used to light it all up to make it more cheerful, kept bad hours sitting up till 1 or 2 and had not such a bad time at all. Isabel had the girls broken in splendidly, though the cook and they had only been with us four months they managed A.1. I had dinner at night so as to be free all day. However, I was glad to get across to Isabel and

John again. We are here and I am much afraid will miss the return steamer and in that case Synod.

Mrs.Watt is in good health and spirits but this is an awful hot place and house. We appreciated our open situation and airy house at Lenakel before, but will do so more from this on. The great fear of the early missionaries was of hurricanes and the sites for houses were chosen for shelter and the houses themselves built low. This house is of that type and so situated that so far as I can see hardly any wind that blows can reach it. The high mountains bring plenty of rain, and mosquitoes work day and night. It is an awfully pretty place but give me Lenakel every time. We have acres of cleared ground, plenty of fresh air, few mosquitoes and a right hearty people. The people here have been so much in contact with whites for the past century almost that they are not the same. The harbour drew all the slavers about and hellish deeds have been wrought in this place.

We have been feeling a bit off. We need a good cold spell to set us up. Nothing serious, but always some little thing, attacks of fever, toothache, earache, etc. John has prickly heat, his back is like that of a measily child. But he does not mind, always on the move and happy. He is a fine wee boy and making great efforts to talk now in both Tannese and English. He repeats whatever is said to him. Nano still is his faithful companion and never asks to leave him, indeed we would have to order her away if we wanted her to take a spell. She is sitting outside the bedroom door last thing at night and is there again at daybreak waiting for John to call her as he always does on awakening.

We are hoping to get away soon. Our Communion Sabbath is the last of this month and always requires a lot of preparation, then if we do go to Synod that would also require more. I would like to go if possible. There will arise several questions in which I am much interested. However, I guess they will be settled just as well whether I am there or not.

Isabel has written so you will excuse more this time. Mr.Watt is hammering away at a typewriter on the same table and it does not help one to write. They are very kind to us and so anxious to please and entertain us. Mr.Watt has now been down 37 years and is now about 65 or 66 years of age, beginning life again, raising a family. He is still fairly strong but I really do not think he can hold out many more years. The McMillans are all well and all well at Lenake; we had news last week. Isabel is feeling the heat a good deal. I wish she could get to Mrs.McMillan, they get on so well and carry on like schoolgirls all the time they are together. The White Sands station is new and well situated being very much cooler. But we must just wait.

I hope Father is better and that the cough is gone.

I don't feel happy about Dan, but as they say he may pick up quicker out of the old country. (Rev.Dan Robertson, elder sister Sarah's husband: they were at home from Manchuria at the beginning of 1905.)

I hope you are keeping strong. How I would like to see you and all the others at home.

With much love,
Your affect. Son in Christ,
J.Campbell Nicholson.

PS. Sunday 6th

Dear Mother,

Mrs. Watt gave birth to a fine boy this afternoon at 3.30 p.m. Both are doing well and Mr.Watt is greatly pleased. We hope to get back by the steamer coming from Sydney on Thursday or Friday. I can come across on horseback afterwards. Isabel was of great assistance, only two hours trouble. The steamer will most likely be here at daybreak tomorrow so Mr.Watt will get his news away without delay.

With much love from,
Your affect. Son,
J.Campbell Nicholson

Lenakel,
TANNA,
New Hebrides.
June 2nd 1906

Dear Mother,

We have been caught napping again. The steamer should not have come for us until Monday but there was not much trade and instead she called for us on the Thursday before. I went on board and told them that unless they could wait at least six hours they need not wait at all. After some bluster they would wait any time required but the rush, etc., nearly knocked us up. I had to fix up the hospital and get rid of six patients, chloroform and operated on one myself as Isabel felt upset. The steamer came at daybreak so that we did not get a proper breakfast. However, by 12 a.m. we got on board and are now at Efate, Undine Bay to call for Rev.Mr.Milne, then expect to be landed at Tongoa tonight. It is so hard to write on board, you can understand that, and only that we must post the letters on board tonight before leaving I would not try to write.

We are both well and John especially so. He is such a cheery little chap and makes all on board his friends, but on board eats all the time, biscuits, apples, cake, etc. and yet is quite ready for each meal. It's wonderful. Nano is not with us. She did not like to leave her husband so soon again, so we have a boy called Nilauas, my hospital boy. He does well and looks after John alright. Not hard to do seeing there is always somebody waiting to get hold of him

We had a glorious communion season. The church members partaking nearly filled the Church and adherents and all children had to sit outside on the Friday. I baptised twenty-three infants and married five couples. On the Sabbath I baptised forty-seven adults and dispensed the Communion. It was a great week but I felt the strain a good deal. At White Sands fifty were baptised and Mr.McMillan had a good time. I did not hear about Port Resolution, but Mr.Watt is far from well. However, Mrs.Watt is well now and the baby is a fine boy.

The northern Missionaries are all on Tongoa waiting for us. We from the south will then have to wait till the northerners are returned which will mean a month away from Tanna. We do not like this but can't help it.

Mr.McMillan is Moderator and Mr.Watt is the Clerk. About the French and English agreement, there is nothing definite. The old cry is raised again. If neither Nation can annexe then divide them up. If France should get Tanna, I'm afraid, in spite of the religious liberty clause we would be put out. The Lord help our people, but this is an old cry about the Islands and the old hands say they have got used to it and expect nothing from it, but the times are changed now and I really think something must soon be done. Isabel is only writing one letter home, she does not feel equal to sitting down below. Good company on deck. The youngsters and ladies are making a great stir. Mr.Watt, McMillan and myself sitting pushing away at the pens.

We had a letter from Sarah from Colombo. We are awaiting good news from Ballyholme. (sister-in-law Jeanie must be expecting an arrival)

Now Mother mine I must stop. This is longer than I expected but we are going round the point called The Devil's Point and a good name for it. We have been thinking and calculating about just going home on our short furlough. Some say we could do it nearly as cheap with less trouble than living in the colonies, but passages are not cheap. Mr.Frater goes home in August for deputation work and Dr.McKenzie is very ill. His furlough is due now.

Love to all from us three. I have had no time for photography but am sending two tone ones you have seen before.

Much love,
Your affect.son,
J.Campbell Nicholson

From Paama:

Lenakel,
TANNA,
New Hebrides,
June 27th 1906.

Dear Mother,

We were so glad to get your letter, written on the 2nd April. It caught us at Tongoa when the steamer came to take the northern missionaries home. We came on as far as here to stay with the Fraters and expect the steamer at any time to return and take us south. The Island of Tongoa is a high table land about 350 ft. or more high. The station is high up and we all felt it very cold as a strong south wind blew most of the time. The buildings were not very comfortable and nearly every man, woman and child were laid up for a day or so with fever or bronchitis, etc. The children all had coughs and John was pretty bad. We were glad to get down here and into a comfortable house. He began to get better at once and is now eating and working like a horse. I never knew a kid to like work so much. He must have wheelbarrows or carts or something to pull about. He is always in a lather of sweat and as hard as nails. He added considerably to his reputation at Synod and men and women alike served and obeyed him. One Sunday they took him to a big meeting in another part of the Island. We stayed at home for a rest. When the missionaries came back the whole talk was John. He had got up on the front seat and faced the audience with a hymn book and tried to sing "Jesus Loves Me" in Tannese. This too during the sermon. Mr.McMillan tried to get him but John fell down. After a bit he got up again and did the same, this time with his back to a post. He was captured but again escaped and did the same. Mr.Mitchelson who was preaching had to stop once and ask the people to pay less attention to the child and more to him.

John is talking quite a lot now. He has learnt so much from the children at Synod, but mixes his English with Tannese. Nano is not with us, her husband wanted her so we have a boy called Nilauas. He is a good boy, a real Christian. We enjoyed Synod and we did not. I had fever and neuralgia and had to get two teeth out. Isabel was off form for a day or two and then kept anxious about John who had fever once and then bronchitis. We are glad we came to the Fraters. They are a fine couple and you must have them at Ellenville if possible. They are to commence deputation in Ireland. God has used them to do a good work, indeed a wonderful work here and on the south east of Ambrim. Frater is a good speaker and so I believe is Mrs.Frater. You will like the latter very much.

The people here are more advanced in some ways than ours. They are richer and can easily get money but in others ours are ahead. Most of the Teachers here are from other Islands, all ours are from our own district and we have sent out two to Mr.McMillan's district. But I hope Frater will be asked to Bangor. Mr.Watson[1] will have all the arrangements in his hands and I am sure will be glad if he is asked to Bangor, which is subscribing fairly well now.

You asked about Somo's age. He is about 10 I think. He lives at Lenakel with his mother. I do hope he will turn out good. I would like to send him to Tongoa Training Institute for Teachers, but if he is not inclined that way I suppose I must do the best for him in some other way.

I was glad to hear about Ballymaconnell and Helen. If you do not state very definitely that the money is to be sent it is just absorbed by the general fund. I am always glad to have some on hand to get things for church or station without having to trouble the committee. Give my kind regards to the Hartes, especially Mabel. I am so glad they are doing well. The Lord prosper them still more, they have made a gallant fight.

I am glad Uncle John[2] *takes an interest in us. We're so glad to know he had been in with you.*

I hope Netta passed her exam well, she likes music better than letter writing. I have now had a letter from Sara and Dan, but not from China. I trust things may go well with them.

There is a good deal of talk at present about the Islands, but we do not think anything can be settled for years. The prevailing opinion now is that the group will be divided by England and France. France will want the Southern half. The dividing line would pass about Ambrym, whether south or north is not said. In case of the French getting the south I am afraid we would have to get out. They would regulate us so stringently that no work would be done. We have got a lot of rose and other flower slips to take home with us. I have gathered so many different kinds of things, but the drought has always killed them. I must some time give you a list of all the different flowers we have.

Mr.McMcMillan, wife and children have been sent up to the Institute to take charge until August. Mr. And Mrs.Watt[3] *will return with us. He is far from strong and may soon have to resign. There will be great changes on the Mission staff in a few years. Some of the men or women are being knocked about too much by fever and some are getting old. We have been kept in wonderful health and have not found life so hard here at all. We try to live and eat as good as possible and neither of us are especially lazy. We always manage to have a good deal of fresh food and vegetables and like to get back to Lenakel for that reason. In most other places tinned meat, fish, vegetables, have to be used nearly all the time.*

Now, Mother mine, I must dry up. We would like if you could come out and see us and John. We have a six months furlough and if we steered for home we could have six weeks or two months with you but it would cost more and the constant sailing might not be for the best. But the colonies do not appeal to us, they are strange lands to us and the looking for digs or a house, etc. frightens us. I wish the Committee would let us stay down for another year (five) and then furlough home. But I suppose it is no use talking. I tried to get these conditions when leaving saying that the first furlough was the principal one.

We got Father's photo. It is very good. But you must get one a real good one too. John was asking in Tannese where gany was. He knows your photo and will now know his grandfather's. But at Synod he called all the elder members 'gannies'.

With our united love to you and Father and Netta and kind regards to all friends.

Your affect. Son in Christ,
J.Campbell Nicholson

Lenakel,
TANNA,
New Hebrides.
28th June, 1906

Dear Father,

We were so glad to get your photo and see you looking so well. There is only the suggestion of more whiteness about hair and whiskers to make you look any different since we left. We always hear now and again about your cough giving you trouble, but I also see you can keep up your attendances at the Council and Guardians[4] *so it must just be a touch of chronic bronchitis.*

Mother says Bobs is too lazy to go about much now. You are feeding him too well.

We are all packed and waiting for the steamer to take us to Lenakel. We have enjoyed ourselves since coming here, but on Tongoa our enjoyment of some society was spoiled by fever and colds.

Mr.McMillan was Moderator this year and all passed off quietly. The political situation is thought to be critical. It is felt that the Islands cannot remain as they are much longer. The French want them. Britain does not. The Colonies, N.Z. and Australia don't want the French to get them but are not too caring for them themselves so that I am afraid it will end in France getting. They are putting a lot of money into them and I believe will pay men to take up land. They impose no tariffs on the French produce and take it away at reduced rates. The Britishers have not a look in, the only thing they can get into Australia is copra. Hundreds of acres of splendid coffee are going to waste yearly, though this coffee once topped the London Market. Our Commissioner is playing into the hands of the French. I hear he has said that's what he is here for. It is terrible to think that after nearly a century (70 years) of work the Presbyterian Mission should be ousted. But maybe things will turn out better than we think. France yet may be glad to get territorial rights in Africa or elsewhere in exchange for any claim they may have on the New Hebrides.

We are very well, but must get out of the Islands this hot season. We are not as strong as when we came down. The climate is not so bad, but it is very taxing and the fever gradually breaks up one's constitution.

Mr.and Mrs.Frater, with whom we are staying till the steamer returns from the north to take us home, expect to be in Ireland in November and will call. They have been very good to us since coming.

I had letters from Sarah and Dan. Though they were written about the same time one arrived after the other in a month. They were written in the Indian Ocean.

John has passed his 2nd birthday and is talking a great deal now. Isabel unites with me in love to you.

Your affect. son,
J.Campbell Nicholson

In the July Jottings (No.53) there is an interesting article of a cruise Grandfather takes round the island: 'Early in February I made my first complete cruise round the island in our boat. For this I had a goodly number of volunteers to pick from, and though we had intended only to take ten, we started fifteen all told. Lomai and George Mahau were my officers and made everything easy and pleasant for me during the trip.

Our people gave us a good send off. With sails spread out before a favouring breeze we were at leisure to have our morning worship. Worship over, we put out our fishing line and stationed a man forward to look out for turtles, then settled ourselves for a general talk. The cry of Iau (turtle) soon had us all agog with excitement. To the cry of where, some shout here, others there, but at last I get a glimpse of it under the boom and bear down upon it.

It lies like a brown patch on the water with head under. It has no ears and so depends on its eyes to warn it of approaching danger. Up comes its head to take a look round and bang goes the rifle, it flounders, turns on its back. Lomai, stripped to the waist, is ready to dive, but ere the boat reaches it sinks out of sight, and we sail over the place of its struggles leaving an aldermanic feast for crabs and fishes.

A mile or two slips past and we enjoy to the full the sea and reefs and landscape. We are sailing north, and wave a greeting to Tapanua, the teacher at Loaneai, who, with his people are gathering for school.'

Lenakel,
TANNA,
New Hebrides.
November 11th 1906

Dear Mother,

It is Sunday evening and Isabel and I are just up from our English service. The people are learning to read the little book we have and are making good progress. They can sing a good many of the hymns. The Church looks well lighted up. We have large 300 candle power lamps. I trust that these services may be the means of great good to the Tannese who are being expelled from Queensland, some of them after being there for many years, some even thirty years.

All goes on very smoothly. We are very busy. The people are working like slaves. There are to be three villages completed before I leave and other new houses erected. The people worry about what they would do and no doctor here with them so I just told them that if they got into new and healthy sites and new houses that they would have less need of always being doctored up. I told some that if they did not look sharp I would come back to see their graves and not them

Our services here are largely attended now by new people from all around. Indeed at Xmas I do not know what we shall do. The Church is almost full each Sunday as it is. I suppose it will mean the open air again and this I do not care about as it is more trying than preaching in the Church.

Mrs.McMillan and children are here. Mr.McMillan was across today and preached here for me in the morning. I went to an outstation in the south and conducted the service there. Things are going well in Mr.McMillan's district too and the people coming out well to hear the word. Tanna has been long of coming in, over 70 years now, but a better day has dawned and the day when all shall at least profess to believe in the true God is not far distant. Teachers are needed and we have none ready to go out.

We are all in fair form. Isabel and Mrs.McMillan get on well and are a comfort to each other at this time. She is a great help to Isabel in advising her about the things best to take and get for the journey home. John, Bertie and James have great times, they make an awful row. John is as hard as nails and does not look a bit like a tropical baby. He can talk fluently now in Tannese. He is a great man for holding meetings, sings with great gusto. At prayer (his) the other night after he had finished he said Ani God bless verandah kin. I could not make out for awhile what he meant but when he said mene (Grandma) I knew he meant his two Grandas, he did not know them being called Grandfather. He always has to bring in the horses and dogs by name.

We are having dry weather and our garden is going back a bit. I have lost a good deal of seed but the things which had got a good start are doing well. We have several kinds of roses, six varieties of lilies, the zinnies, balsams[5]*, mignonette, sunflowers, phlox, chrysanthemums, cosmos, all blooming. We have a lot of native things. Sweet Williams, wallflowers and stock have grown but not bloomed, pinks and carnations flowered a little, three vines are growing well. We got a Virginia creeper for the front of the house and it is doing well. The fruit trees are doing well but too young yet to bear well, but we always have grandiloes, passionfruit, pomegranates, oranges, etc. Of vegeta-*

bles we have only tomatoes, carrots, French beans, parsley, mint and some new things coming on. Okra, Eggplant, which you will not know. In time we should have a good garden. I like it, it is a fine recreation and I always enjoy walking about it.

Our stock are doing well. The cow should calve soon. We have thirty sheep and have been eating mutton and will eat more before we leave. We are going to kill our big bull for the natives before we go. The new young one is doing well. I put a ring in its nose and will handle him so that there need not be so much fear of him hurting anybody. Isabel is afraid of the big one, but he never bothers with anybody.

The people have a lot of maize planted but this drought is against it. We must try for something more profitable to work for the books. I have arrowroot planted but it has not increased much as yet. I lent Mr.McMillan the horse, Tom, to cross today. He was to take him half way and then turn him home to come by himself, he has only turned up now, 9 p.m. He has been having a good feed on the way. I hope he has not raided a garden on his way or tomorrow I will hear about it. I believe definite conversions are taking place amongst us. One sees a grand change coming over many, but conversion can never be the striking change here that it is at home. There often the knowledge is in the head but there has been disobedience to light and knowledge. Here the head is dark and knowledge comes slowly and with it the change gradually that comes suddenly at home. A man here may renounce heathenism and conform so far as he knows to what is right and yet be far from having any idea of his need of a Saviour. Then as he learns and if his heart is reached one sees the sign of the new life coming day by day. Our great tendency is to forget that these people need to be converted again after they are converted from heathenism. They need to be "turned to God".

You seem to have had a great time with the fleet. We too had our fleet. I hope the next man of war will be as nice.

Well if all goes well we should be ready to leave Tanna this time three months and hope that we will get on a boat at once for home from Sydney. I suppose we will have to rough it a bit on the White Star boats but they say sometimes nice people travel by them, at others there are many rough cases on board. By going this way we will escape the heat of the Red Sea and fewer calls which will mean less inducement to spend money.

I had a letter from Dr.Paton. He does not say anything as to whether they like our going home instead of the Colonies or not, but hope for some little deputation work at least. Maybe they will want me to stay a little to do some. In that case Isabel and John will get a longer time with you all.

Love to Father, Netta and Willie and all friends. Much to yourself from we three,

Your affect. son,
James

Notes for 1906

In Britain, at the beginning of the year a strict new Aliens Act was brought in to stem the flow of refugees from central Europe and Russia where civil unrest had been ongoing. Refugees were questioned about their finances and given stringent health checks, both physical and mental.

In the Pacific 10,000 were feared dead after a cyclone hit and Grandfather mentions a hurricane in his January letter that must have been the edge of it. It seemed as if there was no end to the earth's anger; in March, Etna erupted and many were killed and in April Vesuvius blew up leaving hundreds dead. As if that was not enough, on 19th April an earthquake hit San Francisco leaving over a 1,000 dead with millions of pounds worth of damage and looters were shot in the streets. On a gentler note in America, Kellogg's cornflakes were marketed for the first time.

Sister Sarah and her husband Dan appeared to be returning to China after furlough.

The local paper in the summertime listed visitors to Bangor and where they were staying and the subject of mixed bathing was being discussed but certainly not approved of as it was in France. On 4th August the British Fleet arrived in Bangor Bay amongst much excitement. On the continent that year, the Simplon Tunnel was opened and confetti was invented in Paris by an enterprising printer.

The missionary's wife had to be a jack of all trades; nurse, housekeeper, teacher and hotelier. She had to be able to help with nursing (as can be seen in the letters my grandmother was the anaesthetist in the hospital), teach the local women cooking and housekeeping, and remember she was only 25. To be able to accommodate and look after guests – sometimes with very little warning – and last but not least, the organist in the church.

When missionaries first arrived on the islands they thought that the best possible place to site their homes was near the sea, partly for convenience, so that they were able to see approaching ships and for embarking and disembarking, but also for safety in case of the need for a quick getaway. However, it was soon found that some places close to the shore were a breeding ground for mosquitoes and so in later years dwellings were built higher up with plenty of windows to let the breezes blow through. In Tanna still, malaria, or fever, is still a cruel force to be reckoned with and quinine or the equivalent, much valued; cuts and abrasions quickly become infected.

I have a feeling that some of the letters are missing. There appear gaps at times and grandfather's next letter is written on board ship on his way home on furlough.

Chapter VI – The Fifth Year

Tragedy Strikes

The end of 1906 on Tanna brought a particularly virulent strain of malignant malaria. My grandmother had just given birth a month previously to my Auntie May and Mrs.MacMillan had also had a baby at the same time, when both came down with the disease. It was a terrible time for my grandfather and Mr.Macmillan. Both wives were being nursed at Lenakel and while my grandfather looked after them and fed both young babies, Mr.MacMillan looked after the hospital and dispensary.

Lenakel,
TANNA,
New Hebrides.
Jan.13th 1907

Dear Mother,

Just a few lines to yourself and that is about all the mail we will send this time. We have had an anxious time and are having another. Isabel is much better and able to sit up a little every day but Mrs.Macmillan is very ill with fever now and near the valley of the shadow. For three days she has been delirious and in spite of all treatment the fever scarcely remits at all. We had to cut off her hair and either Mr.Macmillan or myself have to be in the room all the time. On Friday night we had a hurricane but not a very bad one, only the rain got into the house a bit. We thought Mrs.MacM. was going. She had a lucid moment and told us she was, in her delirium she sang the 23rd Psalm splendidly so that it could be heard all through the house. At one time I called him to her side as the heart had nearly ceased to beat, but she rallied and has dragged on till now. I do pray and hope she may pull through.

The people are praying much. They had a special prayer for Isabel just before she got the turn for the better and are loud in the Praises of Jehovah for the quick answer.

The fever has been very bad this year, two young strong men went down like ninepins, others came through after a bad time. I am trying to get the hospital closed. We have been unable to operate any since November and though the hospital has kept full of cases they have not got much attention. Mr. Macmillan did the work for over a week whilst I was with Isabel. We are both getting very tired, since the 11th December I have never had more than 2 hours sleep at a time and seldom that. I have to feed both babies with the bottle and that is not easy in this hot weather. Then the three boys and Isabel and Mr. and Mrs. MacM. in their separate rooms. The worst of it is our provisions are running out. We have not a big stock on account of our furlough being near. However, we must keep on, do our best and trust God about everything. It will be grand to get on the big steamer and rest. The MacMillans, if all goes well, will be in the house for a day or two after we leave. I have been unable to hold communion or baptismal services, but let the people have a day's play and about 2000 turned up.

The work is going on grandly. His Kingdom is coming quickly, one would like another consecutive year or two but we know now that we have stayed down if anything too long without a break. These short stays are not good for the work.

The Leggatts have gone for good and I expect there has been a good deal of sickness up north.

I am afraid there will be others who will have to go. Some are getting old and then our fields will be enlarged. There is some doubt as to whether Ewen McKenzie will be back and Yates is not too strong.

This season is very wet and hot. The mosquitoes are very numerous and vicious.

The growth of all things is wonderful, the place looks lovely and the flowers are simply glorious. Barring hurricanes food should be plentiful soon

May and John keep well but John does not want to leave Nano. Today at the table he told me he was not going in the steamer he would stay with Nano till we came back. He said he would cry if he had not Nano with him. Nano is fretting and I think must be talking to him although she denies it.

Isabel is cheery, she feels Mrs. MacM. will get better, why she does not say, only she has got the feeling about it that came to her when she was at her worst. Thank God for sparing me Isabel. I have been in the depths at times.

Your affect. son,
J.Campbell Nicholson

PS. 15th Mrs.MacMillan is no better but still holding her own fairly well, though delirious all the time. Isabel and all well.

J.C.

But the sad news in the July Jottings read:

JOTTINGS 57 JULY 1907

'Tanna will never be the same to me again' was the wail of a lady on Tanna when Mrs.Macmillan died – and that expression found an echo in all our hearts. How often had her bright smile and hearty welcome chased away weariness and given encouragement to us all. My first introduction to her was at White Sands. Soon after my arrival on Tanna a messenger crossed to Lenakel with a letter asking me to come and see one of Mrs.Macmillan's children who was ill. Not knowing the distance across, I set out rather late in the afternoon, and after a few hours began to realize that there is a tremendous difference between the way the crow flies and the way a native travels to a given place. Daylight suddenly failed, and being new to native tracks and bush riding amidst the thunderous roaring of a volcano, I thought I should never reach White Sands. But suddenly there was a cheer of greeting, followed by a flashing of lights, and the warmest of welcomes. I was at the station of my fellow Missionaries on the other side of Tanna. I had never met Mr.and Mrs. Macmillan before, but it seemed as though we were old friends – the joy of

that welcome dispelled all strangeness, and chased away the gloomy thoughts begotten in the stygian darkness of the volcano haunted woods. This was my first experience in a Missionary's home, and what it meant to me I can never fully record. I was then in the stage of disillusionment which comes to most of us on first entering the Mission field. Mrs.Macmillan was a very messenger of encouragement and peace, and by her optimism sent me back to my station and people a better man – albeit she herself was all unconscious that she was being used of God to that end.

The blood of white martyrs has never been shed on Tanna during the sixty-eight years of strenuous effort for its evangelization, but Tanna holds in its keeping the dust of four of the faithful who counted not their lives dear for its redemption, and of these four, three were heroic and saintly women.

The first Mrs.John Paton,along with her child, died on March 3rd, 1859 – the year following her arrival. The next to go was Mrs.Watt, who lived for twenty-five years in the south of Tanna, and who nobly at her husband's side faced the bitterest hostility and lived to see the hatred and opposition change to respect and love. These two were buried at Port Resolution; and now our station at Lenakel is hallowed by the memory and remains of Mrs.Macmillan, who was in all respects their worthy successor.

Mrs. Macmillan, like her husband, was the child of Indian Missionaries, and they were both born in that country. Her father, the late Rev.Professor Robertson, was Missionary Professor in the Duff Memorial College at Bombay, and was called from there to the Chair of Church History in Aberdeen. Mrs. Macmillan spent her girlhood in Aberdeen, and may be said to have been brought up in a Missionary atmosphere; since her home was the meeting place with so many missionaries.

Mr.Macmillan took up his work in the Islands two years before Mrs. Macmillan went out. She voyaged alone to Australia, where Mr.Macmillan met her; and they were married in the home of the beloved Dr.J.G.Paton in Melbourne. Afterwards they went to Tanna, and Mrs.Macmillan began her life work there at the early age of twenty- one.

*The last year, she often said, had brought better health to her than ever she had enjoyed before in the Islands. Her baby boy was born on the 26*th *of*

November last, and her recovery was uninterrupted, mother and child being so entirely "un-island-like" in health and spirits. But early in the new year a malignant malarial fever attacked the natives. Mrs.Nicholson took the fever, and Mrs.Macmillan also. In Mrs.Macmillan's case the fever ran so unrelenting a course that in only a fortnight, on Sabbath morning, the 20th of January last, her spirit passed to be with Christ.

That evening we buried her beside our Church at the foot of a sychus palm. The heavy rain which had been falling all day, ceased for a little, and through a rent in the clouds the sun shone on the sorrowing group at the graveside, speaking a message of hope.

In death, as in life, Mrs.Macmillan was full of faith and hope. A deep peace and rest settled on her when she realized that her end was near. One night when the storm raged outside the house, and the fire of her life burnt very low, she burst into singing, and her contralto voice sounded through all the house as she sang the twenty-third Psalm. In another room we listened spell-bound as we heard the note of triumphant trust swell in the words,

> *"Yea, though I walk through death's dark vale,*
>
> *Yet will I fear none ill,*
>
> *For Thou art with me, and Thy rod and staff Me comfort still.*
>
> *And in God's house for ever more my dwelling place shall be."*

A swift messenger crossed to White Sands with the sad news, and among the poor natives the death wail sounded all around. Men and women wept for one who, of a truth, had been a very angel of light to them. Kokaia, the war chief – now elder in the Church – led across a band of men and women to give to their sore stricken Missionary and his children the one sad tribute – all that they had to give – their heartfelt sympathy.

J.C.N

Hobart,
Tasmania,
JS.S.'Persic'.
March 3rd 1907

Dear Mother,

We left Lenakel two weeks ago yesterday. We had a good passage to Sydney where we stayed one night and then came to Melbourne where we stayed two nights and then joined the 'Persic',coming on here for 46,000 cases of apples and 80 more passengers. We cannot exactly say how we like this all one class business, there is less attendance and one is expected to bring a good many things but we will be able to criticise better after 7 weeks in her.

Isabel has had a hard time since we left. I was having fever every night a little before leaving but thought I would be all right on the sea. But it only began when I got on board and for six days I had the malignant kind that Mrs. McMillan and Isabel had. Then it got easier and I had only 3 attacks in the 24 hours and I arrived in Sydney like that. I got through my business some way and Isabel hers. In Melbourne I began to pick up but the Doctor found I was in bad form, my liver and spleen being large and I was very breathless. The committee have recommended me to take time and get well and sent a strong letter home I believe, not to let me come back till we are fit, so we may be at home more than two or three months. But I want to get back to relieve poor Mr.McMillan. He says he will stay till we come back. We had a good reception in Melbourne. In Sydney we are classed Victorians[1] *and get the cold shoulder.*

This company evidently is trying to become popular. The ship is open to visitors now and is crowded with them, they will even open the door of your cabin and look in. It is not a bit like Sunday with the bairns and I not being able to walk much, we are afraid to venture ashore and look for a church. Isabel wants me to go myself but I hope these people will soon be chased and we will be able to sit and read in quietness.

We have hard cases of both sexes on board and they are not afraid to let it be seen. Whilst many of the people seem quiet decent folk the bulk are the gilt and tinsel, loud laughing, bluff and swagger, no mannered kind of people. We have two parsons on board, one a Presbyterian and the other something else I hope. But I have been put on the list as the Rev.Dr.Nicholson without any reference to the fact of me being medical. This is the fault of the Agent who booking our passages, he must pile on all he can. I am even addressed at times in letters as 'Reverend Sir'.

We expect to be in good form for a holiday when we get home, the rest on board will fatten us, the food is good and plain but rough served. Today serviettes were put out on all the tables and then lifted just before the bell rang for dinner. They were only for the visitors to look at, not to be used. Dessert forks and such odds and ends are not used. We feel the cold here, but have no flannels on yet. It will be warmer all the way after we leave here until we get to the Channel and at home we will be able to clothe ourselves as we want.

John is a terror, we have not seen him for more than an hour. I used to hunt by the hour for him, now I wait till he turns up with a smile and plenty of tar on. He won't wear stockings and his sandals have skinned his foot so he runs barefooted. He talks in Tannese to everybody and they stare. He is very happy, but occasionally talks of Lenakel and Nano and says he is going to cry for them tomorrow. He told me that he had everything at Lenakel and Nano to help him and said he would soon return to it.

5th. We leave here at daybreak. We are going out for a drive with the Presbyterian Minister. He is a brother-in-law of Frank Paton's. We did a little shopping yesterday. John nearly wrecked two shops. Going along the street a man was cleaning a big shop window, he hailed John like an old friend, John returned the greeting cordially. The man explained he was a friend of the carpenter on the 'Persic' and met John in his cabin on Sunday. That's the kind of boy, he knows everybody. The baby is doing well and Isabel is getting more like herself each day. We feel the cold a bit, not much.

Now I must say goodbye. I do not think we can write again before getting home. It will be grand to see you all. May the Lord spare us all till then. It has been an awful time of death lately.

Love to all, Father, Netta and yourself. Isabel wants to stay with her people first. Lizzie says she will have all ready for us. I am afraid we will be a bit of a nuisance with two children.

Your affect. son,
J Campbell Nicholson

A note in the Jottings reads:

"Dr. and Mrs. Nicholson arrived safely in Ireland, all the better for the invigorating sea breezes of their voyage home via the Cape. The sad trying days of their last few months on Tanna had left a deep mark on their health. Mrs. Nicholson had been at death's door while Mrs. Macmillan, her friend, was lying seriously ill – both of them in the home at Lenakel. One was taken and the other left, and the death of one who, in the isolation of the Islands, had become to Mrs.Nicholson like a sister, wrought deeply upon her heart, and had its inevitable effect upon her already weakened health – so that it is a matter for devout thankfulness that the opportunity for the voyage home came just at the moment of need.

It is not quite settled when the Doctor will return. The Victorian Committee recommended, in consequence of the fact that he had stayed a year beyond the stipulated period when, for health's sake, a change to the Colonies is considered essential, that Dr.Nicholson should stay a little beyond the ordinary period. He will, therefore, probably remain at any rate until after Mr.Frank Paton arrives, so that he may have the advantage of meeting him with the Home Committee before his return.

We have felt that it would be unfair at this time – particularly in view of the fact that Mrs.Nicholson is not yet strong – to ask the Doctor to leave home to take meetings. Friends of his work will, we are sure, quite understand and appreciate the situation."

Dr. J. Campbell Nicholson's Report – written from Ireland

June, 25th 1907

I must begin this letter with an apology to all the friends who kindly sent clothing in the case which arrived on Tanna last December. I failed to acknowledge the gifts at the time owing to the dark season of sickness and death through which we were passing at the time.

The last hot season on Tanna was the worst we had experienced there. The winds were from the north, intensely hot, and amounted at times almost to hurricanes. Rain was heavy and very constant.

Worse, however, than the weather, there appeared among our natives a very malignant type of malarial fever. A young teacher and several Church members died from it. Afterwards the dreaded fever entered our own house and claimed Mrs.Macmillan as its victim, also giving us grave anxiety about Mrs. Nicholson. All these trials combined to make the season anything but happy and joyous.

In the midst of it all, I am thankful to add, the work of God was prospering in our district, and extension was made in several directions. Under God, we owe much to Mr.Macmillan for this happy condition of things. He took all the services and dispensary work during December, while my hands were full through Mrs.Nicholson being so ill with malarial fever. I also had blood poisoning first in one hand and then in the other.

It was not until the first week in the New Year that we were able to have our Christmas gathering. The fever had almost ceased with Mrs.Nicholson; and though, even then, Mrs.Macmillan was having slight attacks, yet, so far, no alarming symptoms had manifested themselves. We were thus able at last to fix a day for the natives to gather, though we were obliged to postpone the Communion and Baptismal services at that time.

It was by far the largest gathering ever held on the grounds. The people themselves carried through most of the arrangements and the day passed off splendidly and without anything to mar its peace and happiness. Tug of war, football and races were held. We had also a new departure. Some Tanna men lately returned from Queensland had brought a set of bats and stumps, and the first cricket matches were played on Tanna. Some of the natives bowled and batted splendidly.' Grandfather had been a keen athlete in his youth, playing football for the Ulster Rangers Association Football Club and having been Vice President of Bangor Rugby Club, so this probably stood him in good stead when it came to showing the Tannese the niceties of the games. *The heathen were at peace – in consequence of the visit of the Joint Naval Commission some months previously – and many of them took part in the feasting and games. We strictly enforced the rule that no rifles were allowed in the grounds, and while this law kept some from entering, it made for the peace and security of those who did.*

The new road, mentioned in my last letter as having been jointly undertaken by Mr.Macmillan's people and my own, has been almost carried across the island. Our people have completed a road eight miles long from the west coast inland. They accomplished between thirty and forty chains[2] *each day. As they got further from Lenakel they camped out near their work; and in three days had reached the point of junction agreed upon with the people of the east coast. It is not much of a road, but it is a great advance on native tracks, and Mr.Macmillan and myself can ride side by side over its whole extent. His people have a mile or two to make yet, but when they have finished the distance between our stations will be reduced to sixteen miles. The heathen now and then gave great help – they were not, however, very constant, the fear that the road might prove a highway for their enemies ever seemed to haunt them.*

Other roads at different outstations have been commenced, and, now that the practical advantage of good straight tracks has been demonstrated to them, I think the natives will be encouraged to carry on this work till travelling in our district is made easy. All roads will converge to Lenakel, as the people now really appreciate the Hospital and Dispensary.

From the Editor of the Jottings: *Dr. and Mrs.Nicholson are still in the Home Land. Mrs.Nicholson has scarcely sufficiently recovered strength to return to the Islands, and particularly to return in the hot season beginning about November. The Doctor is improving the time by getting up the latest knowledge on the treatment of tropical diseases; he is also doing some deputation work for us. In agreeing to the extension of his short furlough we are, we believe, conferring future blessings on Tanna, and at the same time carrying out the wishes of the Victorian Committee, who asked for an extended rest for our Missionary and his wife. We are sure the time will be more than made up in the strenuous work that will be put into the West Tanna Mission on their return.*

By the way, Dr.Nicholson will be in London in October, and will be able to take weekend deputation work in and around the Metropolis. Will friends who wish for Sabbath meetings be good enough to give us early intimations, so that arrangements may be made quickly. We are very anxious that any meetings held may be so organized as to bring new permanent interest to the Mission – collections are of secondary importance.

Notes for 1907

Because of my grandmother's poor recovery after the birth of her second child and the terrible bouts of malaria, it was decided to travel home to Ireland rather than spend their furlough in Australia, that the sea voyage and rest at home would be more beneficial.

In England the Suffragette movement was escalating as the women's war for the vote continued. Fifty five appeared in court and fifteen went to prison, but Finland was a step ahead having given the vote to women the year before. That year saw Baden-Powell forming the Boy Scouts and Rudyard Kipling won the Nobel Prize for literature.

Russia continued to be torn apart with strife; pogroms against the Jews, 20 million were reckoned to be starving and on their far eastern borders, the Russo-Japanese war came to an end and the Russians and Japanese troops withdrew, leaving Manchuria once again in Chinese hands, which I am sure was a relief to my great-aunt and her husband, who were due back there.

Grandfather was coming home to more tribal fighting, but of a different kind in Ulster. In August, there were riots in Belfast; Sir Edward Carson spoke out in Parliament against the Irish Council bill that would give Ireland a measure of self-government, saying it would mean 'the swallowing of a loyal Ulster into the government of Ireland'. Cavalry galloped down the Falls Road and four civilians were killed.

Back in Bangor a Mr.J.Fletcher was offering a tourist coach service down the Ards Peninsula, stopping for $1^{1/2}$ hours each at Ballywalter and Greyabbey for 2/6 (*$12^{1/2}$* new pence) and Mrs.Lyttle's Services Registry Office was constantly in need of all classes of well-recommended servants. One Saturday in July the Bangor bakers' shops ran out of bread and biscuits due to the influx of visitors, mostly from Scotland and in August in Belfast, the police went on strike – they hadn't had an increase in pay for 20 years! The dockers were on strike as well. Also in Bangor, Lady Clanmorris, on the committee of the cottage hospital, was of the opinion that the time had come for a new hospital to be built to be able to provide for the town and that the people of Bangor should contribute £50 per annum towards the upkeep of the cottage hospital until the new hospital was built. If these terms were not agreed the hospital would close; no Health Service in those days. The new Drama Club was in full swing and its first production in May of She Stoops to Conquer was a great success. My great grandmother was on the committee for the church bazaar and great aunt Netta was on the refreshment stall. In May, William, or WP, grandfather's evangelist brother, was home on holiday, the County Down Spectator mentions 'a well-known visitor W.P.Nicholson, conducted three services in Bangor on Sunday, the last one being closed with a prayer by his missionary brother James: not for him the limelight. Also on a summer note, Alex.Sloan of Conlig was granted a permit to run donkeys on Ballyholme Beach. Constable Dixon was standing no nonsense with these new-fangled motor cycles; two men were stopped for having exceeded the speed limit of 6 miles per hour and one gentleman was fined for 'not having a distinguishing mark on the back of his bathchair'. Captain Nicholson raised a concern with the Wrackey Loaning, a road in the Princetown Road district. Many years ago, rights were given to men to remove seaweed – or seawrack – from the beaches, that was used as fertilizer, amongst other things, and the loaning was the road up which it came. Mr.Caproni was still enlarging his empire, opening a new shop in Newcastle. In July, HMS Drake, part of the British Fleet anchored in Bangor Bay and again there was much interest and excitement with music played by the Drake's band to help raise funds for the local hospital and cricket matches and teas.

On the family front, Willie, grandfather's brother, was married in Scotland on 15th August and in October, the wife of his elder brother John, gave birth to a daughter.

Captain Nicholson served on the Board of Guardians for the Union Workhouse in Newtownards and it was there during the summer that grandfather acted as locum while the permanent doctor went on holiday. An epidemic of meningitis had broken out in Glasgow and Edinburgh and also in Belfast, causing much concern.

During his furlough home he travelled to London and along with Dr.Daniel Mcdonald of Nguna and Rev.Maurice Frater of Paama, went to see Lord Elgin who was Secretary of State for Foreign Affairs under the

Campbell Bannerman Government. I have mentioned the Recruitment trade and it was with a view to end the practise of recruiting women who of course acted as a lure, that the three lobbied the minister. What had begun as a procurement of labour for the plantations developed into a slave trade early in the 1860s. The missions protested vehemently in the press and to Parliament, strongly urging the traffic to be stopped; many were the cries against them by those who stood to gain. When Bishop Patterson of the Melanesian Mission was murdered by natives on an island south of the Solomon Islands in retaliation against the slave trade in 1871, there was outrage around the world. Queen Victoria told of it in her Opening Speech in Parliament and every newspaper carried the news. This proved to be the turning point although abolition did not happen just yet, a Protection Bill being brought in but the trade continued. (Jottings 56 contains information on the above.) The family were in London from October, doing deputation work and attending meetings, before they sailed for the New Hebrides in January 1908. One meeting at Caxton Hall in London Grandfather spoke with other missionaries to an invited audience: *'Dr.Nicholson's evening address was full of vivacity and brightness. He began by reciting how on one occasion a native of Tanna who had been in Queensland came to him and asked him where he came from. When he replied that he came from Ireland, the man said, 'Then you must be a Policeman!' This was somewhat disconcerting, and the Doctor asked the reason for such a conclusion. The reply was that when in Queensland the native had on one occasion broken the law and cheeked a policeman, upon which the policeman had kicked him vigorously and sent him about his business. The policeman and others he had met were Irishmen, and the Tanna man had drawn the inference that Ireland must be the land from which all policemen came, and that Irishman and Policeman were synonymous terms!*

The devotion of Lomai was a very conspicuous note in Dr.Nicholson's address. The resourcefulness and steady faith of this native Man of God who had been raised up to help the West Tanna Mission was very remarkable. Lomai was not only able and willing at any time to undertake long journeys preaching the Gospel, but he also proved himself a splendid helper at the Hospital. He could be trusted to assist at the most difficult operations, and indeed, on one occasion had gone so far as to say that 'if he could only learn to tie the strings (meaning the veins) he could cut off a leg himself.'

An Editor's note at the beginning Jottings 59 Jan.1908 reads:

"Everyone must have missed the quarterly reports from the West Tanna, East Santo and Paama Mission Stations, and will perhaps be wondering how matters have progressed in the absence of the Missionaries. By the way of illustration there is a suggestive sentence in a letter which Dr.Nicholson has recently received from Iavis and Lomai, who are in charge at Lenakel. "Bring with you," they say to their Missionary, "some new scrubbing brushes – the old ones are nearly worn out!" This looks as though Mrs.Nicholson will find the house spick and span when she returns, and speaks well for her training of the two house girls at Lenakel who are supported by a lady in Newcastle-on-Tyne.

There will be a record crowd and a record yell when the Pioneer lands the Missis and their two grand little boys (should be boy and girl) on Lenakel beach in March or early April. The Doctor and his family sail from Liverpool on the 4th inst, via the Cape. They will take with them the love of many new friends, and may be assured of an increasing volume of prayer ascending for them in their future labours."

Chapter VII – The Sixth Year

Outward Bound and News From Tanna

PALMA
January 1908

My Dear Mother,

We are nearing Las Palmas after a very rough voyage so far. At first we were detained by fogs and after getting out of the Mersey it was so rough we could not get our pilot off and put in to Waterford and landed him there. Since then we have had a series of gales from south to west and north. The ship rolls badly. She has 3,000 tons of corrugated iron at the bottom of her hold and then wire netting and Locomotives above that and then 3,000 tons of Manchester goods on top of that. When she is filled with frozen meat she does not rock any. We are very comfortable and are fed well but the decks have been impossible until today. Isabel has been a little seasick but neither May, John or myself have been. I would have been if I had not been kept very busy. The ship has been so wet and the weather so bad when we left that I have been really working my passage. The Capt. has been laid up and I have had a good many of the crew to doctor. They all like medicine and have great faith in it. We have all told about 230 people on board. I have not got a girl to help Isabel yet but hope to soon. There are a good many in the steerage but we did not want a seasick one. The few passengers in the saloon are very nice. One young man is pretty ill at present with influenza and an old lady with bronchitis. We had no service last Sabbath, all was wet and the people seasick, but I am going to try and have one tonight. The Capt. is not given that way but I have got his consent. I wish John[1] *had been calling at Las Palmas, we might have met, but I suppose it is only on the outward passage he comes here. John was ill last night, very hot and restless. He has been sleeping all day and is better a bit. The baby also had a day off, but she looks so well and they both keep so cheery and bright. I am much afraid John will get a taste for ships after all this travelling.*

*I wish we could get word from here to tell us how you all are, if Father has got in to Council. I have not seen about the barrow yet but have it at hand and will get it fixed up soon. Ned is not much use while the ships rocks like this, but after this we should get better weather. I am much afraid we shall miss the 1*st *of March boat. We'll be sorry if we do, five weeks in Australia costs a great deal and besides we're anxious to get down. I feel ready to start work again. We are like new creatures. The Lord has given us a grand furlough and restored us to health and strength again. Sometimes one fears the future, having to separate from our children and death striking either of us or the children, but we comfort ourselves in the Lord and go forward in His charge.*

It is not easy writing, the ship rocks so much but you will understand the intention if you cannot read the writing.

I hope you are all well. The Lord bless you all. With much love to you and Father and Netta,

Your affect. son,
J.Campbell Nicholson

While Grandfather made his way back to Tanna, The Reverand Macmillan sends this report back to London:

*January,1908 A change has come over these Islands in the shape of a Dual Protectorate. The much-talked-of and long-delayed Convention was proclaimed in Vila on the 2*nd *December, and it may be of interest if I quote a little from an eye witness's account of the event.*

*The French Man-of-War, Kersaint, with the Governor of New Caledonia on board, arrived in Vila on November 23*rd*, and announced that a British war-*

ship, with the Governor of Fiji, was to arrive on the 26th, and that on the 28th the proclamation of the Convention would take place. It was not, however, till the 30th that H.M.S.Challenger arrived, "a magnificent ship", which "put the Kersaint into the shade". The following day was the Queen's birthday, and the inhabitants of Vila were startled by a Royal salute at noon. Then, on the next day, Monday, December 2nd, at 9.30 a.m. the Proclamation of the Convention was read in English and in French, addresses were delivered, and salutes fired by the Men-of-War, and then the Band struck up "God Save the King" and the "Marseillaise", and the New Hebrides had, all unconsciously, passed under a new regime, and although there are articles in the Convention which are, we think, capable of improvement, we are, on paper at any rate, very much better off than before, and only time will show how things will really work out.

The new Resident Commissioner is Mr.King, late Secretary to the High Commissioner in Fiji, who ought therefore to be already fairly well grounded in things New Hebridean.

The first news of the Proclamation was brought here by the French Man-of-War, which paid a flying visit to Weasisi on Thursday of the same week. The trader there sent me word of it, and in connection with this I may go on to relate what happened in the course of the next few days.

On the Saturday, Simon, one of the teachers in training at Lenakel, arrived at East Tanna on horseback with a message from Lomai, the elder in charge, saying that a French labour vessel was scattering drink broadcast along the coast, and had taken, amongst those recruited, a woman without her husband, and a girl against the wishes of her parents. Lomai had gone on board and remonstrated, and the Recruiter had faithfully promised to send these two women on shore again. He simply lied to Lomai; and next day moved further along the coast.

The vessel has a bad reputation. It was here in the South earlier in the year, scattering drink and firearms everywhere, and again in November it had made another of its nefarious raids. By a free use of "grog" it had made a good haul of recruits in November, and had now returned to play the same game, with considerable success too. The only white man on board was the French

Captain. The vessel was practically "run" by a somewhat notorious character, a Loyalty Islander and a professing Christian, Willie Uvea by name, who though nominally the "recruiter", was in reality everything, and the "Captain" was a convenient figure head.

Saturday though it was, and close to steamer time, I decided to go at once to Lenakel, and at once rode over, only to find the vessel had cleared out. But from the people on the Lenakel side I found out that they knew on board about the "Change of Government" at Vila, and therefore they were guilty of wittingly violating certain articles of the Convention, viz., in regard to supplying drink to natives and recruiting of women.

Thinking the affair was over, I merely decided to report the vessel by the incoming steamer, little knowing I should have more to report. However, on Monday a lad who had run nearly all the way from Weasisi, came panting up to me to say that Willie Uvea had carried off a young girl at Weasisi, one named Yahilu, a Church member.

Bobs – my horse – was, as it happened, looking for a tit-bit at the back door, and in a few minutes I had him saddled ready, and was off. Leaving him on the top of the steep hill behind Weasisi, I ran down and reached the beach to see those on board the recruiting ketch heaving anchor. Malin, the trader, who was boiling over with wrath at an insult received from Willie Uvea that morning, said he thought I should still be in time if I put off at once in his dinghy which was lying on the beach.

Asking him to come in case a witness was needed, I jumped in and we were pushed off by a crowd of willing hands and got alongside the recruiter quickly. On stepping on board I asked for the Captain, who came forward with a polite bow. Returning his salute, but declining to see his hand, I asked for an interpreter, and he called for Willie Uvea, who, however, paid not the slightest attention to his "Captain", but kept on, as he had been doing all along, bawling with oaths to the men forward to "Heave-away", – his idea being to get the vessel under way at once. Still bawling and swearing he came close to us, and continued to utterly disregard the Captain, and then I saw and smelt – what I had suspected – that he was under the influence of "grog". When he came quite close I spoke to him directly, and asked him to translate to the

Captain, warning him that I could understand what he might say. Shouts and oaths to the men forward was the only response.

In despair I tried to summon up enough French to speak to the Captain, and as I was doing so, the girl Yohilu of her own accord slipped into the dinghy, the first notice I had of the fact being a rush made by Willie Uvea to the side, and an attempt to drag her back. Failing in this he turned and ranged about in drunken fury for some weapon, while the "Captain" throwing his arms round him besought and "prayed" him to desist, and in a lull of these interesting proceedings he asked me to go into the dinghy.

As nothing could be gained by remaining, I went over the side, and just as my foot touched the dinghy I was suddenly and roughly seized from above, and as my hat was crushed over my eyes I failed to see what was going on for a moment of two. My shirt was ripped, my hat knocked off, and my hand and shirt covered with blood before I was able to see who was pulling at me. It proved to be Willie Uvea. I spoke quite quietly to him, telling him he was very foolish to act so. Presently he let go and stepped back, and then I saw where the blood had come from. Willie Uvea was bleeding freely from a cut over the left eye.

On our side this was the only regrettable incident. It seems that when Willie Uvea attacked me, Malin, the trader, had recourse to violent measures, and hit him with an oar. The other Loyalty Islanders on board tried to get hold of Malin, but he beat them off.

Of course this all happened in a few seconds, and we quickly pushed away from the side of the vessel. Then Willie Uvea seemed to be looking for a "shooting iron", but changed his mind, and made a run aft to the wheel, cut the lashings with his knife, and pulled the helm over, manifestly meaning to run us down. Fortunately the men at the windlass had been so much interested in the fracas amidships that they had stopped heaving anchor and the "mud-hook" was still on the bottom. So Willie left the wheel, and going forward pursued us with abuse. Yohilu came ashore with us of course, but I could do nothing about the other two women except report to Vila, which I have done.

In the end of the same week my two little boys returned from Erromanga, where they have been under the loving care of the Robertsons since Synod time.

Not only were they in kind and capable hands, and staying in a comparatively healthy place, but also, except for this help and the help given by the Bowies in Santo in looking after my boys, I could never have been able to get about on Tanna as I have been doing during the past months; and that was a great matter, seeing that the Lenakel district has also been my charge.

Both my boys are strong and healthy, and have shown no sign of fever as yet this season, even though we have had a very wet and stormy time almost since the day they arrived. For the last two weeks or so of the Old Year and the first week of the New Year we had hardly a glimpse of sunshine, but thunder and lightning, wind and rain, in large doses. The rainfall in that time was almost twenty-six inches.

The arrangements for the Christmas gathering and for the Communion Services for this and the Lenakel districts were that "Christmas" was to be held at Lenakel on 24th December, and the "Sacred Feast," as the natives call it, on the 29th at White Sands. The weather was not too promising, but we hoped for the best. Saturday forenoon was dull but dry, and so at noon a small cavalcade from White Sands started off for Lenakel. On a pack-saddle belonging to Mr.Carruthers I had rigged a kind of pannier arrangement for the boys, and with Bertie on one side and Hamish on the other the horse jogged along quite sedately, and the two little fellows chatted and laughed in high glee, until after a time Hamish went sound asleep. All went well until we were some two hours away, and then the rain pelted us, and though we kept the little ones fairly dry, I decided to return. We got back just in time to escaped some very heavy showers. Some men and women who had started earlier in the day got terribly wet in crossing over. So it was well we returned.

I intended to make an early start on Tuesday (the 24th) and to return the same day, but as Mr.Carruthers very kindly came all the way back from Lenakel (where he had gone in his launch) in order to look after the boys while I was away, I went on Monday and stayed overnight, which was more satisfactory. There was a great gathering, and house-room at Lenakel and neighbourhood was taxed to the utmost.

"Christmas" dawned brightly, but there were heavy clouds to windward. Fortunately we got a fine dry morning and forenoon, and after an open air

service, games were the order of the day till "kaikai" time at noon. There was a noisy, happy crowd busy with cricket, football, rounders and tug-of-war, besides other things, but when I blew the conch as the signal for dinner, the silence was most wonderful. All were seemingly keen for "kaikai", of which there was an abundance, and so all hearts were "good", and certainly there was no lack of smiles when after a hasty dinner I rode down through the crowd on my way back. Many a greasy paw was thrust up to say, "Alofa", after a hurried rub on dress, or lava-lava, or other convenient garment.

Half way across I met the rain, or rather it met me and passed on towards Lenakel, which it soon reached, putting an effectual end to all festivities, I believe, for it was no "Scotch mist", but tropical rain, with local thunder-storms, to one of which I was treated as I crossed the barren plain near the volcano, and did not half like it. In fact I thought it wise to dismount and lead the horse. There was of course no thought of taking shelter for it was evident we were in for a night of it.

The weather continued broken, and in consequence our Communion Services at White Sands were not so largely attended as would have been the case. Still we had a very large gathering, especially on Friday, Saturday and Sunday.

The main service, to which all the others led up, was on Sunday of course, and though we began in fine weather we had to hurry through the last part of the service in a downpour of rain. No building in Tanna could have held the congregation that had assembled, not to speak of a number of heathen who had come to look on, and we were therefore at the mercy of the elements; at least the people were, for we on the platform were in more or less shelter. As I said to the people, we were getting a lesson that we must hurry on with the funds for the new Church.

At this service the Baptismal Font presented for the new Church by the P.W.M.U. in South Australia, "In loving memory of Mrs.Macmillan", was used for the first time, when forty-three were baptised into the Triune Name, nineteen from Lenakel district, the rest from this.

After the baptisms we partook of the Lord's Supper together, and owing to the fact that the service was avowedly one for both Lenakel and White Sands districts, as well as to the further fact that in the absence of the Watts on furlough, the Port Resolution district is also temporarily under my care, I am safe in saying that in spite of adverse weather, it was the most representative "Sacred Feast" that has yet been held on Tanna, as well as the largest. The collection, which is to help with the new Church, was £14 15s 3d., in spite of the fact that very many gave nothing. Unfortunately it was impossible to count the people present. In a building it would have been easy, but out of doors it was impossible, for I tried to do so as the collection was being taken and got completely muddled.

At the three Communion Services in 1907 (one of which should have belonged to 1906) ninety-one of my people were admitted to the Church, and in spite of "weak brethren" perhaps in these ninety-one, have we not great cause to rejoice at the evidence of God's work in the hearts of the people, and to thank Him most sincerely for His abundant answers to our prayers? May this New Year be even more full of blessing than any that has gone before in this island that only so lately was rightly called "dark Tanna". For each and all let the motto be "Tanna for Christ".

THOMAS MACMILLAN

(S.S.) AYSHIRE
Adelaide.
Feb.18th 1908

My Dear Mother,

We are within a day's journey of above port and as the mail goes the day we arrive I am writing early. We are all in the best of health and spirits. The voyage since Capetown has been a fine bracing one. We struck down south and east till we reached 48. Then due east till the day before yesterday, since that north by east for Adelaide (this is for Father). We saw no icebergs but it was cold, dry and sunny. The winds and waves followed us all the way and we rolled along nicely, our best run was 294, about 280 average. If time is no consideration this is the healthiest way to come out. I am very much afraid we will not get the 1st of March steamer for the Islands. We have cargo for Adelaide and Melbourne and will be in the first until Sunday the 23rd and a week at least in Melbourne, so unless I can get off at Melbourne it will be the

1st of April before we start for the Islands. Most of the passengers are for Sydney and Brisbane so it is not likely I'll get off duty till Sydney. They are bound to have a Doctor for anything over 90 or 100 passengers. We took on two saloon and 23 steerage passengers at Capetown.

We had a day at Capetown and saw Jack Dobbs. He works for Willie Smyth who has an oil and paint business and is doing well. We only saw him (W.Smyth) for a minute. He has had trouble with his ears. We had a lovely day and spent part of it on shore, but it makes one very tired carrying the baby about. John and May are in grand form so fat and chubby now. May toddles about a little but the constant rolling of the vessel does not give her much of a chance. She is full of fun and learning to talk and looks so pretty now her hair is long enough for a ribbon at the side to keep it out of her eyes. She is very contented and resourceful in amusing herself still, and sings and claps her hands, etc. She is great on getting a paper and reading out loud to me. John is still John and as full of questions as an egg of meat. Sometimes he nearly drives me wild with them. Tonight he asked me if Jesus could hammer bogie men who made bad boys naughty and if he had a hammer or what to do it with. He said Jesus is a good man, He'll take care of me. But he goes too far sometimes. He went up to a lady passenger and pointing about the middle of her abdomen he asked her if she had a little hole there because he had one. He plays and fights with a little girl called Linda and she asked him tonight if he would give her a hug and kiss when she left at Adelaide. John was not very eager and just nodded a yes to her. She is about four and very precocious and tells John not to be silly. 'I'm ashamed at you John'. 'John don't contradict me', etc. John is known fore and aft and gets messed up in paint and oil at times. He says he's going to be a sailor and work. The Chief Engineer put his wheel on an axle and made brass clips to attach it to the shaft of his barrow. He drilled the hub of the wheel so that it can be oiled. The barrow is a splendid one. Father has put a lot of work into the shafts, legs etc. I will send a photo of John and it home when we get to Tanna. It has all been put together with brass screws. I am going to take it to pieces again and pack it for the Islands.

I have continued the Sabbath Services and the people have turned up well. The Captain, Officers and crew do not come. One feels almost alone. One old man in the steerage stuck to me right through and leads the singing. Very few passengers seem to have bibles and you could count all the hymn books on board on both hands. The Company have never had Service Books and bothered about Services on board their boats. On the other boats we travelled by Church of England prayer books, bibles and hymn books were provided and at least a Church of England Service every Sabbath. I think the Officers think it unlucky to have a Christian Doctor on board, or might be. We have had such a good trip since Las Palmas that they have not been able to talk about bad luck and Jonahs. Whether I have been made a blessing or not God knows, but I know the effort to help others and witness for Christ has been a great blessing to me.

I hear as usual missionaries well abused but am still trying to get one of the abusers to give name, date, place, etc. so that their story might be followed up. I almost give up hope of any of these slanderers ever having been eye witnesses or in touch with eye witnesses of the deeds of some of these awful missionaries. I am afraid it is the same everywhere abroad as it is with us on Tanna and the Islands. The lives and actions of these talkers would not stand investigation and as these are the people (officials, traders, etc.) who travel, they have given rise to what is called P & O Theology, i.e., the blackguarding of Missionaries and that all religions are equally good in their own special countries and it is a mistake to take Christianity to east or south or anywhere it has not yet been carried.

I hope Father has got in again. I wish I had been at home to help him. What a lot of opposition. We were so glad to get your letter at Capetown and to know you were all well. Isabel is dropping you a note. John talks about you all and never forgets you in his prayers. May weighs two stone and John 3. I am up to 11st 2lbs again. If we call Granny or Granda May looks all round for you. I will write soon from Australia again. Write to –

Assembly Buildings
Collins St.
Melbourne

No, to the Islands, I forgot we are so far away again. God bless you all. Love to Father and Netta and yourself from us all,

Your affect. son,

J. Campbell Nicholson

(S.S.) AYSHIRE
Sydney.
March 6th 1908

My Dear Mother,

I have been here since last Monday but leave tonight for Melbourne to rejoin Isabel and the children. I miss them very much but I have been able to get most of my business done here so that when we all come I will be able to help Isabel all the time. They are in very comfortable lodgings and we will like it better even than staying with folk. When you have children the invitations are half-hearted or absent altogether and one cannot blame folk. Adults make little noise in a house but two sturdy children can make any amount of noise. May has now two double back teeth. The mosquitoes bother her a lot. John escapes. We are longing to get to our house, Isabel especially. When John landed in Melbourne he asked a lady 'Is this Tanna and where is Nano'. He asked the fourth Officer 'Paddy is that the Bangor boat'. It was a steamer like her. All hands yet talk of John. He would have been spoiled if he had been on board much longer. They bought him toys and books, fixed up his barrow and horse, made boats, etc. May was always with the Ladies and she is not a whit behind John at making friends.

It was warm in Melbourne and is just as warm here. I perspire freely, but feel very well. The people don't recognise us for the same folk that passed through a year ago. The Manageress of the Hotel we stayed at said she remembered the delicate couple with a very delicate little baby.

I have had to give two interviews since coming to Sydney. There was nearly a column in two of the papers today. I'll get you one. They make me say some things I never said or did not intend to say. It was in the papers at Melbourne that we had arrived etc. They're hard up for news here.

I have been kept so busy since coming to Australia that I really forget if I gave all the news about our stay in Adelaide and the news of Melbourne. I must try and write regularly.

I hope Father and you and Netta are quite well. You'll be glad the winter is past. Is Uncle John still with you? Kind regards to all Friends and much love to you and Father and Netta.

Your affect. son,
J.Campbell Nicholson

Monday 9th.

P.S. I forgot to post this letter in Sydney and carried it through to Melbourne with me. I enclose a photo of baby. She walks all the time now, started suddenly and so pleased to be able to do it. Had good services on Sunday, received a cheque for £5 from a hearer this morning for Church or any purpose. That story 'I talk 10s'. has been used here by Frank Paton and has done the funds services. We have met the Edgars. I saw Bob Bowman but not to speak to. He does not seem to be very prosperous. Mrs.McCausland is far from well. He is doing Locum till he gets settled.

The weather here has become cool suddenly. On Sunday it was terrific, now summer clothes feel light enough. I got your letter and two enclosed, also one from George and Isabel one from Etta. I had a good meeting today and am free now till Friday. Next Sunday morning and evening again and the next week almost filled up. Isabel, John and May unite in our fondest love. John said to me one day I went out 'I thought you had gone to heaven Dadda and I would never see you again'. He ranaway one day from the Patons where we had left him to go to a meeting and created a bit of a stir but was found by a servant girl and brought back. I asked him why he went out and he said 'I thought you would get lost so I came to look for you'.

With much love,
Your affect. son,

J.Campbell Nicholson

My Dear Mother,

We forgot that we can post weekly to you. I think it is more than a week since I wrote last. We are still in the Boarding house but tomorrow are going to another suburb of Melbourne called Malvern to stay with a lady called Mrs. Robinson. She is a widow and well off and promises us a good time. She has engaged her old nurse to come and take care of the children and is planning little outings for us. Her husband was a brother of Professor Robinson of the Assembly's College, Belfast, and I think she is related to the Wrights of Newtownards.

We have been very comfortable here. Mrs.McCue and her daughter came out from the North of Ireland many years ago. She likes to talk about the old times. I had two meetings last week and the Sunday morning service at Erskine Church. We stayed at the Manse over Sunday and they were very good with the children. The children win the hearts of all once they get to know them. Mrs.Alexander, the Minister's wife, is just about your size and her hair is like yours. She took May early in the morning to let us dress and when I handed out May, May thought it was you again. She examined Mrs. Alexander's hair and held her face and looked at it so long that I am sure she had recollection of the time you used to come for her in the mornings. I said Granny get the shawl and baby turned to Mrs.Alexander. May can walk well now and is so merry and good-tempered. John is still her coachman and wheels her about in her little chair. John is very good and can talk well, he has such a lot of new words and is getting a Colonial accent. A lady one day took us all down town for lunch and then kept the children till Isabel and I went to a service. Then we all went to the Zoological Gardens. May was afraid of the big animals, but John had a good time. The same lady brought John and May and Isabel nice books each day.

The weather is very cold here this last week. One would need woollen underclothing but we have none, but tomorrow may be scorching hot again. From all accounts it is well we did miss the first of March boat, there has been so much heat and rain in the Islands this season. It will give us all a better start and the children will be a bit acclimatised after the cold at home and on the voyage.

There was a great demonstration here today by the Roman Catholics on account of St.Patrick. Green was worn and the Irish flag flown everywhere. We have just been packing again for tomorrow. We'll soon be experts at packing and unpacking. But I'll be glad to get home and leave the bags and boxes aside for a year or two. It is not easy travelling with children. We split up one day. Isabel took John down town and I stayed here with the baby. She kept me going, then I took her out in her chair and walked about, then brought her in and wished Isabel was back, but at last she fell asleep and I had a nap with her. I don't know how Isabel keeps it up. I am sure she'll be glad to see Nano again and so will I. Dr.McCausland is here and not settled yet. He is doing Locum work, with Mrs.McCausland far from well. I am afraid it is consumption, she is so thin and has a bad cough. She has three children. I think one of the Edgars is very good to them, also Mrs.Robinson.

I hope Father and you and Netta are keeping well. I'm glad Father knocked out that she doctor. Great-grandfather was still a respected member of the Bangor Council; after a rather acrimonious tussle at the polls with, unusually, a woman and a doctor at that, Dr.Harriet Neill. Did I tell you that Mrs. Milne of Ngura was dead. She had been in the Islands about 35 years, got a chill in NewZealand and Malarial Fever set in and she was dead in three days. Now the Lord Bless you and keep you all.

Love from us all to you all,
Your affect.son, J.Campbell Nicholson

THE N.S.W.ALLIANCE HEADQUARTERS,
SYDNEY.

March 29th, 1908

My Dear Mother,

We are here, another stage on our journey. We sail on Wednesday and D.V. should reach Tanna about the 13th or 14th. We are shopping, it is not easy to do with the children running about our feet and fingering everything, but they are very good. Two Miss Robertson, daughters of Dr.Robertson of Erromanga, came this morning and took John and May out to the Park whilst Isabel and I went to the Cathedral Service. Bishop Wilson of Melanesia preached and we had a chat with him afterwards. He is very nice and spent the best part of a day with us on Tanna once. He preached well taking for his Text "What are these amongst so Many," referring to the Church gifts of money, prayers and missionaries to the Heathen. They were few but Christ multiplied and used the few loaves and fishes so He had done so with the Church gifts.

Miss Robertson is going to relieve us tonight and we are going to a Presbyterian Service. The Presbyterians don't pay much attention to Missionaries here. If one had been in Melbourne there would have been several invitations to take the Services at Churches. I was in the pulpit every Sabbath. Tonight I asked John if he would come and he said "but you'll be going up on the Bridge and leave me all by myself." John is with me now. He was talking about you all. I asked him if he would like to go to Bangor. He hesitated and said no, Nano would cry if he didn't go to Tanna. He is very anxious to get down and would hardly come into the hotel because it was not Tanna. We were out one day here and I said, let us go home now John and he said, to which home Daddy? It is hard on the Bairns this knocking about, but they are good travellers and keep cheery. We had a good journey up from Melbourne from 5 p.m. of one day till 11 a.m. the next. We were very uncomfortable for a bit but the Guard took us out of the second and gave us a sleeping carriage all to ourselves, so that we slept well all night. The Lord has been very good to us over and over. To travel is nice but not with young children, indeed the hardest part of our missionary work has been travelling by land and sea with the Bairns and trying to get into hotels or boarding houses, getting washing done etc. But it's all in the day's journey and the Hand of the Lord has been with us, but we will be glad to get to Tanna again. We hear that many of our boys have been recruited away from Lenakel and my special hospital boy amongst them. The recruiters knowing I was away were often at Lenakel and gave grog away ad lib and spread lies that we were not coming back and have succeeded in getting many. Maybe it will not be so bad as they made out, I hope not.

Isabel and John and May are well. May is so lively and walks so well now. Her four eye teeth are coming all at once but she is not peevish. The mosquitoes bother her and she swells with bites. Now I must go to Church and will add to this again. I hope that you are all well, I'd like to drop in on you this evening.

THE N.S.W. ALLIANCE HEADQUARTERS,
SYDNEY.

Monday 30th 1908

Another day over. We long for Tanna. John and May find the restraints of hotel life very tiresome. John has a cold and May is cutting or trying to cut all her eye teeth at once. They have both slept well this evening so we have got a rest Isabel does not look so well as when she left home, but only complains of feeling tired. Sometimes I think that we could not face the journey again and that we must resign and settle and rear our children somewhere. But the Lord will guide. I have work to do for Him on Tanna yet.

We have all our shopping done and will just amuse the children till it is time to go on board. I have had a variety of purchases to make, Church and some hens, a boat and tin tacks, medicines and pots and pans and all the odds and ends needed about a church, a hospital, a house, a farm, a boat. I have failed to get a dog.

I had an interruption. John awoke and got May up and came out of the bedroom into the passage to look for us. A maid found them both crying. John said 'well what for did you leave us'.

I hope Father is getting through the winter without a remnant of bronchitis and fit for the duties of the Council and does not sit up late at nights. I take after him in that. I like the quiet hours when everybody is sleeping. They are good to read or write in.

I hope Willie will not get knocked up. I'm afraid he'll have to give up preaching.[2]

We envy you the quietness of Princetown Road, tonight an accordian is playing in the streets, loud voices and laughter and the hum of trolley cars nearly deafen one. But the weather is cooler and that is something to be thankful for. There go a set of bagpipes now.

Well goodnight. Give our love to Father and Netta and don't forget yourself. John said to tell you all about May and his new shoes and that his rubber tyred barrow is in the box and that he saw a kangaroo and a big duck, etc.

Love to yourself, your affectionate son,

J.Campbell Nicholson

JOTTINGS 61 JULY 1908

An Editor's note at the beginning of the Jottings reads:

The natural disappointment of Dr,Nicholson and Mr.Frater at the necessity, under the new laws, for proceeding to the Central Island of Efate, and having to tranship there and return, in Dr.Nicholson's case perhaps 100 miles southward again, to reach Lenakel, is compensated for, to some extent at least, by the advantages that should follow the new regulation of the Joint Government. The regulation is as follows:

"The Port of Vila in the island of Efate shall be the sole port of entry for the New Hebrides, and all vessels entering the Group from foreign ports shall report first at such Port of Vila, and all vessels leaving the Group for foreign ports shall effect their final clearance from the Port of Vila aforesaid."

Henceforth irresponsible marauding ships and unauthorised labour vessels will be breaking the law if they call anywhere but at Vila, where they must declare themselves to the Port Authorities and, we hope, be strictly examined as to their bona fides and overhauled for contraband, &c.

from Dr.Campbell Nicholson

We have two cheery letters from Dr.Nicholson, one dated from Melbourne (17th March) and the other from Efate (15th April).

The Doctor filled up some useful time in deputation work while in Melbourne by arrangement with our Hon.Director.

He says of Tanna, "I have had a letter from my people at Lenakel. They give a hopeful account of the work, with the exception that some of the natives have been recruited to Noumea. Mr.Macmillan also gives good accounts of the work. He is very busy as he has for the moment the charge of the whole of Tanna".

"While in Melbourne I had some opportunities of ventilating Island matters. Our feeling is strongly against the recruitment of natives outside the Islands; but Mr.Deakin has published a letter from Lord Elgin saying that the French

absolutely refused to cease the recruiting of labour from the Islands to New Caledonia, and that therefore the British did not feel that they could stop recruiting from the Islands of Fiji".

"We learn that a French Judge has been appointed, and is already in the Islands. The Australian Authorities say they are urging the immediate appointment of a British Judge; but the French are, as usual, ahead of us, whilst Australia is doing nothing to encourage settlement and trade in the group."

In his second letter, of the 15th April, the Doctor says:

"We passed Tanna on Friday night. Now we are at Vila waiting for a vessel to take us southwards, retracing our steps to our own place. The regulations that render this the first port of call are very tantalising and wearisome to us. It was a pleasure, however, to have the opportunity of a talk with the new British Commissioner, Mr.King. We found him very gracious, and we feel that we will always get an unprejudiced hearing from him."

"Our voyage down from Sydney was rough and miserable, and we are longing to get home to Lenakel amongst our own people. I have heard that as many as eighty young Tanna men from the north of the Island were recruited for Noumea in December last – my Hospital lad among them."

If rumour is true, they were disappointed that I did not return in September last, and a trader took advantage of this feeling to lie to them, inventing the base insinuation that I had 'cleared out with their money subscribed for the new church.'"

"I hope soon to get things in order again, but the loss of these fellows is very saddening."

Yours sincerely,
J.CAMPBELL NICHOLSON

Lenakel,
TANNA, New Hebrides.
11.5/08

My Dear Mother,

Here we are safely landed and fairly settled. Oh, how glad we were to be in our own home again. Hotels, boarding houses, steamers, are necessary abominations, tolerable, without children, but with them almost intolerable, because anybody's children but your own or your own's own are always a bit of a nuisance. Well we had a great reception. We had to lie 8 days at Vila, waiting and watching for the other steamer never knowing the minute she might turn up. What a yell we did give when she was sighted. We arrived here on Sunday night, 19th. They landed us with a case of provisions and went on south, returning to us on the following Tuesday, when we got all our goods.

What a joy it was to see Lomai and Javis and Nilauas and all the rest. It was all a lie about any of my special people being recruited. About 30 were recruited from my district, more than half heathen. When we came to the beach the people massed up and gave us such a cheer. Nano was down in the sea. She thought from a letter of mine that we had left John, all because I did not mention his name. She was glad to see him and marched off with him but May was shy at first for a bit. I had to carry her up but Nano had her quite contented and pleased in a minute after we did get up. It's wonderful how she gets on with them. Not able to speak a word of English and yet has them both all day and knows what they want and talks away to them and they to her, baths, feeds and clothes them and full of joy because she has them. We have engaged her permanently now and her husband is our cook. Her boy has gone to New Caledonia and her adopted child died so she is quite free and was so eager and indeed so was Kaati. We have four little girls, three of the old ones came back at once and the other is a girl Nano is keeping for her son if he comes back, so I think we are now settled for a bit in domestics.

Well we found everything so clean and neat. The grass all cut about the place while washing and painting done and everything done that could have been done without us being here. Some of the passengers came up with us. Traders and planters and two Yank tourists. We had milk and tea and ripe bananas, not a biscuit or a piece of bread. We scarcely knew the place when we arrived. Our first four years were years of drought, mostly, but before we left and since we left there had been regular rain. I had planted hundreds of plants and shrubs, only to die, but those I planted before leaving had grown more in a year than things had done in the four preceding years. Trees a foot high on the front of the terrace are now 16 to 18 ft. high, not bad for 14 or 15 months growth. We'll get a little shade now. We have had good rains since coming and I have peas and french beans a foot above ground already. Our vines had wandered about wildly and are now cut back close to the stem. We have hundreds of pineapple plants and when the season is on will have any amount of mangoes, Brazilian cherries, pineapples, passionfruit etc. We have splendid oranges, mandarins, and limes now.

Mr.McMillan says the place was ablaze with flowers when we were away. Sunflowers, zinnias, balsams, cosmos, geraniums, roses etc. There are only a few in bloom now and we have pulled most out for the new seeds Mr.Watson gave us. I hope they turn out well. I have an old man for gardener. He takes a great interest and begs to get staying. He minds the cows (4 female and 2 male) and the garden. We give him a little tea, a biscuit a day, £1 a year and some of my cast off clothes and he takes this in preference to £8 a year and his food from the trader, but with me he is free to come and go and has all the time he wants for his own garden and knocking about. I am keen on the garden but some days never get a look into it. I have not got two hours' work in it yet.

On the Monday after we landed I galloped over the Island to Mr.McMillan. He looked well and his two boys are in good form but it was awful to find no Mrs.McMillan. One missed her at every turn. He had everything nice but she was so tasty and neat, her touch was missed in everything. All the improvements they had planned together he had carried out and the garden was laid out as she had planned it. It was beautiful although he did not speak of her, one felt as he showed one round he was thinking about her all the time and knew I was doing the same. I got a great reception at his place. On Tuesday morning the natives, Heathen and Christian, gathered to meet the Commissioner who had travelled down with us. A trader, a heathen himself, had told the heathen he was going to get the Government to put down the Worship, but Mr.King, the Commissioner, told the heathen he would like to see them all Xtians, although they were free to remain in heathenism if they wished, but he advised them strongly to join and become Xtian. It was a fearful knock out for the Trader – he collapsed. Mr.King also said that any of their customs which were contrary to the dictates of humanity and decency would have to be given up. He established native courts and will uphold their judgment by force and appointed Mr.McMillan, a Trader called Malm, consultative Magistrates, and all correspondence with the officials is to go through them. Fines are to be remitted to Headquarters and corporal punishment is to be inflicted when necessary, by police sent from Vila. I crossed again on Tuesday to meet the steamer here on Wednesday morning and Mr.King had a meeting in our grounds and appointed me as his representative for this coast. These courts and appointments are only temporary till a proper magistrate and police are established on Tanna. I got him four or five fine big fellows for police and he was greatly pleased. Mr.King's visit has done good. The heathen had been roused to expect the Government to expel Christianity and were in high fettle.

After we got the steamer away came the unpacking. The pictures with one exception, came unbroken and everything else was in good condition. We brought some linoleum with us and I laid it in the sitting room and to do so had to take off all the doors (seven) to do so. The floor we hewed level with an adze and finished off with a jack plane. It was an awful job, but looks well and Isabel is proud of her room. The other floors are either painted or just plain. I had a lot of patching and mending to do and have yet, but the work at the Hospital is so heavy I can hardly get an unbroken hour at it. We have had 10 patients in already, 7 are still in and more coming and more to follow as soon as we can take them. I have several operations waiting to be done, but they are things which can wait till I get my mail and the steamer away and Mr.McMillan across.

Mr.MacMillan crossed last Wednesday and left today. His two boys, Bertie (6) and Hamish (33/4) he has left with us, so we have a good-sized family. We worked hard at, what do you think, a Minister and a Doctor, building Latrines for the Hospital. They are up now. Today we had Mrs.Worthington under chloroform. It was touch and go whether I would amputate the middle finger of her right hand, but I think I have saved it. She must have suffered a lot to have swallowed her pride and come to me. When we arrived he did not speak to us. I met him and passed time of day with him. I felt so sorry he looked so ill, but I thought she would never give in even if death threatened them. I prayed about it and was willing to do my part and this was the answer. She came with a guinea in her hand. I told her I did not want the money but would accept it as a donation for the Hospital. She is very humble and nice and I hope there will be no further unpleasantness or cause for it between. They have no heathen to support them and are dependent now on the Xtian people. Once when we were away they listened to their anti-Christ friend on the other side and began to talk his talk. Lomai and Javis went down to him and told him he was very foolish and if he only wanted heathenism they would call on all the Christian people to boycott him. He climbed down and told Lomai he would never speak against Christ and the Worship again, so I hope they have learnt a lesson. I for my part am glad that there is speech between us and that we can help them in case of sickness, otherwise I'm afraid we have little in common.

John and May are happy all day. They go down to the beach and bathe every day. May cried to get in so we had to give permission. They take a lunch down and we do not see them again to 12 o'clock. It is shaded and clean but hot in the afternoons. John says he does not want to leave Tanna again. I have not got his barrow screwed up yet, he is always at me and I must try and do it tomorrow. We cannot get him to wear sandals. May is a merry wee body, she has some Tanna words already, but John refuses to even repeat a Tanna word. He says he knows what Nano says but refuses to try and talk to her or repeat words after her. May is getting her back teeth but they are not at their worst yet. We have a new fox terrier, Pat, John's dog. One of the Buff Orpington hens died. We have quite a lot of fowl and have about a dozen roosters caged up for eating. We have a lot of wild fowl about. I will get them with the gun as we need them. We got eight eggs today, in a week or so we should have plenty. We have 15 sheep, 6 cattle, 5 horses, 110 goats and plenty for them all to eat. We are eating the goats one a week with mint sauce.

We are both in good form but feel tired at times. I forgot to tell you I got Dengue fever at Vila and was ill when I arrived but kept my end up in spite of the fearful pain till Friday. Then I got the rash (like scarlet) and had to lie up. A lot of people came on Saturday and Sunday, some hundreds, but I only spoke a few words to them on Saturday and was not able for the Church on Sunday and was afraid of spreading the fever. I slept in a room by myself and was careful and am glad to say it has gone no further. It was epidemic in Vila and I attended Dr.Mackenzie of Vila who was ill with malaria but some of his servants had Dengue and Mrs.Mackenzie had had it. The other missionaries did not see them, I alone going daily, so I expect the others have escaped. Lomai's wife had a little son the day we arrived. Javis and all the others are fairly well but there has been a lot of fever and I have a big attendance daily at the dispensary. We have grand congregations on Sundays. A lot of people about have been won over. Last Sunday we had over 20 heathen in. I told them to come and hear the word of God and then decide for or against and they came. I hope we win them over. I must say I do not care to see them naked in God's house, but if they continue I'll give them a hint I would like to see them with something on even if they took it off after they went out. Things have gone on splendidly, a good number have been baptised by Mr.Mac. and he says he had a lot of marriages. There have been a few lapses but not many and I think I'll get them all back again. Isabel is well but so busy. She goes to bed early, though I like the midnight oil and quietness. I hope you will have patience to read all this. I could write more but I'll spare you. I hope Father and Netta and yourself keep in good health and I wait for the next mail eagerly. If I get time to open it before the steamer leaves I will send another note, if anything requires answering. Love to all friends from us all. Isabel and John and May and myself send you and Father and Netta our special love.

Your affect. son,
J.Campbell Nicholson

A note at the beginning of the Jottings reads:

"We learn that it is possible that Lomai may go to Australia at about Christmas next for a short time, if Dr.Nicholson can spare him, to address some meetings in connection with a Missionary Forward Movement which Mr.Frank Paton is seeking to promote in Victoria.

*We only wish Lomai could come to Britain for a similar purpose. Facts are stubborn things when looked in the face; and Lomai, the Christian chief of Tanna, is a **FACT!** May God keep him humble."*

While my grandparents were on their way back to Tanna, a Dual Protectorate was declared at Vila in January 1908, the Condominium. Since 1887 an Anglo-French convention provided for the patrol of the islands by two British and two French officers from warships but this failed to bring order. However, the Condominium did establish local courts and in December grandfather writes in the Jottings, *'That native courts should have worked so well as they have is a constant source of surprise to me. The culprits in almost all cases have submitted quietly to the verdicts, and there has been very little friction, except in one part, where the cause is not from a native source. This peaceable working of the courts is in great measure due to the British Commissioner's visit. Mr.King, by his wise and kindly words to the natives themselves, and by making the natives themselves responsible for the good order of the island, without imposing foreign forms of procedure or exacting conditions on them, seems to have tided them over that most dangerous of all periods, the transitional year. He has thus paved the way for the future development of civil procedure under a resident or visiting magistrate.'* (Jot.64)

No letters from August until December so the Jottings admirably details what has been happening at Lenakel:

JOTTINGS 63 JANUARY 1909

Lenakel, TANNA

13th July, 1908

Though two months have come and gone since I last I wrote to you it seems but a few days. We have been kept so busy. However, I am looking forward to the arrival of Mr.Mackenzie next week, and he will take over the charge of the building work. The building material for the Church and Hospital can scarcely come by this steamer, but we have lime ready for the foundations, and there is more than a month's repairing to be done. The people are showing a strong desire to go on as they have begun, and have put in splendid work during the past two weeks, of which I will write in the course of this letter.

After the despatch of my last letter I visited the Northern stations of my district. At first it seemed as if I must postpone my visit for want of time – the Hospital being uncomfortably full – several awaiting operation. However, Mr.Carruthers, a young planter and trader, called here in his motor launch, and kindly agreed to give me a day's run along the coast. I had asked

Mr.Macmillan to come and assist with the operations, but I sailed the day he was to arrive, trusting to an expeditious trip out and back. The weather was in our favour, and as we skimmed over the placid sea I confess to a strong desire to possess a motor boat for the good of the work. How easy and speedy it would be by this means to visit the furthest station to consult with the teacher or people, and to hold services or visit the sick, and bring helpless patients to the Hospital. I am afraid the desire will not die, and may yet ripen into an earnest request, but not just yet. However, I give you warning. A lady gave me £1 towards getting such a boat, and I had half thought to ask her to let me use it for something else, but have decided not to.

We got to our first station – Laepu – early, and on landing got a great welcome – seeing this was our first visit since our return from Ireland. Iaurel and his wife, Iata, looked smart and neat, and very happy. I just wished that Mrs. Wright, who supports them, could have been with us. It would have been a great pleasure to them, and to her also, I am sure. I visited their house and every house in the village. Their house was an example for all the others, and an example worth dozens of my lectures. In a certain sense our work must all be done through native assistants, and though one often feels how little one really does for the people living away from Lenakel, yet, after all, to turn out such teachers as Iaurel and Iata, and plant them amidst the heathen of Laepu is a great advance. Under their guidance and example these heathen will demolish their tiny hovels, vacate their little caves, and build themselves decent habitations – with such furniture as raised beds – and having separate rooms for sleeping and living in. Above all, they will build a good native school or church in which to daily pray to God and learn to read His Word. This is worth more than days of itinerant teaching.

I am firmly convinced that if the Head station can be kept sound, and a regular hive of activities, the people will always turn to it for light and guidance, and thus get a firmer faith in their Saviour and Lord. The Head Station must be the heart and brain from whence shall flow life-giving blood, vitalising ideas, and intelligent guidance.

But, to my narrative. I arranged with Iaurel to bring his people to the next outstation, Lehang, in the evening, for a mass meeting, and then embarked and passed Lehang for Loananbego.

Landing on the reef from the dinghy I was surprised to find only two boys to welcome me. They told me the people were inland. However, I thought I would go and see their village, and maybe the teacher would turn up. Arriving at the site of the village I was surprised to find only a few old houses and no signs of life. Then the boys informed me they had made a new village inland! I had forgotten about my advice to the people before leaving for home, and hastened inland eager to see what had been done. What was my joy to find on ground well above the sea and half a mile inland the welcome sight of new houses and all the people gathered with their teacher, Yolu, and Wahu his wife, smiling and eager to hear what I would have to say.

The salutations being over, I was conducted round, and felt that after all it was well worth having come to live and work on Tanna. The teacher's house was splendid, but he had gone further and actually planted a flower garden in front! There were zinnias, sunflowers and phlox blooming, and crotons and palm lilies had been planted. This, for a Tanna teacher, was a surprise indeed. For, up till now, apart from Lenakel, and hardly even there, the people simply cannot understand why one should plant things that do not produce fruit, or something eatable.

The sight of the houses did me good, but the new church nearly took my breath away. It was only a native church, but it was so symmetrical and so perfectly finished, quite the best I have seen on Tanna. The coral floor, rough-hewn seats, raised platform – with seat and reading desk – and grounds outside neatly arranged, formed a picture which could never fade from the mind of a Missionary who knew the former state of the people and their heathen village.

But one felt sad because Nakaboi – the teacher who had guided the natives in all this good work – had been deprived of the joy of following up his splendid labours, and had resigned before my arrival. His wife had never been a help to him; and of late had, by her foolish talk and behaviour, made her name a bye-word. The people complained that she taught the girls bad talk, and to be idle. Nakaboi felt it was useless to try to continue in such circumstances and resigned. Mr.Macmillan sent Yolu and Wahu from Lenakel to replace the faithful Nakaboi. Nakaboi was here for the Communion, but he feels it would be useless to try teaching again, unless a great change comes over his wife. Lehang thus lost one of the best teachers we have, because of his wife's ill conduct. Unless a man has a real helpmeet in his wife, it is useless for him to go out as a teacher. The best teaching and efforts for a people can be almost completely neutralised by a foolish or bad wife.

I visited Mr.Macmillan's outstation and then returned to Lehang in the evening. Simon, who replaced Kahwa as teacher, is doing well. I found everything in good order. A new church had been built, not perhaps, as good as the last mentioned; but the people are healthy and happy – so different from the people I camped amongst at their old village five years ago. We had a big service. All the people from the other three stations had come, and the church was crowded – many sitting outside. Our service concluded with a wedding; and afterwards, by the help of a lamp, we scrambled down the face of the cliffs and put off to the launch – reaching Lenakel without a breakdown about twelve p.m. Lomai and I were well pleased with all we had seen and heard, and felt greatly encouraged to go ahead in the work.

Mr.Macmillan had arrived, and the next day we devoted our time to the Hospital. It is a great comfort having Mr.Macmillan at one's beck and call to help with operations; and I believe our cooperation in this and other work has had a good influence on the work in the two districts.

Mr.Macmillan embarked from here for Synod. But we had fears that he would have been prevented from going, his horse falling and throwing him heavily. He was badly marked about the face, but he seemed well enough to embark; and we trust to see him back in a day or two, perfectly recovered, bringing his baby boy who has been staying with Mr.Bowie, of Tangoa, and whom we have not seen since our departure for the old country sixteen months ago.

Our Communion services were fixed to commence on July 1st. But previous to this many men came in to help to prepare the lime for our building. Two large pits were burned and several hundred tons of earth were removed from behind the church to make the site more airy and commodious. Our services were well attended from the first, and our days were fully occupied with can-

didates' and teachers's classes, and the extra work at the Hospital, due to the influx of people from all parts of our district. On Friday the people washed the floor of the Church and seats, cleaned the windows, and tidied up the ground about it. On Saturday they washed their clothes, cleaned their houses and the village in general. These proceedings are now a regular practice, and I think you will regard it as a good one. Our Communion Sabbath was wet, and only a few adherents got into the Church, the rest retired to their houses for shelter. No babies were allowed, so that we had a very quiet and impressive service. The dividing aisle between men and women was done away with (I wish we could do away with it altogether, but that time has not come yet) and the men sat with their wives.

Thirty-eight adults were baptised, and two hundred and fifty sat down at the Lord's Table. Our special Scripture for the season was I John, iii, 1-3, and many of the people committed the words to memory. I trust they may bear fruit, "for every man that hath this hope in him purifieth himself even as He is pure."

Sickness, old age, and recruiting, accounted for there being only two hundred and fifty present.

In the afternoon we had our Thanksgiving Service.

The people have now dispersed to their homes, and there is a slight lull in the work before we commence building operations.

With our united kind regards,

Yours sincerely,

J.CAMPBELL NICHOLSON

Lenakel
TANNA
Aug.12th 1908

My Dear Mother,

It will surprise you and all the folk at home greatly to know that another daughter has arrived. It was born on the 4th inst. and Isabel and the baby are doing well. In fact, Isabel has come through it all with normal temperature and pulse, nurses the baby and frets at having to keep to her bed. We did not lose more than three hours sleep, it was born at 9.30 a.m. You have quite a lot of granddaughters now. It was Isabel's earnest wish that nothing should be said about the expected arrival and I respected her wish, so I hope that you will not feel hurt. Now this must be just the baby's letter. She is like John, at least such is the prevailing opinion. I can't see much likeness to anybody. I saw a likeness in May to her Granda Campbell but this one I can make nothing of. She is pretty as babies go, not much hair, but dark coloured what is, has rather a decent nose and is strong, no matter how far you lay her from her mother she can worm her way back unless a pillow is placed between. I guess it is cupboard attraction. May and John are delighted. May at first laughed and laughed when she saw it but was nervous about it and bolted when it gave a cry, but now she will lie down with it on her arm and keeps kissing it. She wants everybody to see it. John also likes to lie with it on his arm and when Mr.Macmillan asked him for it he said, 'you have May and I have no baby', John said 'well you take May then'. Bertie and Hamish, especially the latter, are greatly interested but feel jealous of John a bit. He swaggers about 'his' baby. Nano is delighted and thinks it knows her and listens while she talks to it. Isabel makes a lot of it, more that she did of John or May. She says it is great company and talks a lot to it. The people are all greatly pleased, but I think inwardly sympathize with me about it being 'only' a daughter, but they dare not say so. Isabel has rowed them pretty severely about this idea of theirs. Mrs. Mackenzie has been a great help. We are very glad she came on although we feel sore about her husband not coming. All the stuff for the hospital is lying about, lime, sand and stones all ready and waiting for him and the new church, to come down this next steamer. I am afraid he may not come. The Government want him for a year to be foreman of their new buildings and are offering double of the salary he gets. I think he expects to get keeping in the mission and doing the year's Government work as well. But it would scarcely be fair. He has been brought here by the mission and had a good furlough at their expense and there is a lot of work for him to do. If he does not come I will have to get a carpenter somewhere in the Colonies and that will cost a brave penny. But there is so much hospital and teaching and preaching work to be done that I cannot undertake single-handed building work on so large a scale as the church and hospital.

This month seems to have been lost. We had all worked so hard to have all ready, that Mackenzie not turning up has upset our plans and put us back. I had twenty patients in the hospital last week and six operations under chloroform. To run all this without a trained nurse or matron is enough in itself for one man. I have two hours a day teaching three youths English, preparing them to go to the Teachers' Training Institute. They go for four years and should be of great service when they get back. We need better- equipped teachers as the years go by and the people know more. Some other youths want to go, but I'll get these three off first. I have to teach them to read simple English, spell a little and do simple addition and subtraction. They are smart lads and getting on fine. Then we have the teachers to train here. We have fine congregations now on Sundays, they are learning to listen better. A heathen village have repeatedly asked for a teacher and I have not got one for them. I wish we had some ready, indeed I am almost afraid of some heathen tribes renouncing their heathenism and being unable to supply them with a teacher. However, the work is the Lord's and He will supply.

All goes on quietly and well. We have the house nearly all painted outside. The garden is fine, we have more vegetables than we can use and flowers galore. There has been good rain and everything is so green although it is the off part of the year, our 'depth of winter'. The weather is variable, no steady trade winds. Some days not so cool, many muggy.

The children are all well. Bertie and Hamish will be going over to White Sands soon as Mrs. and Miss Robertson of Erromanga are coming to stay there for a month with Mr.McMillan. This was an arrangement to lighten us at the expected arrival of our daughter. But she came a week or so sooner than we had calculated so that we could have kept the boys. However, it will be nice for Mr.McMillan to have his desolate home filled up a little. He left here today but does not look well. I am sure he has his bad moments about his loss, but he does not talk. A gravestone is coming down this time. I will have to put it up.

I hope that you enjoyed your visit to Scotland and that the grandchild arrived safely. We are anxious to hear what Willie is going to do. I will close for the night. We expect the steamer on the 15th. It may be later, the sea has been rough, but I will have a chance to write after getting the mail as she calls twice at Tanna this trip giving us a day between her calls. (Letter ends abruptly, a page must have been lost)

Lenakel,
TANNA, New Hebrides.
Aug.25th 1908

My Dear Mother,

I sent a letter away to you a few days ago by the usual steamer. The Man of War 'Prometheus' is here and I expect this letter will reach you two or three weeks before the other. Well a little daughter arrived on the 4th. Isabel is up again and gradually picking up her strength. The baby is well, it is a nice one, a 9lb one and has gone ahead from the first. Isabel passed through and after without any rise of pulse or temperature. Indeed we can scarcely realise it is all over.

Mr.Mackenzie is here but the ship's people took away with them some of the timber and we are unable to proceed with the church. However, he is going ahead with the hospital but is not going to stay for the church. He has got a job with the Government, more pay and throws all else up. It is not fair treatment to the committee. He is paid better than any of us and has only been six years with the J.G.Paton committee. He was allowed to go to the colonies to get married and go the furlough home, all on the expectation that he settled to the work. I am sure they will be greatly disappointed. It will mean a considerable loss as it is expensive to bring carpenters so far. Frater has a lot of work and Mackenzie says I have four months at the least. We have had a bad time with lay assistants.

I have been kept busy since the steamer. Mrs.Robertson of Erromanga came down to stay with him (Mr.Macmillan) and look after the children in view of our daughter's arrival. Whilst about to leave the vessel at White Sands, she fell on the deck and fractured her elbow and bruised her whole side. I was sent for and have been across twice and will go again tomorrow on the Man of War. She is doing well but her elbow will never be the same I'm afraid.

We are all well here and elsewhere on Tanna. Things are going well. Law and order is beginning to press heavily on the heathen but the Man of War is paying more attention to murders and crime in general so that things are quiet. I got your letter and Insurance paper. Have written and will write Willie. Love to Father, Netta and yourself.

Your affect.son,
J.Campbell Nicholson

P.S. In my hurry I nearly forgot the principal thing. We wanted to call the baby after you but Isabel said you did not care for Ellen or Helen in her cousin (John's), and says she thinks you mentioned Eileen. Well I never heard your views on the subject but as I have to register the baby at once I'll just call her Eileen and if it does not please you send the name for the next one in advance, for these registrars won't wait. John and May are very fond of the baby, especially May. John is like a lost duck without Bertie and Hamish. I am going to take him across to stay with them.

With much love,
Your affect. son, J.C.N.

By introducing his Public Health methods, Grandfather had not only shown the natives that by keeping their homes clean and the areas surrounding it, that infection and disease diminished, but also instilled a pride and a sense of competitiveness that caused him to try and do better than his neighbour. He says in a report to the Jottings "*We have begun our new village at last. The site was cleared for it on the biggest chiefs on Tanna, and had (in the Jottings a line seems to be missing). Rows of trees had been planted and are growing well. It will involve many months of work, but the people are keen. Being on the hillside, the ground will have to be terraced. I was planning to do as little of this as possible but they have started it more extensively. I expect I shall have to give some verbal encouragement later on to keep them up to their present intentions. Their ambitions know no bounds. I have always believed that 'eyegate' admitted more than 'eargate' (seeing is believing?) and I have always tried to make Lenakel a model and inspiration for the district. This has been more than accomplished, for some of the outstations have actually gone ahead of our native village, and instead of setting the example our people have now to try to compete at building. Iavis is the first to commence building. His site is prepared. I was up blocking out the plan of the house, and feeling irritated a little because he wanted it rather large. Then he began to tell me his plans for the ground around. "I am going to plant grass in the front, like your place, and flowers at the sides. I shall put a fence round it". "But", I said, "you do not want to hide your place, do you?" "Oh no," he said, "I am going to save up and get netting wire, and how much would a lawn mower cost?" If this is the beginning, what will the end be?" (Jot.64 Apr.09 but written in Oct.08).* This for instance, is the Saturday routine: *"Saturday, as usual, was the great cooking and cleaning day. Houses were cleaned, clothes washed and hair cutting and shaving much in evidence. After an anointing with coconut oil the toilet finishes with a good bathe, which leaves the face shining and healthy looking." (Jot.74* Oct.1911) Before this, the natives would rarely go into the sea, now it was a regular occurrence. Tuberculosis was a great concern. Not only was it spread by dirty living conditions but the practice of kava drinking was one of the main sources. This involved the chewing of the kava root – a narcotic plant found in the Pacific – by young boys who then spat it into a bowl where it was mixed with a small amount of water. The men then drank it until they became intoxicated and incapable of standing. Not only was the disease spread from person to person, but animals, the ground and the living accommodation would become infected, so with a great deal of difficulty infected villages were pulled down and the animals shot. *"The old village was a terrible place, both as regards houses and site. I noticed that a constant stream of our patients came from there, and resolved to put them on a new basis. A special visit and long and stormy conference with the people followed. They were loath to undertake the work. At last I told them I did not come to Tanna to bury them or to give medicine to help them to die easy; that it was useless my trying to help them if they would not believe in, and help me, and that if they would not obey and clear away the old insanitary village, I could not give any medicine as it was so much waste to try and help them." (*Jot.71 Jan.1911).

Later news in the same Jottings Grandfather expresses his relief at the effect of the influence of the new British Commissioner:

"It seems almost too good to be true that we have reached December of this

year without the slightest whisper of inter-tribal fighting. The traditional causa belli have not been resurrected, and I trust never will. The recent troubles, that is those occurring during the past year, have been dealt with by native courts and the offenders punished by the infliction of fines, or varying periods of work on native tracks or new roads. Almost all the cases centre round pigs, women or witchcraft.

There is a piece in the same Jottings which, I think, deserves inclusion:
"Lately we had the pleasure of opening a new church at Iakit, a southern out-station. Mayhap a description of our journey there, the opening services and incidents connected with it will help to redeem a somewhat prosy letter. We were all invited. Lenakel and the neighbouring out-stations turned out en bloc. The start was imposing. Mrs.Nicholson and myself on horseback, the vanguard of strong men armed with axes and knives for clearing the way, next our children and the house girls, and along the track hundreds of men and women in single file. The day was ideal and our way was by the shore. Immediately on our right hand the sea beat against the fringing reef, giving a musical combination of sounds peculiarly its own; to our left coral cliffs overhung the track, their whiteness relieved by the gorgeous and varied greens of tropical creepers and trees. At one spot hanging unprotected from the coral we saw combs of honey, and the bees busy at work, but they were beyond our reach. Bees were introduced some years ago and are now to be found all over the island." Jot.64 Apr.09 but written in Oct.08

JCN

'Lenakel',
TANNA, New Hebrides.
December 13th 1908

My Dear Mother,

Our Sabbath is past. I expect you will be upstairs getting on your hat for the morning service. Isabel and the bairns are sound asleep and I hope soon to be ditto as we expect the steamer in the morning. I shall only start the letter tonight and finish it after I get yours. I hope we get news that Nellie has got safely home. Our hearts are much with her every time we look at our bairns we think of hers and her[3].

Having the three services and the hospital I do not go out itinerating on Sundays now but stay at home with Isabel and the bairns. We have a quiet afternoon. John was writing a letter to you on a slate. He said he was telling you to come here and bring his train and a spade and shovel for his garden. He always keeps on about his train in Bangor. I forget almost that he had one. May is a hearty lass and eats more than John. She is far braver than him in the sea and stands any amount of ducking, calling out 1, 2, 3, Daddy, wanting me to plunge her under. She has no bathing dress so Nano made her a fringe of grass of which she is very proud. The baby has been in and enjoys it. She is very fat and strong and happy. Isabel makes more of her than she did of John and May when babies. Eileen is very pretty, better features than May had. May is still in love with me. She is happy as long as she can be near me. She understands English but will not speak it. She chatters away in Tannese. John could teach us now. He is using the native idiom in his English now. We refuse to speak to him in Tannese. He and May speak nothing else to each other._

We are nearing Christmas and Communion now. It will be a busy time, one almost wishes it were over. We got our first rain since August, not much, but enough to fill our tanks except the big one at the hospital. The grass is green again and everything looks well. We hope soon to have flowers and fruit again.

P.S. No letter from Princetown. Sorry Etta is ill. I hope they are not too upset about the baby.

J.C.N.

Dec. 16th.

The steamer came last night and we have got a Mr.and Mrs.Thompson down to replace Mr. and Mrs.Mackenzie. He is an engineer and I am doubtful whether to let him touch the church. However, there is plenty for him to do at house and hospital and by the time he has finished we will know what to expect of him. They are now married and nice so far as we have seen. I must get about now and must try and get a day in Mr.MacMillan's district this week. Isabel had a nice letter from Nellie. She puts us to shame for we scarcely believed God could answer our prayer so much more abundantly than we expected. But it must be awful to have one's house emptied of bairns. Your letters were good, but we were so sorry to hear about Louie. The Lord save him. The drink is a terrible thing. We must pray on and on. Willie is great on his kiddie. It will do him a lot of good.

I am so glad you are pleased with the name and I am sure you would be pleased with the bairn, she is such a laughing little thing and to see her and May roll about the floor is a treat. I am on pins and needles lest May hurts her, but Eileen takes it all in good part. John is going to be a gardener. We have got him a toy garden set and he has a fenced in garden and some things growing. He knows a lot of names of flowers already. We are full up about Communion and Christmas gathering which should be a record one. Thank God there is not a whisper of fighting on all Tanna. May peace long continue.

A dog killed a new ram I got down from Sydney today. I think the people will pay for it though. I shot the dog.

A priest and two nuns were drowned up north. They were capsized in an open boat miles from land. The New Hebrides is a place of tragic deaths. Another man, a trader, has been lost at sea, never heard of. We are now into the hot weather. It is fair blistering. I have put my head under a tap sometimes, the sun is so hot.

We are all keeping well. May is at teething again, nose and eyes running. Isabel fine. She is a grand wee wife. Give our love to Father, Netta and any of the clan who may be with you when this arrives and don't forget your own selves,

Your affect. son, J.Campbell Nicholson

P.S. I have about twenty letters to get ready for Friday hence haste in this. J.C.N.

Notes on 1908

In London the Suffragette movement was still taking up a lot of news space with Emily Pankhurst being imprisoned for six weeks and in June 200,000 people attended a rally in the movement's support in Hyde Park. Herbert Asquith had become prime minister and the papers tell of a 'rising star' called Winston Churchill, taking up the post of President of the Board of Trade. The Old Age Pension was first introduced with 5 shillings for everyone over 70 and 7 shillings and sixpence for married couples, those accused of 'feather bedding' (to work according to their ability), prisoners, the insane and paupers (!) were excluded. Further afield, Oklahoma became the 46th state of the United States and postage to there was introduced costing 1p. Flying was in its infancy with Wilbur Wright conducting a flight of 1 hr. and 32 minutes. The earth continued its unpredictable movements with an horrific earthquake in Sicily with fears that less than half of the 150,000 citizens having survived. Trouble was brewing in the Balkans and the Royal Naval Fleet sailed for the Aegean as the trouble deepened.

The Suffragette Movement was making itself felt in Bangor and one gets the impression from the Press that the Movement was the root cause of the contention. Brother William the evangelist, was home on leave and preaching in Hamilton Road Presbyterian Church. Later in May he went on an evangelical tour in America for two months. January brought severe weather with heavy snow and there were hundreds sledging on Irish Hill in Holywood. The snow appeared later at the end of April! At the Royal Ulster Yacht Club's annual regatta, Sir Thomas Lipton's Shamrock made an appearance and did well and in those days during the summer, (presumably to keep the dust down) the streets were watered, a special cart being used, although that year a ten-ton steam roller was bought to lay tarmacadam. In July the Atlantic Fleet put in their annual appearance but unfortunately when they left, five crew got left behind and had to be put on the train by the local police for the next port of call! In September the Spectator tells with sadness, that grandfather's sister Nellie and James Hanna, lost their little daughter to diptheria – tragically their little boy succumbed as well.

Chapter VIII – The Seventh Year

A Busy Year and Visitors

'Lenakel',
TANNA, New Hebrides.
Jan. 12th 1909

My Dear Mother,

It is hard to believe that a month has passed since last I wrote to you and yet if one had to write minutely of the events of each day it would seem a long month. We have the Thompsons with us and if he is allowed to stay and finish the work he will be here several more months. What he does he does well, but he is a slow worker. Mackenzie could do three times as much, but then Mackenzie has been at this kind of work for years and Thompson is new to it and carpentering is not his line. However, he is a great help whether he will tackle the church or not I do not know. I am nervous about him cutting into the old one. They are very nice and easy to do with, but I often think that Mrs.T might offer to help Isabel. Dust a room or do something, but she does not offer and Isabel does not ask. I would much prefer having a single man, every mouth extra means more work for Isabel in the kitchen as our cook is not much use except to get firewood and keep up the fire, etc.

I better tell you about Isabel and the Bairns. Isabel is in good health and spirits. She looks nicer than ever and is better in her looks. Thank God for giving me such a grand wee wife to accompany and help me out here. Not many women are suitable for the life here. We are keen on roses now and hope yet to have a good collection and we will as we are both keen on it. But as yet we have not got rain enough to wet the ground and the garden has been almost barren for months, not many flowers and no vegetables. Plenty of pineapples, I wish we could send you some. Eileen got two teeth when four months old and since she cut them I allowed Isabel to give her biscuits and she can munch them up fine. She is like what John was, bald, fat and smiling. May has never got her four back teeth yet, they are always bothering her, but she manages in spite of them to get a good deal of joy out of life. She still keeps in love with me and is content to be near me at all times. John is looking well and plays a good deal with May. He talks more about Bangor than ever and thinks everything can be got there if we would only write to Granda and Granny. He told me the other day that the sea was full up with soap, (foam). I think I told you his ambition when he grows up is to be able to take out and put in again his teeth. Nano is still head nurse but Isabel has taken in a little boy instead of a girl. He was always knocking about and was so handy that I told Isabel she could keep him so as two girls were leaving we took him and another girl in. We have never any difficulty getting girls, there is always plenty of help about.

We had a great Christmas, about 2,500 or more turned up and they had a great day. We had big services. 42 adults and 30 children were baptised. 374 sat down at the Lord's table. We had to reserve the church for Communicants only, all the others and children stayed outside and as there was no rain it did alright. But it would have been grand if we had had our church up. I felt fagged a bit after it but had to leave for White Sands next day. Truss, the trader who opposed the work so bitterly died the day after Christmas. A friend of his buried (page of original must have been lost as it ends here. BN)

A piece from Jottings 65 – July 1909 – gives more details of the Christmas festivities and also a note about the trader that may complete the above sentence:

"A new feature was the appointment of twelve men – with Silent William as Captain – to act as Policemen. I had asked that our gates, fences and fruit trees should be respected, and this was the thorough way the natives arranged that the request was carried out.

"The day opened with our "Marathon" race, over a course of about five miles. The interest kept up so completely that all other games were suspended for the time. Several heathen young men entered, and one of them succeeded in winning third prize. The first prize was won by my hospital boy, Nilauas, who was to appreciate advice and take it easy at first. Then all rushed to football, cricket, tug of war, etc., and the day passed quickly for everybody. Tug of war and football are the favourite games. I played the latter myself for some time, with the result that I have foresworn it for the future! Tug-of-war is a tremendous affair with them. We have a big rope and at one time Mr.Thomson and I counted two hundred women pulling!

The grounds, which are fairly extensive and shaded with huge banyan trees, presented an animated picture; and the whole-hearted enjoyment of old and young is very infectious. We spent the day with them. Towards evening we had the scrambling for sweets. There were not nearly enough to give one each all round, and the only way to distribute them with comfort is to creep along the branch of a banyan and sow them over the heads or into the open mouths of the people beneath. I should not care for my sweets served out to me in this manner, but they prefer it so. At sunset the conch shell sounded, and all subsided into quiet again – the distant visitors left at once, and the nearer ones waited for the evening service.

A messenger came across from the east coast to say a trader had died, and that another man was very ill and wanted me to come across at once. I started right away, and found one trader dead, and the other suffering from a large tropical abscess."

Lenakel,
TANNA, New Hebrides.
February, 15th 1909

My Dear Mother,

We are just beginning to wonder if the steamer is detained again by the strike, it is not very late yet and we hope for the best. We have had a very hot month, the hottest we have had yet. Eileen has been very bad with her four last teeth, she is so quick with them, they are still troubling her, one is through and the others just about cutting. She wailed night and day and would not leave

Nano, nor Nano her, but she did not fall off in body, just got white. John had fever and was a couple of days in bed, but is alright again. May has not had any more and keeps very sturdy. If it were not for regular dosing with quinine it would be impossible for them to stay. We all take it, servants and all, once a week on Saturdays and everybody near us must take it. All in the hospital are treated with it when they come in and now again afterwards. By these measures we have nearly all escaped it this year. We are just as busy as ever. I was away three days on the East coast, saw the Watts and got a leper settlement formed. We are going to try and segregate all the cases on Tanna. I have to cross and examine another batch of suspected cases, the people have notified me of. I am going north to see a site for another settlement and set the people to building houses on it. The people are cooperating with me heartily and keep me going reporting suspicious cases here and there. The lepers will be much better on their own land and as I only consent to land which has plenty of water, fruit trees and good garden ground, they will have plenty of food and more freedom

The people of Tanna have now raised £126.10.0, the Aniwans and Erromangans £12.10.0. As the 'Unknown' gentleman did not get giving us the launch he sent me the £200 to use for hospital and church and in whatever way I like, so that we will build a better and proper hospital when I get a carpenter. We have a lot of building before us, hospital, enlarge church, boat house for launch. We keep on and on. We think after this we will have a rest but who knows. The people talk of building a school and keeping the church for services as it is large and not easily cleaned.

I do hope Willie comes down. We will be greatly disappointed if he does not. We could have big services and a time of real blessing, the people are ready for it.

I wish the steamer would come and let us get on with work waiting to be done. One cannot go far away lest she turn up.

Our garden is pretty bare of flowers but we have magnificent roses. I must take a photo of a vase some day to show you what they are like. All the ordinary flowers are just beginning to grow again, they do best from April on. Vegetables will not grow at this time, even french beans fail us, they shoot up weak and struggling. Pumpkins there are plenty of. But, the terraces, hospital and church grounds look well. We have to mow the grass more than once a week, it grows so fast.

We had a lot of earthquakes lately, some times they kept on one after the other for hours and one whole night the bed never seemed to keep still, one quake being alarming and giving Isabel a big fright. One sometimes wonders how long the groaning and creaking house can stand it. The volcano is not very active and I suppose this is the cause of the earthquakes.

We have a full hospital and 6 cases waiting for operation. I would like to get the steamer past first, but must go ahead if she does not turn up tomorrow. It is trying on Isabel, chloroforming in hot weather is not an easy task and very fatiguing.

Willie had great times in the West of Australia, a Municipal reception in the Capital and real blessing at all the services. I wonder where he is now. I wish they were on the steamer bound for here.

I will finish this letter after the steamer comes and we see the mail. (17th). The steamer has come but the strike is still holding out at Sydney and much poverty and misery resulting. Your birthday is past, but we wished you in our prayers many happy returns. Today Isabel is 30 and says she feels old now, but she does not look it and is as pretty and nice as ever in my eyes. The (in the typed copy from the originals, there is a gap here as if the typist could not make out the writing) will be on Saturday and I must drop her a line. John had fever last night and has been in bed all day, but is a little better. Eileen is still teething and has wilted terribly. May is brown and sturdy and does not mind the heat, she had prickly heat, but it is better. We just let her lie naked at nights under the mosquito net, she perspires so freely. You will have received the photos and explanation of their delay. I am glad you like them. Mr.MacMillan should be down next time and that will relieve me greatly. I have the hospital full and ten operations before me, three tomorrow. It is too much for Isabel but what can we do. This has been a very hot season and we long for the end of it. Indeed I want Isabel and Nano and the children to go south to Norfolk Island for a month, but Isabel does not want to as we have to put up two surveyors who are coming next month to survey all the mission grounds here and else-

where on Tanna. The trouble about land is very great and the dispute will cause a lot of heart burning between French and English.

Willie is not coming down at present but may get in July, he thinks. That will be a much better month. I expect to have a busy month after the steamer goes, long rides. With so many earthquakes I do not like to be away at night. But we are trying to get leprosy held in check and the people everywhere are keen. It is a case of striking whilst the iron is hot. I have no time to see about a motor boat at present. I do hope we get a single carpenter for a year. I feel lazy at times but when I take my courage in both hands and go ahead I feel much better for doing so. But there is so much important work to be done one should be free from manual labour. Our schools and services are well attended. Full church on Sunday last. I am able to preach without paper now and that is a great help, but I must keep my careful translations or else ones powers of expression become very limited or awry.

I do hope Father is up and about now. He will be keen on the General Election and seems to be going to win on Tariff Reform. I hope Nellie will come through safe and sound and rejoicing. With much love to you all,

Your affect. son,
J.Campbell Nicholson

'Lenakel',
TANNA, New Hebrides.
March 14th 1909

My Dear Mother,

By this time you will have forgotten about the mail we missed and have received your letters with more regularity. I wish we had the old service back by which our mails went off direct to Sydney. Now they will sometimes go almost at once by the French steamer and at other times be sailing about for a month in the group. The authorities always promise us an amelioration of present conditions. Mrs. Worthington went to Sydney in January and she had to go right round the group to get there. She left Tanna on the 15th January and she passed Tanna on the 15th February for Sydney. Just think if one had to take a family what clothes would be necessary for that extra month of sailing and then we have to pay for the trip round as well, though we take it against our wishes. Such is life.

The Thomsons being away gave us a rest in the house this month or rather Isabel. I don't think we are inhospitable but it is nice to be alone sometimes. The months fly here, each day is so full that the time passes quickly, then again we dread furlough, the travelling and having to leave John in Australia makes the days seem far too short. However, we must not stay down too long. Mrs. Fred Paton, Mrs. MacMillan, Mrs. Mackenzie Mrs. Milne all dead and gone and only the last named passed middle age, all the others young. Mrs. Leggett and Mrs. Frazer had to leave in ill health, also Mrs. McCausland, all since we came down, also Mrs. Yates. It is not good for ladies to be down too long at a time. They do not go out enough. Isabel is a good deal in the garden and is very active which is greatly in her favour. She keeps in splendid health and I will do my best to keep her in it. She is a grand wee woman, gets better all the time. She chloroforms for me, helps me to teach as well as her own work. We are going to try and get across to Mr. MacMillan's house for a week or two. The change will do Isabel and the bairns good. It has been raining for more than a week but as soon as the weather seems settled and I can get things arranged at the hospital we'll to horse and saddles and off.

I have photos of the children taken but not printed but I hope to get some done by this mail. Eileen is hard to take. I have spoiled a lot of plates, she is such a restless morsel, the best has neither hands nor feet to show. John is in his garden. He takes a great interest in it and plants all he can get his hands on. He says to tell Granda and you that he has zinnias, corn, maize, cosmos, millet, frangipani, melons, pumpkins, pineapples, potatoes, itunga, i.e., foreign and sweet potatoes, mangoes, coconuts, geraniums, balsams, roses, creepers, gailardia, chrysanthemums and some other things. He would like to show you them all, they are all mixed up without order. We give him his sweet will and he gets a new thing as soon as he knows and can point out all the other things. This will be a bit of education for him and may incline him to love these things in future. May had another bad turn lately, fever and fainted but is all right again. She is so averse to taking medicine. John asks for quinine regularly. I have children of 3 and 4 years who come up alone in the mornings to drink a solution of quinine, they get so much relief from it they suffer the awful taste willingly

We operated four days last week doing seven cases. I felt tired after them, but they have all done well and with one exception are about again and the exception had a tumour of between five and six pounds removed. The work goes steadily forward. The services are crowded and the people hearty. The heathen coming in weekly and those who do not are keeping very quiet. The name Christian was a despised one formerly and still is in places, but now the change has begun and to be called a heathen or 'ieiem ilna' an outsider, is felt not to be such a grand title after all. The danger in future will be of getting converts not because of conviction but because of fashion. The people have kept in wonderful good health. Lomai, Javis and all the teachers fit for duty right along. We sent three away to the Training Institute last month for four years training, that is six away now. Soon we hope to have more ready.

Our garden is a blaze of bloom now. Zinnias principally but other things coming on quickly. We have splendid roses. I think they would nearly do for showing. Isabel and I like the roses best, they respond more to effort on their behalf than any other flower we know. Our vegetables will now grow and in the hot season it would take rain every day to keep them going and then they mostly become too rank. Peas will not do at all. Our difficulty here is to find out the right time for each thing. I wish you could see our garden. I am sure you would be pleased. I will send this time or soon a photo of our first terrace, the grass and shrubs are in splendid order now. I must begin and do some photography. People are asking for photos of their teachers and Mr. Longridge always wants photos for Lantern Slides. They think it is only a little thing to ask but it means a lot of extra work for me, besides I am not keen on it. I hope you are keeping well. Your talk of Christmas made us a bit homesick, but we are all very happy, especially Eileen. She is the personification of joy. May is still courting me and is very jealous. The man or woman who has never had the arms of his or her own child round their necks have never experienced one of the greatest joys this life affords, at least so I think.

I'll keep this letter open till the steamer comes, so goodnight. John asked, Dadda where was it horses went round and an organ played and who took me. I think Father took him to the hobby horses, ask him. John has forgotten Melbourne and Sydney and gone back to Bangor.

The steamer has come, 2 letters from you. Glad to hear all well. Enclose photos. Mr. Macmillan came down a run but has been elected Moderator of South Australia Church and has to go back next month and remain up for 6 or 7 months for his duties.

With love to all,

Your affect. son,
J. Campbell Nicholson

'Lenakel',
TANNA, New Hebrides.
Apr.8th 1909

My Dear Mother,

I was so glad to get your two letters and to know you were all well. We have all had fever, nothing serious in any case, except May's. The house is shaking at present but we have had no bad earthquakes so far, but this swinging backwards and forwards would almost make one seasick. I hope it does not waken the wife and bairns. I have just read your reference to the Italian one and it makes one think more of our little shakes.

Isabel has had pains in her back and shoulders and feels weak today. Eileen's attack made her look white and wan. Last Sunday John retired to his bed and without any fuss had his but was all right on Monday. May, however, made us anxious. Her temperature runs up and keeps so high that the she twitches all over, and at the climax has a convulsion. This last time it only lasted a minute or so, before we could get hot water she was out of it. I have to lie with her and hold her. It is pitiful to hear her say, Dada Jakamus (I am sick). Today she is much better and was quite lively. She takes her medicine readily now and makes Nano take one at the same time. When delirious she called out, gany ihia (where is granny). John is very good to her and so pleased when she asks for him and he is allowed to go and sit with her. He is a tender hearted soul and I am afraid will not make a doctor (how wrong he was!). We have had Mr.Macmillan across for three days helping me with operations. I got nine done comfortably and all doing well.

Mr.Macmillan has been elected Moderator of the South Australian Church but as it will detain him in the colonies till September, he made it conditional to getting a run down to see his people and reorganise things a bit as at present, and indeed since he left in November, there has been a great number of heathen coming in all over Tanna. It is really wonderful to see the work of the Holy Spirit awakening those who sit in darkness and the shadow of death!! It is so quiet and gradual, day by day and week by week, that only those praying and working and watching are cognisant of it. But we need a revival amongst those in the Worship. I have no doubt that many attend the schools and services now who have never had a serious conviction about the matter. They renounced darknesss because others related to them did so, but the root of the matter is not in them. However, they are daily being taught the word of God and the illumination of the Holy Spirit must come and I trust come soon. It used to be very hard to break heathenism. There is no longer, or at least not often, any great persecution of those who do so now so that whereas we have quantity the quality is not always so certain. However, to get men and women under the instruction of the 'Word' is a step in the right direction. After all, ours is the command to teach and preach. It is God who converts or regenerates.

The steamer calls for Mr.Macmillan on Monday the 12th and so we get a mail up with him and to let you have letters regularly we must post again on the 13th or 14th otherwise. But indeed I don't know how the mails go now, we just take every chance. Our letters can go by French or English steamers and we can use English or French stamps as we like, our Postmaster General is a Frenchman.

Things are moving slowly politically. The dual protectorate is not going to run very smoothly. The French do not enforce the law. The British do and in consequence the British traders are complaining and wish themselves under French law. We missionaries are blessed for the stringency of British law and find little favour in the eyes of the traders. However, the protectorate has made for good so far and may be the foundation of something better.

There has been a hurricane up north and a lot of damage done. We got a little of it but not as much as we expected from the glass. I lowered our flag post and made all snug but it passed off.

The Worthingtons have had a lot of fever. Mr.Watt, his wife and bairns have all had it and it is rife amongst the natives at present. We are getting plenty of rain and we can now begin to plant. The garden is a blaze of colours, zinnias and cosmos principally, but most of the other flowers are coming on. Vegetables, such as peas, haricot beans, are growing and it will soon be cool enough to plant all kinds of seeds.

I was so glad to hear about Dan's appointment. It is a most important one, none more so, for China's millions must be moved by Chinese Evangelists and preachers. I wish they would write to us. Both Isabel and myself have written since coming out and as yet no answer. I will write again soon.

We are wondering about Willie, Alexander and Chapman[1] *should be in Australia now. I hope Willie comes with them and can get a run down here. We have been down a year almost, the time flies. I have come far short of the year's work I laid out: not getting our Church up has acted like a brake. However, much progress has been made. It has been a good year: a year of goodness and mercy.*

Father is a wonderful man for his years. I wish you both could come and see us in our home. I am sure you both would find much to interest you. We would not need to work up entertainment for you. I will write again in a few days.

With love from us all to you all,

Your affect: son,
J.Campbell Nicholson

From the Jottings Grandfather tells of a new innovation:

This year we had our first Harvest Thanksgiving service. It came about quite naturally, and our only surprise was that we never thought of having it before. Tanna heathenism had a hard and fast custom that no one should eat of the new yams until general permission was given by the "yam man" of the district, who was supposed to inherit from his father the power of making the yams grow. He was fed and paid by his own people to make him strong and willing to work for the good of the yams of all in his district. New yams, pigs and kava were presented to him following the yam digging. "Sing-sings" were held afterwards, and the day was called Nian Vi, "New Day," analogous to our New

Year's Day, as their year dates from the first new yam to the next new yam.

So, at the desire of the people, we proclaimed the "Nian Vi", or New Day. The people brought of the first fruits of their gardens to the Church. Every man, woman and child about Lenakel brought their tithe, and all acknowledged God as the "Giver of every good and perfect gift". The Church was tastefully decorated. We never had decorations before, and I took little interest in the matter, but on being sent for to come to the Church I was overcome with surprise. The yams, pumpkins, taro, maize, nuts, bananas, etc., which we despised for decorative purposes, with the aid of crotons and other variegated leaves, had transformed our Church. The yams had been piled up in front of the reading desk; their earthiness relieved by the white, green, red and yellow of different crotons. Great bunches of different kinds of nuts, bananas and oranges were swung from the tie beams or walls. Plants had been potted to make them keep their appearance over Sunday. I was so pleased that I tried to take a photo, thought it was not very successful.

On the Sabbath we had the Thanksgiving Service, and on Monday the yams, nuts and fruit were taken to the hospital, with the exception of a part which the people set aside for us and our household.

Due to the absence of Mr.Macmillan, Grandfather was in charge of his district and tells of a visit he pays to White Sands on the east coast:

After the gathering the people took me to see a waterfall back in the mountains. The road was impossible for the horses. We had a lot of ups and downs before we struck the course of a broad mountain stream. Following this, crossing and re-crossing it, a mighty sound of water began to assail one's ears. At last the watercourse had come to an end, and such an end. I have never seen anything so beautiful in nature before! The stream flowed out of a natural amphitheatre, sheer and overhanging cliffs enclosed more than three sides of it, and these cliffs stretch up into the mountains, one of which is 3,500 feet above sea level. The cliffs were clothed with glorious greens of moss and fern and other plants. In the centre of the top of the horseshoe cliffs there was a cleft, and through this a mountain torrent shot straight out and fell perpendicularly for 120 feet into the pool of water that formed the floor of the amphitheatre. It fell on to a large flat stone – which lay just below the surface of the water – and was shattered into a cloud of spray, which rose in a ring round the descending column. The sun striking this from over the edge of the cliff produced a perfect rainbow. We all sat down and gazed in awe, speaking was not easy, and besides seemed out of place.[2]

With the help of some young men I ascended the cliff to where the water rushed out, and viewed the scene from above. It was magnificent, and passes description. The volume of water would be about three feet in diameter, and from the markings on the cliff it must sometimes be nearly three times that in one diameter, and would then shoot out clear from the cliffs a corresponding distance. I would like to see it after a very wet season. (Jottings 66 October 1909)

'Lenakel'
TANNA, New Hebrides.
June 11th 1909

My Dear Mother,

I am waiting for the steamer to call and take me to Synod. She may be here any moment or not for days and as she only calls for me, I have to be ready to get on board at a moment's notice.

I expect you will get this letter at the same time as last month's but am not sure. We spent the last fortnight in Mr.Macmillan's district. We all crossed on horseback, John and May in panniers on the horse I gave Mr.Macmillan, Isabel on Bruce, I on Tom and our goods packed on a horse of Mr.Worthington's. I am sorry we did not get a photo of the cavalcade for you. Eileen was carried by Nano and Hyan and I took her and May by turns on my saddle. We got across in about 8 hours and dry, stopped twice for food.

We had a good holiday. Isabel and I rode to the different outstations and to Port Resolution. We had Communion and baptismal services. 200 communicated and 36 baptised. It was a time of Blessing. Mrs.Watt persuaded Isabel to stay with her at Port Resolution while Mr.Watt is at Synod so I took them there by boat. It was a rough day but only Eileen was sick, she vomited a lot. John was none too good and when we got into the Port he said 'they have a very nice sea here'. May's yells as I was leaving still haunt me. She can hardly let me out of her sight night or day. I have to let her sleep with me. I smacked her but she does not mind that, keeps the whole house awake if I do not let her come and after a whacking she tells me I am so good and nice and she loves me – what should I do? John sleeps by himself.

Eileen has got four back teeth now: except for a cough they do not give her much trouble which is a comfort. Isabel and the bairns all were better of the change. The Thomsons were glad to get alone. They have not been much alone since they were married and they get on well in the house and with the people. He is working like a Trojan, seems to have wakened up and is at the Church early and late. He is getting on splendidly and doing the work well. He is a good stamp of a Christian and a real missionary at heart. I heard lately he gave up a good post and a good salary to come down.

I expect to hear from Willie this time. I do hope he gets down. It would be a good way to begin our new Church with regular Evangelistic services. I don't know how he would like speaking by interpretation but am sure it would be a grand thing for our Church members.

I hope Nellie has got rid of her Guinea Worm. We do not have them here and I am not fretting for them. I hope Louis pulls up. It would be grand to hear he had decided for Christ.

It is nice and quiet here at White Sands. The volcano explosions make the house shake and the doors rattle every now and again. It is awesome at night, although I have heard and seen it much worse.

All is very quiet now on Tanna. The mad Russian is still mad but does not come out of Weasisi. I was always afraid of his coming to White Sands lest he might frighten Isabel. He is full of delusions and afraid of witchcraft.

Since the death of Truss and the departure of another trader things have gone very smoothly. The former's death created a great impression and all the natives looked on it as a judgement. It looks as if the end of heathenism is not very far off. We may yet be able to write that there are no more heathens.

I am glad father keeps so well and indeed you all. With much love to you all,

Your affect: son,
J.Campbell Nicholson

In August, my Grandparents, along with many of the natives, paid a visit to the most southerly station, Infeitana:

One Friday recently Mrs.Nicholson and I, together with people from all over our district, visited our most southerly out-station, Infeitana.

It is situated right up in the mountains. Moi is the teacher there. He tells me it is sometimes so cold they have to sit all night at the fire, and that without a fire everything in their house gets covered with mildew. Yet the people cleave to their mountain and cold, and will not be persuaded to come lower down nearer the coast. They have cleared the scrub along the native track, and zig-zagged a path for us over a spur of land which before had made it impossible for us to go by horse.

Even as it was, they described parts of the roads as being like "soap", and the description we found true to the nature of some of the clayey ascents. Going up, the unshod feet of the horses took a good grip; but returning downhill we did some rare sliding, sitting well back on our horses and wondering what would happen next.

When we came in sight of Infeitana we were well repaid for our rough riding. The road for a few hundred yards before we entered had been well made, and we cantered in amidst cheers and exclamations of surprise. Not a few of the natives saw the "big pigs", as they called the horses, for the first time. Moi, and Nepiko, the chief, had come to meet us, fearful lest the road should be too difficult for Mrs.Nicholson.

We found the old kava house gone, and a substantial native church in its place. Around it was a garden of variegated shrubs and flowers. We were sorry we could not speak to many of the new people we met, their dialect is totally different from that at Lenakel; but Lomai, who knows all the dialects of Tanna, acted as interpreter, and we had a very attentive audience. Nepiko came forward with an offering of £1 10s. to help defray the cost of the addition to the church here.

The usual feast was served out, and on leaving, the people lined the road, asking us to let them see the horses galloping, which we did to the wonder and awe of the strangers. (Jot.67 Jan.1910)

TANNA, New Hebrides.
Oct. 7th 1909

My Dear Mother,

We were glad to get your two letters and to hear you were all well. Who is Mr.Andrew Bailis, I don't remember the name. We have enjoyed the visit of our two girl guests very much. We had not so much to entertain them as they entertained us and our bairns. Frances Robinson is just a big, overgrown girl with her hair still down her back. I think her mother thought she was growing too quickly and had better have a rest from schoolwork. Her companion is older and very nice too. Mr.Mackenzie of Santo brought them from Melbourne and will take them there again. He has had to leave the Tropics and is going to Korea instead. The Committee were unwilling to take him but he would take no denial and offered to go for a year without salary. He has no children. It must be pretty hard on his leaving Nogugu where is wife is buried and where they were permitted to do a grand work. We had intended to spend a week at White Sands and let the girls see the Island, but cases kept coming to the hospital and we had ten operations in less than that number of days. One was a sad case of life or death, a girl with a cancer of the upper jaw choking her. We could hear her at night over in the house. I was afraid, but did what I thought was for the best. I got the tumour and jaw away and the chloroform stopped and was feeling well pleased to have been able to get through such a large operation single handed. I was putting in the last stitches when she collapsed. We brought her round but she went off again – after three hours and a half we had to give up. I felt bad, how bad I could not describe. Two others were waiting for operation but I could do no more that day. The next day was Sunday and I was glad of it, but on the Monday felt all right and the other two patients lay down on the table as if nothing had happened and we got them finished comfortably. The same day two more patients came for operation. On Wednesday we were all ready to start for White Sands but it rained so we put it off. I expected that the death of the girl would create a panic, it has been our first death from operation, but it made not the slightest difference and we have several more in and must operate again as soon as possible. The girl was from the White Sands district where we were going on Thursday. We made a start but we got so wet four miles from home we had to return.

Isabel decided not to go as the weather was uncertain and we were afraid for the children. On Friday I crossed with the girls and we had only one shower and by pressing on got across in $4^{1/2}$hrs. Our packhorse and the boys got a bad drenching as they were longer on the road. On Saturday we visited the volcano and on Sunday had a big united service in the morning. Miss Beath played the organ. After it was over the elder asked me to wait as the people wanted to speak about the hospital. Representatives of the village, heathen and Christian alike came forward with sums of money to the amount of £11.4.0 to help to make the hospital bigger and to make my heart strong to stay with them and not go to Vila. They said they were going to begin to work and get more and would try to have £100 by Christmas. Not a word about the girl and several crossed with us for operation. It really was more than one could expect from people, some of whom were yet in heathenism and the majority of the rest not long out of it. During our four days stay not a word was spoken about the girl lest it might hurt my feelings. About £26 has already been given and about half of this from heathen and it is only given as the surety of their promise they will give any money I need to make the hospital as large as is necessary. They call it the 'seed of our intentions' meaning it will grow. I never thought that they appreciated the work done for them so much from north to south and east to west of Tanna and Erromanga the seed has come in. It has given me back my nerve and filled my heart with deep gratitude to God.

On Monday the girls and I went to Port Resolution to see the Watts and the scenes and graves of Dr.Paton's early years on Tanna. We crossed today and had a dry crossing finding all well at home. Mr.Macmillan is not to be down till April of next year. His church say they cannot do without his services so I will have his work and my own till then, but as all is going on smoothly and progress being made, it will not be so hard. I have written definitely that I do not see my way to leave Tanna even for a time. I think they will get Crombie or Bowie, both would like to go to Vila[3]*. Willie is doing grand work in Australia. He writes as if he might come, and speaks of Heminger*[4] *coming. But as I promised at least half expenses I am beginning to get afraid, as I could not pay or be responsible for half expenses of a party of them. But it may be arranged in time. I want Isabel to have as easy a time between this and June as possible as we will most likely have forty at Synod and it means a lot of* *work and planning. They have to bring nearly all their own beds and bedding and towels, so that is a great help. Then there is cutlery, lamps and things that belong to Synod so that it is not such a big expense to the missionary whose station is visited. We are having real blessing in the work and our church is well filled on Sundays. Our lines have been cast in pleasant places and we have been privileged to see a wondrous work on Dark Tanna.*

Willie says he would not like his influence confined to the limits of a small island, but the best thing in life is just to be in the place where God wants you and to do the work He gives you to do to the best of your ability. A wider range of influence cannot give you any greater peace and joy, than that it can only give you as much.

John and May and Eileen are looking well and are a trio of mischiefs. I am rich in my wife and bairns, none richer. With much love to Father, Netta and Louie and his and all, not forgetting your own dear self.

Your affect: son,
J.Campbell Nicholson

In a letter undated, but obviously August 1909, Grandfather writes in Jottings 67 (Jan.1910):

In October the family had visitors and they accompanied my Grandparents on a visit to Lokavit, a village that Grandfather had been to a few months before and remonstrated with the people on the condition of the place:

Let me tell you the result. We have two young ladies from Melbourne staying with us, Miss Robinson and Miss Beath, and they came with us. Mounted on Mr.MacMillan's horses and my own, the three ladies and myself soon found ourselves passing along a real road, straight, level and wide enough for a buggy, and through gardens and past cocoanut and fruit trees, we travelled for seven or eight miles. We passed two men busy cleaning the road. They are convicts under the new native law. Instead of being shot and getting others shot for their misdeeds, as in the old days, they have now to work out their sentences on the roads. Our way now begins to ascend, and the aspect is quite unlike the usual island one. There are but few trees, and only coarse grass and a variety of shrubs. The ocean lies behind us, and is rough enough to make us glad to be on horseback and not in the Pioneer. To our left the mountains, away to the north, stands out bold and blue, and before us lies a broken range of hills. After some miles thus, without the sign of habitations, we pass through a break in the hills, and now our ears are assailed by the shouts and laughter of many people. In a minute a cheerful scene lies before our eyes. A new village with a church in the centre. In front of this a cleared space, and there some four hundred men, women and children, not fighting and quarrelling, but at healthy play. Some are at tug-of-war, others at cricket and football, and some at island games. Our appearance is greeted with a cheer, and soon we are amongst them. Our horses are led away, and the ladies almost overpowered by heathen women. There are some real 'man bush' women here today (?) This is Mrs.Nicholson's first visit. It is the first time white women have been in the place. I leave the ladies to admire and be admired by their own sex. Miss Robinson's hair, in a plait down her back, comes in for some handling, and the men folk wanted to drive their women back, but were not allowed to do so. After I came back from a talk with the teachers and some of the chiefs I found an exchange had been made of safety pins and small coins on the one hand, for bracelets made of cocoanut shells and pearl shell neck pendants on the other. I had three couples to marry, and so we had a marriage ceremony in lieu of the usual service. Then the puddings and pork are carried out with all due ceremony and apportioned to each party of visitors.

We lunched in the teacher's house. It is built of rough-hewn slabs of timber, roofed with corrugated iron brought from Queensland by a relative of the teacher's. It has four rooms, and we sat on chairs at a decent table. We brought our own sandwiches, but the good native wife had some taro ready and served it up on enamel plates, with bananas to follow. We walked through the fourteen new houses, and several not quite new, and duly admired the gardens, which are a mixture of vegetables and flowers (the sunflowers rub shoulders with the cabbages, and gaillardia blooms cheerfully beside shallots). But they look nice. In one house a table was decked with flowers, in bottles for vases, and we even saw a neat potted plant.

'Lenakel',
TANNA, New Hebrides.

Nov.17th 1909

My Dear Mother,

I was dusting my desk before settling to writing and lifting the blotting pad to my amazement and consternation found your letter and a packet of photos which should have gone last month. I had no envelope big enough and had gummed up the letter and photos in paper and to make it stick put it under the pad and there it remained. I am sorry for I wanted you all to have them at Christmas in lieu of Christmas cards. It is too bad. I must be getting old as I have made mistakes in dates, etc., frequently of late. No letter last mail but three this time to make up for it and good news in all. It is splendid that Father is able to go about even to Liverpool and Conway. He is quite fit for a trip out here and if he came he could help me with the launch which I have no time to order, Mr.Macmillan being away and as I cannot get a carpenter to build a boat house and lay rails down to pull the launch up on I have not ordered it yet. I have not time to do building myself. We had 39 in the hospital at once last week and our services here are growing,, the big church full every Sunday. We have been having very bad weather, very hot and muggy. I wish the hot season was over. The children do not seem to mind it but one is always afraid of them getting about in the sun without a hat. John was talking about you at tea tonight, he cannot understand about the old wheel barrow and George, the rubber tyred one knocked that out of his memory. He remembers his Granda taking him walks and asked us if we remembered the bees chasing him at the Dodds. I think he pulled the top of a hive. May asked if Granny was a herahigal like Nano, i.e., an old woman. Poor May feels out of it with John's reminiscences. He seems to realize the meaning and necessity of prayer already. May has not reached that stage yet to all appearance but always says her prayers. She is a great singer and picks up the tunes well. Eileen tries to but makes everybody laugh. I wish that it had been possible to have had the children grow up with us but we have put our hands to the plough and must just trust our God. It feels as if the time flies, we never know till it is mail time and there are only twelve mails in the year. Our garden is pretty dry now, only roses are doing anything. We have a good show of them, 54 varieties blooming now and some of the blooms are fine. We have always roses in the house. Isabel is the best up and can name them all on sight but I get mixed up. I can't always see the difference between light yellow and sulphur yellow and deep yellow, and rosy pink and flesh pink, etc., but if I have an hour to spare it goes very quickly among roses. We have few vegetables now, pumpkins, carrots and cabbages about all. The heat is too great and the rain scarce, a month since we had a drop.

We have a youth in the hospital called Freeman from Anietyum, he was born there twenty years ago and this is the first time he has been off it. His father died lately and though well off would not let his family leave the island. He has three sons and four daughters. The eldest son ran away and one or two of the girls cleared out to Sydney and got something to do there but they are all weakly and two have had tubercular disease and some of the others are infected. I feel sure the boy here has picked up but I am urging him to go up to Sydney for a time. I think he is afraid. He has many native ways and is not happy unless with the natives. He does not care to talk with white people and when walking with us will persist in dropping (a page missing?

The tracks are kept clear by prisoners sentenced by the native Courts but all new tracks are made by the people working one day a week. It is an easy matter now to carry the sick to the hospital, it was almost impossible before on the old tracks and the food for the hospital can be collected over a wide area by cart or with the pack saddle. The people have raised £68.10.0 and by Christmas are going to make it £100 to enlarge the hospital. We expect a huge gathering at Christmas and at the Communion and Baptismal services. The hearty willing spirit and appreciation makes hard work easy, but we miss Mr.Macmillan. Without the hospital I could do both districts but with it I cannot get about as I should, but by it I am kept in close touch with all parts of Tanna and in close touch with the heathen who have given very liberally to the hospital.

We are all keeping well. Isabel feels the heat some days but the children don't seem to mind it, they are all looking so well. Your namesake is a terror, she tries to imitate John in everything and looks down on May. I think May gets left in the cold as Eileen with her laughing and antics attracts all attention. But May is still in love with me, she can hardly bear me out of her sight and sleeps in the cot beside me, reaching in at night to feel if I am there. John is developing fast and tries us with his questions. He was sent to the hospital to get a cut bound up, I was praying with a man who was dying and when I came out John was standing with the tears streaming down his face. He asked me a lot of questions keeping his back to me and I could only pray for guidance to answer him aright. One could not help feeling that it might mean so much in after life to the wee man. Eileen is a great girl, strong and big, and gives May a bad time sometimes. She is very like what John was, scanty flaxen hair, big laughing face and it is impossible to pass her.

I had no letter from Willie this time but a P.C. of baby from Ellie.(Willie's wife was called Ellison) They are in Western Australia. Willie is to get January off but a month would not be time enough to run down, besides it is at the very worst part of the year. I do hope we get them. If Hemminger comes I don't know how we'll put them up, it will be a tight fit. We have only one spare bedroom. The committee would help with expenses.

I had a very nice flattering letter from the home committee asking me not to leave them or Tanna. They have not got any man for Vila yet, this the Victorian Church. Crombie may go.

We had the Man of War and Mr.King the Commissioner down last month. They intended to stay over Sunday. Mr.King would have come to the services but there was a terrific sea and I could hardly get the boat out. They had to clear out. I met them at the other side to help the Commissioner in some inquiries and had dinner on board and a very pleasant evening. The French are striving tooth and nail to get a foothold on Tanna. A French schooner was selling grog and ball cartridges and took away a girl. I tried to get her back but on going alongside the vessel pulled away. The blasphemy and vituperation and threats were terrible. They cleared for Vila and reported I had threatened them with a rifle, had boarded their vessel with twenty natives and given them a bad time. They wanted to be protected from me. The Commissioner (French) pretends he thinks it is true. He blames me for the native hatred of the French. If they get on Tanna I will have a troubled time. We have no French on Erromanga, Tanna, Anniva, Fotuna or Anietyum, that is south of Vila, and this gets on the French nerves and they are most anxious to have some claim. This dual protection or Condominium will not work for long, a crisis must come. I wish we could get rid of the French for good. What with quarrelling about the North Pole, flying like birds, budgets, etc., the civilized world is kept busy. What next.

Isabel is feeling the heat but is in good health. We ride now and again and she always feels better after being out. I am going to try and get a second-hand sulky so that we can take the children and go drives. The cart comes and goes for hospital food so that the roads are fairly good now. It is a very different Tanna from a few years ago. We cannot realise we are on Tanna at times. A stranger would not notice it because he does not know what the former things were. The people have done well and if they only keep it up the dying out process will cease. For two years we have been increasing I think.

I am sorry about Nellie. Could James not get on some other mission. I never could agree with J.T.Mission[5] methods. I don't know how they do on £100 a year. It is not right to ask people to go abroad for that.

I hope Netta is well. She is very quiet surely. I am sorry about Louie's wife's hand. Tell Louie and his wife we were asking about them and George.(Louie's son). I would like to see Louie.

Pray for us that we may get through the work and this season well. With love to all at home, Father and yourself,

Your affect. son,
J. Campbell Nicholson

From Jottings 69 July 1910

Lenakel, TANNA
28th December, 1909

We are cut off from the outside world at present, and have received no mail from home or Australia since November. The steamer going to Sydney called to say they had received a cable from Noumea by the French Man-of-War, informing them that, in consequence of a coal strike, the December steamer could not leave Sydney, and no one could say how long the strike would last. On account of the October steamer arriving late in Sydney we did not get our provisions in November, and they are still on the wharf at Sydney. We would have preferred to have missed any other steamer call in the year. I had to put a letter from Santa Claus in my little boy's stocking to say that the steamer would bring him something later on.

However, Christmas is past, and we had a very happy one. Our Christmas party was very large, somewhere about 3,000 people turning up. The day was fine, and a cool southerly breeze made it possible for us to move about in comfort, and for our guests to disport themselves at football, tug -of- war, rounders, races, etc., without heat stroke or collapse. It would have been most interesting for you or any of our home friends to have spent the day with us among the people. I am sure you could have made a special Christmas number of Jottings snapshots, and with pen sketches of the games and contests, and the groups and individuals among the natives.

From early morning people kept streaming in by the five main roads leading into Lenakel. The near villagers were burdened with huge puddings, baskets of cooked pork, and young coconuts for liquid refreshment. One thing is very noticeable to us by its absence, you would not miss it, is the rifle. Not one did we see. After rushing through the hospital work a messenger came up to say that all was ready for the opening service. Under the banyans a great concourse had gathered; and to lead the singing of our Christmas hymns one is compelled to mount a chair and at last stand up on the table itself. The message of Christmas may get fixed in some heathen mind by a chorus, and so we repeat it and then explain it to them.

After the service the promised subscriptions of tribes – heathen as well as Christian – for enlarging the hospital, were laid on the table. The naked heathen with painted face and plaited hair was there – rubbing shoulders with his clothed and unpainted brother, and one at heart with him this time as he comes forward and lays down the contribution of his tribe. The lowest subscription was five shillings, and the highest £2 13s. One chief himself gave £1. Soon £31 17s is on the table (making the total amount in hand £95 4s). The southern people are to make a hospital collection at Port Resolution on the first Sunday in the New Year, and at least £7 10s. has been subscribed on Erromanga. Aniwa has not yet come forward. But the Tannese have done what they said they would and more. For when Mr.Watt gives me the south-

ern money, more than £100 will have been raised on Tanna for enlarging the Hospital on Tanna.

Now to play. Seven or eight young men line up for the five mile race. Nobody thinks of anything else till this is run off. Away to the south they go along the main road, and we wait impatiently for their return. At last cheers break out and three come in sight, a big strapping heathen leading. He leads till the last thirty yards, and then Nilauas runs in an easy first; our heathen friend loses second place and comes in third. We felt sorry for him, as he had led all the way and made the pace so hot that only three finished.

Now the football is let loose, the big tug-of-war cable stretched out, and soon several acres of ground are covered with people bent on enjoying themselves. Under the shade of the banyans, groups of old men gather together. Do they contrast the old times with the new? This used to be their fighting season, and even at the Christmas gatherings, on these very grounds, secret councils of war were held. Just four years ago today such a one was held; and on the Sunday following, men, women and children were cruelly murdered. If the old men indulge in contrasting the past with the present the contrast is but adding to their enjoyment of the present, or else I do not read their faces aright. Up on the slope of the hill the chiefs from all of the north of Tanna have gathered. One after another arises and speaks. I ask a man what the talk is about, he replies "Roads, courts, laws!" What a change! I did not intrude, but I was told afterwards that the chiefs were "making each other strong" to maintain peace and suppress "old talk" of fighting and witchcraft.

Thank God. Thank God.

And so the day wears on till the hush of the midday feast. Afterwards jumping and racing, then a scramble for 28lbs of sweets which friends in Victoria had sent down by the November boat. Girls are displaying their prizes, boys their knives, mouth organs or trumpets. A mother is fitting her baby into a very tight fitting shirt that she has run for.

My afternoon was spent in preparation for a magic lantern display at night. We had a record gathering. The little acetylene generator I brought out from home is a great improvement on the kerosene lamp we had before.

Our Christmas gathering was held on the Friday. On the Wednesday and Thursday preceding we had two services each day, as well as Candidates' Classes in preparation for the Communion and Baptismal Services on the Sunday. Saturday was given up to cooking and cleaning. In the evening we paid a tour of inspection. The women were putting the puddings in the earth ovens for the morrow. The beach is thronged with bathers. Here and there little groups of men are shaving each other. The village street is brushed clean, and after the evening service the curfew order is given; for the services tomorrow will engage most of the day, and we not want the after effects of Christmas exercises to be in evidence.

After the morning preparation service the elders and deacons arrange the candidates for baptism; and put the communicants in their places. The latter are admitted by ticket. Men are seated beside their wives. Our audience is only mixed at communion seasons. I wish the elders could think it right to be always so, but they think that time is not yet.

The baptismal service comes first, ninety-nine adults are baptised. After that the Lord's Supper is administered and 534 of us partake. The service, although it lasts three hours, does not seem long, and the southerly breeze keeps the Church cool and comfortable. In the afternoon another service, at which thirty-five infants are baptised. They are unusually noisy, and we were glad to make the service short.

In the evening we had another service, at which an elder from Mr.Watt's district in the south, and another from Mr.Macmillan's district in the east spoke. They had come to help my two elders, Iavis and Lomai. Each spoke in his own language, so that every one gathered heard from one or other of the addresses of the Gospel in his or her own language. It is very possible that, as the result of Christianity on Tanna, a common language may evolve from our babel of dialects on this little island. I cannot understand the southern language a bit, but the East Tanna tongue I can follow fairly well in conversation.

As our Church was crowded out at all services, I got Lomai and one of the teachers to conduct a mothers' meeting under a tree at some distance from the Church. It was a grand idea, and one we must never give up. Why did I never think of it before?

It was a grand time, and the Lord was with us.

Lenakel now seems deserted; but away along the coast, on the mountains and in the bush, men, women and children will talk for long of the good Christmas of peace and joy at Lenakel.

Notes on 1909

In southern Italy, only three years after Mounts Etna and Vesuvius erupted, Messina was devastated by an enormous earthquake leaving 200,000 people dead with many missing. Liberal Chancellor Lloyd George implemented the start of the Welfare State and in April introduced a radical budget attacking the propertied classes. Germany was looming as a threat and the new tax was aimed at financing rearmament and the new old age pensions; naturally the Tory Party condemned this. Men were still attempting to conquer the skies and Louis Bleriot became the first person to fly across the Channel. The Suffragettes hadn't given up their fight for the vote and 14 were in prison, some using the tactic of going on hunger strike; the warders retaliated by having them force fed. In America, President Taft decided in favour of a naval base at Pearl Harbour – Japan was posing as a threat, and the Union of South Africa was proclaimed with Louis Botha as its Prime Minister.

The Bangor Council had been in correspondence with Mr.Andrew Carnegie who had agreed to donate money towards a free library and technical school, the Council would raise the rest. Bangor was certainly working on a number of improvements; what had been James Bowman's brickyard was, within the next few years to become Ward Park. Near the seafront in Southwell Road, a Mr.Gray had opened a large roller skating rink, complete with ample room for 300 skaters – or rinkers – and orchestral music was provided by skilful musicians, Bangor was known as the 'Brighton of the North' in those days. Travel abroad was reasonable, with a first class ticket by sea to America of £10 and an'assisted passage' to Australia of £3. Dickson's roses were as well known then as they are today, carrying off the Championship Challenge Trophy in London for the best 72 roses at the National Rose Society Show. In August the opening of the new reservoir at Ballysallagh was carried out by Mr.McMeeken,

Chairman of the Urban District Council, who turned on the water. It seems as if half of Bangor was there, all guests listed, with both sets of my grandparents present. My other grandfather was Manager of Bangor Gas Works. 13 acres, 15 roods and 3 perches of land was sold at Ballyholme for the high price of £595 and a tailor-made suit could be bought in the summer sales for 39/ 6 s. (about £2). At the end of the year the town completed its urban improvements by laying the foundation stone for Bangor Hospital. The Spectator also gives coverage to Grandfather's brother William, or WP the evangelist, who at that time was in Australia on an evangelical mission. My Grandfather had high hopes of his brother taking the steamer down to visit Tanna but William, as he said to his brother in a letter, 'would not like his influence confined to the limits of a small island.' I am sure my grandfather was disappointed.

Nowhere does the statement 'cleanliness is next to Godliness' become more accurate than on Tanna. My Grandfather introduced Public Health and once the people began to realize that by living in a clean, orderly fashion, they improved their health and way of life. Grandfather's idea was to lead by example and with hesitant steps and occasional back-sliding, the people could see with their own eyes that it was a far better way to live. Leprosy, another disease introduced to the islands from Queensland and New Caledonia, was becoming a serious problem on the island and Grandfather was the first person in Vanuatu to start a leper colony, to separate these poor people from the healthy and by living in decent surroundings so improve their condition.

There is a distinct lack of letters at the beginning of 1910 and the reason became apparent when I read the April edition of the Jottings. The Editor writes:

That a coal strike in Australia should affect the issue of Quarterly Jottings seems an exaggerated and dreamy suggestion – but it is true nevertheless.

Owing to a coal strike one of the monthly trips of the steamer had to be abandoned, and thus no mails could be sent or received. In consequence we are reduced to the task of Pharoah's bondmen – that of making bricks without straw.

But we have managed to get some stubble together, and trust the result may be not altogether flat and uninteresting.

Friends will notice with regret – a regret which we share keenly – that we have no report from West Tanna this time. We take it that the coal strike is responsible. We have, however, some recent photographs, and these have been made up into a double page inset suitable for framing. Possibly the pictures may to some extent make up the usual interesting word-pictures that Dr.Nicholson supplies of his work. In the next number we shall hope to have a big budget of Tanna news. (Jot.68 April 1910)

Isobel, May & Eileen on Sydney Bridge

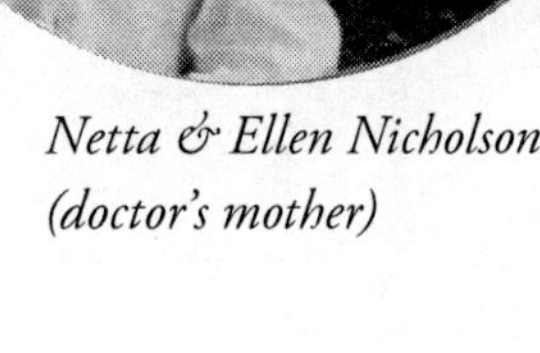

Netta & Ellen Nicholson (doctor's mother)

Netta, Sarah & Nellie

Dr. & Mrs. Nicholson, John and May

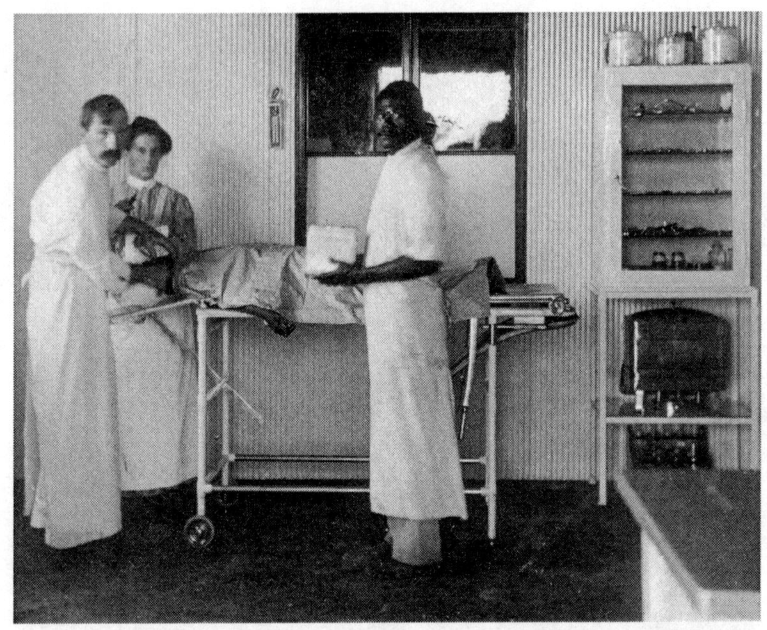

Operating Theatre, Dr. & Mrs. Nicholson & Nilauas

Isobel and John

Lomai

Hospital Staff, Nilaus on right

House Staff

Lenakel Hospital

Chapter IX – The Eighth Year

Hurricane!

In Jottings 69 July 1910 a letter dated March 1910 from my Grandfather is included:

NEWS FROM WEST TANNA

Lenakel,
March, 1910

After Christmas, we went to White Sands; Mrs.Nicholson and myself on horseback, the two elder children in boxes arranged as panniers across the back of another horse, and our goods packed on Mr.Macmillan's horse. Our baby slung on the back of her nurse and quite content with her mount. The new track is such a blessing, and makes the journey much shorter and pleasanter. The former narrow bush track rendered panniers or a packhorse, quite out of the question. We got over dry, a thing to be thankful for at this time of the year. While on the other side we visited Mr. and Mrs.Watt, and as many out- stations as possible; held services and had another "Christmas" for the people there. Anything in the nature of a holiday, the people call "Kirsmas".

As I had to cross and re-cross to attend my hospital, and nearly always in rain, I was very glad to get the family back to Lenakel after eight days' stay.

We are now within hoping distance of the cooler weather. Though tonight I have more perspiration than inspiration whilst writing to you – and believe me, the former weakens the latter considerably, indeed, almost destroys it.

This has been a real hot-wet season, night and day alike. Even the natives complained of the sun, and of the heat at night. And we had other things besides heat. The mosquitos have been very active. They appear to have worked in relays – I suppose to get in as much work as possible – the Stegomia have worked vigorously during each day, and the Culex and Anopheles were on active duty at night!

To exterminate mosquitoes in the rainy season is an impossibility, they breed in holes in the trees, in plants which can retain water, and amongst dense undergrowth. We put up a fairly good fight against them, and about our hospital and house reduced their numbers greatly; but we only touched the fringe of their breeding places.

Then earthquakes have been frequent. One night it was impossible to sleep. The noise and vibration continued till morning. One could only lie still and wonder how long the creaking and groaning house would hold out. But so far in March we had no hurricane; and that is something to be grateful for.

Fever we combated with a great measure of success by regular prophylactic doses of quinine. Every patient in the hospital and all the natives about us, got their weekly dose. Our house girls had light attacks, while Mrs.Nicholson and myself, Lomai and Nilauas, and almost all hospital patients, escaped. Those who did develop fever had only the one attack as they were thoroughly treated with quinine for days. It may be possible in the future, to institute a system by which our people can obtain free, or at a nominal cost, quinine during the fever months. As it is, each teacher is given a supply, but the people should have it themselves and learn to use it, to prevent fever during the worst months.

I have been occupied this hot season with a still greater problem of public health – the suppression of leprosy. I had succeeded in getting some cases isolated, but the matter has become pressing; and I have had to start educating and agitating on every possible occasion. Things are shaping well at present, and the people are awake and anxious. On the east coast, after some delay, the people set apart a piece of good land for a settlement. I told them they must select a situation with natural boundaries, good water supply, plenty of fruit trees, and good garden ground. These conditions led to the rejection of several sites; but now we have got leprosy settlements started on the east and west coasts, and expect to have another on the south coast soon. The people made gardens and built houses before any leper was asked to move in. About a dozen cases are segregated. No case is allowed in the settlement until I have certified this as necessary. If doubtful, the person is isolated from the village till I can have a further examination.

Leprosy has been introduced by returns from Queensland and New Caledonia – principally the latter place. It spreads rapidly amongst a semi-civilised people, in what way is not yet known. I have amputated a foot each in two cases. Whilst at the hospital they have a small house to themselves. It may be thought a dangerous proceeding to take such cases into a general hospital; but experience proves that, with cleanliness and care, such is not the case. I saw a leper in the Seamens' Hospital at Greenwich when in London. There will be a lot of work to do once the rains cease. With Mr.Watts and Mr.Macmillan's cooperation, I think we can get all pronounced cases segregated and the spread stayed.

The chiefs asked me what they would do in case a village refused to have a leper or lepers segregated. I told them that the only thing to do was to proclaim that village a leper settlement, and tabu it. This pronouncement has had a salutary effect already.

Segregation is not the terrible thing in our island that it would be in a civilised country. The lepers will live their ordinary lives; build houses, plant gardens, and their people will supply them with anything they want. Relatives can see them at their boundary fence and talk with them at a convenient distance. In time arrangements can be made for services, or if possible they may have schools of their own. The settlement will not cost the Mission funds anything, with the exception of medicine. I marked out a house for the lepers on the east coast settlement to commence to build; and have promised to visit them soon, to see what progress they are making. They seem delighted, and work will do them good. Their gardens are splendidly kept, and they said they did not know what they would do with all their food. The natives who came with me would not cross the boundary, but stood afar off whilst I went in. It is as well that it should be so at present.

We are expecting Mr.Macmillan back soon now; and it will be a relief to have his district off our hands, and to have his cooperation and help in our own work in the hospital.

You will be glad to know that the people have now raised over £140 for the extension of the Hospital, and are still going ahead. I have received £5 4s. during these last few days.

March 23rd. Mr.Macmillan has returned. He landed here and rode across to his home station, where the steamer would be calling in a few days. Two Frenchmen have landed in the south of Tanna to commence trading there. Mr.Macmillan kindly returned here a week later to help with operations, and we are delighted to have the opportunity of hearing the news from Australia.

We have also with us a Mr.Vance and his two assistants. These gentlemen are engaged upon the survey of the Mission lands and other British claims that have to be surveyed in anticipation of the Land Court which is shortly to be instituted.

On Sunday before Easter we had our harvest thanksgiving service. The people spent the Saturday decorating the Church; and it looked very well. Indeed our guests said they had not seen anything better in Australia. The season has been a productive one. Yams and taro will be in abundance. The coconut and orange trees are weighted with fruit, and all kinds of native fruits and nuts should be very plentiful.

With our united kind regards;
Yours sincerely, J.C.Nicholson

Lenakel
TANNA, New Hebrides.
April 10th 1910

My Dear Mother,

Seven years ago this Easter time we landed on Tanna and since then have seen many changes, but Easter Sunday morning showed us a change we did not think probable, our station was simply a wreck. If two Dreadnoughts had bombarded us all night they could not have done much more harm. We knew we were in for a blow and spent Saturday getting things ready and snug for it. I did not go to bed as the glass was fast falling and the roar of the wind terrific from ten p.m. to three a.m. I fought single- handed keeping doors and ventilators closed. Our doors are double, the outside ones are venetian doors and open out, the inner doors open in. The tremendous pressure of the wind suddenly relaxed would make the outer doors spring their bolts and bang outwards like the report of a rifle, the inner doors would then bend inwards and I had to crawl out on the lee side and get round and close the outer doors to prevent the inner ones from being burst. Isabel could not sleep much but the children slept well, I got drenched repeatedly. At 3 a.m. the glass was down to 27.76 and the needle waving about wildly. A ventilator burst open and the inside doors of the house between the rooms began to go. I was trying to hold the one upon which most depended and getting the worst of it. When the surveyors came out of their room with their help we nailed up and stayed the doors all round leaving one sheltered one to let us out in case we had to run. Natives began to arrive in a pitiful condition. Their house had been blown down and I found out that the hospital was gone and crawled across to look for the patients. 10 ft. sheets of galvanised iron were flying about like paper, wood, branches of trees, filled the air. Sometimes one had to lie down and hold on. I found one poor fellow stripped naked by the wind and wailing but could not lift him so wrapt him in a blanket lying handy and went back for help. But there was plenty of work for me with my own. We got the children and Isabel into the sitting room, one corner of which was dry, the rest of the house was like a shower bath, our guests thought we should clear for the cellar, but I determined to wait as there was no sign that the house was giving anywhere. We got bags and old canvas, anything and piled as much as we could on beds or tables and covered them up. We saved most of our books, pictures and odds and ends in this way. Beds and bedding were all wet and we had to keep the girls mopping up the sitting room floor to keep our one dry corner for the children. These thought that the whole matter was a great adventure. John was very quiet but May and Eileen laughed at all the topsy turvy. We waited for daybreak and when it came we were appalled at the sight which met our eyes, no church could be seen, trees bare and broken or thrown down, the new village on the hill wiped out, also the old one down below it, the hospital scattered everywhere, only the walls of the operating room standing, Lomai and Niauaus new houses at the back of the hospital torn to pieces and thrown all about, timber, sheets of iron, stretchers, were scattered to a quarter of a mile and more, boat and goat houses, fences, all smashed up. Our house had escaped with the exception of the front verandah but sheets of iron were flapping and one missing. Mr.Vance went up at great risk and nailed them down and then we all got a new sheet of iron and by carefully keeping its edge on to the wind got it up and nailed. One time it got turned and threw us about and was torn from our grasp. The natives were no help, dazed, dumbfounded, they could not move to get someone to help their women and children and patients. I at last got hold of a piece of wood and frightened them into their senses. I did not strike any but after that I was obeyed, they evidently thought it was better to risk the hurricane than my hurricane of a temper. I have a big copper urn for heating water at the hospital and we got this and its kerosene stove going and soon Isabel had hot tea flowing round and things began to brighten. We (the three surveyors and myself) outside, Isabel and her girls inside, worked right on till 3 p.m. to make our 60 or so refugees comfortable and to make the room for the children comfortable. By three I got dry clothes on and a hot drink, John and May got on a sofa beside me and after 24 hours straight on end I had the nicest sleep of my life. From six to nine we worked again making all fast for the night as we expected the last and worst blow from the west, face onto the house, but the glass was rising and at nine the crowded cellar and house was fast asleep. Daybreak came and though the wind was blowing strong yet we had sun instead of rain. The three white men started at once to put a new roof on the kitchen. It had only walls left. I got a horse and went about bucking up the people and got them started to build small houses out of the remains of their broken ones. By Saturday of that week we had nearly all under cover again. The kitchen roofed, also the operating room at the hospital and the frame of a temporary hospital put up (now ready for use). Our cellar has been the hospital till now. Two patients died from exposure or wounds, the others are doing well. In our district the death roll has reached 7 and many were hurt. Only one village had any houses left standing and its school was only damaged. It was built under a cliff and so escaped but here and at every outstation all schools and houses have been destroyed. We meet in the open air now, there is no shade as the trees are leafless. The people the

Sunday after the storm gave £7 towards a new church and seem keen to go ahead and do all they can to get a new church. They have given £140 for the hospital and I have £200 more on hand for it.

But I must get outside help to build a church, the people will be poor for years. They must do their best and will do it. The roads are all blocked with trees; I will not be able to get about for a long time. The leper work must be suspended and one will have to stick in at the hospital and station work.

John has been getting fever every now and then and suppurates every time he gets a scratch. May has kept well and Eileen is nearly her old self. John asked me one day 'Dadda am I only tired or am I sick for I am tired all the time'.

After the storm our garden was bare. Mr.Watt and Mr.Macmilan had their share but they got it off the sea, we got it shot down on us through gullies from the mountains and fared worse. The church at Port Resolution weathered it, also the dwelling house, not much damage there. Mr.Macmillan lost part of the roof of his kitchen, nothing more. The wooden churches at Kwamera and Weasisi both destroyed. The traders all suffered more or less, but their loss will be the want of copra for a year to come. Our damage as far as I can estimate it is near £2,000 but our mercies are not to be numbered, our house riding out the gale and our lives and limbs preserved. The church is an awful wreck, the platform furniture and organ are useless. If I could get men we could save many of the seats, others are smashed up, part of the church is right down the hill, beams of hardwood must have been flying about like straws, and I suppose I looked glum a bit, whilst surveying the barrenness and mess John said 'Never mind Dadda, things will grow again.' That word did me real good.

Isabel keeps well and cheery. These three guests are very nice and easy to do with in the house, but for Isabel's sake in the cooking line I will be glad when they move on. As they are engaged by the churches we have no option but to take them in. Still I think the church has no right to simply command us to board and lodge these men for two months as we must do and yet never offer to defray the expense of their keep. We cannot send out and get what we want here and it takes two months to get anything from Sydney so that housekeeping for unexpected guests requires some skill here and Isabel manages splendidly.

We did not get any Spectators last mail, you told us there were many things of interest in them and this makes our disappointment the greater. We are now wondering what news the steamer will bring from other Islands. It is possible they may have escaped as we seemed to be about the centre of the hurricane. We have escaped many of their blows.

As we now look forward to cooler weather you are looking for warmer. I hope you will all get through March without colds, it is a trying month in all parts of the World.

We unite in sending our love to Father, Netta and yourself.

Your affectionate son,
J.Campbell Nicholson

Ap. 21st. Steamer very late, not here yet but letters sent over from Port Resolution.

The hurricane was local, the Northern Islands did not get it. Many thanks for the receipt and all well.

Your affect. son
James

At the beginning of Jottings 69 (July 1910) the Editor writes:

The news in this number of Quarterly Jottings will be a startling reminder of the risks and difficulties of Missionary Work in the New Hebrides. Isolation, malaria and climatic conditions can to some extent be short of their terrors; but hurricanes and earthquakes defy mortal powers, and destroy the works of man with terrible swiftness and ease.

To put the bad news briefly, our First Mission Station on West Tanna has been destroyed!

Church and hospital, boathouse, fences; the neat little cottages that were visible evidences of the material benefits of Christianity; trees, crops, flowers, native villages, and even the very mould of the gardens, are one tangled mass of ruin and death. Worse still, men and women and little children, hurled away, crushed to death, or sorely wounded.

All destroyed except the Mission House, which, in God's Gracious Providence, was spared. It proved a sanctuary for the poor wounded patients, who used their little strength to crawl from beneath the debris of the sick wards of what had once been their clean and beautiful House of Healing.

These buildings must be reared again, and this means £1,000 at least. Can we raise £1,000 towards the cost? It is an urgent, instant need. He who gives quickly gives twice in this case.

We never make an appeal in these pages. We feel that the record of solid self-denying work is the best of all appeals. But this is an exceptional case, and we do appeal now; – earnestly, eagerly, and we are confident that we shall not appeal in vain.

Speaking of motorboats the friends at Tunbridge Wells and Weston-super-Mare who subscribed all the money for the motor boat for Dr.Nicholson's Station on West Tanna may be wondering how it is that they have not heard of the advent of their gift. We explained previously that Dr.Nicholson had decided to see the Paama boat before ordering his, as he required special adaptations for carrying sick natives to the Lenakel Hospital from comparatively long distances.

He was on the spot, and was as eager as ever for his motorboat, but somehow he had felt that it would be wiser and better in the end to "make haste slowly". Listen to the sequel. The West Tanna boathouse, as will be seen from the photographs, has been demolished by the hurricane. If the motorboat had been there its bow at least would have been smashed in, as it would have been longer than the Pioneer – which was just missed, by a few inches only, by a falling tree!

Is not this a new case for humble praise and thankfulness in the midst of the loss and havoc? No doubt our Missionary will carefully see, when the new motorboat does arrive, that the boathouse is sufficiently strong to protect it, and especially he will be careful that there are no big trees near by that might prove destructive agents. The "John G. Paton" will plough its way around Tanna on its mission of mercy we hope directly the more immediate needs of the new situation are met.

Lenakel, TANNA
April, 1910

At the beginning of March I wrote, "So far we have had no hurricane; and that is something to be very grateful for."

Now I must report that we have had a terrible hurricane, and yet we have very many things to be grateful for.

On Good Friday afternoon, I had to go up the coast in the boat. We had only got a few miles, when we realised that the wind and sea were rising, and that we could not make the passage we were bound for. So we put about, and started for home – beating against the wind and tide. Rowing was out of the question. After a hard struggle we got home at 8 p.m.

The barometer was falling slowly, and continued to do so all night and all the next day. In the afternoon, as the wind increased steadily, we made all things as snug and fast as we could. By evening branches of trees began to break under the wind pressure; and to save young trees we had to lop off the branches, and to cut down shrubs and roses to save them.

After darkness had set in, Mr.Vance and his two assistants (Mr.Smith and Mr.Leicester) and I, went round the hospital and Church, saw to the boat, and called on our neighbour, Mr.Worthington, to see if we could render him any assistance. The wind was now blowing at hurricane force, and the glass very low and still falling.

All retired but myself, and from 10 p.m. till 3 a.m. I was kept working. The roar of the wind was awful, and branches were continually striking the house. Ventilators and doors kept blowing open and the rain began to drip through the ceiling.

At 3 a.m. the glass was down to 27.76, and the needle was swinging about wildly. The pressure on one's eardrums was most uncomfortable.

Then the doors inside the house between the rooms began to burst their catches, and one wondered what the end would be. I was now joined by our three guests, who had risen; and we went round and nailed up doors and ventilators; some we found it necessary to stay up as well.

Our house girls came in to say their house was blown down. Other natives arrived with the news that their houses had been smashed up. Just then our kitchen roof was wrenched from its fastenings by the force of the wind and carried away.

The news then came that the hospital was missing; that the new houses and kitchens built by Lomai and Nilauas had been rooted up, and, to add to our anxieties we heard amid the roar of the wind, news that the Church was smashed to pieces.

As I had twenty-one patients in the hospital, I had to venture out to look for them.

It was an extraordinary experience. Sheets of iron and pieces of wood were carried past me as if shot out of a gun. Sometimes I had to lie down and crawl; and my lamp went out. I found one poor boy lying naked beside the ruins. Hurriedly wrapping him in a blanket which I found caught in some wood, I went back for help. Two of our guests returned with me, and we found the boy blown away into a fence and his blanket gone. We carried him into the cellar below our house, and there found some of the other patients who had escaped from the wrecked Hospital building.

Next we searched for Lomai's house but there was no sign of anyone, or anything but ruin and devastation. When we got back we found many more people had arrived. They said both old and new villages were completely destroyed.

I was urged to get Mrs.Nicholson and the children down to the cellar, in case the house might go; but I determined to wait a little. The only place in the house where a shower bath could be avoided was a corner of the sitting room, and into this were gathered wife and children.

We fought on till daybreak. The refugees were so beaten with wind and rain that they were quite dazed and unable to help; and the women and children were in a most distressful plight. When the day dawned what a revelation met our gaze. Our station was destroyed. Nothing remained but a tangled mass of trees and wreckage! No church. No hospital. No house but our own. We began to search for the patients; one little girl was found stuck in a wire fence and buried under sheets of corrugated iron and pieces of wood! She was terribly cut and bruised. A poor woman had been struck in the eye by a piece of wood, the rest of the patients, so far as we could ascertain, had crept into the cellar unhurt.

Mrs.Nicholson, with the aid of a kerosene stove, was able to serve hot tea all round. Mr.Vance, and his assistants, at great risk, got on our roof and replaced a sheet of iron which had been blown away, and nailed down others which were flapping about. If they had not done so we should have lost at least the roof of the house.

At this time the glass began to rise, and the wind had swung round to the north. Rain lashed us like whips as we went about making people and things snug for the final blow, which we expected from the west. By the time we got into dry clothes it was 3 p.m. The glass continued to go up, and the wind kept steadily in the north. By night our cellar was full of people. Old bags, pieces of canvas and sails were pressed into service; and the people had so far recovered that Lomai conducted a service.

We had to make up beds somehow. Every mattress but one was soaked through. By 9 p.m. we had so secured ourselves that we slept – exhausted with fatigue – and heedless of the roar of the wind and the swish of the rain. We awoke at daybreak to find the rain gone and the wind considerably abated.

When the sun rose a terrible scene of desolation met our eyes. We seemed to be in another country. Before the hurricane the trees were heavy with foliage and fruit of all kinds. Now they were stripped bare of both, broken to pieces, or torn up by the roots.

Our hospital was lying a shapeless mass of ruins. The operating room alone was standing, but it was roofless. The Church was smashed to matchwood and hurled in three directions. It must have burst, and then been blown to right and left. The new village on the hill blown to bits, and the old one on the level, all gone but two houses, and these but shapeless masses.

The country had been swept as by fire; and even the earth in the garden had been piled up here and there by the force of the wind. With the exception of the front verandah, our house had escaped. We owe this to double doors and having no gable ends. The roof is hipped bungalow fashion.

But it was not a time for moping or lamenting. I got the natives to begin at once to build kitchens out of the ruins of their houses; and tried to show them there was a bright side to it all, as there really is. I rode about hunting up laggards, and soon they were as busy as bees, and laughing and putting a good face on the event.

The one very sore point was the church. They expected me to cut up badly about it; but I told them it meant they would have to build a better one, and that meanwhile we might manage a school out of the ruins of the old one. They said "Ooh nuparhien" (Yes, truly), and seemed greatly relieved.

I rode down to Mr.Worthington; and had great work getting the horse through. His house had been badly damaged, the store and kitchen gone. Coconut trees had been snapped by the hundred, and coconuts and oranges were lying about everywhere. It will take a year to tidy things up. Our boathouse was wrecked, but the boat escaped. Our goathouse and yards destroyed, and five goats had been killed by a rafter from the hospital. Everywhere sheets of iron, warped and twisted, were lying about, even a quarter of a mile away. Rafters and studs of hardwood were stuck about the ground like so many spears. One gable of the hospital, about half a ton in weight, had been blown right over the trees down the hill. Fences were down; and about twenty acres of maize, in all stages of growth destroyed.

As one said, our seven years' work seemed to be blotted out in a night. Not so, however, for the work that counts is not in buildings or stations, but in the hearts and lives of the people. They said, "As soon as we get up houses for shelter, we must begin and make all the coconuts which are down into copra, so that we may have money for a new Church and hospital; for there will be no coconuts again for a long time." I said, "What about food?" "Oh! we shall get enough somehow, and there is always better health when there is not too much food."

Whilst I was riding about, our guests had been busy re-roofing the kitchen, and have worked early and late roofing the operating room, and building the frame for a temporary hospital, which the people will thatch. We count it one of our great mercies at this time to have had these friends with us.

On Monday night the woman, whose orbit had been pierced, died. It was too late to bury her, and, indeed, we had no place in which to lay her dead body, so Lomai and Nilauas prepared the body for burial, and tied it up in a tree out of the reach of dogs.

On Tuesday the boy died. The girl so badly wounded we chloroformed and spent an hour cleansing and sewing up her terrible gashes. Two women and a man were killed by the fall of their houses. A woman running for shelter sank down and was found dead in the morning. A woman carrying one child and leading another was crossing a stream when she stumbled, and the child tied to her back slipped off; she stooped to catch it and lost her hold of the other, and both were swept away and mourned as lost, but the elder of the two was found twenty-four hours afterwards. The poor little thing had been caught in some branches, and had crawled along them to land. The baby has not been found. One man had been killed by a falling tree; and we have heard of ten or so wounded.

All our outstations, with one exception have been completely destroyed. The latter was built under a cliff, and only part of the houses and native church were destroyed. All the heathen villages have been wrecked.

The people fled in many cases, to the beach, others to caves. One house here in the old village which stood was filled with people; they carried beams of wood inside and stayed it up, and then men, women and children hung on to posts and rafters all night. Iavis was amongst them, and said it would have been lifted but for their weight.

The absence of foliage makes the country look like home in winter. We never saw the trees all bare before. The force of the wind must have been terrific; beams of hardwood, twelve feet by five inches wide and three inches thick were carried a hundred yards from the hospital; and studs four inches by four inches and twelve feet long, we found sticking three feet and more into the ground on the levels below. A tin dish which was hanging in the kitchen we found near the sea.

But the photographs will tell you more than anything I can write.

I expect if we went into details the loss at Lenakel would not come far short of £1,500

If our house had gone the wreck would have been complete. And yet our hearts well up with gratitude; and we are prone to speak of what might have been. I dare say, as the days go on, we will feel our losses more; but I trust we will not lose our gratitude to God, who was our Rock and our Shield, for that would be the greatest loss of all.

Besides, as my little boy consoled me by saying when looking at the bare garden, "Never mind, dadda, things will grow again." Yes! Church, hospital, village, all will grow again, gradually grow, and the latter will be better than the former, I trust. It is just seven years ago since we landed here on an Easter Monday. What an anniversary of our arrival!

We held our Sabbath service, a week after the hurricane, under the leafless banyans, and took up our first collection for the new church. It amounted to £5 19s. and that, together with £54 that the people had raised for enlarging the Church, gives us a good start for our new one.

With our united kind regards,

Yours sincerely,
J.CAMPBELL NICHOLSON

JOTTINGS 70 OCTOBER 1910

In the opening page of the Jottings the Editor reports:

We understand that Dr. and Mrs.Nicholson go to Australia in December or January next for a short furlough. After their anxieties, and the rush of work following the hurricane, an invigorating change is essential. While in Australia the Doctor intends to supervise the building of his new motorboat, and to get thoroughly acquainted with the working of the engine.

Their rest will be darkened by one heavy cloud, in the fact that they will be leaving their eldest child of six in the Colonies for his education, as well as for his health's sake; he has not been clear of fever for the past seven or eight months.

Lenakel, TANNA
July, 1910

"Since the hurricane," "Before the hurricane." With ourselves and our natives these have become almost daily sayings. I trust we may never have another such hurricane. Since the disaster our work has consisted of cleaning up, repairing,

rebuilding, reorganising and encouraging. Most providentially a carpenter, Mr.Robertson, from Melbourne, arrived a month after the hurricane. He came to build the boathouse for the launch, and to make preparations for her arrival, as well as to enlarge the Church and Hospital. But that programme was not to be at present; in its stead work sufficient for two or more years lies before us.

Our first and most urgent task was to collect the wreckage and erect temporary buildings for the Hospital, etc. With this work we had progressed satisfactorily when the Synod meeting at Port Resolution had to be attended. We left Mr.Robertson to continue the building at Lenakel, and embarked to engage in the business of Synod, and to enjoy the fellowship of our fellow labourers, some of whom we had not met for over three years.

Port Resolution is redolent with the memories of the early years of our Mission. The Autobiography of Dr.J.G.Paton has made the place known throughout the world – wherever the command of our Lord is heard and obeyed. But Port Resolution is also associated with John Williams of the London Missionary Society, for it was here that his last service in life was done for Christ. He settled Samoan teachers on Tanna, and passed on to give up his life for Christ on Erromanga the next day. Turner and Nesbit settled here shortly afterwards, but only for seven terrible months, and they passed on to Polynesia for many years of fruitful service there. Then Dr.Paton and his heroic wife came; the latter with her infant son to stay till the resurrection. Four years – the travail of which is known to all readers of his Autobiography – completed the labours of Dr.Paton. He was driven out never to settle here again. I am wrong in saying completed the labours, for when Dr.Paton settled on Aniwa, fourteen miles distant, his hope and aim and prayer was that from there he might yet do something for the salvation of the Tannese who had expelled him. This hope was realised in his lifetime, and Aniwan teachers have taken a large part in evangelising Tanna.

Here, at Port Resolution, is the little graveyard, and I can do no better than quote what the late Mrs.Watt wrote about it in her letters, which are published in book form, and should be read by all who are interested in Tanna and its stubborn resistance to the Gospel since 1839.

Mrs.Watt writes: "I know not all who lie in this little 'God's acre,' but I know some. Here Mr.Johnston rests, having only put his hand to the plough. The club of the savage did not break his skull, but he never recovered from the shock he received when he saw what a narrow escape he had had. Here lies also the first Mrs.Paton and her infant son. Here, too, several native teachers rest, and a goodly number of little children, and here was buried all that remained of a trader who was blown up with his own gunpowder while in a state of intoxication. So shattered was he that only one foot and his chin were left to be buried. Near him lies Dana who, while out shooting on the Sabbath, accidentally shot himself and died of tetanus.

"Close by we buried poor Bell, who was shot by the Tannese. What a strange medley, gathered from many parts of the world, Scotland, England, Nova Scotia, Germany, Raratonga and Aneityum. The helpless infant and the sinner old in wickedness: all awaiting the resurrection morning."

Now Mrs.Watt herself has passed to her well earned rest, after twenty-five strenuous, years, many of them, terrible years' work for Tanna, and her body also lies at Port Resolution.

It is hard today to realise these former things. They have passed away. On this Sabbath there is peace, intertribal warfare and cannibalism are no more; members of all the tribes of the South and visitors from all parts of Tanna are gathered together in the open air to commemorate the death of the Prince of Peace. On the Wednesday all are landed. What a bustle! Two score of willing converts shoulder the bags, boxes and bedding, and by evening all are settled in their different quarters. The men in native built barracks, and the ladies and children in Mr.Watt's house.

The natives have contributed yams, taro, bananas and fowls for our sustenance, and all arrangements for our comfort have been made to the point of perfection by Mr.and Mrs.Watt.

On Wednesday evening Synod was opened, and from that till the evening of the following Monday we were kept at it, morning, noon and night. It was a large Synod, only three members absent, and these all at their stations, none being on furlough.

"It is hard for you to realise what Synod means to us all, and even to our children. It is for the latter often their first introduction to the society of white children. The ladies have a Synod peculiarly their own, and into its details the mere man dare not enter. This year there was no time for a picnic or any social function except a few hours one evening for what we call our Moderator's reception."

Our Moderator this year, as was fitting, was Mr.Watt, and a note of sadness pervaded the gatherings owing to the fact that it was his last year with us. After forty-one years' strenuous service he resigns at the end of this year. Mr.Watt was the Moderator of the first Synod, and for twenty-four years was its Clerk.

The weather was not too good, strong southerly winds accompanied by rain brought colds and revived latent fever. Mrs.Nicholson suffered from her first attack this year, so that when the steamer came and wished to take us home via Aneityum, with the chance even then of not being able to land at Lenakel, we decided to try and get home some other way. We had hoped the Captain would consent to take us direct to Lenakel, a four hours' run, instead of keeping us on board in such rough weather for a night and a day.

"On Saturday, Mr.Robertson sent us across the following disquieting news: 'Dear Doctor, If you have experienced the earthquake anything like ourselves, you will be in measure prepared for what I am going to tell you. The Temporary Hospital has suffered badly. The instrument case was thrown flat on its face and all the glasswork smashed. The big bottles came to grief. The pipe from the tank to the wash-hand basin was severed, but I managed to stop the water with rags. The dispensary is a very sorry sight: liquids, tabloids, powders and glass all mixed up in a mess on the floor. The house got rather a bad shake, down each side of the brick piers the joints have started, one pier is down altogether, blocks of concrete have fallen. The store room floor is covered with tins, broken bottles, loaf sugar, etc. The glass churn is no more. The chest of drawers in your bedroom is lying face down on the children's bed. The shelves in the study are minus many of the books, only some pictures are down in the sitting room. I suppose you will think me a Job's comforter, telling you all this. I am sorry enough for doing so. I don't want a second dose of

what we had."

"The sea continued rough and prevented us getting down to White Sands by boat, from whence we intended to cross the island by horse to Lenakel. On Saturday morning, however, the sea looked a little better, though not good enough for ladies and children to go. Mr.MacMillan, Mr.Woolacot (the Solicitor who is seeing to our land deeds) and I therefore set out. Our boat was heavily laden with Mr.Macmillan's goods, which the steamer had been unable to land at White Sands. We had a fair wind, and the boat raced along at an exhilarating speed, but when we neared the passage through the barrier reef at White Sands things wore a different aspect. However, nothing was said, and the boat put in line with the guiding marks on the shore. Mr.Macmillan was steering, and I was standing holding on to the stay and mast to give the course – when sitting the guiding marks could not be seen for the heavy seas. A tremendous roller caught us and we rushed on its crest into the passage. We felt our chance of getting through was one in a hundred. The smooth water was near, the sunlit beach was but fifty yards off, but we were caught in the terrible backwash of water, which in big seas always rushes out through these openings or passages in barrier reefs. Our good boat lost way, then stopped, and was sucked back towards the passage. I turned and saw the next roller coming like a wall of water towering over us. It blanketed us, and our sails hung limp. I slipped off my oilskin coat and saw Mr.Woolacot kick off his boots. Hold tight all! It was on us, our boat rose a little, but not enough. The waves swept over those in the stern and the boat filled, we touched coral and the helm sprang away. Mr.Woolacot jumped over the stern, the right thing to do in surf on an open beach, but the most dangerous thing one can do in a passage where there is the dreaded outrush of water. Another roller, and after that confusion! One shout I remember, a young teacher of Mr.Macmillan's yelled, 'get hold of our Missi,' and he and another stood by him. As for myself, I could only laugh for joy because Mrs.Nicholson and the children were not with us. I remembered the time we were both thrown on the reef in our early days. I next found myself swimming for the shore with my coat under my arm, but duty called, and I swam back to see if any needed help. Mr.Macmillan had been caught in the cross current, but Lamai, the teacher I mentioned, and another man, were on each side of him. Mr.Woolacot had, fortunately,

got on a high growth of coral, two natives were with him, and he swam to the boat, calling loudly for his box of deeds and papers.

Soon the canoes were launching, and Mr.Carruthers, who had witnessed the accident from the beach, came out in his dinghy. The water seemed alive with men, women and children, who had swam out to help. They had been watching the coming of the boat, crying out to warn us off, but the waves hid them and drowned their shouts.

Waiting the inevitable, they hid their faces. But now that they found us all safe, there was joy and laughter. They were swimming here and there after packages and boxes, bags of rice, tins of kerosene. So far as I know only one oar and the rowlocks were lost. The boat, which had turned over, was righted as soon as the mast and sails were got off her, and was pulled up on shore unhurt.

Soon afterwards I started for home, quite satisfied with the day's experience, and not a bit desirous of any more. The horse I rode I had lately broken in. When we began to ascend the mountain rain came on. I laid the reins on the horse's neck and unstrapped my coat from the saddle and swung it round to put it on. Instantly I found myself lying on the ground, and the horse rushing up the track. Metaphorically kicking myself for forgetting the horse was young, I gathered myself up and for the second time taking my coat under my arm, started after him. He waited every now and then to see that I was coming, and then went on. For about a mile uphill this went on, at length he got tired and let me mount him and away we sped.

Arriving at Lenakel, my first concern was the house. Mr.Robertson had understated the damage to the foundations. Several brick piers were thrown in at the back and out at the front. It will take some time to get lime burnt and the walls built again. The house had been cleared up inside. About the station there are several cracks in the ground, but not very serious. Mr.Robertson said the ground could be seen moving, and the trees swayed and rustled as in a big wind. The sea was agitated, but there was no tidal wave. The natives rushed in all directions; our cook left the kitchen and got up a tree, not knowing what to do. It was well the lamps were not lighted, as several were thrown down; the glasses in others were broken off by the vibration. The dispensary suffered badly, the loss of drugs is great. Our large underground tank is empty and broken, but can be repaired.

The earthquake caused landslips, and parts of the roads across were so shaken that the ground was quite soft. Some heathen near Lenakel were drinking kava when the earth beside them fissured on two sides and gave them a great fright. The natives tell me that yams in the ground were broken by the shaking and that it is thirty years since there has been so severe an earthquake.

But we have many things to cheer us. The Missionaries gave us their Communion collection for our Church, amounting to £7 14s; the members of Mr.Macmillan's Church gave us £6 5s. 7d, though they are building a new Church of their own. Then, too, it was fortunate we were absent during the earthquake. Mrs.Nicholson and the children have had quite enough of hurricane and earthquake experience to last for some time.

It was with real pleasure we welcomed Dr. and Mrs.Taylor to the Islands. I had met them both at home. They are to be settled right in the most northern station, so our opportunities of meeting will be few. We are glad to have fellow countryman and countrywoman to help us to represent old Ireland away here.

Yours sincerely,
J.CAMPBELL NICHOLSON

Lenakel, TANNA
September, 1910

Earlier in the year I had looked forward to this cool season, believing that it would bring leisure for a more systematic visitation of the outstations, and itineration amongst the heathen. We had planned to have a week or fortnight of Bible study with all the teachers, and arrangements were made to develop the Hospital and Public Health work. All these hopes and plans were, however, upset by the hurricane. God knows what is best, and one can see now that His way is right. To reach green pastures and still waters the shepherd must sometimes lead through rough and arduous paths.

It has been a real pleasure to see the people working to rebuild their villages and churches, and this at the time when their new gardens require to be made. As you know, a new garden is made every year. Fresh ground is cleared, burnt and tilled and heaped into mounds for the yams. This means a lot of work, and some of it, I think, unnecessary, but the people are keen experts on growing yams, and take a great pride in it.

In my letters last year I spoke of our gatherings at the different villages. Sometimes we went to the opening of new Churches, and sometimes to celebrate the completion of an absolutely new village.

The hurricane made a clean sweep of everything; and lately we have been repeating our visitations, to see yet newer Churches and villages that have sprung up. The first village to invite us was Lehang, where Simon is the teacher. Mr.Robertson, our carpenter, came with me. We sailed north on the Saturday, camping out on the beach for the night. We had a splendid gathering of the people from the neighbouring villages as well as the people of Lehang. As the Church could only accommodate one hundred and thirty, we had a short dedicatory service inside, and then had two services in the open air.

This is the third village these people have built since we came to Tanna.

I should say that in all these visits the elders and our lads in training are our companions.

Our next trip was to Iakit in the south. Neropo is the teacher at Iakit, and is in the forefront as a builder. His Church is better than any of the others for finish. The village is a picture, flowers bloom all about. Our surprise came this time in the shape of paint. In the old days the people painted their faces with coloured earth mixed with coconut oil. Nerepo and his people carried out this idea in a new and better fashion by painting the woodwork of their houses with this homemade material, giving them a brightness and finish. We had a splendid service, and a very happy time. I wish we could conduct some British visitors to inspect Iakit.

Ikamar came next. It is only about two miles from Lenakel. Kati is teacher here, and Nerro is his wife. Nerro was our nurse and Kati was our cook. Nerro is the "better man" of the two. She had helped me as nurse in some cases in the hospital, and when our boy was born she came to us. According to native custom Nerro, as nurse, is the "mother" of our three children, and a real mother she has been to them. While we were at home Kati and Nerro filled a vacant outstation as teachers; but after our return Nerro wanted the children again. Kati preferred teaching to cooking, but Nerro's tears won the day. As they had had no children of their own for years we felt they were fixtures, and were glad to have them to look after our four housegirls as well as our own children. But the unexpected generally happens, and Nerro gave up our children without a tear to nurse a little daughter of her own called after ours, Eileen.

Ikamar being near, I had worked it from Lenakel, with the help of assistant native teachers. The bulk of the tribe are heathen, and we had persuaded those won over to come down to the coast and begin to build a new village. As the village had grown, I felt it time to settle a teacher with them, and asked Kati and Nerro to go. They did so, and are doing good work. The people have rallied round them, and it was to open their Church that we went down this time. The building is small, but in some ways it is the best. The frame is very neat and strong; the thatch was all sewn together by the women before it was put on; and part of the walls are wattled, and plastered with clay – finished with what I took to be very fine lime. I was surprised to learn that Kati and some of the Ikamar people had gone to Kati's mountain home in the north (more than fifteen miles away) to fetch this white substance which they call white clay. I did not know there was such a thing on Tanna. The village proper is not built yet, but we have marked it out, and now that the Church is finished the people are going to begin building their new village in earnest.

Melibus is an inland village where Lahwa is the teacher. An excellent teacher, too, who, with a little training, would become a first class carpenter. He had a surprise for us all. He had made a wooden floor for this Church and twenty excellent seats, which would not have disgraced a Mission Hall at home. He, and his people had felled large trees. He then got a big cross-cut saw, wedges and a plane from me, and they split the trees into planks, adzed and planed them, and made pews with inclined backs. If they had known about book rests I believe they would also have added them. Mr.Robertson, as an expert carpenter, was delighted, and said it was a marvel of work for untrained men, and that a trained man with such primitive tools (no square or rule, and trees freshly felled to get timber with wedges and an axe) could not have done better.

The effort will do the people good, and I expect to see them beginning to make furniture now that it has been shown what can be really done with the material at their disposal. (Jot.71 Jan.1911)

With kind regards,

Yours sincerely,
J.CAMPBELL NICHOLSON

The April 1911 Jottings gives an excerpt from a letter written to the Mission Fund from my Grandfather of their trip from the islands to Australia; unfortunately there is no date of when he left, but it must have been October:
The steamer came all too quickly. The saying of goodbye was not easy on account of the uncertainty of what was to be done about the French recruiters firing on the natives and the natives returning the fire. But what the natives felt most was the ordeal of saying farewell to our little boy. His nurse, Nerro, wept as if her heart would break, and the girls and women followed suit. The men also turned their heads every now and then when the tears began to be too visible. John simply could not say goodbye, but crept into the boat and hid his face. He seemed to realise it was his final farewell to home and to Tanna, although we had not told him so. He had lost his playmates, Bertie and Hamish Macmillan, they had gone away and their father had returned without them.

Our passage up was a rough one and we were unable to get ashore on either Norfolk Island or Lord Howe. We were glad at last to sight the Australian coast and to glide into the quiet waters of Sydney Harbour. The weather has been cool and to us, bracing. As usual our fever comes with us and Mrs. Nicholson and the children have had several attacks. I escaped. People tell us that we are not like those they expect to see coming from the tropics." Further on, referring to the troubles with the French, he says: *"As I did not get any news from the Islands north of Tanna, I do not know what has been done about the French recruiting. My teacher and the other native taken with him have been returned to Tanna and no further investigations have been made on Tanna, so I suppose matters have been settled; but if there was any attempt at justice, the Recruiters should be punished." (Jot.72 Apr.1910)*

Assembly Hall,
MELBOURNE, Victoria.
Nov. 13th 1910

My Dear Mother,

Yesterday I received your letter of the 9th ult. I am glad that Father has no pain but am anxious to hear how he is again. What a lot and a variety of visitors he has. I wish we could call too, but it can't be helped, it will not be long till our trip home is due.[1]

Mrs.Robinson has us all in her house, she is the heart of kindness and tries to make out it is a case of us obliging her, her son and daughters are all very good to us and the children. The grounds are so nice and they have a croquet lawn and a tennis court and plenty of room for the children to do as they like. Isabel had a smart attack of fever but is now better; Eileen is also much brighter. I thought she was going to develop acute dysentery but it yielded to treatment and feeding. She was very peevish and petted on her mother but is now glad to see and go with anybody.

We have been here a week and had a fine passage down in a splendid steamer. I have been kept very busy but have managed to get tennis and bathing with Jack Robinson. I had an interview with the Minister for External Affairs and he was very sympathetic and gave me some good news. He said the Australian Government would not permit the French to get the Islands and unofficially said that the French Judge who had been going for the Missionaries was going on furlough and would not be coming back. The French Captain of Police who took my teacher has also been removed.

John and May are awfully pleased with Melbourne. I think John will be content to stay after the parting is over. We have got a very nice home with five other boys, all Missionaries' sons. I liked the lady and the boys and when John gets interested in school he will be alright. I feel it bad whenever I think about it and Isabel has her own share. However it is for Christ and His Cause.

I need not write too big a letter as I will write soon again. With our united love to you all,

Your affect. son,
J.Campbell Nicholson

P.S. I have had two weekday meetings and a church service on Sunday but am now off till February. They have a big programme planned. Many speak of Willie.

J.C.N.

Assembly Hall,
MELBOURNE.
22nd Dec. 1910

My Dear Mother,

I received your welcome letter but although I had been half expecting to hear that father's eye had to be removed to save the sight of the other one, yet we were a bit cut up when the news came. I had told Isabel that the delay in removing it meant either that the injury had not been so great or else was extremely dangerous for the sight of the other. I do hope it has healed well and that the sight of the other is unimpaired and we wish we were with you for Christmas.

We are staying on with Mrs.Robinson. It seems awful imposing ourselves on a friend like this but she makes out that we are doing her a favour as her son and the governess is away and she likes to have a man in the house and the children for Christmas. It will be a fine Christmas for the bairns, they are full up about Santa Claus, and John mourns because he has only socks. The girls tell him they will give him a pillow case. We go to Hobart at the beginning of the year, 8 adults and three children, we should have a good time. The weather is splendid, very often cold, but we complain less about it than the Melbournites.

The people in Melbourne have been very kind to us and we have joined the Church here for John's sake as much as our own. The Minister is a splendid man and has the Missionaries' children every Sunday night at his house. I think I told you that Miss Murray has Dr.Crombie's boy and three boys from Korea. When we come back from Hobart I have to travel about on deputation work. John and May are going to a Kindergarten school and we will all be living at a very nice boarding house near here.

I have been busy seeing about the motor launch and have at last got it nearly settled. I am getting it built here and will send you a photo of it in March if all goes well. We have had no more fever and look well if all that is said to us is true. I am in better health than I have been in 4 years. John is very inquisitive, it is nothing but questions all the time, but he is learning a lot. May and Eileen are beginning to speak English but amongst themselves it is always Tannese.

Willie will be home by this time. I am glad he is to have a month. He should take a complete rest. I hope father and you go for drives and see your friends.

We are waiting anxiously for news from the islands. I wonder what the French have been up to. Now I must close praying that you all may have a happy Christmastide and a New Year of peace and prosperity.

With much love from us all to you all,

Your affect. son,
J.Campbell Nicholson

Grandfather's concern regarding the French is evident in the previous three letters and the constant protestations of the *Jottings* and Christian people at home bore fruit when questions were asked in Parliament:

THINGS POLITICAL IN THE NEW HEBRIDES

Our protest in the January Jottings brought encouraging sympathy from many influential quarters.

The following question and answer in the House of Commons are a direct result:

House of Commons

15th February, 1911

Question: Viscount Castlereagh asked the Secretary for the Colonies "whether his attention has been called to the reports of the Bishop of Melanesia and the Presbyterian Missionaries on the violation of the Anglo-French Convention in several of the New Hebrides Islands by the sale of liquor and cartridges to the natives, and by the kidnapping of women and the recruiting of children for illegal purposes; and will he say what action he proposes to take in the matter?

Mr.Harcourt: "My attention has been drawn to the reports to which the Hon. Member refers, and I am in communication with the High Commissioner for the Western Pacific on the question of the liquor traffic, and of alleged improper recruiting in New Hebrides. I am fully alive to the importance of the matter."

We learn also that M.Colonna, the French Judge, and at one time Acting French Resident, has gone on prolonged furlough; and that there have been, so far, no reprisals on Tanna.

Dr. Nicholson made some frank and fully sustained public statements on the situation when in Sydney; and was backed by public opinion. The Bishop of Melanesia and others also emphasised the undoubted fact of the illegal sale of grog in the Islands, and the constant troubles arising from cases of illegal recruiting – especially of women.

The Land Court has been formally constituted at Vila, and conciliatory speeches were made by the President and British and French Judges. The real work of investigating rival land claims was to commence at the end of March. The operation is beset with tremendous difficulties. Verbal native evidence is certain to be discounted, but such evidence is of vital_importance; and every detail will require to be sifted and tested with the utmost acumen, care and patience.

Upon the finding of the Court the future of the Islands largely depends.

May God defend the right.

This excerpt appeared in *Jottings* 72 April 1911.

Notes on 1910

Severe floods heralded in the New Year in Paris with the River Seine running at three times its normal 7ft level and there were growing fears that the Louvre would be flooded. Across the Atlantic the first film was made in Hollywood and Mark Twain died, only this time the reports were not 'greatly exaggerated' as he had put it himself when an erroneous report had appeared before. Dr.Crippen became the first criminal to be caught with the aid of radio as he and his mistress attempted to escape by ship across the Atlantic and in Russia, a shocking epidemic of cholera had swept the country killing 60,000 people. In August, at the age of 90, Florence Nightingale died with many mourners lining the London streets as horses drew her hearse to St. Paul's Cathedral. In Britain the country was beset with workers' strikes. Dockers nationwide were given 24 hours notice of a lock-out as were cotton workers in Manchester. In Wales the Cavalry was called in to the Rhondda coalfields. On a sad note, December brought a fearful mining disaster at a Lancashire coalpit with 350 feared dead.

At the beginning of the year in Bangor a notable event took place: the opening of the New Library and Technical College. The Marquis of Londonderry performed the opening ceremony at the premises in Hamilton Road that was attended by many well-known names of Bangor. My great-grandfather, at the venerable age of 80, was still serving on the Council and lodged a complaint to the Council, that at 8pm. the lamplighter for the Princetown District had not lit the lamps on the Princetown Road. It was agreed that the lamplighter should be warned that if he could not light the lamps at the proper time his services would be dispensed with. The motorcar was still in its infancy and there were big crowds to watch a hill climb competition for motorcars and motor cycles held in Central Avenue in April. In May Edward VII died. Full details of the funeral were given in the Spectator, with columns and advertisements lined in black and Mehargs advertised mourning hats. The Urban District Council adjourned their monthly meeting after an eloquent speech by the Chairman in deference to the late King. Mid-summer saw the arrival of Sir Thomas Lipton's 'J' Class yacht Shamrock for the annual Royal Ulster Yacht Club Regatta. Smaller 15 and 12 metre boats racing as well – made them big in those days! The glorious weather in July saw the town filled with 60,000 people and Pickie swimming pool had a record 936 people through the turnpike. Fashion saw the arrival of the hobble skirt, measuring one to one and a half yards wide it was considered suitable for walking but not for tennis. On October 7th a huge gathering attending the opening of the new hospital by Lady Clanmorris. Grandfather's brother WP, was in America when his wife gave birth to a son at the beginning of December in Bangor, but he arrived home at Christmas for 10 days before setting off again on another evangelical tour.

In Jottings 70, Oct.1910, there is an interesting article by J.Nairn Marshall of Glasgow who visited Lenakel that year:

"On New Year's day morning, armed with fraternal greetings from the John G.Paton Mission Fund Committee to the brethren labouring in the New Hebrides, we steamed out of the far-famed Sydney Harbour for a two months' cruise. If it was hot on shore it was cool and stormy enough at sea. The steamer made calls at the interesting islands of Lord Howe and Norfolk, the latter island showing the roofless ruins of the old convict prison, which, if all stories are true, was often the scene of horrid cruelty. One of the first places of call after clearing Vila was Lenakel, Tanna. It was early morning, but not too early for the energetic Dr.Nicholson. He came on board at once, secured his mail, and invited Rev.William Mackay and myself to breakfast. One of the most delightful features of a cruise amongst the New Hebrides is that there are so many opportunities of landing and enjoying the warm and hearty hospitality of the Missionaries and many of the traders.

A considerable group of natives were on the shore awaiting our arrival. First we were introduced to Lomai, of whom we had read and heard so much. He is a man who does not disappoint one. With quiet, self-possessed dignity, and yet with open- hearted frankness, he shook hands and welcomed us warmly in a few words of English.

The first glimpse of Lenakel is very beautiful. It is not characteristic of the New Hebrides exactly, for the luxuriant tropical growth is kept in check, and stretching up from the shore is a magnificent lawn, shore and sea. Dr.Nicholson's horse, held by a boy, waited restlessly. Directly the Doctor mounted, the horse galloped up the track as if all the lives on the island depended on speed. We followed leisurely, passing a tolerably clean and tidy village by the way. At the Mission House we were heartily welcomed by Mrs.Nicholson and her chil-

dren, and were soon seated at a fine fresh homely breakfast, which tasted all the better after the more monotonous menu of the ship's table.

We then accompanied the Doctor on his round to the hospital patients and the hospital. The hospital is small for the work it is doing, but fortunately the patients do not lie in bed during the day if they can possibly move about, so that often there is not a single person inside, and only one or two resting on beds on the verandah. The other beds are all taken out, and left all day in the bright hot sunshine, and thus disease germs are killed and the bedclothes freshened.

Many of the cases were very interesting, a little girl had her arm in splints, and as the Doctor moved the stiffened fingers, a silent tear trickled down the dusky cheeks. A man was brought in with some broken ribs, and here and there in his back were small holes made 'to let the pain out'. Another girl came and begged for re-admission. Tuberculosis had appeared in her finger, which had been amputated, and now she showed a large open sore above the wrist. This wound was washed and dressed, and then, with a glad contented look, she joined the other patients who were well enough to help in the weekly Friday 'spring-cleaning'. This consisted in cutting the lawns, raking and weeding the walks, and lifting all the debris and rubbish that might be lying about. The whole buildings and grounds are thus kept in splendid order.

Perhaps the most amazing performance to a European was the 'slick' way in which the natives disposed of their medicine. They came up one by one to a little window of the dispensary, and the doctor handed out medicine – mostly tabloids – one, two, three or four, as might be necessary, and these were scarcely put into the eager hand, till they were passed to the mouth. Instead of the expected struggle there was scarcely an appearance of swallowing on the solemn impassive faces. One and all had perfect faith and completest confidence in their medical adviser, and swallowed with unquestioning satisfaction all that was given them. The assistant, Nilauas, was most helpful and attended to the details of cleanliness and order. He knew intimately everybody, and looked after their comfort with a quiet discretionary discipline that would have done credit to much higher paid men in the homeland.

Dr Nicholson and I then got on horseback and I had the most interesting tour of inspection I ever enjoyed. Not only have many acres around the hospital been reclaimed from the bush and planted with grass but many more have been sown with maize, which promised a good return. Besides greatly improving the appearance of the place, the clearing of the overgrown bush adds to the healthiness of the district. We also visited the native gardens, which are wonderful examples of patient, elaborate toil, especially on the part of the women. The ground is first cleared of surface growth, and then the roots are picked carefully out of the soil. The earth is passed laboriously through the fingers and made fine and pliable, and then raised into mounds four or five feet in diameter. Into the mounds are planted several yams, which soon send out tender shoots, like vines or convolvulus, and these are carefully trained along reed trellis work; without touching the ground, for many yards, sometimes in so many radiating fences from the mound, and sometimes in circles around it. In the garden are often planted bananas as well, and sometimes cocoa palms, but seldom is a garden used for more than three years, and so it happens that all through the overgrown bush the remains of old gardens are sometimes visible.

Another scene greatly interested me, and that was a new village that was being built on a site higher than the hospital. The site on the slope of the hill was admirably chosen. With great labour a broad shelf, or plateau, was levelled out of the slope, and on it was built a long row of neat little reed cottages of two or three apartments. The outside walls were not the common irregular wattle, but the reeds were so woven as to show an ornamental diamond pattern. Inside there were fixed bedsteads, which allowed the natives to sleep about three feet above the ground, and so escape the many dangers from sleeping on mats on the often- damp floor. In front of the cottages – the village street – there was a broad footpath and then a neatly kept narrow grass lawn, and towards the edge of the plateau a border of garden flowers. Truly, what a contrast to the filthy, dilapidated collection of pig styes the natives call their homes that I saw in other parts. As we rode along well cleared roads through the bush, we came to an ancient banyan tree, which had been the scene of many a heathen feast. As one thought of the life and din in former times, the place, in the subdued twilight under the trees seemed oppressively quiet. Dr.Nicholson called a native, who seemed to be living near, and he explained many of the old customs and sites where they danced and feasted, and pointed out, stuck in the branches of the banyan tree, many bones, some of them human, and relics of former feasts.

It was here also that there was a sort of City of Refuge, a horn of the alter as it were, a trunk of an old tree on which, if any victim or captive, – black or white – could lay hold, his life and person were perfectly safe. It is to be hoped that at least some of the poor trembling creatures who were appointed unto death knew of this haven of safety, and had at least a temporary respite from a horrible death.

It was our good fortune to be present at a wedding in the large and beautiful church adjoining the hospital at Lenakel. The conch shell was sounded, and twenty to thirty people gathered. On the seat in front of the platform pulpit sat the bride and bridegroom, with several of the office bearers and friends. The other witnesses occupied the side seats. The service was not a prolonged one, but seemed to be perfectly understood by all, and at the close we all with hearty handshakes, congratulated the bridegroom and his shy and modest bride. Lomai was there, and led in one of the prayers, besides making all arrangements for the comfort and convenience of all concerned.

I had presented Lomai with a Gospel, printed in large black-letter type, which, though English, I hoped might be useful to him as he grew older. After family worship, a knock came to the study door and Lomai asked if Mr.Marshall would accept a few shells? Of course I would be only too glad, and he gave me ten fine large brown mottled shells which I shall always prize and which will remind me of the giver and of a pleasant and profitable visit to Lenakel. These shells proved to be the beginning of quite a little collection of shells and other interesting curios given to me as I called at the other Mission Stations.

In looking back on my pleasant experiences in Tanna, and comparing the conditions of "Dark Tanna" only a few years ago with its present happy circumstances, I cannot but exclaim "What hath God wrought?" There are still many heathen, but they are mild and harmless and they return a nod with a friendly smile. All the people, heathen and Christian alike, almost worship the Doctor. He is their guide, philosopher and friend, and they apply to him for advice in all the concerns and difficulties of life. His position of responsibil-

ity is not an easy one, and his work is hard and constant, yet he nobly keeps before himself a high ideal. In such a busy life, where so much time must be given up to medical and social work, and having to be ready to mount his horse and gallop at a moment's notice to any distant part of the island, one might be expected to grow languid in evangelical fervour, but this is not by any means so. Dr.Nicholson's fear is that in present circumstances the natives may become civilised but not Christianised, and his principal aim in preaching and in all his varied work, is to first of all exalt Jesus Christ, that He may draw all men unto himself.

In the evening of Saturday I was admitted to the inner circle, the sacred centre of the Mission life. It is Dr.Nicholson's practice to meet on the eve of the Sabbath with his elders, Lomai and Iavis, and receive their reports on their work in their districts, confer on the work generally, and spend a considerable time in intercessory prayer. Nothing could be more helpful in preparing for the Sabbath services, and to me it was both solemn and impressive. Lomai and Iavis prayed with much freedom and earnestness in Tannese, while Dr.Nicholson, Rev.W.Mackay and I prayed in English. Surely, as we knelt at the mercy seat, our prayers must have risen to a prayer hearing and a prayer answering God, and the anticipated blessing would descend on the Sabbath gatherings, and on the district.

It was with regret that I left to go on board the steamer, which sailed the same evening, for I was fain to accept Dr.Nicholson's pressing invitation to wait a month at Lenakel and assist him in some of his interesting and eminently successful work."

At the beginning of the Jottings 70 Oct.1910 there is mention of my father:

"Dr. and Mrs.Nicholson will have a cloud over them during their short and well earned furlough in the Colonies, in the prospect of leaving behind their eldest boy – for his education. Grace to endure comes from on High, and we are sure many prayers will ascend to Heaven for our Missionaries in their trial.

As will be seen from his letter, Dr.Nicholson is having his motorboat built in Australia. The engine has gone from England – one of Thorneycroft's best motors. It was shipped on the 18th ult, and will we trust arrive in time for the Doctor to see it securely fitted into the boat, so that the whole thing may be taken under his own care to the Islands.

A new chapter of Tanna history – brightened by the amelioration of suffering and swift succour in distress – which will open up with the advent of the "John G. Paton", as the new motorboat is to be called. Dr.Crombie has called his motor by this name; but Tanna must of course take precedence, and the Wala boat will require to be re-christened!

Doctor James Nicholson in army uniform.

Boathouse

Granny on horseback

Motorboat John G. Paton

Dr. Nicholson and Church members, Iavis on Dr's right and Lomai on left

Eileen and May with local babies

Lenakel Church (still in existence)

Isobel, May, Eileen and Peggy in buggy

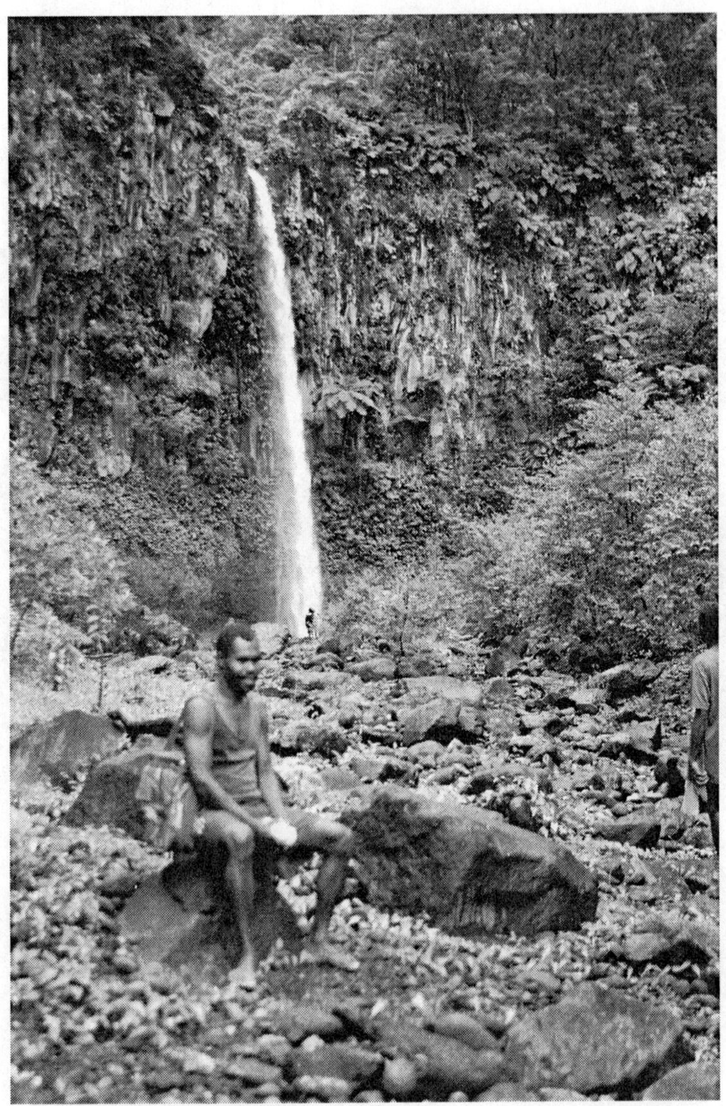

Chief Jelsen Denny Hoseah at Fekar Falls

Author with Chief Peter Marshall on her left and descendants from Iavis, Nilauas and members of Isini village

Chapter X – The Ninth Year

Tasmania and New Transport

From Hobart.

Assembly Hall,
MELBOURNE, Victoria.
9.1.11

My Dear Mother,

I received your letter on the 4th instant and you had not heard when writing of our arrival in Australia. We were glad to hear father was so much better but awfully sorry to hear that Louie would not go to a Sanatorium.

We crossed here leaving Melbourne on the afternoon, 2 p.m., of the 4th and arrived in the early hours of the morning of the 6th. It was smooth all the way, like our trip Sydney to Melbourne. We feel the cold a little here but that is just what we want. The air here is like that of your summer at home and the scenery magnificent. Mrs.Robertson, her three daughters and Miss Beath who was at Lenakel with Francis Robinson. We make a large party. We are staying in Hobart till Friday of this week and then go to a little seaside place called Brown's River (half an hour in a little steamer takes us there) where we intend to spend the days on the beach with the children. We intend to return to Melbourne the first or second week in February. I have meetings from Sunday the 12th onward. Next Sunday I am to take the Morning Service of St.John's Presbyterian Church.

We are all looking well, the children have colds yet and chapped hands and legs but otherwise are quite robust. Isabel is just splendid and looks as nice as ever. I have a sore throat, it has lasted a week but is feeling better and I hope it will be all right for Sunday. We have felt the keen edge of good appetites since coming and all make a good show at meal times.

I am reading the reports of the Edinburgh Conference. It is fine and heartening reading in the main although some facts brought out about the church at home and abroad are not very encouraging. Still Christ is becoming the desire of the Nation and the Light of the World. I believe we are soon to see a regular Pentecostal advance especially in the East, China, Korea and Japan. If we were all as faithful and devoted as we should be to the Lord personally and obedient to his commands the world would soon be evangelised.

This Island has a curse on it. It destroyed the native population like vermin, rounded them up and shot them. It is the gambling centre of Australasia and derives £60,000 for Government purposes alone from gambling.

We have not met any yet who met Willie and Hemminger. Willie asked me to call on a Baptist Minister here, but I don't think I will have time as we leave Hobart soon.

I hope we get a letter from you this week. The cultivated country square fields make me feel homesick.

With love to you all from us all,

Your affect. son,
J.Campbell Nicholson

T.R.Skegg's
Jubilee Hotel
LOTTAH,Tasmania
Sunday 12.1.11

My Dear Mother,

It is quite a long time since I got a letter from you but I am sure there is one if not more in Melbourne and Isabel will have them by this time. This village is right up in the mountains (a tiny mining village) about 19 miles from the east coast. We did not intend to stay here but after miles of climbing and whilst we were coming down this side a front wheel came off. The driver was so quick with the brakes that the car stopped dead so that we were hardly shaken at all. On the side of the road was an almost sheer drop of 7 or 800 feet. We felt thankful to escape so easily. As some bolt was broken we could do nothing but come on here and take men and a cart back and we got to bed at 2 a.m. this morning. We have had a very quiet Sunday. There was only one service here today, a Methodist one and a very good one it was. Many of these villages have only a service once a month, some every two weeks and there are hundreds of people settled on the land who never have services or Sunday schools and many no day schools. What the children will be like who grow up in this way is hard to conceive of. The Home Mission work of the Churches of Australia and Tasmania is a big problem and not easily solved. Many of the Home Missionaries have a parish half the size of Ireland with the people scattered far and wide through it.

My heart feels sore as we travel about for the natives who have been completely wiped out, not one is left, not a foot of ground was ever bought from them and they never resented the settlement of whites, but they were so brutally treated by the early settlers and especially escaped convicts and driven back to the hills where food was scarce that they became revengeful and attacked the invaders of the lands and were then shot down like crows. Indeed men, shepherds used to boast of having shot so many 'crows' in a day. If they had been a fierce race like the Tannese not a settler would have escaped. By a series of big drives the natives were rounded up and shot down or driven over the cliffs, and at last through the mediation of a Christian man the remnant of the people were put on an island to die out. One feels a curse rests on the land, a land rich in all things with the best climate in the world bar none and which has been stagnating for years and is yet.

I am to cross to the mainland on Tuesday or Thursday and begin deputation work in Ballarat next Sunday, three services I expect in Dr.Cairn's Church. He comes from between Comber and Newtownards. Isabel and the bairns crossed on Thursday last with Mrs.Robinson. I have not had a letter yet but will get one tomorrow if we get on to Scamander, a place on the east coast. I am getting tired of camping out, we had some very wet nights and it is hard work each night pitching our tent and doing our own cooking and washing up. We help out our larder with fish and game.

Dr.Gibson was not very well yesterday. He fished, wading to the hips a whole day and although he says he never feels it I am sure he does. I'm quite content with the bank.

Mr.Hughes who is with us and does the driving is a handy man, been at sea, had a farm and some other things and is now in the motor car business.

I hope you are all well at home. I would like to hear about Father's eye and Louie. I have not heard from Willie for a long time and have been feeling anxious about Sarah and Dan. We need to pray for them and the Church in Manchuria in their severe affliction and trial.

Give my love to Father and Netta and all the kin you see, with much to yourself.

Your affectionate son, J.Campbell Nicholson

Assembly Hall,
MELBOURNE.
27th February,1911

My Dear Mother,

I received your letters up till the 19th January, that was the last one. I expect another today as the mail arrived in Adelaide on Saturday. I got back from Tasmania on Friday week and Isabel and I went on to Ballarat. I had the morning and evening services in the St.Andrew's Church (Dr.Cairns, a Comber man). It is a magnificent big church and we had big congregations. I also spoke at the adult bible class and Sunday Schools, so had a full day. We stayed with an old fellow student of mine, Dr.Sloss, and he took us round in his motor. We were down a gold mine and saw all that was worth seeing in Ballarat, returning on Tuesday night as I had a meeting on Wednesday. Yesterday I had the both services in Malvern Church (our Church) and also the fellowship. I beg off Sunday School and bible classes as I go off my sleep after much speaking, though I do not suffer much from nervousness at the time. I am free so far as I know this week and then have three church services next Sunday. I often wish Ministers would take the devotional parts, but so far they have been absent or preferred to have a day in the pew. When absent the Churches so far (St.Andrews and Malvern) have treated me as a supply and I get £4.4.0 for the Sunday. This has been very useful as we have gone in for a holiday almost regardless of expense (from our point of view) thanks to Uncle James.

Isabel had fever on the Steamer returning from Tasmania but she looks well and has a better complexion than most in Australia. John is very keen on his school and can not get out quick enough in the mornings, but he objects to May going as she persists in sitting with him amongst the boys. However, May today went again and says she can sit anywhere, but we will only allow her to stay till one. John goes to Miss Murray's for lunch, it is near the school and this will prepare him for living there.

We spent Saturday afternoon with the little Macmillans, they look and are splendid. John said right out 'I will stay with them' but Mrs.Wilson would not take any more. However, he is living in the anticipation of spending next weekend with them and I have the Church services over there and will be staying near him and bring him back. I think that by April John will have become so settled that he will prefer staying to going. Eileen wants to go to school but is much too young and would be a nuisance. The Church, School and Miss Murray's are all close together and in the middle of a circle of good Christian friends we have made. God has been good to us and we realise it.

I spent an afternoon with Mr.Andrew Agnew. His wife and daughter are to call next Thursday and arrange a day for us all to go across. They have a fine big house and plenty of ground. He is very keen on the North of Ireland and was at school with Uncle James, you and your sister Jane, he says. He is to go home next year if all goes well. One Edgar and two Mrs.Edgars go home soon. Isabel met some of those going yesterday and so if you meet them they will be able to tell you about Isabel and the three bairns.

We get our photos taken tomorrow so as to keep you all from forgetting what we are like. The work goes well on Tanna but the French recruiters are still troubling us.

I was sorry to hear about Uncle William, you have been having exciting times all round. I wish we had news from Sarah and Dan. With much love to you all,

Your affect. son,
J.Campbell Nicholson

(address in future) Lenakel,
Tanna, New Hebrides.
(From Melbourne)
Ap. 4th 1911.

My Dear Mother,

Your letter to hand yesterday telling us about the death of the baby. It is not often so young a baby pulls through but it does not make the loss easier for Lizzie and her husband.[1]

We are now very near to the parting with John, he is so interested in his school work and so interesting to us as he progresses that it is getting harder and harder to face the parting. But we must do what we believe to be our duty at present but still the consideration of whether one's duty to one's children is not first will be largely in our minds during the next two years. May God who has guided us make us guidable in the future. John knows but we never talk to him about it, but I must soon. He said to Isabel, 'who is Miss Murray, she does not belong to us, why don't you send me to Granny, she belongs to me'. But John does not want to go to Tanna again, he says. He likes civilization and that is always a comfort to us.

We went a long motor drive with Mr.Agnew yesterday. John and May were with us and we had a great time. It was kind of Mr.Agnew and we had dinner at his house at night. I have nearly finished meetings now and have only two Sundays and a long country trip to do. I have applications for many more from Ministers and must say I like the quiet Sabbath services best.

It is very cold today. We are shivering but a walk would soon warm us up. The children look well and we are getting so hardy and fat.

I hope you and Father keep well, also Netta. Any news from Sarah? With much love,

Your affect. son,
J.Campbell Nicholson.

Copy of Newspaper Cutting enclosed with this letter.

'Warrnamabool (St.John's). – Dr.Nicholson from Tanna, conducted the services on Sunday, 19th inst. In the forenoon the very heavy downpour of rain prevented any large attendance, but in the evening the church was quite full. Dr.Nicholson's address of 80 minutes on his work in Tanna was listened to with rapt attention. It is rarely the privilege of the congregation to listen to a missionary's address showing such sane and sanctified common sense in dealing with the inhabitants of these islands of the New Hebrides. It was refreshing and stimulating to hear of the never-failing effect the old time religion from the same Old Bible had upon the lives of savages.'

'Lenakel',
TANNA, New Hebrides.
July 10th 1911

My Dear Mother,

I was so glad to know by your letter of April 11th that you were taking a holiday and enjoying it. You have had a good run round. It is our great loss that we are so far away that you cannot visit us. I think you would really have the time of your life if you could get a month or two here, everything would be so new to you. Father too could find much to interest him and I think almost anybody. We have the launch now and it is a good one. It came last month. We have done about 170 miles without a breakdown.

I just got back last night from Aniwa, spent Sunday there and had a busy enjoyable time. We had to cross in a big sea. Isabel was not with me as we expect a new arrival in September and she is not taking any risks. I was glad she was not as the spray came over us in sheets. Coming back the sea was bigger but we were running before it and did not take any sea on board. We did the forty odd miles in 5 ½ hours and the engine only going quarter speed most of the time, but we had the sails set. I had my two white helpers. Mr.Robertson was very sick going and coming but Mr.Bell who acts as engineer kept his end up though squeamish. As long as I have work to do I never get seasick. The Aniwans gave us a great welcome and had put in a lot of cleaning. I visited every house and saw every individual and think we will get on well. They have a fear of me as a sanitary inspector and though they have a bad reputa-

tion for being dirty, nobody would have believed it if they had gone round the villages with me. The Elders said they worked very hard to clean up. Dr.Paton laid good foundations. These people for twenty years without a resident missionary are a grand testimony to the power of Christ and His Gospel. We had hearty services. I had to use an interpreter of course, but one felt a great spiritual uplift.

We are working hard at the hospital and hope soon to have part at least ready for patients. I have a lot of surgical work to do and the launch will bring in a good many patients. I have been overhauling the engine and my hands are skinned and stiff. It is dirty work but one must get to know it in all its parts and moods.

We still are heart sore for John but he is doing well. He told a friend that he wished Jesus had not made any black people then there would be no need for Daddy and Mama to leave him. He prints letters to us and how we puzzle over them and prize them. May and Eileen are very well and enjoying themselves. They talk a lot about John. I am glad now I did not go to Synod.

The Volcano has become almost extinct and the natives were afraid that it meant something dreadful. I hope not. I went up to see it and the sides of the crater have fallen in and partly filled it. It has a most uncanny quietness about it and absence of smoke, but we had only one very slight shake since.

I was glad to hear about Sarah and hope we meet at home. They must have had a very trying time indeed with the plague.

Father must be strong yet to walk out to the ? and back. What about his taking a car. Tell him the launch is fine but the smell and noise is not as restful and nice as sails, but better than a native crew perspiring at the oars.

Our garden is picking up again, but two years blow out at the very time all the flowers and trees are at their best has hurt it a good deal. I get very little time at it now. We have so many things on hand that one wonders when we will be able to get back to a normal pace of work at Lenakel. However, we are all well and strong and that is a great matter.

With our love to you all,

Your affect. son,

J.Campbell Nicholson.

P.S. Did you get our photographs yet? J.C.N.

It was back in 1908 that Grandfather put forward the idea of a motor-boat for the Island and in 1909 it was ordered, along with one for the island of Paama. He had decided to wait and see the Paama one first as he required his to be a 'sea ambulance' which would need modifications; however, the hurricane put in an appearance first, so it was all to the good. While the family were on furlough, Grandfather was going to oversee the building of the boat, a Thorneycroft engine being sent out from England, but unfortunately, the engine arrived after he returned to Tanna; people in Tunbridge Wells had raised the money for the boat and now that Grandfather also had to oversee Aniwa, an island 40 miles to the east, the motor boat would greatly help. July in Tanna saw the arrival of the much-awaited motor boat. Grandfather writes in the Jottings*: "The engine runs splendidly, it has never delayed us at sea. Sometimes it has refused to start, but the fault has been ours, and when we have found out our mistake and given the motor a fair chance, away we go. One listens to the beating of the little engine as one would to the heart or lungs of a patient, and learns to regulate the spark and supply of benzine and air till at last its rhythmic throb is like the sweetest music. Even the smell of benzine and oil, which at first made most of us look overboard and lose our sustenance, has become, if not pleasant, at least not unpleasant. The motor has already done splendid service to doctor and patients, and saved many weary hours for both." (Jot.75)*

Grandfather writes in the Jottings about the natives' reaction to the sudden stillness of Mount Yassur:

This month the people on the other side almost got into a panic and, in the absence of Mr.Macmillan, I went across at once. The news was that the volcano "had died". It had ceased to roar or belch out smoke. The stillness when I got over was uncanny. Mr.Carruthers and I, followed by some natives, went up to the top of the mountain and found that hundreds of tons of earth from the sides of the crater had fallen in, partly filling the great orifice. There were none of those gigantic explosions which have been experienced every few minutes night and day for generations, and, as a native said, you could walk about the bottom of the crater now. Huge cracks showed that more ashes would yet fall in. I walked round the crater, but could see no signs of activity. The people prophesy big earthquakes or some calamity. I told them that all over the earth were to be found extinct volcanoes, and that their volcano might just have "gone out", and would give them no more trouble by clouds of falling ash and sulphuric acid to destroy their gardens. So far the volcano still remains silent, and the people are feeling easier in their minds. (Jot.74 Oct.1911)

In Jottings 75 Jan.1912, Grandfather did not attend Synod, he says for several reasons and I think one of them must have been because Granny was expecting. Peggy is mentioned in the next letter, who was child number four.

'Lenakel',
TANNA, New Hebrides.
Oct. 16th 1911

My Dear Mother,

The Man of War did not give us a chance to send off letters as we had hoped, so I will send that one on and just give you a line to let you know we are all well. Isabel is riding about again and Peggy beginning to see and hear and take notice. We had good news of John, May and Eileen are well and robust.

The work goes on well. I had nearly a week under canvas up north and had a good time.

I suppose Sarah and Dan have arrived. Tell them to write us big letters to let us know how they find people and things.

With much love from us all,

Your affect. Son
J.Campbell Nicholson

At the beginning of October the Melbourne office of the Mission received the following telegram:

"Hurricane wrecked Tanna launch shall we build another." A reply was sent: *"Build another, presume engine saved"* This message came back from the Doctor: *'We are paralysed and full of grief to tell you that our beautiful motor boat has been completely lost!*

She had just been overhauled, and we had her launched to try the engine preparatory to a series of voyages – to Aniwa and to three northern stations. The night was fine; there was no wind, and the glass good, so that we felt safe in leaving her quietly at her moorings. But before daybreak a big sea came up from the south, and huge seas rushed over the reef into the calm where the launch rode at anchor. The boat was swirled around and the mooring chain got foul of the coral and shortened and the strain of the enormous rushes of the seas snapped the chain, and quickly drove our boat on to the reef.

The alarm was raised, and the natives rushed with me to the rescue. By this time, however, her bows were smashed in. We managed to get a rope fastened to her, and with two horses and the natives pulling, tried to drag her ashore to save the engine, but alas, in the midst of our struggle the rope snapped and a great sea drew the helpless boat back into deep water and engulfed her.

Mr.Robertson and the natives have dived into the sea to discover her whereabouts, but no trace of our boat can be found, and we are thus bereft of one of the best aids to our work that has ever been sent to Tanna. It is as if a terrible tragedy had been committed before our eyes, and the natives go about softly and speak in whispers of the occurrence.

The boat had just been with us long enough to make us realise her value, and I am certain we cannot go back to the slow and uncertain service of the sailing boat without a distinct set back to the work in every direction.

So much do we feel this that we will guarantee £100 at once towards the cost of a new motor if our supporters will make up the rest. To have charge of Aniwa without a motor to cross over to that little island is impossible, as I cannot leave the hospital and my patients if I am to take the risk of head winds and calms and the consequent long periods of absence, which are the necessary concomitants of a sailing boat in these islands.'

The reply quickly came back from the Mission Committee that a boat must be ordered and that somehow the money would be found-just another £100. £200 for a large motor boat doesn't seem like much today but then it was a lot of money. Poor Aniwa! Cut off again and not knowing why until another boat arrives. In the April Jottings the Mission Committee reported that they had enough money for rails and tackle to haul the boat up into a place of safety as well. The new boat had arrived in June. (Jot.75 Apr.1912)

Jottings 77 gives an overall picture of how the hurricane had affected everybody:

Eight natives from Erromanga went by steamer to the Tanna Hospital lately to place themselves under the care of Dr.Nicholson for their sicknesses. Tanna is becoming a centre of light and healing instead of the "dark Tanna" of a few years ago. How great is the reward of the patient and persistent effort of sixty years.

The accounts from every Island and District in the New Hebrides go to show that hurricanes during the past hot season have been the worst experienced for many years. The records are sad reading indeed. Our little Mission has been sorely tried.

From Grandfather there is this report:

Lenakel, TANNA
October, 1911

The loss of our launch upset the timetable of our work laid out to be done before Christmas, and disarranged our Communion Services. Aniwa has suffered most, as I have been, and am, unable to visit the Island now. To go by steamer means a month away from the hospital, and would necessitate clearing out all patients. If the Pioneer, our sailing boat, were seaworthy, it could be done, but she is old and leaks so badly that the natives refuse to go in her any distance from the land.

Then, too, we are so very busy building, painting, etc. However, we were able to spend the best part of a week in the north of Tanna, where I had to open three new Churches. We ventured in the Pioneer, but she leaked in a dozen places. Still, as we had a fair wind, and the sea was not too rough we tried the experiment – taking extra sails and buckets to bail. With an extra mainsail as spinnaker we made a record trip – almost as quick as the launch could have done – but two of the boys had to keep constantly bucketing the water overboard. The people at Laepu were ready to receive us, and we soon had the whaleboat pulled up, and by means of the sails a comfortable tent was made.

We had a good service at Laepu that night, but the opening of the Church was not to take place until Sunday.

On the Friday we went inland to Ikalau. A big crowd had gathered at this the most populous village in Tanna. One of the outstanding features of this place is the large number of young children. Since the hurricane in March 1910, the houses have shrunk in size. I was sorry for this, but the reasons given were too good to be put aside. The village is situated amongst the mountains, and is swept by every wind, and the rainfall is very great. Also the thatch of the houses only lasts about a year, and material to make it is not very abundant. However, like most highlanders, they are a healthy, long-limbed lot. Their Church is large and well built, but lacked the lines and finish of some others. Lomai and Iavis assisted me in the services, and we had a good time. An abundance of food was provided for all comers.(Jottings 77 July 1912)

'Lenakel',
TANNA , New Hebrides.
29th December, 1911

My Dear Mother,

I did not get a letter from you by last mail but Isabel did. I hope that you all have had a very happy Christmas and will have a good New Year. We are late having our Christmas Communion but next week our services commence and the Sunday after next will celebrate the Lord's Supper.

The Steamer is calling in here on her way to Sydney for Mr. & Mrs. Worthington. They have sold their place and we have got a very nice young couple instead, Mr. & Mrs Griffiths. The former is an Englishman and the latter a Victorian from Melbourne. I hear they have or are giving £4,000 for the place. I think it is too much to spend in an isolated and bad climate like this. However, there is no opposition and not likely to be any and with care and graft they can soon get their own. Mrs. Griffiths is a very capable woman and she can do more than her husband in such a business as theirs and so for that reason as it gives both an outlet for their energies the place may be worth the money. I think it will be for the good of all that we are having a change. The Worthingtons have always and consistently been opposed to the Worship, especially Mrs.Worthington. She was and is a fair terror and we are not sorry she is leaving Tanna. The Griffiths say they are going to attend the English service, on Sunday evenings I have a white congregation almost, the brothers Christian and their wives (one works for the Griffiths) and Mr.Robertson and now Mr. & Mrs.Griffiths. However, I shall continue my simple English addresses to the natives and trust that the whites may get some pickings.

We thought we were in for a hurricane last Friday and got all ready but it passed off. Our people fled for the caves, they were taking no risks. We are all keeping well. Peggie is splendid and has won all our hearts. She is always smiling and happy. Eileen is a bit brighter but her tonsils still keep very large. May is as hard as nuts and is a very good girl. Isabel is in robust health and rides about on horseback, but is too fond of the galloping.

Mr. and Mrs. Christian are both great helps. I wish I had got them years ago. It would have saved me so much manual labour. The Hospital has 25 in-patients and the people are coming from all parts of the Island. We have missed the launch badly. I feel almost like crying when I think about her. I hope that you are all well at home. Did Sarah and Dan cross for Christmas. I suppose Willie has gone to America now.

Next week we will be very busy, services and crowds on the go all the time. I hope the weather keeps fine, that is a very important matter when so many people come to stay. I will write you about our week by the ordinary steamer. With love to all.

Your affect. son,
J. Campbell Nicholson

At the end of December 1911 another hurricane flattened the almost completed church. Luckily it was just the frame that was up and after reviewing the damage and altering the design of the construction, they were able to rebuild it. One good aspect of the hurricanes – in February 1912 in the Jottings, Grandfather reports that they have had four of them in 23 months, three doing great damage – was that it swept away all the old dwellings and new ones, in better and cleaner locations were able to be built. In one village that Grandfather visited he came across a little boy called Kooki. Kooki had been like a foster brother to my Father, being about the same age. He had visited Lenakel, met my father and decided to stay, sleeping under my Father's bed, the two becoming firm friends; my Father informed his parents that 'Kooki was going to stay with him', which he did until my Father was sent to Australia after which Kooki ran away. When Grandfather met him he cried bitterly and the Doctor had to leave without a smile or a word. He obviously hadn't forgiven him. (Jot.77 July 1912)

Notes on 1911

Back in Britain in March, a shop workers bill was brought in to abolish the 80 and 90 hr. week with a limit of 60 hrs. Eton school abolished the birch and George V was crowned on 22nd June, ruler of the largest kingdom, one fifth of the world. In Belfast, 31st May saw the launch of the sister ship to the Olympic, the Titanic. Britain was not a good place to be that year, as in Wales, riots intensified as railwaymen came out on strike in support of the dockers who had been on strike for some months seeking a minimum pay and better working conditions; six died in the riots and three were shot by troops. A nationwide strike had brought the country to a standstill with people taking to the streets and many cities fearing famine. August that year saw a record-breaking heat wave – 97 deg. in London – with many dying.

In France, after fierce riots, where thousands of bottles of wine were broken, settlement was reached over the application of the term 'champagne' and Paris saw the theft of the Mona Lisa from the Louvre.

The end of December saw the Norwegian explorer Roald Amundsen, winner of the race to the South Pole, beating Captain Robert Scott.

In Bangor, due to severe depression in the building trade, employment was at an all time low and many children were leaving school early as their parents were forced to emigrate. At the end of May, virtually the whole population of Bangor turned out to see the Olympic sail down Belfast Lough. Great-grandfather was on the Coronation Committee that organized bonfires to be lit all round the bay and an old 67 foot lightship, fully laden with explosives, was set alight for the occasion. Mixed bathing was seen at Ballyholme for the first time and still on the coast, a sunfish, roughly 8 ft. in diameter and weighing 5 to 6 hundredweight, was washed up in Bangor Bay. Mention is made of William, or WP, being in Glasgow, but going back to America; I wonder did he find time to visit Bangor?

In the New Hebrides, despite the Convention between Britain and France and a Protection Bill being brought in 1906, the French continued to flout the rule with regards to recruitment, sale of grog etc. (An article in Jot.71 Jan.1911). In November 1910, Mr.Frederick White MP, put a question to the Secretary of State for Foreign Affairs as to whether he was aware that the President of the Condominium Court and the Public Prosecutor were both ignorant of the English language, being Spanish; the gist of the reply was that a translator would be supplied but admitted that it was 'an undoubted disadvantage'! Britain appeared to be doing little to alleviate the problem; the Missionaries were deeply worried and never a quarter goes by that the problem isn't aired in the Jottings.

Chapter XI – The Tenth Year

Continued Hard Work

~

Since there are no 'home' letters for the beginning of the year, I have included one from the Jottings:

February

I am sure readers of Jottings must be tired of reading about hurricanes! But how much more tired of them must they be who have suffered from no less than four of them within twenty-three months – three of them doing great damage. Well, at the end of December we had the tail end of one which did us not much damage but made us "sit up". The islands north suffered more, and a steamer belonging to an island firm foundered near Malekula and twenty-five lives were lost with her. On the 30th of January the glass again went down, and the wind blew hard from the northeast. In the teeth of the wind there came up a terrible sea, which swept upon the beach with terrific force – destroying our boat rails and causing us to hurriedly pull our boat out of the house right up into the grounds. The hurricane had commenced far to the west and swept far east of us, coming close to the north of us. Towards evening the wind suddenly dropped, and the glass rose a little, but we made all buildings as snug as possible.

We had the frame of our new Church up, and put on extra braces, but as the weatherboards were not on we did not feel especially anxious as the wind had free play through it with little resistance. About seven o'clock when it was getting dark, the wind came suddenly out of the south-west, and seemed for a bit as if it were going to lift the house, but we were ready, and the glass was still rising. The patients in the Hospital were in a panic, but that building will stand any wind that comes I think! Lomai and Nilauas and their people fled into the cellar of the Hospital.

As the wind began to abate and the glass still to rise, I started out for the village to prevent the people flying for the open and sleeping out all night.

On my way, to my utter dismay, I found the new Church had been blown flat down! I could scarcely believe my eyes, and I felt my heart sink. However, I had to push on to the village, and found the people had crowded into two of the largest houses, ready to fly to the beach. But, having great faith in the barometer, they were quite reassured when I told them it was "good".

When I got back with the news of the disaster there was real dismay. Mr.Robertson did not believe me, I think, at least he went out to verify my statement. At first this was a real knockdown blow. We knew that to get new material from Sydney would take three months, and that the inaction would have a very bad effect on the people. In the morning, however, we went carefully over the wreck, and determined to alter the construction of the roof so that we could work in other timber to replace that which was broken. To our joy we found we could do this and go on at once with the re-building without decreasing the seating accommodation of the Church at all. Thus, by the time we are ready for it, the extra material will arrive from Sydney. All hands were accordingly set to clear up, and the carpenter began to make new plates, etc; and now we are going forward as if these kind of things were just ordinary occurrences – which indeed, they are really getting to be!

The country usually looks its best at this time of the year; and our garden was in splendid order with roses in great profusion. Now we must start clearing up the mess of fallen leaves and branches, and pulling trees up to a perpendicular position with block and tackle; all the time trying to keep smiling.

One good thing is that at this time of the year growth is so rapid that in a month or so the damage will have been covered over in new foliage and bloom. But we have some months yet in which to wait and watch for another hurricane. We are anxious for news of how the islands around us fared. The native gardens and plantations have suffered a good deal. The breadfruit trees and some other native and fruit trees have their crops spoiled. Bananas, too, have suffered. But the native houses were rebuilt so strongly after the last big hurricane that they have only lost some thatch.

With our kindest regards,

Yours sincerely,
J.CAMPBELL NICHOLSON

Lenakel,
TANNA, New Hebrides
March, 31st 1912

My Dear Mother,

We received your letter of the 17th Jan. by last steamer. You had a great time in Scotland and your letter was full of interesting news. I do hope George[1] *gets on well and feel sure he will. I must write him by this mail.*

I am writing your letter early as we are to have our Church opening and Communion on the 14th of April, the steamer date. Mr. & Mrs Frater came by last steamer and their two boys and we are enjoying their visit very much. Mr.Frater will baptise Peggy. We are to have a Harvest Thanksgiving, Baptisms, Marriages, Church opening and the Sacrament all in one week-end. I do hope the weather keeps good as the people in many cases will have to camp out. Mr.Frater brought the good news that the Islands are to pass into the hands of the British in exchange for African territory. Thank God for news like this, it will give a better chance to white and black of getting some justice. The French are in a terrible state I believe and a great deal of French property has been put on the market. We should get some official news by next mail.

We are all keeping in good health and have got through the hot season so far with very little fever. I did not get any news of the launch but Mr.Frater says he was one of three who ordered it in November, so surely it should soon be here. Committees, however, are not the best arrangement to get a thing put through. I would soon trust an individual.

We are having good services and the heathen are coming in fine. We have had a revival going on amongst the Church people since January and expect real times of blessing at our united services and Communion.

I do hope Sarah and Dan are keeping well. I also am sorry we did not meet. How did Netta get on with Nellie's baby. Father would help her. He would be delighted with Peggy, she has the fat smiling face of John in his babyhood but not the blue eyes. Peggy is the joy of everybody here. I intend to finish this letter in a fortnight when the steamer comes and will tell you about Communion then.

April 16th.

Dear Mother, We are waiting for the steamer and it is very rough, but I think we could get a boat out alright.

We had a great series of meetings last week, Pre-Communion services, Baptismal Classes, Harvest Thanksgiving, opening of new Church, eleven marriages. On Sunday we had four services. 80 adults and infants were baptised and 460 people communicated. It was a grand day and we finished up with a testimony meeting.

Many of the natives told how they were first led to decide for Christ. The Holy Spirit works the same the world over and when others least think it. Souls are in concern and conflict.

Peggy was baptised and took the water as a joke on Mr.Frater's part. She laughed right out. Mr. and Mrs.Frater are feeling anxious about getting away as Synod is at their place and they need to get back to get ready.

May and Eileen have had a great time with the two boys. We are all keeping well and looking forward to the cool season.

With our united love to you all,

Your affect. son,
J.Campbell Nicholson

'Lenakel',
TANNA, New Hebrides.
May 5th 1912

My Dear Mother,

I was very sorry to hear about Sarah having to undergo an operation but glad to hear she had come through so well and was making a good recovery. I must write to her by this mail.

When the steamer came last time the sea was so rough she would not anchor. I put off at once in the dinghy hoping to coax her in but at last had to pull out into the open ocean to her. I lost an oar and nearly lost a man but a skilfully thrown rope from the steamer's stern got him and he was pulled on board. Mr.Frater had gone out with me expecting the steamer to come to anchor and when the Captain said he was not to anchor, Mr.Frater stayed on board and went on to Paama leaving Mrs.Frater and the two boys with us. I got my mail and just by a chance had taken out part of my letters to post so got them away. Our goods were not landed and our neighbours and ourselves have been a bit short in some things this month. As Mrs.Frater has Synod coming off at her place next month it did make her anxious not to stay another month here, but she has been helping Isabel at dressmaking and me at preaching and her month has gone quickly enough.

I was away for three days north camping out. I have a little tent and take a pack horse so am independent of native houses and fleas. I had fine weather but just got back in time as a wet spell has set in. Just after the steamer left last month it rained for a week and then one night we had a flood such as I could not believe possible to happen. The sea round the coast was reddish yellow and covered with driftwood. Our garden and walks were washed out, the ground was torn up terribly and our neighbours, the Griffiths have lost about three acres of ground they had just brought under cultivation. It has either been carried away or is so torn up that it is useless. If it had happened in the daytime I am afraid many lives would have been lost as it came so suddenly and swept down all the roads in torrents. It's a great country this and the next and only thing nature can supply us with is a blizzard. We have had fire, hurricane, earthquake and flood.

I hope the baby has continued to thrive with you. I suppose he is in Edinburgh with his mother. I am hoping to hear from George by this mail and am sure he will do well. I had a letter from Willie who is having great times in America. I would have liked him to settle in Carruthers Close but he does not seem drawn to it. It is hard lines that the house in front should remain so long unlet. I hope the McConnells will stay on at Ellenville.

We are all keeping well and getting into the cool season. Isabel looks fine and is hearty. May and Eileen are very happy with the Frater boys. Peggy reigns over all and is so bright and merry but has not got a tooth yet. She is better if anything than John was when a baby and very like him.

With love to Father, Netta and yourself,

Your affect. son,
J.Campbell Nicholson

P.S. May 16th We were shocked to hear of the death of Nellies baby. It is terrible, four children and all dead. Poor, poor Nellie. Mrs.Frater has got on board this time. All well.

'Lenakel',
TANNA, New Hebrides.
July 10th 1912

My Dear Mother,

I am writing this from Mr.Macmillan's house. I spent Monday night here and now again tonight (Wednesday). On Monday morning Mr.Carruthers went out to milk a cow and a short time afterwards staggered into his wife covered with blood and his forehead laid open. He could not give any account of what had happened. I galloped across as soon as I got news and found his skull fractured by the kick of a horse. He is in a bad way. I saw him again on Tuesday and then crossed to Lenakel to look after things there, returning today and will D.V. cross tomorrow and back again on Friday, in this way attending to him each day.

I had been very busy all June. We did not get to Synod on account of the confinement of Mrs.Griffiths and we have been busy completing our Church as the carpenter leaves on Friday. The steamer is to call for him and so we get a mail away straight to Sydney instead of spending four weeks in the group after we post it. We got the Church completed for the Sunday and had a splendid gathering and great joy and blessing. The Griffiths got their baby baptised (my first white one) Mary Winifred was the name. The Church is very complete even to a little Vestry. It is grand to be back in a Church and to have all one's audience *inside*, *not a lot sitting outside as we have had for the past 18 months. The Station now is very complete and the Church is known as the Cathedral of the New Hebrides. The Lord has been good to the Tannese and us. We never thought to have such a Church and hospital and school and station. The Lord must expect great things from our people.*

Well, I left the mail to this week expecting to have plenty of time for it and instead of plenty of time here I am tearing back and forwards across the mountain daily. Isabel and the children are all in the best of health. Indeed Isabel looks just splendid, she is a little stout but not too much and her face is round and fair. She has not the yellow look of most women down here. The three girls are like what John was when you saw him. Eileen and Peggy are very like what he was at their ages. Peggy is queen of all our hearts, so healthy and happy. I don't think any baby was ever loved so much. Her followers are waiting their turn for a word and a smile. She won't crawl but can pull herself up to her feet and calls Mama and Dadda to us every time we come near. She calls out to me at the Sunday services and several times I have had to order her out as she kept yelling Dadda. May and Eileen are devoted to her, May especially. She stands and looks at her in adoration and says over and over again to whoever is near, isn't she a nice wee baby. Isabel says she has got more love and joy out of this baby than the babyhood of the others. She will not let any body else bath her if she can help it.

We have now got almost all our building done at Lenakel. We only need a consumptive ward and a maternity ward to finish. I have the timber for one and the money for the other.

The French are troubling our people again and we never seem to be without some recruiter at anchor at Lenakel. A good many young heathen men have gone, but at present nobody seems to want to leave and so the vessels are losing money waiting about.

I hope Father's leg is better. Tell him always to put his feet up on a chair when sitting or else replace his armchair with a couch. I hope you are all keeping well. Willie is to have a summer with you and will keep you all lively. Now I must turn in and I hope to sleep, but the explosions of the volcano shake the house and make me jump every 8 or 9 minutes. Since the volcano has been so active we have had no earthquakes but the falling ashes (hundreds of tons) keep one's eyes sore. We have had to sweep down our roofs and shovel the ashes out of the gutters (spouts).

With much love to all,

Your affect. son,
J.Campbell Nicholson

This excerpt from the Jottings, although a May letter, explains why Grandfather was 'tearing backwards and forwards across the mountain':

WHY THE 'JOTTINGS' LETTER FAILED

AN EXCITING STORY OF THE TANNA MAIL

May 20th, 1912

The most uncertain thing here is the mail service, especially the outgoing mail. To explain to those who have not lived in the New Hebrides, or on Tanna, all the elements of uncertainty is not easy. When we miss a Jottings letter next time, think well of our disabilities, and remember please that orders for drugs, food for the hospital and ourselves, and the many things necessary for the working and upkeep of a large station miss the mail at the same time. True, the steamer will be back in a month, but it will be three months from now before our goods can arrive from Sydney, and the want of a drug may hinder a recovery.

Let me give you an account of our efforts to catch the last two mails on Tanna. It will help you to understand. In April the steamer came into sight, but did not anchor. She stood off a long way, but I went out to sea and got my mail, or rather half of it. The rest was carried on to be delivered when next the steamer happened to anchor at Tanna. A few letters that I carried on board were sent on, but not a letter could be answered. No goods were landed, of course. A month later – in May – we did receive our mail and most of our goods – though a huge case of drugs, and two bags of hospital rice were over-carried.

Now, as to the outward mail. I was asked to have my letters at White Sands, which meant a journey across Tanna, early on Friday morning. To make sure I took the mail bag myself, sending a relay horse on the night before. After being up nearly all night writing letters and orders I set off at daybreak. It was a dark morning and soon the rain came down in torrents. After an hour's riding I picked up the relay horse and pushed on, trying to save my mail bag as much as possible from the rain. At the top of the mountains the rain was terrific, and the tracks soon became running streams in many places. I found that one part of the road had been carried clean away by a landslip, and debated whether it was worth risking the horse's limbs or life. I lost a valuable horse two years ago in a similar way. However, I decided to risk it and, leading the horse, scrambled on to the slope of loose wet clay. Half way across the horse refused to proceed and began to slip, but by dint of coaxing we regained the track by a series of plunges and scrambles. Congratulating myself, we slithered down the steep mountain track, only to find the road on the level a running stream. Barring holes this was alright, but there were holes, and into one of these the horse fell, rolling on its side with my leg under! A nice snapshot. A horse's head and a man's leg, arm and head showing above water! In the struggles of the horse to get up and out of the hole my knee, side and neck suffered. The mail bag (supposed to be waterproof) was dripping and covered in mud. Up we got and on again, with water half way up my leg – another hole would mean swimming for man and horse. In this way we skirted the lake and at last reached dry land. Then I had to gallop as hard as the horse could go. Near White Sands I met a native galloping a horse back towards Weasisi – rushing with Mr. Macmillan's mail. The steamer had passed White Sands and Port Resolution, as the sea was considered too rough to wait at either place, and Weasisi was the next and only chance. Congratulating myself that I had succeeded, I gave the boy my mail bag and rode down to Mr.Macmillan's. After a bath and change I felt happy that I had undertaken the risky journey as I had anyhow caught the post and saved a month. But, alas, the native returned WITH THE MAIL!! The steamer had not called even at Weasisi, and my Jottings letter is still on Tanna, as well as my orders and bag of correspondence.

I hope after this account friends will appreciate their post offices and pillar letterboxes, and their four or five mails per day!

J.CAMPBELL NICHOLSON

The joys of the post on Tanna; and the inward mail was sometimes no better, having to go out by boat into the open ocean if the steamer couldn't anchor

Lenakel
TANNA, New Hebrides.
Sept. 12th 1912

My Dear Mother,

Your two letters of the 6th and 27th June arrived by last mail and we were glad to know you were all well. Nellie and Sarah and Dan at home is a family rally, I wish we could have seen them but we are such a far flung family it does not seem possible we can all meet at one time again on earth. Yes, at the end of next year or the beginning of the next we intend (D.V.) to come and see you all. Peggy will be a year old tomorrow. How time goes. I am beginning to realise my age. Thank God we are all kept in good health and spirits. We have Mr. and Mrs.Wilkes staying with us. He is to be Magistrate for Tanna and the Southern Islands and will live on the East coast of Tanna near Mr.Macmillan. I expect we will have them for a month, then they are to get the use of Mr.Carruther's house till their own is built. They are both from New Zealand and very nice Christian folk. He sang a gospel solo at our Sabbath evening service and is keen on the good work on Tanna. It is wonderful the way we are kept supplied with visitors. We never seem to be alone now. We are seldom away from Tanna or home but people seem to like coming here. Dr.Gunn of Fotuna is to be with us a month arriving in October. He will help me with the Communion and I will arrange special evangelistic services for him as well. He is not much of a doctor but he is a very spiritual man and a keen evangelist. His wife and children are now in Sydney and he is going to retire shortly. He has done thirty years down here.

Our launch arrived last month and is now running well. We have done about 230 miles, Aniwa and all our coastal stations. The natives are well pleased and she has filled up the hospital to overflowing but as she brings in food from distant villages we do not mind the rush.

We had eight operations this week. Mr.Wilkes is learning to be assistant but Isabel still is anaesthetist and I want no better and no one else for it. May likes the launch but Eileen can't stand it, she gets sick and says it smells like a dirty lamp. One day Eileen told me cars were very nice things. I wondered what she was driving at but she soon came to the point and asked me to take the engine out of the launch and work it with cars which she says would hold it steady and would not make a smell.

Sarah wrote me a nice long letter and would like us to come home by Manchuria and Siberia but with four children I am afraid it is out of the question. I hope Willie takes a good rest. With love to you all from us all.

Your affect. son,
J.Campbell Nicholson

In November, Grandfather crossed the 40 miles to visit the Aniwans:

PASTORAL VISITS TO ANIWA
By J.C.Nicholson

Lenakel, TANNA
November 13th 1912

The arrival of the launch has enabled me to take up the work of Aniwa in earnest. The Aniwans are a different race to the Tannese; they are more akin to the Polynesians – such as the Samoans or Fijians. Lighter in skin, finer in feature and quicker intellectually. They are prouder too, and quick to take offence. Hitherto intercourse with them had been through their principal men, and in a great measure I did not get to know the rank and file of the Islanders. I was getting discouraged but at last I came into direct contact with the younger generation and found that they were all keen to go forward.

I have now visited Aniwa three times in as many months. On one of these occasions Mrs.Nicholson accompanied me, and we spent the best part of a week there, Mrs.Christian, the wife of our assistant, meanwhile looking after our children at Lenakel. Some times the mosquitoes are so bad on Aniwa that the natives put out to sea in canoes and spend the nights fishing. I had a very bad time once. On the other occasions a strong south-east wind was blowing and the mosquitoes were cleared out or else remained in their hiding places.

(Jot.80 April 1913)

Lomai had been at death's door from a sharp attack of pneumonia, but happily he had well nigh recovered when the last news came from Tanna.

There is an interesting account in the Jottings regarding the French that Grandfather had written:

Towards the end of 1912 and well into 1913, the French were doing their level best to cause trouble in Tanna; stirring up the heathen who in turn threatened the Christian natives, as Grandfather explains in detail in his letters and also in the Jottings (Jot.80 Apr.1913) where he says that the Condominium has been declared a farce, but is now assuming a more dangerous phase, and the sooner it ends the better for all concerned. Towards the end of the year the ever present problem with the French took an unpleasant turn when a French man-of-war called with the Assistant French Commissioner on board; his visit unknown and unannounced to the Condominium Agent a Mr.Wilkes. Their express reason seeming to be to stir up trouble amongst the natives to whom they gave the impression that they were about to expel the missionaries and take the Christian chiefs prisoners. Grandfather was accused of threatening behaviour, even seeing off the Captain of the French ship with a gun! In December this article appeared in the Jottings: (Jot.81 July 1913)

THE SEQUEL TO THE FRENCH THREATS OF DISTURBANCE ON TANNA

December 19th 1912

Following my report of the 12th November I got the surprise of my life. I voyaged to the seat of the Dual Government at Vila only to find that the French had made no report whatever against me, but that the Government Agent stationed on Tanna had assailed me – evidently with the object of standing well with the Government officials. But the report created a ridiculous situation. I was supposed to have driven a Captain of the French Navy and a company of his men helplessly along the beach at the point of a revolver!!

Fancy the French sacrificing the character of their Navy by accepting such a story. Its absurdity to put the poor Government Agent into a fix, and the upshot was that the French wished bygones to be bygones!

The sequel was that the British Resident Commissioner brought to Tanna the French Commissioner and his Assistant. They called at Lenakel and we entertained them. They inspected the Station and Hospital and the next day I got the natives together and acted as interpreter for the Joint Commissioners who, instead of stopping our Native Courts, as had been threatened, put them on a sound and permanent footing.'

Grandfather was still very concerned about the recruiting of natives as can be seen from this article: *"During the past year at least one hundred young men have gone, and one hundred households would make a large village on Tanna. Whilst the birth rate exceeds the death rate, and has done so for several years, I believe the recruiting of young men has prevented the increase of population which otherwise was assured. Very few of these men ever return, and when they do so, although they were taken away as recruited labour they have to pay their own way home, and come back as best they can. They are passed out of the New Hebrides as recruited labour, but they are entered into New Caledonia as 'immigrants' and sold at from £15 to £20 per head! And we hear now that the last three shipments have been sent to the nickel mines for terms of five years – poor fellows!*

I have written of the arrival of the new motor boat elsewhere, and will only say here to the friends at Tunbridge Wells, Weston-super-Mare and elsewhere, who sent us this new gift, how great is our rejoicing. The Lord, who so gloriously helped through His servants in re-building our church and hospital also made it possible to replace the launch. To all those whose hearts the Lord touched to help us so generously in these matters I convey the heartfelt gratitude of our people and ourselves, and assure them that our sincere prayer is that God may richly reward them both in this world and the world to come.

As regards their church and ours, Mr.Frater calls it the Cathedral of the New Hebrides. The Hospital, too, is all we could wish, and the operating room, erected to the glory of God and in memory of Ernest, late son of Mr.Marshall, of Bangor, Ireland, is thoroughly up to date, and worthy of a better surgeon than it has got.

During its first year the hospital has had 228 in-patients, representing all the five southern islands. We have performed 123 operations under general anaesthetic. Nilauas, my hospital assistant, is increasingly useful. He has himself been on the operating table twice during the year for a radical mastoid operation and bone disease of the leg, but he is now in splendid health, and I trust will be long spared to us all.

The people as usual supplied all native food for the hospital free of charge, each village bringing its share in rotation. The people have also contributed £20 towards a maternity ward. The increase in maternity work has been a marked feature of the year's work. (Jot.81 July 1913)

All known cases of leprosy, except one, are now isolated in a settlement, and the nearest teacher to the settlement conducts services at the boundary on Sundays.

Our people are now making a start towards supporting their own teachers and our aim for this year is to raise the salary of six of them. I believe it will be done as I believe the people feel their responsibility. They contributed generously to the cost of the former church and hospital, and now that they are free from this responsibility I believe they will do their duty as regards their teachers.

Mr. & Mrs. Christian, descendants of the mutineers of the Bounty, from Norfolk Island, have come to assist us and already are making themselves indispensable. Mr.Christian is a good all-round man, as much at home between the handles of a plough as at the tiller of a boat; and he knows something about boats as he has been engaged in whaling. He has made the Mission plantation a new thing, and if we could only get a market for produce I believe we could make the whole work self-supporting. We have acres of sweet potatoes, pumpkins, cabbages, maize, all planted amongst growing coconut trees. The hospital bill for feed next year will be very small.

We are still planting, and in a few years the plantation should produce enough revenue, together with voluntary contributions of the people, to cover the upkeep of Hospital, teachers salaries and general expenses. This has been our aim since coming, but it is dreary waiting for coconut trees to grow and produce copra. In connection with building operations, the people contributed their labour willingly and freely, and they take as much interest and pride in their head station as their Missionary does.

We intend shortly to have a special service for praise and thanksgiving to God for all His goodness to us since the hurricane, and at that service those who have so kindly and generously helped us will not be forgotten.'

Notes on 1912

The Home Rule question in Ireland was making front page news in Britain, with the Liberals unable to book a hall in Ulster for Winston Churchill to put the case for the Government. Sir Edward Carson said Home Rule would mean using the army to maintain justice for the Protestant minority and declared that 'If we cannot remain as we are, we will take matters into our own hands.' Britain was in the grip of a 'big freeze' in February with temperatures dropping to –35 deg. On January 17th Captain Robert Scott reached the South Pole only to discover the heartbreaking evidence that Amundsen had been there a month previously. April 15th brought one of the worst sea disasters when the Titanic hit an iceberg on her maiden voyage and sank with the loss of more than 1,500 lives. In London Churchill was worried about the increase in German ships and men and said that naval expansion is a luxury for Germany, a necessity for Britain.

In Northern Ireland the threat of Home Rule was causing grave concern with emotions running high and posters appeared in Bangor advertising meetings for the drilling of men for the Ulster Volunteer Force. Great-grandfather had not run for the Council but was still on the Board of Guardians for the Workhouse. The coal strike in England was being felt in the Province and the Belfast and Co.Down Railway found it necessary to curtail some of their services. Reports of the sinking of Titanic began to filter through and one Bangor lady, who had been a stewardess on the Olympic and had transferred after it was involved in a collision to the Titanic, was lucky enough to have been rescued. After nearly three years of procrastination, Ward Park, which it was finally called, was opened and a great success with tennis, quoits, croquet and for the children, see-saws and sand courts (I think it means pits). Ulster Day, 28th September, saw the signing of the Covenant (to keep Ulster British and no Home Rule) by many with some signing in their own blood. The Census had been the year before and the results showed an increase in the population with Bangor rising to 3,946 – it is now about 90,000.

Chapter XII – The Eleventh Year

Home On Furlough and War

Since there are no letters for the beginning of the year, Grandfather's letter in the Jottings dated January, will fill the gap:

Lenakel

27th January, 1913

We have entered the New Year with good hope that it may be a prosperous one in the work of the Lord here. Everything is quiet, and the recent activity of heathenism seems to have passed off. Whilst the heathen show a greater willingness to hear the Word, there are few signs of movement towards Christ and the worship. However, without sowing there can be no reaping, and it has been laid upon us to urge the Church members and teachers to pay more attention to individuals, speaking to them privately by the wayside, in the gardens or houses, and to pray for some one particular person.

We have been greatly rejoiced to hear that Mr. Frank Paton is to visit the New Hebrides, and are hoping that he will give Tanna a month at least. If he does, he is assured of a great welcome, as he has never lost his place in the affections and prayers of our people.

It is not easy now to find items that will interest the readers of Jottings. The usual rounds of services and schools and hospital work afford little that one has not already written about. I will try and take you, if you have imagination enough, a trip north with Mrs.Nicholson and myself, together with Mr.Christian, Lomai and other natives. We have to settle a new teacher in an old station, to visit our Leper Settlement and take the lepers a present of food and clothing. We have also to get hardwood fencing posts for the station here, as there are almost no hardwood trees growing near Lenakel. As we are to be away three days, due preparation has to be made. Food, bedding, medicine case, cooking utensils, soap, towels, etc., have to be packed. Rice, tea, sugar, salt, tinned meats, dresses, shirts, and kerosene tins made into buckets for the lepers. Saws, axes and wedges for the fencing posts. The John G.Paton and the old Pioneer, under Lomai in charge leaves soon after daybreak. Before starting, I have the hospital work to do, outpatients to see, and instructions to give to Nilauas about medicine and treatment. It is eleven o'clock before I have finished. The launch is lying at her moorings ready to start, and soon we are speeding down the coast after the Pioneer, towing behind us a little cedar dinghy which came from Melbourne by the last steamer. The dinghy is very necessary, as it is not safe taking the launch into many of our passages, or alongside reefs. In the absence of a dinghy we used to have to wait for a canoe to come off, and thus lost much time.

The day is fine, the wind fair, so the sails are set and the coast line flies past at eight miles an hour, and in less than two hours we are at anchor at Laope. The Pioneer is already beached. We make ourselves snug first, as this is the rainy season, and the rains at Laope are something to remember and protect oneself against. We put down two anchors. To avoid mosquitoes, Mrs.Nicholson and myself are to sleep on board the motor boat. The after part of the boat is fitted with awning, and with side curtains it looks like a little cabin. A hammock is slung, and under it a stretcher is placed. Our assistant, Mr.Christian finds a sleeping place by turning the Pioneer bottom up and sheltering under the boat.

After a cup of tea we go up the hill with Iakapas and Wap, the new teacher and his wife. Iakapas succeeds his brother Iaruel who was the teacher here. Iaruel has volunteered to go to another Island to teach. He is our first volunteer for foreign service, and we are greatly rejoiced that the call has come to him. I cannot remember any other Tanna man who has volunteered for Foreign service. Mrs.Wright, who supported Iaruel and Iata, his wife, will now take over his younger brother Iakapas. Iakapas was one of the first who went from our district to the Training Institute on South Santo. Now, after four years' training, Iakapas is beginning his life work. He has kept up his Tannese well, and is not puffed up with his knowledge of English. Besides his evangelistic work in the language of the people of Laope, Iakapas is going to start an English class for boys and girls from adjacent villages. There is to be a preliminary examination for this English class, and any boys or girls who cannot read fluently in their own language are to be sent down till they can do so. The villagers are very pleased to get Iakapas, and have made ready his house, and the puddings are ready to feast all who come to assist in his settlement.

After greetings and conversation with the people the bell rings for the service. Lomai, Kahwa, who is Iakapas's older brother, and Iakapas assist me, and we have a very hearty service. After the native feast and good-byes to the strangers, we go back to the beach for our evening meal, and soon to our beds – as the journey to the Leper Settlement is a rough and tiresome one, and we must make an early start. We sleep well, the rise and fall of the boat to the swell is not unpleasant, and severe heavy showers of rain caused us no inconvenience.

'Soon after daybreak we are all busy. Mr.Christian and some boys are away to cut the fence posts. A party of men and women have gone before us. The bags of rice are slung on poles and carried by relays of men, the lighter things are slung on the backs of the women. Our track is straight inland, up hills at first, and then down into a deep gully which cleaves its way between the mountains. The people have very kindly cleared it with their knives, so that we make good progress on our horses which have been brought up by some boys. Kahwa keeps close to us and sometimes we have to dismount as the ground on the descents and ascents is very slippery. The horses are used to it, and follow me down, sometimes, however, sliding past me, crashing through the undergrowth to get a foothold. It was in this district I lost a horse, he slid over a bank and fell thirty feet into water. By noon we get to the entrance of Loanalien. Two low fences have been made by the lepers, in the space between these fences we place our gifts. A hollow tree is beaten to announce our arrival, and soon the lepers

begin to gather. Some who are badly disfigured are ashamed to be seen. I am the only one who goes inside and shakes hands with them. Then I give to each some new garments and speak a word of cheer to them individually. After a few words and prayer they take the present of food. The tea, sugar and salt they are especially delighted with, but complain that I have brought them no soap. I promise to send them some, and they are quite satisfied. I asked our Church members to make a collection for this present to the lepers, but they only gave twenty-five shillings (£1 25p). Next Christmas, however, they have promised to do better, and I believe they will. Mr. and Mrs.Christian and ourselves supplemented the gifts of the natives, and our united gifts, added to the Mission box clothing, made a fairly decent show.

Kahwa and his people have services here on Sundays, but since the death of a Christian leper there is no one in the place who tries to conduct a service or teach. All the male lepers are heathen, and only three women have been connected with the Church. The lepers make very good gardens, and their friends bring presents of food when they visit them.'

I should say here that as far as Grandfather was aware, Tanna was the only place in the Islands where an attempt had been made to combat leprosy. The Condominium was doing nothing and it spoke well of the Tannese that they were willing to follow Grandfather's instructions on the matter. After leaving the lepers, Grandfather headed for home on the launch towing the dinghy loaded with wood posts behind; Granny took the horses home overland. The next day he set out for Aneityum in the south but they had no sooner cleared the coast when a big head wind came up so they headed back, calling in at Lenakel and then continuing north and running down the east coast hoping to call in at various stations, but there were tremendous seas everywhere and it was impossible to gain access through the reef. Grandfather now always carried a glass on the launch and it was falling, so they put into Port Resolution, which is an open bay, and they anchored there for the night. In the morning they headed for home and pulled the launch into the boathouse and it was as well they did as huge seas piled up shingle and the sea came right up under the boathouse door. There must have been a big blow somewhere else that accounted for the sea, but they weren't taking any chances.

(Jot.81 July 1913)

'Lenakel',
TANNA, New Hebrides.
Apr.15th 1913

My Dear Mother,

We expected the steamer yesterday morning and as she has not come yet we will most likely not get time to answer the mail she brings so must get our home letters written at once. The home letters and John's or Miss Murray's we always open with a certain amount of trepidation. What will the news be and what then the burden of our prayers.

We are all well except that I have been laid up for a few days by an accident. I hope you are all well and enjoying fine spring weather. This month has been our hottest with plenty of rain, everything is looking its best, gorgeous is the only word which fits it. But here there is always at hand the hurricane to stay nature and keep her from running riot. Mr.Christian was telling me this evening that maize which he is drilling up is six and more feet high and even from a rise in the ground he cannot see the boy with the scarifier working a few drills off, yet we only planted it five or six weeks ago, so it is with nearly everything, the roads grow up as quickly as you clear them.

I think I told you that the French are doing all they can to get me expelled from Tanna. Our poor little condominium agent, Wilkes, has sold himself to them, body and soul. What the price is we can only surmise, but it consists largely of promises.

Mr.Mahaffy[1] *came down in the yacht, a beautiful steam one like the big ones you see in Bangor Bay, at regatta time. I was his guest for three days visiting the East coast of Tanna, Fortuna and Erromanga. He let me see all the official correspondence. He went for Wilkes and gave him the chance to withdraw his lying report. Wilkes refused. He then told him not to be surprised if he found himself in a bad fix. The position is a delicate one. To clear Wilkes out at once would be to give the French the chance of saying it was done because he showed favour to them and they pay half his salary. But whether soon or late Wilkes has spoiled himself. The charges brought against me are that I threatened to put a bullet through the first of two boat loads of French Man of Wars men who put his foot on mission ground and that they had to clear out!!! No wonder they have been laughed at if they acknowledge that. That I told the French Captain it was useless to ask him for his word of honour because Frenchmen did not possess such a thing and that I insulted the French flag. These are the main charges but there are other trifling ones such as that I nearly galloped over the French Captain and when he tried to get to his boats I shook my clenched fist under his nose and prevented him. It really is no wonder that the report is read with peals of laughter by all who are fortunate to get hold of it. The Captain did not understand English and the report was got up by Wilkes and the Interpreter on board the French Man of War. These two have made a fool of the poor Captain.*

Fortunately Dr.Gunn was with me all the time. Mr.Mahaffy has so far only tried to show them the foolishness of the whole affair but if they will not step down by the way he keeps open for them then he is going to attack not defend. As it is, it seems likely that I will be made a shuttlecock, an international one as it has already reached the French Government and so must go to ours. The French Man of War followed the yacht down here and spent three days, Wilkes being with them most of that time. I am very sorry for his wife. She told me she knew nothing about the report and wept sore. I have seen her since. He is not treating her very nicely. Life is full of tragedies. Poor Wilkes in smooth waters might have sailed along fairly but he is unstable and the French pressure and threats upset him. In trying to justify himself he said the French would have put him out of Tanna if he had not done what he did. Then again the sequel of the visit would stagger any people but the French. Their Commissioner in the company of ours, Mr.Mahaffy, came down to say the French Man of War's visit was due entirely to a misunderstanding on their part and that they were sorry and wished byegones to be byegones. They stayed for two days and addressed a large gathering of natives. I acted as their interpreter and told the natives they were to have their courts, and in fact everything the French had tried to abolish, and now after all that they begin again. Mr.Mahaffy has given me leave to publish this. Happy are the missionaries who have no French to contend with.

On our way back from Fortuna the yacht called here and took our launch in tow to Erromanga. Cerebro Spinal Meningitis has broken out there after the visit of a French recruiter – 16 deaths. I did what I could and am sending back medicine by the steamer. The yacht left that night for Vila and we for Tanna. We ran into dirty weather, heavy squalls and tropical rain, but kept our course and got into the lee of Tanna in 7 ½ hours. When we got into smooth water and were running down the coast for home and bed I put the engine to full speed. Mr.Christian took the wheel and the boy keeping a look out. I lay down in a deck chair feeling happy we had got across so well, but was not down twenty minutes till there was a terrible bump. I rushed for the engine and stopped it and then the launch heeled over. We were all overboard at once and found we were right up on the reef, the waves breaking over us and carrying us forward. We tried to hold her but at last had to get out two anchors and making them fast to the stern casting them over the edge of the reef into deep water. This held her. Then we had three hours holding her up every time a wave receded to keep her from getting smashed. One time my feet got fast in the reef and she came down on my thighs. I thought all was up with me but Christian and the boy and a wave lifted her and I got clear, glad to find my bones unbroken. It was bitterly cold, sometimes we tried to keep right under the water as protection from the cold land wind. At last we felt her lifted up and by pulling in our anchors after a few bumps she was in deep water; we left our anchors. The engine started at once and we went full speed astern. She steered well and was not leaking. With a hearty Praise God we steered for home. I was very stiff and sore but after a few hours sleep we went back in the launch and picked up our anchors, diving for them. The launch has hardly a scratch. I got about somehow the next day but the muscles on the front of my thighs gave out and I had some fever and a few days in bed. Today I am able to walk a little without wanting to yell, so all is well that ends well. The boy admits he fell asleep. Christian says he does not know whether he was asleep or not. A launch is quick and the noise of her engine prevents one hearing the break on the reef unless it is very big. I am not telling the committee about it, it would only worry them. I must take an extra boy for long journeys.

This is a long letter written as I lie on the sofa, but it is bedtime. We are all bright and cheery. With love from us all to you all,

Your affect. son,

J.Campbell Nicholson

In May Grandfather writes in the Jottings of further repercussions from the French debacle of December 1912 that he had thought was finished with:

"Whilst I should have preferred a thorough investigation as regards Mr.Wilkes' report, I was content to let the matter drop as the British Commissioner suggested.

Any ordinary mortal would have been justified after this in believing that the whole matter was settled and done with. Will it be believed, that all that had transpired was but a blind on the part of the French, who were at the same time urging their Home Government MY EXPULSION FROM TANNA!! The official correspondence, as well as reports by Dr.Gunn and myself have been sent to the Home Government.

The French charge against me, based on Wilkes' report, is that I insulted their flag; that I threatened to put a bullet through the first Frenchman who entered my grounds; and that I told the French Captain that I could not ask him for his word of honour as a Frenchman did not know the meaning of the word.

Of course I addressed no such words to the French Captain – neither did I offer any insult or injury. Mr.Wilkes had played a role of unheard-of duplicity, induced primarily by fear. This is evident from the fact that he tried to justify himself to the British trader here by remarking that 'If he had not attacked me the French would have got him removed from Tanna.' As Mr.Wilkes went off to the French Man-of-War on the evening of the affair and remained some hours on board I suppose the report was drafted there. The language of the report is certainly not British.

He further goes on to say: *'The British Commissioner paid me a visit and walked with me across Tanna. He also had a tramp through the mountains in the south and visited the magnificent waterfall in the heart of the mountainous district.*

I was his guest on the Government yacht, and went with him to the Island of Fotuna, where we met Dr.Gunn. Fotuna is just one huge mountain top with the peak cut off straight across. The natives of Fotuna are Polynesians. How they got there will never be known – probably from the Tongan Group near Fiji. They are all Christian now and a fine looking race.

The island of Fotuna is thought to have large phosphate deposits – like Ocean Island. If this is true, and the phosphates are ever worked, it will not be for the good for the Islanders.

Leaving Fotuna we called in at Lenakel, and taking my launch in tow went to Erromanga. An epidemic of cerbro spinal meningitis had broken out here as the result of a visit from a French recruiter from New Caledonia. Seventeen people have died, and I saw several who had recovered but were partially paralysed.' Closing the subject he goes on to say: 'The conditions of affairs in the Group is becoming more and more serious, and must surely reach a climax. The Joint Court is incompetent to deal with French outrages proven up to the hilt, not by Missionaries but by officials, and in some cases by the highest British official we have here. The cases were handed over to the French National Court, and nothing done!' (Jot.82 Oct.1913)

Lenakel,
TANNA.
7TH June, 1913

My Dear Granny,

The Euprosyne arrived just about midday today. Mr.King and the Captain and an officer of the Yacht came on shore and spent some hours here and are now away to visit the Griffiths.

Mr.Mahaffy left Vila about a month ago. He will be at his home in Fiji by this time, so we shall not see him again. Mr.King is just back from England. He spent from October to March there and says he did not feel the cold at all, so there is hope for us.

James had intended riding over to White Sands this afternoon. Mr.Macmillan's Communion is on the morrow. We cannot go now and will just have to leave early in the morning. We had a visit from Mr.Macmillan and his bride shortly after they landed. She is very bright and I am sure will make Mr.M. a good wife.

I have been doing a lot of sewing lately, getting ready for our trip home. It seems a long time to look ahead but there is so much to be done one needs to make an early start. We don't think of leaving now till about the end of January from Sydney. We shall miss the worst of the winter in that way. I have just written Lizzie about getting a house for us. We both think we would like one in Mayfield. I would not like to be right on the Road like Ellie. I could never keep these wild youngsters of mine in the house all the time. They are used to having so much freedom here. I often think about John on the Princetown Road with his wheelbarrow and wonder how he escaped being run over by a motor car or some other cart or other. He will be quite able to look after himself now as he is used to all that – it will be different with the girls.

We expect to see Mr.Frank Paton in a few days and hope he will be able to spend some time here but all will depend on the steamer arrangements. Mr.Fred Paton is bringing out a wife from Canada, a cousin of his first wife's. They should be on board too, also Mr.Gillan.[2] *The Doctors in Melbourne have forbidden Mrs.Gillan to come back to the Islands. It is a great disappointment to her. I really don't know what they intend to do. In the meantime Mr.Gillan is coming back and she may with a few months' rest be able to come back. She underwent an operation in Melbourne some time ago.*

Mr.Macmillan saw John in Melbourne and says he is looking very well and has got a bit shy. That is something new for John. He sent us a small parcel by Mr.Macmillan with some little article for each of us and his lesson books for me to teach May. May is not very keen on learning and gets tired before many minutes are up. Mr.Macmillan says she is quite time enough, that children learn quicker when they don't begin too soon. Eileen is calling for me to come and get the eggs. I am afraid to trust her with them for she is such a terror breaking eggs and smashing things. She is too quick.

With love from us all to you all,

Yours affectionately, Isabel

Lenakel',
TANNA, New Hebrides.
July, 11th 1913

My Dear Mother,

We are anxious to get this mail and hear about Willie and Father, I hope both have recovered and are well again. It was a pity John was prevented from getting to see Willie. Jeannie must have had an anxious time about John. I am sure she often wishes he had a position on shore.[3]

We got Mr.Paton safely across to catch the steamer and were very sorry that he could not stay a month. We had such good hearty meetings and he saw about a little, but it was all such a rush. It was wonderful that he should have remembered the language so perfectly after being cut off from hearing or speaking it for nearly eleven years. He and I are the only two whites who can speak it and so have only each other in the world competent to criticise. Isabel knows it but would not give an address in it. I think Mr.Paton was as much pleased as he was surprised to see the development of the work since he left. He said 'there is no 'dying out' about these people, they are a different race to the other New Hebrideans'. But he never noticed that when he was down before and when we came here the people were decreasing. We heard a good deal of praise of the place and work and I hope are not unduly 'uplifted'. We have tried to lift the native by showing how things can be done – a whisper for yourself. After our trip round the group eight years ago I determined to try and show some missionaries how things should and could be done and I hope I have succeeded a little. One said, 'This is the 'showplace of the mission' and I was glad to be asked, 'tell me how you do this, show me how this is done'. 'What do you use for that', 'how do you cultivate those', etc., and the whole thing is simply, find out the best possible and do it the best you can and keep it the best you can, and last but not least, pray about everything, for if 'any man lack wisdom let him ask of God who giveth to all men liberally'. When I ordered my launch I told the builders that I wanted her built and finished so that if not kept clean she would cry out against me. Mr.Carruthers after seeing and getting a trip in her said, 'there is only one thing I don't like about her, 'and what is that?' I asked in surprise, 'oh', he said 'I would always be afraid of making her dirty'. That was a compliment to the builders carrying out my instructions. Mr.King, the Commissioner, was in her and said, ' there is only one thing you need and that is a glass case for her', and that was after she had done 14 months hard work and run 2 or 3000 miles.

But boasting is not good, but you are my mother and father and so can be imposed on. Isabel is very well and active. We may have news before this letter goes. May was very ill with fever and an attack of appendicitis but is alright again. Eileen was never so well as at present, she is a little terror. Peggy is very like what John was at her age and is a source of delight to all. You will all like her if the voyage does not spoil her. She is very healthy.

I had four days in Aniwa and held Communion services. We had a good trip both ways. The garden is a mass of bloom, gorgeous is the only word for it. We are having plenty of all kinds of vegetables and have a lot of potatoes, about half an acre, coming on splendidly.

I have not had to ask a penny from the committee for food and general expenses of the hospital for the past year. What with native contributions of food, what we grow and fees from whites, the whole has been covered and a little to spare.

We had good news from John, his cough has almost gone and he is doing well at school, also with his French and music. (I am leaving the letter open till steamer arrives).

No news and mail must go, but Isabel is in best of health and spirits.

With love,

Your affectionate son,
James Campbell Nicholson

The Jottings of January 1914 also include a piece from Rev.Frank Paton, one of the sons of Dr.John G.Paton, who had been stationed at Lenakel for seven years before Grandfather, when he made a visit to Tanna in July 1913 which Grandfather mentions in his letter

'Every inch of the ground was now full of sacred memories as we rounded point after point till we saw Lenakel Bay, where just seventeen years ago Mrs.Paton and I landed from the little Dayspring to make our first home and to begin what we fondly believed to be our life-work. The rattle of the anchor chain recalled me from my reverie. It was time to go ashore, and in a few minutes we were clasping hands with Dr.Nicholson, Lomai, Iavis and a host of others whom we had learned to love in the old days of "dark Tanna".

Ten years had failed to heal the wounds made by the uprooting of life plans, and words refused to come as we gripped hands in tense silence. Joy and pain were mingled in the deep tide of feeling raised by that meeting to which I had looked forward with such desire and such shrinking.

One after another came forward, and it was quite a long time before we began to wend our way up the old familiar road to the house. But what wonderful changes these ten years had brought about! The first thing that arrested our attention was the new Church half way up the hill- a beautiful structure fit for any European city. To the right of the Church and circling round the brow of the hill is the new home-village which the natives have dubbed "Sydney". While the Tanna "Sydney" is centuries behind its Australian namesake, it is just as many centuries ahead of the old Tanna villages. It marks the beginnings of a new civilization on these fair islands – if, alas, man's inhumanity to man does not blast the promise that it holds. To the left of the Church, higher up the hill is the Mission house, and between them is perhaps the most wonderful garden in the New Hebrides. The Doctor's hobby is to make his house beautiful for the woman who left her lovely Irish home to face with him the trials and hardships of life in the South Seas.

There is the Hospital with its beautiful operating room and neat wards; and away up the green slopes, behind and around the station, rise row upon row of stately young coconut palms in place of the wild reeds that used to be.

Lest Melbourne should feel left out in the cold, the Tannese have built another village about three miles inland and called it "Melbourne". "Melbourne" is in the bush and "Sydney" at the Port; but "Melbourne" has bigger houses and a wider street, and it possesses a Courthouse!

At the house we were welcomed by Mrs.Nicholson and Mr. & Mrs.Christian. The children too looked well and strong.

Great as were the evidences of material progress all around us, it was the people in whom our intense interest centred. Such hosts of them, and looking so strong and virile. Boys and girls in all directions, just as mischievous and happy as children should be. My heart filled up with joy to see what strides the Gospel had made in all directions under the faithful and consecrated ministry of the Dr. and Mrs.Nicholson; and rose in thankful praise to see Lomai and

Iavis fulfilling the promise of their early faith and zeal, and also to find the sons and daughters of the first converts more than maintaining the tradition of their fathers.

The Captain arranged to pick me up at White Sands on the east coast of Tanna on his return from Aneityum two days later. We all gathered in the Church. Think of the inspiration of that great congregation of 500 souls. How they sang! It thrilled me as my mind recalled the first service held at the foot of the hill just seventeen years ago, when only five natives gathered with us to worship God.

Sitting in the front seat were Lomai and Iavis, the two elders. Immediately behind them sat Tavo, a silent man but true as steel and one of our comrades in the dark days. Not far away sat Siak, the sainted Iaker's first and only convert. Near him was Ian Selok, our first house boy, who married Iesua, Mrs. Paton's first house girl, and afterwards volunteered for Kwamera and then for Nalebot – two of Tanna's hard and dangerous posts. A little further back sat Iauiko, the first man in a fierce central tribe to accept the Gospel. Not far away was Neropo, who returned from Queensland with his wife Sarah and remained faithful when others went back. Next I noted Kahwa, who went into the heart of Tanna and faced death for Christ's sake and the Gospel's. Near him sat Nilauas, who was one of our keenest boys, now assistant head man at the Hospital under Dr.Nicholson. To his left was Tauero, who tried to come between me and death at Lonebotbot. Face after face among men and women called up memories that made my heart well up in thankfulness to God. Many others were there – strangers to me, having been added to the worship during the intervening years.

Dr.Nicholson conducted the singing, as he did everything else, with military precision. I could not have believed that mortal lungs could raise such a volume of sound as burst from that full-throated congregation. It was tuneful sound too, with enough music in it to convince any sceptic as to the deep earnestness of the worshippers.

When I stood up and faced the people memories thronged in upon me, and it was hard to speak. On the very pulpit at which I stood were two tablets – one to the memory of Numanian, and the other to the memory of the ever faith-

ful and gentle Titonga, each of whom had a big share in the building up of the New Tanna. It was a memorable service, and I did wish Mrs.Paton and Mr.Hume could have been there to share the joy of that day.

Next morning after another service we rode out to the Christian villages within reach – along broad and clear roads, such as we only dreamed of in the olden days. The villages were models of neatness and cleanliness with flowers and variegated shrubs making them home-like. The Doctor's garden had evidently inspired the natives to beautify their villages.

On the way back we called on Mr.and Mrs.Griffiths, who have bought out Mr.Worthington; and here again memories were awakened; the plantation looked at its best. The maize was above our heads though we were on horseback.

Later we set out in the motor boat John G.Paton, to visit Neropo's and Kadi's villages to the South. The launch ran well, she is a perfect picture of a boat. The good old sailing Pioneer was on the beach awaiting repairs – she still has some go in her. The splendid order of the villages revealed the immense strides Tanna has made during the last few years.

On our return I went for a quiet walk with Lomai and Iavis and had a long talk over the old days. In the evening we again gathered in the Church, and I told the people about Korea, and Mrs.Griffiths kindly sang a solo.

Next morning we had to leave. I had only had a brief glimpse of Lenakel, and it seemed cruel to have to leave. At the foot of the hill a long line of natives were awaiting us, and we dismounted to shake hands with each. Some pressed baskets of mats upon me to take to Mrs.Paton. It was indeed hard to say good-bye. There was old Litsi Sore, who nursed me when a baby, and then came to Tanna with us as Titonga's wife, and many others whose life-story is written on the tablets of our hearts. When the last of the long line had shaken hands, we mounted and galloped off into the heart of Tanna. (Jot.83 Jan.1914)

Reading the Jottings it seems as if my Grandmother was ill later in July but Grandfather says in them that the natives' concern was touching and unlike previous times when your misfortune was due to something you had done, believed it was something that they had done and resorted to prayer for forgiveness in order that the cloud might be lifted from my Grandparents' house. Nursing my Grandmother meant that Grandfather had to rush four months' of work into two. He reports that in five days, with only native helpers he had twenty-seven operations under general anaesthetic and he says it speaks well of Nilauas and his staff that they did all the preparation work, and except for a serious abdominal operation, did the dressings afterwards. When my Grandmother left in October he says that 'we nearly all broke down' but were relieved by a choir of young men stepping forward as the boat left singing thank-you and farewell in English.

'Lenakel'.
Aug. 4th 1913

My Dear Mother,

Our boy was born and died on the 1st of Aug. Isabel was laid up for a week before with influenza and since her confinement has developed very bad malarial fever. She misses the bairn so much, it was the biggest and nicest we have had, was to have been called after me.

Mrs.Macmillan was with us and was very helpful. She is going across today as she is looking far from well and I am afraid lest she also be laid up on my hands.

On account of big seas we did not get a mail away in July, but hope that the Government Yacht may come down before the Aug. steamer and so permit us to get our letters and orders and this letter away.

I am feeling very anxious about Isabel and never leave her.

Your affect. son,
J.Campbell Nicholson

An excerpt from Jottings 85 gives other details:

One scene I shall never forget the service conducted by Lomai, Iavis and Nilauas at the graveside of our baby boy. Mr.Macmillan being unable to be present.

Mrs.Nicholson left Tanna for Australia with one of the children in November, as it was essential that they should both be away before the very hot weather set in. At present therefore I am alone with two of the children to look after.

When the natives came to say goodbye to their "Missis" they nearly broke us all down. The situation was only relieved by a choir of young men stepping forward as the boat left the shore and singing a farewell in English a mingling of thanks and good wishes – to a tune I had never heard before.

Lenakel,
TANNA, New Hebrides
Aug. 13th 1913

My Dear Mother,

The mail I hear got away by the Government Yacht last week so you will have heard of the birth and death of the baby boy and Isabel's illness. I am sorry to say she is very little better but one feels more hopeful. She had a hard labour haemorrhage, then fever and her breasts and now pelvic cellulitis. I have been with her night and day. I do not know what we would have done without Mrs.Christian who cared for the house and the children. The natives have been very kind and sympathetic and a great volume of prayer constantly ascended to God for Isabel. I do not know how people can live apart from the consolation of Christ. If one had not the Throne of Grace to go to at such a time they would be most miserable. God has answered and will answer prayer. May, Eileen and Peggy have been very good. May and Eileen prayed constantly and looked for an answer. We never told them about the baby nor yet did the natives. I do not know whether this was the best thing but Isabel was so afraid they would be constantly asking her questions about it. Isabel would like to get Peggy in with her. One day I gave in and it did her good as Peggy was sleepy and both went sound to sleep. But Peggy is not always so content to lie still. Isabel is taking nourishment freely now but mostly milk. We have tried her with everything we know or books could tell us. At first she would not look at milk but has taken a fancy for it these last few days. I have been unable to do any work. Nilauas has had full charge of the hospital and the elders the services.

I will send you a cable if I can arrange it, but it will not get to Norfolk Island till the 20th of next month.

I hope Willie has got home safely. I do not feel like writing much this mail. Will you please give the news to the Princetown folk. Tell them I hope Isabel will write herself next mail.

With much love,

Your affect. son,
J.Campbell Nicholson

18th. Isabel still improving and bright.
J.C.N.

'Lenakel',
TANNA, New Hebrides.
Dec. 10th 1913

My Dear Mother,

I am writing my last letter from Tanna as we expect to embark the day after tomorrow to get to Sydney just before Christmas. The month, since Isabel and Eileen left us, has passed very quickly, there was so much to be done that we had not time to fret though we missed our misses and Eileen very much. I had Communion services here and at Aniwa. Whilst I was at the latter place Peggy had fever but after the second attack had no more. I had then to visit and fix up the lepers and all the time the hospital here was crowded out. I had a lot of operating and one time did 27 in five days. For the last 5 months I have had 200 in-patients and 99 operations under ether or chloroform. Then we had to overhaul buildings and have all the station cleaned up, launch overhauled, Christmas holiday, etc. It has been a rush, now we are doing the odds and ends and settling up reports and accounts. But there should be some rest on the steamer. I am sorry we are not going right through home, but it would not be best for Isabel and Eileen to do so. I do hope they had a real good time and that we find them much improved in health. Isabel was very nervous about travelling alone, but the experience will do her good. The smallpox in Sydney is the only drawback but I hope will not interfere with us and our movements.

I have been much touched by people coming from all parts of Tanna to bid me farewell and telling me that I have helped them and done some good to their island. They accredit me with stopping the awful inter-tribal fighting that used to go on and when I come to think of it the three 'peaces' I got patched up in the north, south and here have all held good and there has been no fighting since. Those all occurred the time I was left alone on Tanna just after I came out.

May has been very good and a regular little mother to Peggy. It is pathetic to see her sitting down with Peggy on her lap putting her to sleep. We slept in different rooms at first but I felt so lonely I brought them into my room. Mr. and Mrs.Christian are indispensable. They are both good and splendid workers. He just works as if the place belonged to him and is the quietest and best-tempered man I have ever met. They have been a gift from God to us. They are going with us for a two month holiday. She will come on to Sydney to help with the children as I have business to do there and return by the same steamer to Norfolk Island for a month there, then they both return to Lenakel. He has signed for another three years.

Now I must to bed for tomorrow will be a rush. I hope Father and you and Netta are all keeping well. It will be good to see you all again.

With much love to you all,

Your affect. son,
J.Campbell Nicholson

Visiting Aniwa just before returning home he tells in the Jottings of the entertainment they provided for him before his departure:

'One evening a programme was handed to me, and at the top was written "A Concert to Dr.Nicholson." The body of the programme was made up like this: Vani's company, Rangi's company, etc., but no indication given of what was to be sung. Vani's company came first, and Vani appeared leading nineteen young men all in white shirts and trousers with black cummerbands and gay handkerchiefs suspended from one wrist. They stood in two lines facing each other. To my great surprise they imitated the gramaphone giving the hymn, "When the roll is called up yonder I'll be there," singing it well, and at the end of each verse imitating the pianoforte accompaniment with variations and all. Then with a round swing of the arm the coloured handkerchiefs fluttered overhead, a deep bow, and out they marched two and two. There were thirteen items on the programme and nearly all were action songs such as one sees at children's services, but these strong fellows went through them with a

seriousness and vigour wonderful to behold. It has given me a new idea and a new conception of the native character. The piece that brought the house down was "Three Blind Mice" in English the three mice having tails of palm leaf easy to be cut and which the dressed up farmer's wife cut off with a butcher's knife, much to the glee of the people. Lomai was sitting near me and laughed to exhaustion." (Jot.85)

When Grandfather left Tanna on furlough at the end of December, he was greeted with the news that the volcano on Ambrim – an island about three hundred miles north – had blown up with terrible loss of life and the complete destruction of the Medical Mission Station; he felt that the French would use it to their advantage, recruiters persuading the dispossessed to work on plantations and that as Tanna had an active volcano it could be next. It was on this note that he sailed for home.

FLAMING MOUNTAINS AND RIVER OF FIRE ON AMBRIM AN EYEWITNESS'S ACCOUNT OF THE VOLCANIC ERUPTION

BY THE REV.MAURICE FRATER

Paama, New Hebrides.

December 20th 1913

On the afternoon of Saturday, 6th December, I drew the attention of some of the natives to dense volumes of smoke that were hanging over our neighbouring island of Ambrim. The active volcano in the region of Mount Marum is so often enveloped in clouds of smoke that little or no attention is paid to such a phenomena. But the smoke of that afternoon was a long distance from Marum, and covered such an extensive area that it looked as if several new volcanic vents had been formed. The natives first thought that bush fires were raging; and as the island had been parched by a drought of several months duration, this explanation seemed reasonable.

The approach of darkness, however, settled our speculations, and revealed one of the most awful, and at the same time one of the most magnificent sights that it is possible for the eye of man to behold. For over an area of twenty miles the earth seemed to have opened up, and along this huge fissure tongues of living flame were shooting up into the sky. In one place at the centre of the disturbance no less than six volcanoes had formed within a short distance of each other, and from these six furnaces, real pillars of fire were belching. So intense was the glare that the whole district was illuminated and reflected the red glow, and the inhabitants of the surrounding islands beheld a spectacle such as had never before been seen within the memory of living man.

From the newly formed craters rivers of molten lava were flowing, in a flood so powerful and fierce in volume that this liquid fire burst away from its single channel, and high up on the mountain side the lava river divided into separate channels, each tearing down in its destructive course till it reached the sea. One flow raced northwards in the direction of Ranon, another followed a southerly course, and hissed into the sea near Port Vato. From our station on Paama we could follow the whole course of the Port Vato flow. Its path was clearly defined, and in the darkness as it wound in and out among the hills, the track of the red -hot lava was like the trail of a huge serpent.

It is easier to imagine than describe the fearful cauldron that was formed when this huge mass of red- hot lava mingled with the waters of the ocean. To such a height was the volume of steam shot up that it looked as if a new crater had been formed in the sea itself. Outbursts from the numerous volcanoes continued every few seconds during the night, each one like the boom of thundering guns reverberating in the night air. The sight was awe inspiring and grand in the extreme, but the thought that the rivers of fire, in their destructive courses, might be overrunning native villages and destroying human life made the scene intensely tragic.

In the midst of the terror a report reached Paama that the Ambrim hospital had been overrun by the fire, and at once the two traders and I set off in our launches to render what assistance we could. Long before we reached the Ambrim coast we could see crowds of natives assembled on the stretch of sand near the Pansileo boat landing. They were waving branches of trees to signal us to approach, and were all terror stricken. They were natives from the fire zone round about Port Vato, and were eagerly waiting in the hope of escaping across to Paama. In the excitement they gave us vague rumours that the volcanic fire had overrun the Mission Station at Dip Point and destroyed the Hospital and all the Mission buildings.

Information so alarming gave pause to our original intention of rescuing at once these waiting natives. They were congregated well away from the fire zone, and were for the present safe, while others farther along might be in imminent danger. I therefore promised them that I would return for them as soon as possible and raced off at top speed for the Hospital district.

The journey down the coast of Ambrim was frightsome in the extreme. A heavy pall of livid smoke lay over the island, ash and cinders were falling all around, and the sea was covered with debris and scoriae. Several volcanoes were belching forth at places which we knew were near the site of villages. At intervals, tremendous explosions occurred, and all nature seemed to reel. The scene reminded one of pictures of the Judgment Day which old painters were wont to depict. "Dies Irae," with its "heaven and earth in ashes burning," seemed a fit description. On rounding Craig Cove Point we were thrilled with surprise and dismay. A new active volcano was actually belching out fire and smoke from what was before the site of the Hospital. Hailing a boat of refugees, I was greatly relieved to learn that all the patients and the whole Hospital staff had escaped and were sheltering on Malekula; but the sad information followed that hundreds of natives who lived in the Dip Point district had been overtaken in the devouring flames. To approach near the location of the Hospital was impossible; the sea all around was simply boiling hot, and as no natives in that part were left to rescue, we sailed across to Malekula to ascertain the state of Dr.Bowie and Mrs.Bowie and the patients. The Doctor was ill with fever, but from the nurse and patients we got the story of their wonderful deliverance – which was briefly as follows:

During the Saturday night, December 6th, and the early hours of Sunday morning, December 7th, Dr.Bowie and his staff had watched the volcanic fire, never dreaming that their place or their lives were in danger. The worst that could happen, the Doctor imagined, would be a flow of lava coming down the valley behind the Hospital; and yet as the place was encircled with a high ridge of hills, this seemed to be almost impossible. Considerably to the north-east of the Hospital a river of fire was flowing, and when it reached the sea the Doctor imagined that, having found an outlet, the danger was over. But about daybreak on Sunday morning terrified natives rushed up with the news that the earth had opened some distance up the valley! This meant escape or death, and instant preparations were made for the removal of the patients.

The launch was filled up with the more helpless patients and sent away with the carpenter, Mr.Robertson, in charge, across to Malekula. The whale boat was also filled as quickly as possible and followed. But there still remained a number of convalescent patients and some of the native workers; and no boat was available, and no help forthcoming. Dr.Bowie and his assistant, Mr.Bayley, remained with these, and managed to pacify them with the assurance that their plight would be observed from other islands, and relief would soon arrive. They remained on the beach while Dr.Bowie returned to the Station to make sure that every one had gone. Just as he started a crowd of terrified natives from the bush villages tore down to the beach in headlong flight, shouting to all to fly as the fire was on them. Nevertheless, the Doctor persisted in returning, having searched the station, and ascertained that the place was clear, he ran for his life. He had barely reached the beach, racing at top speed, pursued by the fire, when the earth reeled and a terrific roar burst upon their ears. A quick backward glance revealed to his astonished gaze the fragments of his house and hospital hurled high into the air and a volcanic vent formed and blazing in the very centre of the hospital grounds.

The position now seemed hopeless. But relief was at hand. A braveheart, over on Pentecost, Mr.Filmer of the Church of Christ Mission, had been watching the fire all night, and as he saw the line of flames gradually encircling the Hospital and Mission Station, he had hastened across the sea in his launch to the rescue. In the Providence of God, he arrived in the hour of dire extremity, and was in time to save. But, even now, it looked for a time as though death would overtake them. They were in the launch it was true, but the falling ash was so dense and hot that the position could not be maintained. So hopeless, indeed, did their case seem that they actually discussed whether it would not be preferable to meet death by drowning rather than be burned alive by the falling cinders. The Good Hand of God was upon them, however, and after a time, the atmosphere gradually cleared, and they got away from the burning zone. At sea, they met a schooner which had come from Malekula to the rescue, and transferred their living freight.

And then these lion-hearted fellows actually turned and went back into the mouth of hell to rescue the crowd of helpless natives. By this time the Hospital launch had reached Malekula with its patients and the news of the disaster. Immediately, launches and cutters and schooners sped across to the rescue, and all the day long the efforts to save the beleaguered natives were strenuously continued. The timely arrival of the French steamer made the work of rescue easier, as the launches, instead of having to undertake the long journey of fifteen miles across to Malekula with their burdens of refugees, transferred the people at sea, and went back immediately for fresh loads. By this means during the first day over a thousand natives must have been rescued and transferred to Malekula.

It is impossible to conjecture at present how many natives perished, but we fear that some hundreds must have been overtaken by the fire and destroyed. After the fire had somewhat subsided, Mr.Merton King, the British Resident Commissioner, called at Paama, and asked me to visit with him the scene of the disaster.

We found the configuration of the whole district around Dip Point so changed that it was difficult to state precisely the exact location of any particular place. So tremendous had been the forces from beneath that a new range of hills, about 500 feet high, has been thrown up near the site of the Hospital right across the valley! Near the head of the Meltugan valley four active volcanoes were still belching away, while over the entire district, numerous jets of steam were issuing out of the lava, until the place suggested the steam issuing out of the power house of a giant factory. Everywhere over hills and valleys and plain there was a state of turmoil. The Meltugan district and the valley behind the Hospital had been thickly populated, and no hope could be cherished that any natives caught in the fire could have escaped.

To our amazed eyes, there in front of us – in the place where we thought the Hospital stood, a land locked boat harbour had been formed! A harbour of water boiling hot!! No boat could venture on that boiling sea, but Mr.King took his boat sufficiently near for me to get some photographs. And that it was perilous is evident from the fact that while the sailors were leaning on their oars at the entrance to the harbour there was heard beneath us the dull boom as of an explosion under the sea. No second warning was needed, the boat was speedily turned and directed towards the yacht, which was lying out at sea in safety.

Three weeks after the eruption at the Hospital, two new volcanoes burst out at S.E.Ambrim to the north of our station at Taviak. At daybreak, on the morning of this fresh outburst, the inhabitants of Paama were startled by a series of rumbling shocks, followed by the kind of tremor which we now know precedes the opening up of a new vent for the volcanic fire. Instinctively, all eyes were turned to Ambrim and there, in the light of the morning sun, dense volumes of smoke were belching out of a new volcano and curling skywards in the most fantastic shapes. Then another roar, and a second volcano burst out near the first. Fortunately, both were up on the hills far way from native villages though we could not tell in what destruction the lava streams might be working.

A trader from Epi was here at the time in his launch, and he and I and the local trader, set off in our launches to see if the natives were in danger and to rescue them. On the way across the channel we met native boats from Ambrim filled with refugees and we were assured by the terrified people that we were going on no useless errand. We sped on, and on reaching the boat passage found hundreds of terror stricken natives assembled. The three white traders, too, had abandoned their stations, and were waiting with the natives in the hope of the arrival of rescuing launches from Paama. At the time of the outbreak the dust and cinders had come down in such heavy showers that the villages were nearly submerged.

The frightened natives had run hither and thither, not knowing which way to turn to escape the ash and cinders. But soon they realised that their sole hope of safety lay in making for the boat passage, and by the time we arrived great crowds were congregated on the sands. All day long the three launches, assisted by native boats, ferried the people across to Paama. The motor launches were small, and owing to the heavy seas that were running it was dangerous to overload, so that we had to proceed with the greatest caution. But on the first day we must have rescued at least 400 natives. At nightfall, owing to the bad boat passage and the big seas, the work of rescue had to be abandoned. Indeed, one boat, the best and largest of the native fleet, when returning from Paama, was caught in the darkness and wrecked.

It was trying to have to leave the crowd of helpless natives huddled up there all night on the sands, but at daybreak on the following morning the work of rescue was resumed. A few natives absolutely refused to leave, but, altogether, we must have ferried over 700 people. They are now divided among the Paama villages, and will remain there until the danger is past.

In the two outbreaks at Dip Point and S.E.Ambrim, the native boats, in common with the launches of the white residents, plied all day across the channel in the work of rescue. But the system in vogue among heathen races is very different from that which prevails among people of Christian lands. When the Titanic sank, women and children had the first consideration, but in times of stress and danger in the New Hebrides men and boys are the first to be saved. At one place near Craig Cove a crowd of natives had congregated and were waiting their chance of rescue, a native boat came in and took way as many men and boys as the boat could carry. No attention at all was paid to the women and girls. Fortunately, a trader's launch was on the spot soon after and rescued the crowd of women and girls. When I arrived at the boat landing on the day of the outbreak at S.E.Ambrim a crowd of men made an attempt to rush the launch. But I informed them that that was not the British way, and that the women and children were to be rescued first. They then very quietly retired and helped the women and children into the launch.

In times of danger the strange idiosyncrasies of the native temperament reveal themselves. Some natives absolutely refused to be saved. Rather than leave the patch of ground they called home they preferred to be swallowed up in the devouring flames. One rescuer tried to reason with a native that unless he left his land he would perish, but the native coolly and stoically replied, "All right, me die." Some natives would insist on carrying bundles of yam. One woman refused to be saved unless she was allowed to carry her load of yams with her. But there was no room in the boat for yams, and she was left. The rescuing boat had not long left the beach when she was swept away with the fire. Another old woman asked the rescuers to wait for her until she had cooked some yams.

The natives are puzzled to account for the catastrophe that has overtaken them. They have no idea of the operation of natural laws. Some person or spirit, they argue, must have done it. The heathen tribes accused each other of making the fire, and began fighting over the matter, so that while the rivers of molten lava were destroying life and property the heathen were killing each other with knives and axes and muskets! To the Christian natives the visitation is every bit as mysterious. They think that God was angry with the heathen natives, and sent the fire to destroy them.

For several nights after the outburst the heavens were ablaze with fireworks. The amount of heat given forth into the atmosphere from the numerous volcanoes had so charged the air with electricity that great flashes of light shot out every few seconds. The French steamer could not get its wireless to work owing to the disturbed state of the atmosphere.

In haste, yours sincerely,

MAURICE FRATER.

Later Details.

January 25th, 1914

In my last letter I stated that about seven hundred refugees from S.E.Ambrim had been safely removed to Paama. Glad as the natives were to be saved from the ash and smoke of the volcano, no sooner had the launch cleared the boat passage and began tossing on the big seas, than many of them wished they had remained on Ambrim and taken their chance with the volcano. Few of the women refugees had ever been off the land before, and the sight of the big rollers threatening to engulf the launch frightened them to death. They expected a watery grave before they reached Paama.

When we reached Paama the refugees were landed at the Mission Station, and for a day or two they camped on the clear ground in front of the Mission house. An open air life would have done them no harm if the weather had been good; but in the middle of the rainy season it was necessary for them to be provided with shelter.

A meeting of the Paama chiefs was called, and it was arranged that the Ambrim refugees should be lodged among the Paama villages until such time as it was safe for them to return to Ambrim.

The Paama people have indeed proved themselves good Samaritans, the villages vying with each other to carry off the greatest number of refugees.

To illustrate the vast changes that Christianity has made, I was struck by a conversation with an old chief, possibly the oldest chief on the island. When we were arranging about hospitality for the homeless he told me that the farthest back thing he could remember was a big eruption on Lopevi, when crowds of natives escaped in their canoes and landed on Paama. I said to the old man, did the Paama people of those days show as great kindness to the Lopevi people as they were now showing to the Ambrim people? He smiled and said, "OH, WE ATE THEM!"

The Ambrim refugees had been three weeks on Paama when the two Resident Commissioners arrived in the Government yacht and invited me to accompany them on a tour round Ambrim. From Vila they brought a large stock of provisions in case the refugees should be in want of food. But no one applied for relief, though there can be no doubt that if the natives had had to remain on Paama for an indefinite period, Government assistance would have been necessary. On our return from the tour the Commissioners intimated to the natives that they thought the violence of the outbreak was over, and that they might now with safety return to their homes. A large number followed the advice of the Commissioners and went back, though the people of the villages in the vicinity of the volcanic outbreak are still sheltering here.

The natives of Ambrim have passed through a time of severe trial and suffering. In the crisis the teachers showed up well, and proved themselves Christian heroes. Many of them stood by their people to the last, helping them into the boats, and only escaping themselves after all their people had gone. Some, like Jamie Taltase and Joseph of Asi, refused to leave Ambrim. They thought it their duty to remain and pray with the people who did not leave Ambrim.

It is difficult for the people to understand a visitation like this. They came to me in a body and asked for an explanation. They thought that God was angry with them and was punishing them for their sins. Poor things: they have indeed been passing through a time of stress and suffering. May an all-wise and an all loving God comfort and sustain them. I trust that all those who have the interest of the New Hebrides at heart will remember them in earnest prayer to God.

The heathen have their explanations and their remedies for extinguishing the fires. With no idea of the operation of natural laws, their perceptions of cause and effect are hopelessly muddled. Anything in nature they cannot account for is attributed to the action of unseen spirits. When the volcano at Dip Point burst out the ash fell in heavy showers on the villages in the S.E.Ambrim district. An old chief, a former sacred man, made a bunch of certain kind of leaves and after performing some incantations, waved them frantically in the air and entreated the spirit of the volcano to extinguish the fire. From some craters ash of a greyish colour was thrown out, from others ash of a dark colour, but from the volcano which the old man tried to stop thick showers of Pele's hair fell and covered the ground with needle like bristles, resembling the hair of a pig. The old man's explanation was that some one had killed a pig and, dipping the skin in the blood, had thrown it into the crater of the volcano. The spirit of the volcano was enraged, and was now throwing back the hair in showers. But the old man's remedy was ineffectual and, with the others, he was forced to flee. Some others tried to appease the offended spirit with gifts of coconuts. The first attempts to reach the lip of the crater were fruitless. The fall of red hot cinders made the journey impossible. Later on, when the violence of the outbursts had somewhat abated, a few natives managed to climb up on the windward side, and were successful in throwing in loads of coconuts, which, they declare, were the means of extinguishing the fire.

At the time of the last big eruption, in 1894, the British Man-of-War, Dart, was in the Islands. A few weeks after the outbreak some officers made an expedition into the interior. They found a fissure extending the whole length of the island, and upon the lines of this fissure were the lava springs and the craters, living and dead. At that time the line of fire followed the fissure, and on this occasion the fires again seemed to follow the same fissure.

With kind regards,
Yours ever,

MAURICE FRATER

NOTES ON 1913

In Europe, unrest continued in the Balkans and in Britain the Suffragettes were becoming more militant, destroying telephone lines and bombing Lloyd George's new house – luckily no one was hurt. The sad news came from the South Pole that Captain Scott and his companions had perished just ten miles from safety. Throughout the year flying records continued to be broken, both with distance and looping the loop for the first time. Civil war broke out in Shanghai and the trouble spread with Japan threatening to step in if any more Japanese were killed. On October 10th, the last obstacle between the Atlantic and the Pacific Ocean was removed with dynamite and the Panama Canal linked the two for the first time.

The strength of feeling against Home Rule in Ulster was increasing. In Helen's Bay in January, the local Unionist Party burnt an effigy of the Prime Minister, Mr.Asquith, holding a copy of the Bill and later that year, the Unionists formed their own 'parliament' with Sir Edward Carson as Chairman. A Royal Proclamation banned the import of arms into the country. Bangor saw the year starting with a spate of burglaries with 10 local youths being arrested and sent to Borstal for 3 years. The Drama Club was in full swing with its latest production held in the Dufferin Hall to packed audiences, many standing at the back. April, known as the start of the emigration season, saw 20 Bangor couples sailing down Belfast Lough on the SS Manitoba on their way to America. June saw the arrival of the First Battle Squadron of the Home Fleet in Bangor Bay and what a sight it must have been, from warships to pinnaces they filled the bay. The Vice Admiral's pinnace was landed on the pier with the aid of the winch on a coal boat! Unfortunately the festivities were marred by tragedy when three members of the crew of HMS Temeraire were drowned when their pinnace overturned while racing in the bay. On the sea front, Mr.Caproni opened another ice-cream parlour; his fourth.

One of the unfortunate side effects of the spread of Christianity was the increase in kava drinking. 'The heathen are sinking into a state of torpor. Now that they have peace from inter-tribal fighting and active witchcraft, they are indulging more in kava drinking, and have more of it than they can drink because their numbers are so much less than formerly.' (Jot.82 p.13). However, the good side of Christian faith was portrayed when Grandfather tried to split up Communion by holding it at different places; the Elders showed his reasons to be unsatisfactory as before the different tribes would have been split up, but now they were one and therefore one Communion at Lenakel for all, where the people would come from all over the island and meet together, the local people helping the visitors to build temporary huts and providing gardens to supply the visitors' needs, was much more satisfactory. True, that the 'sing-sings' the heathen held, the natives came together, but except for their rifles they brought little in case it was stolen and it was known amongst them that the fighting usually started with the sing-sings'. Grandfather accepted that they were right. (Jot.82 p.13)

Unfortunately, there were no more letters after 1913. Whether they were destroyed or lost is not known, but the Jottings still exist in the British Library in London and it was from them that I was able find out what happened to my grandparents from when they returned to Tanna in 1915 until they left early in 1917. They maybe lack the insight that one would obtain from letters home to his mother, but there is a wealth of information in them that makes it worthwhile including them.

Chapter XIII – The Twelfth Year

A New Year and No Doctor on Tanna

1914

The British Government found itself in a grave situation at the beginning of the year: Bonar Law, the Tory Opposition leader, warned that if they persisted with Home Rule for Ireland there would be civil war, Winston Churchill threatened to resign as First Lord of the Admiralty unless there was higher naval expenditure, the Chief of the General Staff resigned and Western Europe continued its military build-up; added to that, by June, 2 million workers were on strike. At the end of the month the event that sparked the beginning of World War I occurred in Sarajevo; the heir to the Austro-Hungarian throne, Franz Ferdinand and his wife were assassinated and on 4th August war was declared. The ugliness of war came not long afterwards; a bloodbath at Mons saw the Allies in retreat and the Russian Army was hopelessly overwhelmed by the Germans at Tannenberg, wielding bayonets against machine guns. Meanwhile, the Suffragettes continued their campaign, burning mansions in Scotland and one slashed a Velasquez in the National Gallery.

In Ulster feelings were running high because of the Home Rule Bill and in March the local papers reported how despite the embargo on armaments being brought into Ireland, 70 tons of ammunition was landed at

Donaghadee at night, carefully avoiding the Coastguards and the Police. My Grandparents arrived home in March and would view with apprehension the current situation although my Grandmother would read with interest how the fashions were changing; the hobble skirt had been introduced, which as one wag said, made running for trains a little difficult! For the first time in Bangor the local cinema showed talking pictures and during the summer the yacht racing continued, but on 4th August, the black cloud of war that had threatened for so long, finally broke. At this time the local authorities were expected to shoulder the burden of looking after the families of those men that had joined up, until such time as the Government had set up a Distress Committee and immediately because of the war certain areas were 'off limits'. In Conlig near Bangor, a suspected German spy was arrested; also an Austrian who was valet to a local gentleman, and two men on board a vessel lying near Grey Point were taken into custody. Grandfather took the opportunity to address Mission meetings, particularly stressing the French situation. Local authorities were asked to reduce the use of electric light, which caused a few grumbles and at Clandeboye there were over 2,000 volunteer troops under canvas. At Christmas the local people helped to brighten up the troops with entertainment and Canada and America sent five enormous cheeses, each weighing 80 lbs., to the local people.

The Mission magazine reported my Grandparents' safe arrival in Ireland and also some snippets of news of what was happening on the islands:

JOTTINGS 84 – APRIL 1914

A note at the beginning of these Jottings reads:

Dr.& Mrs.Nicholson and their children arrived on the 18 ult., and are now at home in Ireland. Mrs. Nicholson is much better for the rest of the voyage, and but for occasional attacks of fever, the children are well. By and bye, after a good rest in the summer, we trust it may be possible for the Doctor to address some meetings. We are sure his story will be heard with deep interest, as Tanna has a great fascination for all readers of Dr.Paton's book.

Dr.Nicholson's evidence will be of great service due to the crisis in connection with the Joint Control of the Islands. First hand testimony is of immense value, and will assist our cause. Happily the case of Judah has stirred up considerable feeling, and many friends have arisen in unexpected quarters to help forward the plea for justice and fair play to these unhappy Islanders. Of this some particulars are given on page 14.

This number of Quarterly Jottings marks the "coming of age" of our little magazine. It has been a very real privilege to be spared to prepare and distribute during these years the record of work done for the Kingdom of Christ. Perhaps it was a bold venture, in view of the crowds of magazines that are published, to launch yet another, but if the increase in circulation (from 2,000 to 7,500), and the many kind things that have been said of Jottings, may be taken as a vindication of the venture, then we have good cause to be thankful.

Owing to many adverse circumstances, the supply of New Hebrides arrowroot has fallen off of late. It is difficult to get any now, as the stock held by the Hon. Agents in Scotland is exhausted. We are hoping, however, that a fresh supply may be forthcoming before long.

We have been given the following remarkable story from a most reliable source:

The French Government yacht, Gallia, recently sailed for Tanna, bent on the arrest of Lomai and Iavis. For what misdemeanour no one can conjecture – probably a part of the organised scheme that the French are carrying out of incarcerating all the prominent native teachers. Shortly after sailing from Vila fire broke out on board the French Government yacht. The flames spread until they obtained the mastery, and the Gallia had to be beached and burnt to ashes!

While my Grandparents were home on furlough, Lenakel was in the capable hands of Mr.and Mrs.Christian. They were born on Norfolk Island and were direct descendents of the mutineers of the Bounty; Mr.Macmillan had overall charge of the island. Mr and Mrs.Christian sent back regular reports to Grandfather and Nilauas and Lomai wrote as well. The local traders attended services that helped set a good example to the natives, including when either Lomai or Iavis were preaching.

On the island of Malekula, north of Tanna, where the natives could be particularly fierce, an interesting report came from the local missionary, with a sequel that illuminates the injustices that were practised by the French:

JOTTINGS 83 January 1914
QUARTERLY JOTTINGS
Issued by
"THE JOHN G.PATON MISSION FUND"
JUDAH – A MIRACLE

From Shorthand Notes of two Addresses by the Rev. Fred J. Paton, New Hebrides

"Wherever a Missionary settles in the New Hebrides there are volunteers from other heathen Islands, natives who have become Christians – ready to go with him and to share, under his oversight, the burden and dangers of the work.

Such a teacher was with me at my main station. He knew the native language and was able to help me greatly. By and by he offered to go wherever I wanted him, and as a village specially noted for fighting had attracted me, I went there prospecting. No white man traded in that direction and no one cared to go as one white man observed, "It is not healthy to go ashore there!"

Well, the fighting village agreed to have a teacher. Perhaps because they wanted the matches, calico and other things that a teacher might give them. We bought a small piece of land there put up a house for the teacher and started 'school'. No one came, but we decided to keep on. Then there came a crisis. The teacher came to me saying that pandemonium reigned at the village. A heathen of a neighbouring tribe had decamped with the wife of the leading chief. A great heathen ceremony had taken place at which hundreds of pigs had been killed, to secure the aid of the spirits in tracing the whereabouts of the culprit.

Murder was in the air. The betrayer – a notorious villain had been guilty of murder after murder. His village was instantly raided and burned to the ground, and his tribe took to the bush.

Directly the news reached me I went over, and when passing through the dense forest occasionally I gave an Australian "Cooee" and here and there from among the undergrowth a face would show itself with the enquiry, "Have you seen my father," or "Tell my little child I am hiding here." Every man carried his gun.

Then the horror deepened. A little native girl, the daughter of the betrayer and murderer, was found by the fighting tribe. She was seized and dragged to the village square, a hole was dug there, and into the hole that little girl was thrown and buried alive! That was the beginning of the Vendetta.

The search continued, and another poor little child was seized and shared the fate of her sister. A third girl was brought in, and the chief and his men had laid aside their guns to dig the grave for her living tomb. Just then a Frenchman who was passing, rushed in, covered the grave diggers with his Winchester, and ordered the release of the child or alternately the contents of his rifle. There was no gainsaying that potent argument, and the third victim was delivered over to the Frenchman who bolted to my house, as life was precarious to the robber of the vendetta. The child ran away and escaped.

The pursuit of the betrayer was still relentlessly carried on. The buried children had not satisfied the blood lust of the pursuers, who were soon hot on the track of the guilty pair. They were almost caught, when, to save his own skin, the betrayer left to her fate the woman whom he had dishonoured and plunged into safety alone.

Alas, for the woman. She was seized and dragged savagely by the hair to the village square weeping in terror. In order that the vendetta might be restricted to the family, her own son was told off to shoot his mother. To refuse would have meant his own death; and to save his life and avoid the vendetta spreading, the son crept behind his mother and shot her through the back with an arrow. Her body was thrown into a shallow grave and the dogs and pigs dug up the body and ate it. When I went there some days later I saw some of the bones lying about.

Then I went to the chief of the fighting village and said, "There has been murder on murder. Can you not now make peace?"

"No," he replied, "there must be yet another death to equalise matters."

He however agreed to my plea that the vendetta should at least be confined to the family or relatives of the man who had sinned adding, "If the other side agrees to that we will keep each to our own territory."

I passed the message round and a sort of peace was patched up, but the hunt for the betrayer and murderer did not cease. He was chased from village to village along the sea coast.

One morning at dawn I was going to the Mission School when the murderer's younger brother came to me, saying, "They want to kill me for what my brother has done." I had built a stone fence round my place and the heathen had agreed that inside that fence was sanctuary for refugees. I had told them of the Cities of Refuge of the Bible. My store was within the fence, and the brother slept there. One night as I was prowling round the fence I saw the gleam of a rifle barrel pointing straight at the door of the store. I crept up, knocked the barrel off, and asked what was the matter? A native, if you give him time, will always find an excuse. (You would think he belonged to our own race in that respect!). The native said he had thought that a walk might do him good and so he happened to be there! I suggested that it must have been a nice little walk for him, ten miles in the dark, including the crossing of a river infested with sharks. Well, I told him to be off, and he went.

Shortly after, at five in the morning, I heard the sound of voices near the fence and went out. Two men were there talking. One of them was the betrayer of the chief's wife the multiple murderer, with a record of crime from boyhood up to thirty-five years of age. I thought he wanted sanctuary, and said, "No, I cannot take you; your brother has done no wrong and he can stay, but you have murdered men, ruined the woman and sent her to her death, and children have been buried alive through your course of evil."

"Oh," he answered coolly, "I have just come in for my brother because our old mother is crying for us, and I want to show her we are still alive."

I said, "I told your mother you were both alive."

"Yes," he replied, "she believes that when you are talking to her. But she wants to see us both."

Now I had heard it whispered that this black hearted man was intent on murdering his younger brother – so I faced him the question, "Are you not here to kill your brother?"

He smiled, and looked me straight in the eye as he replied, "Missionary, do you think I would kill my own brother – the son of my own mother? No." His brother and he had been drinking a bowl of tea together, and I watched his hand as he raised the bowl again to his lips – there was not a ripple on the tea. That test showed him not to be excited but perfectly calm. I trusted his word, and the brothers walked towards the wall fence together. The elder brother vaulted the wall and held out his hand for the gun which the younger man was carrying. I noticed with some anxiety that he afterwards retained the gun instead of handing it back to the younger man.

I went in to do some translation work, but could not settle down. A native came in and said, "Missionary, you will never again see the younger man alive. Come out with your telescope and watch." I went out to the beach – it was low tide – and put the telescope to my eye. In the bush some distance away I descried some fifteen men, all armed, standing among the trees. We tried to warn the brothers by lighting a fire on the beach, but could not attract their attention.

I watched the elder man walking opposite his brother, and then I saw the fifteen men step out; and instantly, with lightning rapidity, the elder man turned, slipped behind his brother, and with that borrowed rifle, shot him in the back. He staggered a few steps and fell and the murderer fled into the bush.

I called for volunteers to accompany me, but none came forward – all were involved in the fighting and expected to be shot – but the teacher joined me. We swam the river and rushed and crawled from tree to tree until we reached the fatal spot, and there lay the younger brother quite dead. We buried him there.

The teacher went back home and I went on to plead again with the chief for peace. "Yes," he said, "Now I will agree to peace. An equal number of deaths have been paid and there shall be no more shooting." But each village had to consent to pay so many tusked pigs, and they reluctantly agreed.

For two or three days thereafter things were at a standstill a severe storm had turned the river into a flood – but I went down, as I thought I could swim it. When I reached the other side, along the beach lay a great tree torn up by the roots, and behind it I thought I saw a man lying down with something in his hand that looked like a gun. To run would have been fatal, so I made a rush towards the tree, and swinging round the upturned roots, I grasped the corpse of the murdered younger brother!

The sea had washed the body out of its shallow grave – the sharks having been kept back by the storm. The superstitious natives were terror stricken. No one would help me bury the body. I did it alone, and went home.

Subsequently there was a fierce hurricane, and for a week no crossing of the river was possible. But one day I saw a native standing on the other side frantically waving to me to come across. I plunged in, and when I reached the shore there was that ghastly corpse loose again, and I was asked to bury it. But I refused, and suggested that the elder brother – the murderer – should be forced this time to bury his brother's body; and at the muzzles of several muskets he was made to complete the task. This he did, as calmly as if it were a matter of daily routine.

But all the time the terror of it was eating into that callous heart.

A period elapsed without any word or sign of the murderer. I knew nothing of his whereabouts, till one day he startled me by re-appearing at my place and astounded me by avowing his desire to be a Christian. But my faith would not reach that far. This man wanting to be a Christian – this, the most treacherous scoundrel in the Island, the murderer and betrayer. No, I could not believe it.

But I forgot the Grace of God.

I forgot that his very desperate condition of heart might have driven him to Jesus Christ.

Doubtful and incredulous, I sent him with a letter to a Missionary in the north of the Island.

Six months elapsed and he returned with a letter testifying that he had done splendid work, and was the finest man that that Missionary had ever had!

But still I could scarcely believe this astounding miracle, and I sent him away to the South for further testing. This time he was gone for two years. And at the end of the second period he returned bearing assurances that he was really a new creature – an absolutely changed and Christian character! He had learned a new language, and the Missionary in the South urged that if I would not baptise him and appoint him a Church member, he himself would be glad to do so, and to receive him as a native teacher and evangelist.

I said, "The new Missionary wants you to be a teacher, and I am willing to baptise you if you are ready to go to him."

"No," came the determined answer, "Missionary, if you think that I am good enough to be a teacher, then I want you to send me to my own village where I did all the evil – where I ruined the woman and murdered those men, and where I was regarded as the worst man of the tribe. Send me there, and let me try to bring them to Christ"! Now that was a test indeed! I would have shrunk from that ordeal – it was a harder task than I would have faced – or suggested. There were warriors in that fighting village with hearts still full of bitterness, mindful of the wrongs that this man had committed.

But he persisted, and I at last believed in the Grace of God, and baptised him – Judah.

Soon after, Judah left for his self-selected post of danger; and the first news that I received of him was that when the fighting village fell on a native of another tribe to club him to death, Judah rushed in as the clubs descended, swung weapons off here and there, and wrested one club away; but offered no resistance – not a vestige of the old slaying spirit was left. The blood lust was gone, though the courage remained. The lad who had been attacked came to me streaming with blood, but his life was saved.

The heathen were awed by the mighty miracle of Judah's conversion, and before long, chiefly by his own efforts –he actually won the whole village for Christ.

Then Judah came to me and begged to be sent to another village where there were a lot of so-called "civilised" natives, i.e., men who had been to Queensland and had learned about Jesus Christ, but nothing more – some were indeed worse than real heathen – drunkards and gamblers and the lowest of the low. They dared not return to their own tribe, but were just "hangers-on" to Christianity because it offered them a whole skin and safety from violence.

To these abandoned men Judah went. They refused to listen to him declaring that they knew more than he did (which was true, for many of them were better scholars); but the difference lay in the fact that Judah knew Jesus Christ and these only knew about Him. Well, Judah lived and strove there; and under his influence and teaching these natives one by one came to know Christ for themselves

One day Judah came to my house bearing in his arms a little girl about eight years old; and laid her gently on the floor. I said, "What have you got there, a dead child?" He answered, "I am not sure – feel her pulse." I found she still lived, though she was a skeleton.

She was an orphan, and there are no orphanages in heathenism. When her parents died the child – as was the heathen custom – was cast out into the bush – nobody wanted her and nobody cared. At last a native took compassion, but "the tender mercies of the wicked are cruel." He saw she was near death, so he just picked her up and threw her out on to the edge of the scrub, too lazy to bury her! Judah heard of it, and ran to find the child. Just in time he brought her gently to me, and by careful feeding and a course of medicine she recovered. Judah said, "I think the Lord let me know of this dying child, and now that she has recovered I think He means me to care for her," and that little child became Judah's adopted daughter, and is now one of the brightest children in the village.

Yet further evidence. Women and children are nothing to heathen as heathen – and these cases I am relating confirm the change in Judah's heart and life. A young widow – a mere girl of sixteen or seventeen, who had lived about my premises; her husband when dying had begged us to take care of her – went into the bush to see her heathen mother. On her way back she was kidnapped and dragged into a heathen village.

The girl's brother found me and pleaded with me to try and save his sister. Judah heard of the trouble, and ran to me to offer his help. We set out to rescue the girl. The natives had surrounded her, and guns were ready to fire on the rescuers. Judah, unarmed, volunteered to take the risk with me. We rushed in, held the ringleaders, and saved the girl.

Every insult was heaped upon Judah now that he was a Christian, but he stood it all.

It seems that his wife had been nagging him – she had let her tongue run freely since Judah became a Christian – and in a paroxysm of rage she had smashed a bottle over his legs. In regard to this incident I received a message from Judah, saying that he was not fit to be a teacher. I returned an instant answer, "You are the best fighter in the district, and when it is known that the wife of the best fighter thrashed her husband without getting killed, that news will do more good than fifty sermons – keep on teaching."

Just before I left for my tour in America and Britain it was necessary to appoint three Elders to be in immediate charge of our Church, and to preside at the Communion services.

I left the appointment to the vote of the Christian natives, and the first man chosen was Judah – ex-murderer, ex-cannibal, ex-betrayer of women. This was the man considered fit to be an elder of the Church. And there in the open air – in the place where once they cooked and feasted on human beings, there with the pure streams of the valley glistening a hundred feet below, and amidst the banks of tree ferns and every form of fern life, with the sweet scent of the roses near by, and with the everlasting hills towering behind us; in that lovely place we sat round in solemn communion with our Lord. A hundred and thirty all told – every man and woman present were living proofs of the power of the Gospel. A Communion never to be forgotten.

That is what the Grace of God in Christ can do.

A sceptical heathen native came to me one day proclaiming that he did not believe in Christianity. I answered "What about Judah?" "Ah," he said, "I had forgotten Judah. When he was a heathen we were never safe, at any time we might be killed even in our sleep; but when he became a Christian we knew that we were safe. Now we send for him when there is fighting, for Judah makes peace. I had forgotten Judah."

Greater miracles are occurring now than ever occurred anywhere in the Bible, except the Death and Resurrection of Jesus Christ – which causes these miracles. This is a greater day than Pentecost."

THE SEQUEL
ARREST OF JUDAH BY THE FRENCH INQUISITION

But Judah was destined for a yet severer test. On the 4th of August 1913 a French warship anchored near Onua, Malekula, and a landing party arrested Judah. He was handcuffed as though he were some dangerous criminal, he himself having not the least idea why he was being arrested.

It appeared subsequently that Judah was charged with having twelve months previously prevented a Frenchman from shooting a native called George for gathering nuts on his (George's) own land!

There, on British ground, this high-handed act was perpetrated by the officers of a friendly Nation, claiming joint control over the New Hebrides Islands.

As the French led him away handcuffed Judah turned round to the surrounding natives and said, "You pray, we pray – goodbye."

He was taken to Vila, the capital of the Islands, and incarcerated in a French prison; and there he lies today, still awaiting trial; a victim of the base despotism of an ostensibly civilised nation.

The Rev.Frank Paton reached Vila a few days later in August, and sought an interview with the British Resident Commissioner about Judah. Through the British Commissioner, permission was obtained from the French Resident Commissioner for Mr.Paton to see Judah.

Mr.Frank Paton writes thus on the subject: conditions were laid down as regards my interview with Judah as follows:

1. *An official from the French Residency must be present.*
2. *I must only speak in beche-le-mer English.*
3. *I must make no reference to Judah's arrest, or to the causes of his detention in a French prison.*

"I had perforce to accept these conditions or leave Judah unvisited, so I presented myself at the French Residency at the time appointed. A policeman at once took me before the French Resident, who repeated the conditions of the interview, and on my accepting them I was led into a room where Judah was standing with a puzzled expression on his beautiful face.

His looked changed to one of joy at the sight of a friendly face, and my heart went out to this Servant of Jesus suffering persecution, whose only crime was that twelve months ago he tried to dissuade a Frenchman named Theuil from shooting a native for collecting coconuts on the native's own ground.

There were three French officials present, the Assistant Resident Commissioner, the Commandant of Police and another. I felt completely gagged, as we were not allowed to speak about the thing that was uppermost in both our minds. After saying a few words and giving a message of love from my brother, I asked the Assistant Commissioner if I might pray with Judah. He looked blank, and the Chief of Police frowned, and as they didn't forbid it, I turned and prayed with Judah. This ended one of the most painful interviews of my life.

Is not this an utterly intolerable situation? We are under Joint Control – the British flag floats in the breeze beside that of France, and yet a Christian teacher, a man whose saintly character is beyond all reproach, is arrested and handcuffed on British soil, and taken to the French prison without knowing of any single offence that he has committed against the French or the Condominium Government.

His own friends are not allowed to see him except under a gag. He cannot get into touch with his lawyer, and even the Native Advocate, appointed by both Governments for this very purpose, is politely told that he has no standing as this is a Man-of –War affair. And all this brutal oppression and cynical injustice goes on under the British flag.

Is it any wonder that all who love justice and mercy have resolved that this Condominium must end, and that if the British Government cannot be moved by official channels, it must be compelled by the rising indignation of the British people to bring to an end this reign of injustice and oppression beneath its own flag."

Ready shortly in booklet form.

JUDAH
A MIRACLE

Copies may be had of any of the Hon.Secretaries of the John G.Paton Mission Fund, or of the printers, Messrs. Francis & Sons, 60, High Street, Southend-on-Sea.

Price, a halfpenny – by post 1d

JOTTINGS 84 APRIL 1914
Page 14

THE DUAL CONTROL INJUSTICES
Judah's Trial

The many enquiries that have come to us following the efforts that friends have been so good as to make in the case of the false arrest of Judah will add special interest to the latest news of the false and unjust proceedings in connection with Judah's trial.

The Joint Commission, we are informed, "tried" him, and sentenced him to two months' imprisonment "for extortion"!

But what a trial. His application to be represented by Counsel was refused, and the Commission also rejected his Counsel's application to be heard as a witness. Judah therefore had no opportunity of calling a single witness to prove his innocence. Surely no Court outside the New Hebrides, of any civilized nation would condemn a man in such circumstances, but such is "Law" in these Islands, as administered by the Joint Commission of two of the leading nations of the world, just because a man has a black skin instead of white.

The Rev.T.Watt Leggatt, in a private letter to us on the subject, makes the following comment:

"I cannot trust myself to speak on the injustice of the whole proceedings. I know the man. I instructed him in the Christian faith, received him into the Church, and had him as one of my teachers, and a more kindly, gentle soul as a Christian never lived.

We have not yet heard the last of this trial. A report is being drawn up on the subject, and if we cannot get fairness from the French, we can at least hope for an honest explanation from the British as to this gross miscarriage of justice.

It was while my Grandparents were at home that war was declared and the Mission wondered how the natives would view it. They had preached peace and goodness and here they were doing the exact opposite. It was also a worry that their supporters would not be able to help them as much as they had previously. There was hope, though, that as Britain had gone to the aid of France that the French would relinquish their hold on the islands and in the meantime have a sense of fair play; but not so, a French Man-of-war had been down to Tanna to try and arrest Lomai and Iavis. However, the Jottings was asking their readers (they had 7,500 subscribers) to write to their MPs and other influential people to plead the case against recruiting and it was beginning to have an effect; questions were being asked in Parliament and prominent people were taking up the case. The Jottings reports (Jot.87 p.2) 'we have heard of Frenchmen embracing British in the exuberance of their friendship' (In the Group).

Just before Grandfather left home in the Spring of 1915, a letter arrived from Tanna: *'The natives of the Islands of Tanna, so recently cannibal savages (and some still remain so) have of their own initiative collected, entirely among themselves, the large sum of £70 and brought the amount to Rev.Macmillan asking him to send the gift to England for the widows and orphans of the British soldiers killed in the War'.* As Grandfather remarked it showed the feelings of friendship that the natives had for the British, and particularly as the War had affected the natives' trade. (Jot.88 p.5) This came with a letter that appeared in a later Jottings (88) *"Recognising that much good has come to them in past years from subjects of his Majesty, the natives of Tanna desire to say that they are not unmindful of what has been done for them and for their fellows in the New Hebrides by men and women from various parts of His Majesty's great Empire.*

They cease not to pray that victory, clear and complete, may rest with the forces of His Majesty and their Allies, and further, the people of this small island humbly request that His Majesty King George V will be pleased to receive an expression of practical sympathy from them in the accompanying contribution, most willingly and heartily given, for the relief, in some small measure, of suffering amongst those of His Majesty's subjects whose husbands and fathers have given their lives for King and country in this great war." (note: somehow I feel that the natives had help in writing this.)

From all over the globe from parts of the Empire, gifts of money and men were coming in to help the war effort; from Hong Kong, British Guiana, Sierra Leone, parts of Africa including the Northern Provinces of Nigeria who sent from the Native Treasuries the princely sum of £6,542.

Lack of letters and reports, as grandfather was at home.

In Jottings 86 October 1914, there are a number of interesting articles to do with Tanna and the New Hebrides as a whole:

Jottings 86 October 1914

MR AND MRS CHRISTIAN

of Lenakel, TANNA

As the friends of our Mission are aware, Dr.Nicholson has the great advantage in his work at Lenakel, Tanna, of the assistance of Mr. and Mrs Christian, who came to the New Hebrides from Norfolk Island.

They were born on Norfolk Island. They are the direct descendents of the mutineers of the Bounty. The parents of our assistants were brought to Norfolk Island from Pitcairn Island, when that Island was considered to be overcrowded.

It is now nearly three years since Mr.& Mrs.Christian took up their work at Lenakel. Dr.Nicholson speaks with warm appreciation of the splendid help that he has received from his assistants. Mr.Christian, he says, can turn his hand to any kind of work, and is equally at home on land or sea. He has had experience in whaling and is quite used to the sea and ready for any roughing it in the launch.

"Mr.Christian," the Doctor goes on to say, "is no speaker, but is to us and the work, better than a dozen orators. We have been together through rough times and tight places, but I have never heard a grumble or a despondent word pass his lips. As regards work my only complaint against him is that he does too much in such a climate.

"The work, the Station, Hospital, Church, launch, &c., are to him as if they were his own; and the natives are all sincerely attached to him."

"Mrs.Christian also is a real helper. She takes a class to teach the natives singing, and also carries on in our absence the sewing class for native women. She has indeed been a great help to Mrs.Nicholson and myself in many ways."

"Since we left I have had reports of the work from Mr. and Mrs.Christian. They tell of the schools still conducted regularly and well by the teachers, and state that the Sabbath services are just as good as when we were there. Lomai and Iavis take the services in turn, and it is interesting to state that they have among their congregation, besides the natives, Mr.& Mrs.Christian, Mr.Robertson, who built the Hospital and Church after the hurricane, and who has now taken up land and started to plant near Lenakel, and Mr.and Mrs.Griffiths, our neighbouring planters. Thus a good example is set by the white residents to the natives."

"Mr.Macmillan is in charge in our absence."

"Nilauas, my Hospital assistant, wrote to me on the 11th June, and I give

below a translation of his letter. I have always called Nilauas "Neruk", my son, and he therefore calls me father."

Dear Father Doctor Nicholson,

I am writing to you in order that you may know we are all well. Lomai, Iavis, the teachers, our women and all the people.

We never forget you in our prayers I and Nauam and Kakob and Mr. Christian pray always for you.

I am not now as strong as I was, as I have a swelling and pain in the bone of my leg every day, and am putting it each day in a warm carbolic bath. If you were but here you would give me relief for my pain, but God will help me to bear it.

Iaruel has returned from Malekula, where he was helping Mr. Fred Paton. The new church at Lokavit has been completed, and they are soon to call us up there for the opening services.

My news is finished for the present. I have no more words to write to you, Doctor.

I, who write, am Nilauaus. Goodbye and may God bless you and Missis and the children of you two.

(In the same Jottings)

We learn from two sources that the French officials in the New Hebrides are making persistent endeavours to arrest Lomai and Iavis the two Christian chiefs of West Tanna. That the effort is official is clear from the fact of the French Man-of-War having been to Tanna on this wretched business. No one knows what pretext the French can formulate to "whitewash" this unworthy and unjust raid on innocent and upright natives.

Of all the natives on Tanna, Lomai and Iavis are, by general consent, the noblest and best. Of course they are staunch friends and helpers of the Missionary; and it looks as though this fact is the underlying reason for the effort to arrest them. But the French are not good hands at inland journeys. Lomai and Iavis have not forgotten their experience as trained warriors in the old days, and probably know a trick or two of bush hiding that will stand them in good stead in outwitting the French. But what a disgrace it is that in the Pacific the sons of France – France for whom this country is bearing such sacrifices – should be so lost to all sense of fair play

Chapter XIV – The Thirteenth Year

A Hazardous Return

It was in February that Germany started to blockade the ports of Britain, Allied merchant and naval ships taking heavy losses and those at home learned of the new horror of tear gas and chlorine gas which the Germans had introduced into warfare. Early on in the year, severe floods in the Thames saw Windsor Castle surrounded by water and the milk and papers being delivered by punt. American neutrality was being severely tested when the passenger ship Lusitania was sunk without warning by a German submarine fourteen miles off the south west of Ireland: 1,400 people lost their lives. And at auction, Lot 15 bought by a Mr.Chubb, saw him the proud owner of a famous ancient monument; Stonehenge. If one good thing could be said about the war it was that views of what women were capable of had changed forever. Gone was the 'shrinking violet', the frail creature who might take a 'fit of the vapours' if confronted with something unpleasant and in its place was the fact that in some factories where women took over from men, were now two and a half times more productive than before. In Brussels, the British nurse Edith Cavell, was executed by the Germans on a charge of treason – she had harboured French and English soldiers – and on the Greek island of Skyros, Rupert Brooke the poet, who was in the Royal Naval Division, was laid to rest after dying of blood poisoning at the age of 28:

If I should die think only this of me
That there's some corner of a foreign field
That is forever England. There shall be
In that rich earth a richer dust concealed;
A dust that England bore, shaped, made aware,
Gave, once, her flowers to love, her ways to roam,
A body of England's, breathing English air.
Washed by the rivers, blest by sons of home.
And think, this heart, all evil shed away,
A pulse in the eternal mind, no less
Gives back somewhere the thoughts by England given;
Her sights and sounds; dreams, happy as her day
And laughter learnt of friends; and gentleness,
And hearts at peace under an English heaven.

In the Jottings of January 1915 (Jot.87), the editor makes this observation:

'The question is often asked, how the War affects the New Hebrides. At first it seemed possible that actual hostilities might have taken place in the Islands, but that danger is largely removed, though not perhaps entirely. The main troubles are the uncertain running of the steamer from Sydney and the trade depression by reason of the chaos in the markets. If copra is not purchased the trader and the native alike suffer, but the trader more particularly, as the native can live on the products of his land.

As everywhere, of course, the uncertainty causes paralysis and a shifting of trade in new directions may have an effect on the Island, but whatever the economic readjustments may be there will, we sincerely trust, come a definite and final change in the conditions under which the Islands are held and governed.

One change is already evident, the attitude of the French in the Group towards the British. We have heard of Frenchmen embracing British in the exuberance of their friendship. If the changed feelings will only last, the future may bring brighter and better days to our little field of Missionary effort.

One thing about the natives that helps to dispel their puzzling questions about white men at war is their unhesitating trust in the British sense of justice and honour. When told that Britain is at war to protect the weak and insist upon the fulfilment of treaty obligations, the problem is settled for the average native, and he is fully satisfied. It is strange and very gratifying how soon the Islanders distinguish between good and evil in white men, and how universal is the sentiment of confidence in the British.'

'Dr.Nicholson, as will be seen from another page, has not yet returned to the Islands, mainly because of sickness in the family. The hoped for improvement will set him free and he will be back on Tanna, we trust, by the spring.' It was due to serious illness and surgery that my Grandparents didn't leave Ireland until April 1915.

***From our First Mission Station* Jot.87 Jan.1915**

Dr.Nicholson expects again to sail for Tanna somewhere about the time this appears in print. Sickness has prevailed in his home circles since his arrival and he himself, and also Mrs.Nicholson, has undergone operations.

The steamship service from Sydney is affected by the War, and it may not be easy to get back; at any rate delays are almost certain.

In the meantime, the Doctor has kindly sent us a letter and jottings from a report that he has received from Mr.and Mrs.Christian, and from Nilauas, the Hospital assistant, as follows:

'Mr.and Mrs.Macmillan paid a visit to Aniwa in August last. The sea was rough both ways, but Mr.Macmillan's launch is a fine sea boat and behaved splendidly.

The Aniwans were well, except Tausi, who had been suffering from pleurisy and pneumonia, but was recovering. Sabbath services and schools had been held regularly and well attended. Communion was held on the Sabbath that Mr.Macmillan was there and proved to be a time of blessing.

Among the letters that have come to me from Tanna is one from Mr.Robertson. It may be recollected that Mr.Robertson came down to the Islands from Australia after the great hurricane, and that it was he who rebuilt the Church and Hospital, etc. Mr.Robertson has now returned to Tanna, and settled near to Lenakel as a planter. The natives are delighted to have him back on the Island, and have sold him land.

In his letter Mr.Robertson reports that Mr.Macmillan came across for the Communion Service at Lenakel, and that about four hundred native Christians were at the Sacred Feast. In the evening a thanksgiving service was held. The collections for the support of teachers amounted to £7 18s. A lady who was on a visit to Mr. and Mrs.Macmillan was present and sang a solo, and the natives sang hymns in English.

The news of the Declaration of War reached Tanna on the 15th August. Almost instantly the price of copra dropped from £20 to £6 a ton, and the price of goods rose by 33 and a third per cent. At the same time the white people in the Islands were warned that possibly it might be months before the steamer could come down again. A British warship in the Group cleared for action the moment the news reached them, and in two hours was repainted!

From Mr.and Mrs.Christian I learn that quite a large party of tourists landed at the Lenakel Mission Station by the July steamer and made a tour of inspection. They appeared to be very pleased with all they saw.

Women and children come about the Station, asking to be allowed to work for dresses, etc. The little boys are found useful jobs about the Mission premises and get loin cloths and shirts for payment. Mrs.Christian adds that some of the native women have asked that their dresses may be "a little flash", and have offered to work a day or two extra for the advantage of being in the fashion! The "fashion" being a few pieces of coloured braid and some lace here and there about the dress. It is not all vanity this natural love of something pretty, but shows that the people are keen to keep themselves neat and smart in appearance. Mrs.Christian has noticed this specially of late at the Church services – even the little babies, she says, have pretty white dresses. Nilauas's little baby was brought to Church, if you please, in a white bonnet and a dress once worn by Peggy!

It is particularly gratifying to note that the neighbouring planters attend the Communion Services at Lenakel, and thus set a good example to the natives.

The British Commissioner and the British Judge of the Joint Court have been to Tanna, and stayed the night at Lenakel. Judge Roseby, who had not visited the Mission Station before, seemed very pleased with all that he saw.

In August, after the Declaration of War was promulgated, the Steamship Company plying between Sydney and the Islands intimated that the sailings of their vessels might be considerably curtailed – it was intimated that possibly even as much as five or six months' interval between the calls might be experienced. Unless a good stock of provisions is laid in the commissariat may be in a somewhat straightened condition before long; and the lowering of the value of copra will make it hard for the traders.

The Elders, Lomai and Iavis, are conducting all the services well and regularly, and the attendance at the schools and services is good. Nilauas the Hospital assistant, has a bad leg. He wanted Mr.Macmillan to cut it, but there seems to be need for a skilled operation to remove some of the bone.

Mr.and Mrs.Christian close their letters with expressions of love for the children of the Missionaries, whom they miss so much, and whose absence is harder to bear the longer it lasts.

The last letter is addressed to Dr.Nicholson by Nilauas, and is here given in full.

From Tanna to Ireland.

August.

My Dear Father,

I, Nilauas, write this letter to you that you may know about the Holy Feast. Missi Macmillan came across and we had good meetings. Twenty-two adults and infants were baptised, and we had good singing in the evening. I would like also to tell you that Iavis and Lomai, the Elders, as well as the teachers and people are in good health. There have been two deaths – one at Lenamout and one at Isapiel.

As yet the people at Loananbaint have not got another teacher, but I am rejoiced to tell you that they have their schools and services and are strong for the Kingdom of Jesus.

We have now no castor oil and the dressings and bandages are finished. Will you send us some. The people have sold Mr.Robertson a piece of land so that he may settle amongst us.

We all send you our greetings our Missionary, and pray that God may bless and help you and the Missis and the children of you two.

I am Nilauas, your son."

JOTTINGS 88 – APRIL 1915

(Excerpts therefrom)

The difficulty of keeping open the lines of communication to use a war phrase – is becoming a menace to Quarterly Jottings. Happily the Censor does not trouble us, but ships wait on trade, and when trade is dull steamers do not find it worthwhile to sail so often, hence delay to mails.

War ships – British and French – used to patrol the Islands, and occasionally by their good offices letters were despatched between steamer times. But no one knows where the Men-of-War are now. Incidentally, there are compensations, due to the absence of certain ships of war, but it were better perhaps to be discreet in regard to this subject at this juncture.

In consequence of serious sickness in his home circle Dr.Nicholson has been obliged to delay his departure to the Pacific, but we are expecting daily to know the date fixed for sailing. The June steamer from Sydney is the earliest that can be caught now. The hearts of sick and suffering Tannese must often turn towards Ireland, praying for the advent of the succourer with his "sleep medicine" and his skill.

On East Tanna, where the Rev.Thompson Macmillan is at work, the rainfall is sometimes phenomenal. In ten days there fell ten and a half inches of rain, and the record torrent by a rain gauge was found to be three quarters of an inch in ten minutes! No wonder that the plants are of emerald green in these lovely islands of the sea."

JOTTINGS 89 JULY 1915

(Excerpts therefrom)

We received tidings of the safe journey of Dr. and Mrs.Nicholson as far as San Francisco. From there they were continuing their voyage across the Pacific. The Atlantic crossing however, did not pass without one thrilling incident in that a German submarine fired a torpedo at the vessel and missed, in God's great mercy, perpetrating another ghastly and shameful deed of wholesale murder – and this by the orders of a civilised nation!

What rejoicings there will be on Tanna when the Doctor and Mrs.Nicholson arrive. For long weary months the sick have cast longing eyes at the Hospital, bereft of its surgeon, whose skill called forth their implicit confidence. All the activities will revive on his return. The drooping spirits of the diseased and wounded will spring into life again, and pain will be exorcised in many a weary body. How great a privilege to be thus used of God for "the least of these" in the uttermost parts of the earth.

The Government Yacht called at East Tanna lately, and kindly conveyed to the post at Vila a letter from the Rev.Thompson Macmillan, who reports that Tanna is expecting Dr. and Mrs.Nicholson by the next steamer, due in May. We fear those high hopes were doomed to disappointment, for it would be a record to have accomplished the long journey in that time.

Mr.Macmillan, Dr.Nicholson's fellow Missionary on the East Coast of Tanna reports a revival lately among the Tannese. Vigorous meetings, he says, are being held in all directions and many heathen are attending.

My grandparents had left all four children in Ireland; whether they were all together with my great-grandparents I do not know.

It will be seen from a little note "From our First Mission Station," on page 13, that Dr. and Mrs. Nicholson have safely reached the end of their long voyage, and are once again among the natives of West Tanna. There has not been time for a full report, but we expect to hear soon of the glad welcome and the "full speed ahead" that always follows the arrival of the Doctor.

Lenakel, Tanna

15th June, 1915

Just a note to let you know that we arrived safely yesterday evening and found all well.

Lenakel looked splendid, and all was ready for our reception, so that we settled down as if we had been away only for a week or two.

Mr.Christian and the people have kept the Station and buildings in excellent order. I never saw them better. Our people look healthy and well, and the crowds of little children were refreshing to look at. The Tannese are not a dying race. Please remember that. The Gospel has lifted them right up out of the pit and placed their feet on a sure foundation.

Progress has been made, and heathen have been won over since I left.

Tomorrow we take in patients, and the next day begin operating. The Matron and Nilauas have been busy all day.

Since the 10th of April we have been speeding across the world, and travelled in five steamers, and we were quite happy to get on shore yesterday (the 14th June), the more so as in journeying we did not see a more beautiful place than Lenakel.

But all around us are reminders of our children, and one almost expects to hear their footsteps and voices at any moment.

With kindest regards,
Yours sincerely,
J.CAMPBELL NICHOLSON (Jot.90 Oct.1915)

In the Jottings of January 1916, Grandfather gives a more detailed letter of his journey from Ireland to Tanna:

Lenakel, Tanna.

10th July, 1915

You will be glad to hear that we reached Tanna. We were able to make our connections on boat and train so as to arrive here on the day we hoped. We sailed from Liverpool on the 12th of April, and reached San Francisco on the 25th of the month – in spite of a German submarine and a torpedo firing at our vessel. We sailed from San Francisco on the 28th of April, and reached Sydney on the 26th of May, calling en route at Tahiti, Raratonga, and Wellington, New Zealand.

Everywhere we went we heard "Tipperary" sung. Foreigners seemed to regard it as our National Anthem! When we left San Francisco some Maories from the Exposition gathered at the end of the pier and farewelled us with "Tipperary"; at Tahiti French Reservists embarked on our boat and a brass band played as the natives sang and "Tipperary" rose in the air from the throat and gramaphone and piano; and on board ship it was sung and whistled at all times.

Two German cruisers had shelled Papeete, sinking a gun boat and steamer, wrecking houses and riddling corrugated iron roofs. The people fled to the hills, and some remained there for days. But when news came of the Falklands Islands battle, and sinking of the Scharnhorst and Gneisenau, the cruisers which had shelled Papeete, there was great rejoicing. As a native told me, "My word, we glad plenty and everybody sing 'Tipperary'.

We had five and a half days in Sydney for shopping, and I went through to Melbourne to see Mr. Paton.

We left Sydney on the first of June, and got to Vila on the night of the 10th. At Vila we transhipped on to a small steamer, and reached Tanna on the 14th of that month.

From the time we left home we have sailed in five steamers, and travelled three thousand miles by train; whilst I did another thousand miles in the train in Australia.

Our steamer was gathering the Missionaries for Synod, but once we saw Lenakel we wanted no more steamer or travelling.

We had heard in Sydney that there had been a hurricane in the southern part of the Group, and that some houses had been destroyed. But when Lenakel came into view there, to our joy, were the different buildings – Hospital, Mission House, Church, School, and the native village; and the green of the foliage and vegetation showed us that our station had escaped. Lenakel never looked better, and in all our long journey across the world no place appealed to us as did this little island spot.

The Captain very kindly placed the launch at our immediate disposal, and we hurried off at once to the shore. Our people awaited us at the landing, and gave us three rousing cheers of welcome, and there was hand shaking all round. We were delighted with everything, and like children, wanted to see all at once.

Mr. and Mrs.Christian and the natives had the buildings, grounds and everything in splendid order, and we were soon settled down in our home, as if we had been away only a week. Iavis and Lomai looked well, and the crowd of bright looking boys and girls showed that the Tannese are not a dying race. Nalauas had been ill and required an immediate operation, but he had managed to get the Hospital put into readiness for immediate occupation.

Next day we began admitting patients. The Hospital was soon filled and in two weeks we got through seventeen operations! I did two more the next week, but contracted blood poisoning in my left arm which put me out of action.

I have twice visited the East Coast, and the last time saw many patients at White Sands. As they knew of my movements, they had carried and brought sick people to the roadsides. I had heard that many were coming to the Hospital, and to prevent being overcrowded, I rode across to pick out suitable cases.

Next Sunday we are to have Communion and Baptismal services, and if my arm permits, I shall start operating again.

The people are now gathering in for the preparatory services, but of this I shall write later.

During our absence a drought of nine months' duration was experienced and bush fires broke out, but our station escaped.

On the East Coast they had a most unique experience, and one which caused much alarm. One night bits of ice clear as glass fell in a shower. The natives and whites thought stones were falling from the volcanic outbursts, but on going out they were struck with invisible missiles which the natives felt to be red hot. Many shouted that the last day had come, and began to rush about. By the aid of a lamp the ice was seen, and dreaded still more, as it was something completely outside their experience. When handled, they dropped it, say-

ing it was red hot – never having experienced the sensation of extreme cold. At last they were reassured, and now feel themselves more privileged than their fellows on the West Coast who have never had such an experience.'

During the middle of the year, Friday services were held in different villages instead of Lenakel and there is this report in Jottings 91:

"Our first such visit was to Melban. The people here honoured the city of Melbourne by giving their new village its name. It is the best native village I have seen. It is situated about three miles inland on high ground, and commands a wide view of land and ocean. It is built on each side of the new road we cut across to the East Coast. Each side of the road is planted with creamy yellow hibiscus, trimmed to a neat hedge. Every house lot is divided by cross hedges, so that each owner has a little garden surrounding his house. In these are collected and planted a good assortment of crotons and flowering native plants. In addition, they have flowers and roses and lilies from our garden. The roses were splendid. They seem to do better in the high ground than with us. There were some blooms which would have delighted Mr.Watson, and done credit to his firm of Alexander Dickson and Sons, of Belfast.

The houses are neat and good, and best of all, the people are doing splendidly in every way. Amongst their young men I have my most loyal helpers, and they are forward in every good work. Lahwa, the teacher, has made his mark all round, and deserves great credit. Mrs. Nicholson and I drove up, and Mr. and Mrs. Christian rode.

The number of young children is one of the features of the thriving "city", and as they cheered us down the road, their merry voices augered well for the future of the people of this happy Tanna village.

The Hospital work has been easier this month, principally because we ran short of chloroform and ether. The former is always called "gloryform" by the natives, and great is their faith in it. Any skill on the part of the operator comes second to "gloryform". They have no faith in local anaesthetics, even though pain is absent.

I was able to repair the old circulating pump of the motor engine, and it worked so well that last week our mileage totalled about 180 miles. We went one day round the north of Tanna and down the East Coast to Port Resolution, making four calls, and picked up about one and a half tons of native food for the Hospital. The sea on the South Coast was too rough for a heavily laden boat, and so we had to come back north instead of completing the circle of the island.

Our people here have cleared and planted a banana plantation for the Hospital, which, however, will not bear for a year. Certainly the people are showing keen appreciation of the Hospital.

Our schools and services are being well attended. At the school of which Mrs. Nicholson has charge there is an average attendance of eighty young people, and the scholars have, and are, contributing in coconuts for special writing desks, whilst they buy their own books and material; so that they are not "rice" scholars, but young people really keen to learn.

We have the notorious Willie Uvea recruiting on a French Schooner called "the Good Mother"! He is anchored quite close to our passage, but has not got any recruits so far.

With our united regards,
Yours sincerely,
J.CAMPBELL NICHOLSON (Jot.91 January,1916)

September saw my Grandparents and Mr. and Mrs. Christian sailing once more to Aniwa. As Grandfather reports: *'On the morrow the services begin. The ladies being with us makes all the difference. No bother to look after meals – and they are real meals, and not scratch affairs, as they would be if we two men were alone. Mr.Christian is, if anything, is less inventive and worse at cooking than myself, so that only a very hungry person would care to face our spreads when we are alone!'* (Jot.92 Apr.1916). Grandfather was pleased to discover that in his absence they had more or less become self-supporting; having planted coconut trees and with the proceeds purchased two whale boats and barbed wire to fence in their pigs. There was even enough over to contribute £8 towards the widows and orphans of British soldiers killed during the war! Because of improved cleanliness their birthrate had increased, although there was a disparity of too many boys to girls. On Grandfather's advice the length of church services had been reduced and after a week on the island, the last day was declared a holiday with a concert in the evening at which the young men sang in the wonderful way peculiar to Aniwa[1].

On his return to Tanna, Grandfather paid a long overdue visit to the leper settlement in the north of the island. He had promised before he left for furlough that he would have new houses built for them and as there wasn't enough money to pay the natives to build the houses, he promised them that their pay was to be banked in the 'Inasmuch' account.[2] Equipped with his tent and sending the men along with his horse by land, he set off in the launch to arrive at the nearest village to the settlement. I include a piece here from the Jottings which paints a picture of what the scene was like. '*We arranged about the building of the houses, and settled to begin at daybreak. Some natives were to cut down the timber, others were to carry it to the settlement, others to clear the ground and dig the holes for the posts. Women were to prepare the thatch and reeds; and children to get the material for tying (special bark vines) and the leaves of the pandanus. Nature is lavish here in the profusion of material. She supplies almost ready for use the wherewithal to build comfortable houses.*

It was my part to supply the nails, to select the site and to mark out the size and shape of the houses by pegs driven into the ground. I had gone on in front to consult with the lepers, and they pointed out to me a very good site. I then started my helpers to work. They soon cut a new road to the site, as they are afraid to use the lepers' tracks. As if by magic the scrub was cut down and rooted out and the ground cleared as for a garden. The place became like a hive, young men carrying the timber, women the reeds and grass, children bundles of pliant bark and tough vines. Some of the men were digging holes for the posts, others trimming and cutting the timber to size.

Old snider rifles are now put to good use (fulfilling the prophecy of Scripture, Isaiah ii, 4). The barrels had been wrenched from the stocks and the muzzles had been heated and hammered flat to a chisel edge. These formed excellent crowbars for driving into the hard subsoil and breaking it up. Then the holes were scooped out.

Soon in true Tanna fashion the people were urging each other on, and a competition set in as to which house should be finished first. It was most entertaining.

The lepers, frightened by the crowd and noise, had fled; but presently one and another were seen peeping through the bushes. One called to Lomai and asked, "Why is the doctor paying all you people to work like this?" "The doctor is not paying us," Lomai answered. "Who is then?" "No one" "Well, why are you all working – see, even the chiefs are working." Lomai told them afresh of the Lord Jesus, and how we were all trying to show love and kindness to them in obedience to His command. Lomai told our people on our return, "The lepers were amazed and lost in wonder."

By nightfall four good houses were completed and the people will boast of the accomplishment for years to come. These houses are superior to almost all others about, and the building of them will be an education and stimulus for the building of better houses elsewhere in future. I gave the lepers a present of salt, sugar and tea; and at Christmas, or such time as I am able to go up to burn down the old houses, I hope to have, from Mission cases, gifts to gladden their hearts."

I visited all the inland stations in the extreme north, and the natives knowing I was soon to come, had cleared the tracks and made travelling on horseback possible and comfortable. The heathen are all scattered about.

I visited a good many, but one seldom finds more than one or two families at the most in one place. The older men are drinking deeper of kava than formerly, and this is the great obstacle with them all. They are willing to forfeit what they acknowledge to be their best friend in this world, and in the world to come life eternal, just for the fleeting and doubtful pleasure of a few hours of absolute unconsciousness. If it only held the men themselves back it would be bad enough, but, in consequence of the drinking, they keep their women and children from accepting and serving the Lord.

These northern people live at a fairly high altitude, and are hardier than most other Tannese. They have little fever, and, apart from influenza, have had no epidemics in my time. (Jot.92 Apr. 1916)

Chapter XV – The Fourteenth Year

Farewell

As the year opened in Britain, the war machine continued to require more men for the front and again women stepped forward to fill their places, in the factory, on the farm, working as bargees, wherever they were needed. The 'pinch' was being felt everywhere, taxes were being levied on luxury goods and the wealthy were being asked to cut down on their affluent lifestyle. At sea, the battle of Jutland saw the sea awash with nearly 10,000 bodies, and in July, the Battle of the Somme opened with 60,000 casualties in the first few days for the advance of just a few miles. Meanwhile war was raging in East Africa and the Middle East.

In May, Irish rebels took the opportunity of the nation's problems with open rebellion against British Rule, seizing control of the main post office in Dublin. A Naval gunship shelled the rebels' headquarters and all seven rebels were eventually captured and shot. In America, President Wilson advocated peace, and was reluctant to enter the War, although there were many that disapproved. In Britain, the price of bread soared to 10p (approx.4 new pence) a loaf and Lloyd George succeeded Herbert Asquith as Prime Minister. The year closed with the bleak news of stalemate in the trenches, despite the shocking death loss.

At home people brought in the New Year quietly and the Council postponed all elections until the war was over. There was strong feeling at the fact that farmers' sons in the South of Ireland were not joining up; the newspaper considered them slackers saying the women could take over the work so there was no excuse. Paper pulp was at a premium and so newspapers were reduced in size and total prohibition was being advocated in Bangor so more men could enlist. The local paper made grim reading with many local men killed or wounded and the 12th July was not celebrated except for a 5 minute silence in honour of those men of the Ulster Division who fell at Thiepvel. Enterprising Mr.Caproni from his Confetterias, would undertake to make up boxes of biscuits, cigarettes etc. and send them to the men at the front and J.S.Balmers' chemist, were advertising Trench Ointment for destroying vermin. Food was becoming scarce too with the Council renting out their field in Bryansburn Road for allotments so people could grow vegetables.

Grandfather's penultimate report appears in Jottings 95, issued in January 1917 but dated July 1916 which gives an idea how far the natives had come in such a short time:

On Tanna the work continued, both spiritual and physical as Grandfather reported in the Jottings, although six months had elapsed since his last report. I take it this must be due to the lack of steamer sailings that there is such a gap:

He says that the attendance at the Communion Service was very good and that seven elders and thirteen deacons had been ordained. These men would be responsible for the spiritual guidance of the people in his village, for the upkeep of the church and for the day-to-day running of the village in general. Schools had been opened in conjunction with the church as has been mentioned before, but simply learning to read the Scriptures in their own language was no longer enough for the natives, now writing, arithmetic and English were also asked to be taught. Consequently young teachers fresh out of the Training College were preferred to the older men, but this was not always to the good. Grandfather had on one occasion to remove a young teacher at the request of the villagers; this teacher had 'got above himself'. He had successfully opened a school, but instead of lessons lasting an hour in the morning as was normal, they lengthened out until noon! The better students left on board a recruiting schooner and the parents of the boys and girls who normally would have had their help after school in the gardens and plantations, kept them away. The teacher neglected to itinerate amongst the heathen and as he had closed down the school made up for it with lengthy sermons lasting two or three hours, which for the natives, unused to church services and combined with the heat, did more to deter than to encourage. Grandfather had the teacher removed to another village where he continued to teach, but under the supervision of the village elder.

It was becoming more apparent that the natives were beginning to run their own affairs and Grandfather tells of the natives raising the money themselves to pay the teachers salaries.

At the beginning of the Jottings there is this interesting note from the Editor: *'The news in Dr.Nicholson's report of the organised effort that is being made by the Christian natives of Tanna to support their own Teachers, and to plant productive trees, etc., that will ultimately bring in considerable profits for the maintenance of the Hospital, is specially encouraging at this time. The Doctor's statesmanlike policy and encouragement to thrift in his people will we trust bear rich fruit in the near future.*

If men of the stamp of Lomai and Iavis should, in the good Providence of God, be converted from heathenism in all the Islands; and if, as we fervently hope, the Government of the Islands should pass into the hands of a competent single authority, enlightened enough to support these Christian native chiefs and uphold their authority, the outlook would, indeed, be bright with hope.' (Jot.93 July 1916)

The unceasing work of the Mission seems to be beginning to tell with my Grandfather. Normally, despite illness, he tirelessly works on; but here he mentions he is tired which is rare What I have not mentioned, but which will become apparent later, is that on my grandparents last furlough home he had informed the Mission that due to my Grandmother's pernicious malaria, he felt they could not remain in Tanna much longer. By the tone of his writings in the Jottings, he was making everything as orderly as he could before he left.

There is an added note of enterprising endeavour on the part of the missionaries: *"It is interesting to learn that the cultivation of cotton is being tried on Tanna – in the Mission grounds – and on Tangoa Island, in connection with the Native Teachers' Training Institution.*

Sea Island cotton has, we have heard, a high value and it would give an immense impetus to the peaceful development of the New Hebrides if the cultivation of cotton should prove to be a remunerative industry. It is something to the credit of the Missionaries that they are pioneers in this effort." (Jot.93 Oct.1916)

In this issue of the Jottings there is also news of Judah. He had settled back on Malekula after his release from prison and was continuing his good work.

In the same Jottings Grandfather paid his last visit to Aniwa and as was usually the case, so many wanted to go with him that the whale boat was brought into use to tow the extra passengers. The journey over took seven and a half hours owing to a big sea and most got drenched, but a fire was lit and all had soon dried off. He reported that the Aniwans were all in good health and if it wasn't for the disproportion of males to females that their numbers would increase rapidly. The visit went well and after nearly a week there they returned home.

The Editor gives a report on the Mission's views on Grandfather leaving Tanna to join the war effort and also gives Grandfather's last entry before leaving Tanna for the final time:

"The War and Dr.J.Campbell Nicholson.

Countless must be the ties of love and blood and nation that this tragic war has severed. There can be scarcely a home that has escaped and certainly no hamlet or village but has its Roll of Honour. When Churches and Societies are suffering sad blanks in their membership we could hardly expect to escape from our share in the universal sacrifice; and thus it comes about that, in addition to giving up our friend, Dr.Ewen Mackenzie, for temporary service with the Forces, we are now called upon to say good-bye to Dr.J.Campbell Nicholson, who has left Tanna and joined the Australian Forces as Medical Officer.

This severance, unlike Dr.Ewen Mackenzie's, is permanent. After fourteen years of close relationship in the work, it is a sad trial to realise that the Doctor will not again return to Tanna and our hearts go out with deep yearning and sympathy to the people of North West Tanna thus deprived at one bitter stroke of their trusted leader and healer.

To the natives of the Lenakel station the Doctor's withdrawal will come as a stunning blow and indeed all Tanna, dependent upon the Hospital and trusting its Principal, will grieve and sigh over their deprivation. The "Dokotor's" skill has been their call in all sicknesses and distresses; and they have proofs – in number beyond their reckoning – in their midst of the good results of his surgical skill. What a blank will be theirs with no Doctor at hand as the days bring their inevitable toll of sickness and pain. We cannot think of Lenakel now without deep sadness and anxiety.

It is only right, however, to add that the cloud has hung over our horizon for more than two years. When Dr.Nicholson came home on furlough early in 1914 he informed us that the persistent attacks of malarial sickness to which Mrs.Nicholson had been subject to on Tanna had caused him after grave consideration to come to the conclusion that there could be no prospect of his remaining permanently on Tanna.

At the time the outlook was so dark, in view of the war and its drain on qualified medical men for the Army, that we felt there was no prospect of securing a successor. Consequently, we earnestly begged the Doctor to reconsider the matter, and to return to Tanna at least for two years, by which time we hoped that the war would be over and the way open for securing a suitable Medical Missionary for Tanna.

To this proposal – pressed very urgently to him – the Doctor at length agreed, and he and Mrs.Nicholson returned to Tanna early in 1915.

Quite frankly let us admit that we cherished the hope that the period of two years would be extended if perchance the war had not then terminated, but this hope has not been fulfilled.

Dr.Nicholson's qualifications as a surgeon had no doubt been brought to the notice of the Australian Commonwealth, and that they should endeavour to enlist his help for the troops caused us no surprise. All the same, gain to the

Army means real and serious loss to the Mission.

Regrets, however, are of no avail, and it is now for us to face the new situation. Elsewhere we have stated briefly the steps that have been taken to this end.

One detects a note of censure here, almost as if Grandfather is being underhand. Yet how the man must have been torn between love for his wife and family on one hand and duty to his God on the other. It is maybe hard for us today to understand that then their Christian beliefs put duty to God above all else.

DR.NICHOLSON'S FAREWELL

The hurried nature of the Doctor's farewell letter is no doubt due to the suddenness of the call; but that the call was anticipated is shown by the preparations that are revealed therein.

He writes, "Before leaving Lenakel I visited the whole district and the Leper Settlement, and we had a united Communion Service. I had managed to get all the Mission buildings thoroughly repaired and painted, and all the fences and gates put in order. Apart from the motorboat, which sustained some damage through the parting of the chain during a heavy squall, I can say that the Station was in the best order.

The immediate care of the Station will devolve upon Nilaus and Jacob; and the Schools and Church services will be under the charge of Iavis, Lomai and the other Elders. But, of course, the general direction and oversight of the whole work will be in the hands of the Rev.Thomson Macmillan, of East Tanna, for the time being.

It would be unwise to let Mrs. Nicholson remain on the Island through another hot fever season, as she is still troubled with malarial neuritis.

I cannot describe how I felt at giving up the work at Lenakel. It was just as if my life and all service was ended, and I had only to wait for the final call. I do not know how to thank you all for your constant kindness to us in all these years of service.

I am sorry to say that Lomai will never be strong again. He has tuberculosis of the spine. It was hard indeed to say goodbye to him.

Yours sincerely
J.CAMPBELL NICHOLSON"

A new missionary was found for West Tanna, the Rev.Campbell Rae, but due to the war, medical missionaries were scarce and so he was asked to give as much time as possible to medical and surgical study and to gain practical experience at Mission Dispensaries before he embarked for the Islands.

On 3rd December 1916, not long after Grandfather left, Lomai died. There is a tribute to him in the Jottings which I include:

LOMAI OF TANNA

Alas, Tanna has lost a Leader indeed. Lomai, the Chief whose life has so brilliantly testified to the saving grace of the Gospel, has been called to his reward. The story of the uplift of Tanna has, at least for the friends at home, largely crystallised around Lomai's name. Mr.Frank Paton evidently felt that the personality of the Chief permeated the years during which the Tanna Mission was in his book (now out of print), "Lomai of Lenakel".

Iavis and Nilauas, and others, have probably given service equally solid and great, but somehow Lomai has grown to be the outstanding figure of the Mission on West Tanna; and his loss will be felt almost as keenly in the homeland as on Tanna.

The first time we met Lomai, so to speak, twenty years ago, was in reading Mr.Frank Paton's description of "a short thick-set savage of magnificent proportions, with shaggy hair and bushy beard" and yet "with a soft winsome voice and manner"; and ever since the Chief has not ceased to captivate our interest and affection.

Dr.Nicholson's ominous report of Lomai's health gave cause for grave anxiety, but we cherished the hope, for Tanna's sake, that a further period of service might be in accordance with God's will. This, however, was not to be, and our Mission has lost an attraction that it will not be easy to replace.

The following brief article from The Messenger gives details, culled from vari-

ous sources, of the last days of the beloved Chief:

Mr.Ernest Robertson, of Lenakel, writes as follows regarding the sad event: "It is with great regret that I write to tell you of Lomai's death. It occurred on Sunday morning, December 3rd. I saw him in the morning. He knew me, but could only say a few words. Towards the last he had little or no pain, and passed away very quietly. A week previous to his death he gave me a message for his Missi – Mr.Frank Paton. He told me to say that 'though his body was weak, his heart was strong when he thought of what Jesus had saved him from. Tell Mr.Paton,' he said 'I remember what I and all the people were like when he first came and taught us about Jesus, how we were walking on rotten places; but now, through the Gospel, our feet are now on firm rocks. And my heart is full of joy because God has used me to teach the people."

The Rev.Thomas Macmillan adds a note to Mr.Frank Paton as follows:

"You will be very sorry indeed to hear of the death of your old friend and convert, Lomai, on the first Sunday of the month. Poor Lomai. He suffered a lot of pain, though latterly he was free from it, and passed very quietly away. The last thing he did was to exhort Iavis to stand fast in the faith for which they had both contended through many years of darkness.

His death is a great blow to Lenakel, for he was decidedly the best man there. It seemed quite strange not to meet his bright smile when I was over a day or two after his death and many thoughts, especially of the old days when we were on Tanna together, crowded in on me as I stood by the spot where they had lain him. His memory will forever remain with all who knew him. I know how the news will come as a blow to Mrs.Paton and you." (Jot.97 July 1917)

The people from all over Tanna collected £40 for a headstone for Lomai's grave and asked Mr.Robertson to obtain the stone and for Rev. Frank Paton to add the inscription.

Chapter XVI

Service of a Different Kind

1917

1917 brought Britain to the nadir of the War. It was now costing £7 million a day, the losses both at sea and on land were appalling and food was becoming scarce. In March the Czar of Russia abdicated and on April 6th, America entered the War. The Third Battle of Ypres took place in August and due to double the rainfall, it was hard to tell whether there was more danger from the mud than from gunfire, a stray step off the duckboards and a man was sucked to his death. Over 90,000 men were reported missing and 40,000 were never found. From home, entertainers, including opera singers and jugglers, joined the war effort to boost the moral of the soldiers, giving concerts along the front lines and light relief to the 'tommy' who would be back in the trenches the next day.

Northern Ireland also was feeling the pinch; large advertisements appeared in the paper: 'Do you own land? Then till every inch of it that you can manage to till this Spring' and people with land were asked to lend it or rent it to people to grow their own food. The Council received over one hundred applications for allotments, although it was frowned on to work on your allotment on Sundays by some. The Board of Agriculture crusaded against sparrows, but house sparrows only, because they ate grain, encouraging children to rob nests and kill the fledglings: this would cause an outcry today! In April there is mention of grandfather arriving home and of his joining up. August brought grim news from the Front where the Third Battle of Ypres raged. The Ulster Division were involved and took heavy casualties at Languemarck. There were now many homes in Bangor that would not see their loved ones returning and morale at home and at the Front was low. Most of the Spectator is taken up with the war and the consequences of war: the Irish Food Control Board issued cards to householders for the control of sugar which could only be purchased from registered retailers and jam recipes using saxin (like saccharine) were printed in the paper. There is mention of my grandmother helping out at a church sale of work and presumably my grandfather was serving in the army. Christmas came and the Picture Palace Cinema opened on Christmas Day and Boxing Day for 'Top Hole Entertainment' in an effort to take peoples' minds off the war.

Unfortunately no further correspondence regarding my Grandfather's departure from the Islands is available, but I was able to obtain his war records from the Australian National Archives that have detailed information. My Grandparents must have departed from Tanna in October or early November as his records show him joining up on 27th November and departing Sydney 29th December. Whether my Grandmother sailed back with him or embarked for Britain before that, I don't know, but he arrived in Plymouth on 3rd March 1917 and reported that day to 3rd Training Battalion at Tidworth north of Salisbury. Six months later he reported for duty at Hurdcott and May the following year found him in Wimereux just south of Calais attached to the 22nd Corps. His service in the Field didn't last long however, recurring attacks of fever eventually had him invalided home on sick leave in August that year. It wasn't until October that he took up the position of Medical Officer in charge of the Casualty Section in the Australian Munitions Workers Headquarters in London until he was discharged in October 1919.

In March 1919 there is a note in the April Jottings (No.104) that a 'New Hebrides At Home' would be held in Caxton Hall. Chaplain Fred Paton – he was also in the AIF (Australian Imperial Force), Mrs.Ewan Mackenzie whose husband was serving in the forces and my Grandfather all spoke. It says of Grandfather: 'and of Captain Dr.Nicholson what can we say better than that he was Dr.Nicholson – racy, humorous, forceful! How he slapped Lomai in the face when he was about to faint while helping at a serious operation, just illustrates our Doctor. No use for sentiment in the face of an emergency. That is how the work on Tanna won through.'

When the war ended, Grandfather was demobbed and came home to Bangor to open up a practice at 30 Hamilton Road, in Bangor. He was at work in his morning surgery on 28th October 1934 when he was suddenly taken ill and died that evening of a heart seizure. His hard unceasing work had eventually taken its toll: he was 61. His obituary in the local newspaper says this of him: ' A skilled physician, keen on his work and interested in those who sought his ministrations as friends as well as patients, a genial, kindly man whose entry into a house of sickness brought brightness and confidence in its train, Dr.Nicholson will be missed by a wide circle, and by none more than the poor crippled children at the Home of Rest, where he acted in the capacity of honorary visiting physician. He could not see suffering or sickness without being impelled to lend a helping hand and by his death the poor people of the district have lost a kindly and generous friend.' This was taken from a cutting that a Nicholson relative had kept.

An untimely end for a truly remarkable man.

My Grandmother lived for another 25 years, taking much to do with her children and family. John became a GP, despite what his father had predicted! He married Aline Mitchell in 1936 and they had two children, my elder brother, also John and myself. May married and had four children, Eileen married another GP and had three children, Peggy became a nurse and married a consultant and had a child and Sheila, who was born in Ireland after my Grandparents returned from the Islands, had three children. Sadly, my father John, died comparatively young at 53 from tuberculosis, two years before his mother.

One Sunday, while visiting her daughter Sheila, my Grandmother was sitting in her favourite wingback chair after lunch, her grandchildren playing nearby, when one of them came to my aunt and said that Granny was asleep. When Auntie Sheila looked in, thinking that Granny was taking a nap, it was to discover that in fact she had quietly slipped away: she was 79.

I include here a reference from Grandfather's superior officer:

COMMONWEALTH OF AUSTRALIA

Headquarters,
Australian Munitions Workers
84 Cromwell Road
South Kensington, S.W.7

24th October, 1919

It gives me great pleasure to state that Captain J.C.Nicholson was attached to these Headquarters as Medical Officer in charge of the Casualty Section for a period of ten months (1918-1919), and it was with great regret that I parted from him when he was demobilised.

He not only had to do the regular professional work in connection with the Department, but was also responsible for the Medical Records, History Cards, etc. of a large body of men – approximately 5,000 – scattered over many different centres in England and Scotland. I cannot speak too highly of Captain Nicholson's energy and resourcefulness in meeting the many difficulties and special emergencies that arose in connection with his post. He is an enthusiastic worker, and has the very valuable quality, from the point of view of a Staff Officer, that whatever special difficulties arose he instinctively endeavoured to ameliorate them without discussion or adding to other people's worries. I have found him in every way most helpful and efficient.

I feel I should also add as one of his marked characteristics that he always showed much real sympathy for the men in their difficulties, and he was also very skilful and helpful in all negotiations – of which there were many – dealing with claims for compensations caused by sickness or injury to men in the course of their work. I feel I can very confidently recommend him as a most useful member of any administrative staff.

(Sgd.) S.H.E.Barraclough
Colonel,
O. i/c Australian Munitions Workers

Chapter XVII

A Return Visit to Tanna

I returned with my husband to Vanuatu in November, 2005 to see what changes had taken place there since our last visit in 1989, and to view the island and its people that my grandfather loved so much through the perspective of a hundred years.

With the advantage of the Internet, not available the last time, I was able to book a delightful guesthouse in Port Vila, the capital of Vanuatu on the island of Efate. The guesthouse, the Seachange Lodge, is owned by Rick and Wendy Tendys, who have established a beautiful spot on the edge of a lagoon, employing the local people to help them create it. They also give 10% of their profits to help the people of the islands in the north of the archipelago, outside aid being almost non-existent.

After a warm welcome from the Tendys we spent our first evening with old friends whom we had met when we were last in Vanuatu. The following morning we made our way to the John G. Paton Presbyterian Church in Port Vila, which has changed very little. I spoke to Johnny Albert, a pastor there. He was able to explain to me the history of the church since grandfather's time: in 1948 the Presbyterian Church of Vanuatu became independent from the mother church, raising money themselves and training their own ministers, women ministers too. New Zealand, Australia and America still continued to support them with exchange missionaries and practical help with income-generating projects. From 1900s – 50s the Missions ran the schools, then duriing the 60s some schools were handed over to the government, although the church is now in the process of taking some back. Education is compulsory in Vanuatu from the age of 5, fees are chargeable, but there is partial government assistance, although according to Mr.Albert it is getting less. Children being educated in either French or English. At the end of that time, approximately at the age of twelve years, students sit for High School Entrance examinations. These are very competitive and only about 20% gain entrance. Some go to technical college, but the rest return to their villages and subsistence level living. Junior High School lasts 4 years, then another examination for entrance to Senior High School for a further 3 years, again extremely competitive. For those ones lucky enough to receive a scholarship, they will finish their education either at the University of the South Pacific for those speaking English, or to universities in France or New Caledonia for French speaking students. A good education is highly prized but because of the lack of help from the government, parents have to foot the bill, the fees being much greater for High School education. The church runs fee- paying technical colleges and an agricultural college and we got the impression that on Efate anyway, the Presbyterian church is striving towards progression in all things; 'we are now reaping what your grandfather sowed', Mr.Albert said.

Medical care was handed over to the government in the 60s and 70s, but there is no National Health Service and care is limited. The people pay for anything minor including consultations in urban areas, the government taking care of emergencies, including flight costs from the islands. There are few doctors in Vanuatu, but most villages have a nurse. Dental care is basic, although there are clinics in Vila and Santo, normally staffed by dentists from China. Maternity care is rarely sought after. In the villages local women give assistance to those women giving birth, as they have always done. When it comes to those at poverty level, the extended family looks after their own.

Mr.Albert took us to meet Anne Naupa, the Librarian at the Museum in Port Vila which had been opened in 2002. It is a beautiful building, heavily used as a local community centre, with a very good collection of local artefacts and well worth a visit. The library was started in December 2004 and Anne is in the process of collecting any material relating to the Church in Vanuatu, so she was interested in what I was doing and took copies of the photos I had of my grandfather's time in Tanna.

We flew to Tanna a few days later, a bigger plane than before, the journey taking only 35 minutes instead of an hour. Gone was the grass runway of our last visit and in its place a surfaced one with a very smart terminal in place of the grass hut of the last time. The roads hadn't improved however, and it was a twenty minute bumpy ride to Leneai Palms outside Lenakel, our home for the next few days, where we stayed in our own spacious chalet with a verandah looking out to the shore a few hundred yards away. Ron and Anne Harland, who own the resort were extremely helpful to me, contacted the pastor of Lenakel Presbyterian Church for us and we arranged to go the next day to see him. The local chief, Peter Marshall, came with us to see the Pastor, who unfortunately was down at the harbour as an overdue supply ship had just arrived, so Peter showed us the church which with age had fallen into disrepair and was no longer used. They would like to rebuild it or erect a new one, but until all Presbyterians on the island agree, nothing will be done. Both the mission house where my grandparents lived and the hospital have gone, blown down by a hurricane in the 1970s, only the foundations remaining. A new hospital, which was there when we visited Tanna the last time, is further up the hill and run by an Australian doctor who was here for a period of six months, the doctors coming out on a six monthly rota. The hospital at Lenakel is managed by VIVA, a group of doctors from Victoria Island in British Columbia who are paid a small amount from the Vanuatu Health Department and helped by various drug donors; the upkeep is the responsibility of the Ministry of Health. Tanna Rotary Australia and Ausaid are jointly upgrading the Hospital, dispensaries and schools. As the people are so poor, medication and hospital care is free.

On an overcast day we visited the east side of the island, taking a four-wheel drive to do the twenty –odd miles as the roads are regularly washed away by torrential rain and any other vehicle is useless. It was interesting to note that the concrete piece of road which was being built by the UN and Vanuatu Government when we were here last is still in good condition. The lake beside the volcano had gone, having burst its banks in 2002 and flowed into the sea so we proceeded across the dry bed, past Mount Yassur which was quietly grumbling to itself, but letting out the occasional deep-throated roar.

We pressed on to a small mission station on the thickly wooded slopes of Mount Tukosmera. On the way we picked up Chief Jelsen Denny Hoseah, whose district this is, as we were going to trek into the bush to see the Fekar Falls that my grandfather had mentioned in his letters; the Chief was going to guide us. This is a new venture allowing the public in to see the falls and was only agreed to in 2005 by a consensus of local chiefs; the river and falls are sacred to the Tannese, a place of myths and a spirit resting place where trespassing has often been given as the reason for natural disasters and sickness, but tourism is increasing and with it a means of generating income. Yanamillan – named after Reverend McMillan? – presented a dismal sight with the rain pouring down and trees dripping with moisture, as we left the car and started up the hill to the American translator's house. We passed children playing football in the square below, including the translator's two little girls. He and his wife and family live here, a strange life in the back of beyond although they seemed happy enough.

A few days later we met with Chief Peter Marshall again at his village of Isini, or Sydney, where the people made us very welcome. There we met descendents of people that had been my grandfather's friends; grandsons of Iavis and Nilauas, but unfortunately none of Lomai. We visited Lomai's grave and I showed them photographs and read some of the letters. When we returned to Port Vila I spoke with Chief Tom Numake, who was once senior chief on Tanna and grandson of Nilauas, and from him I received the same message as Chief Peter Marshall; that by writing about my grandfather and the island, I have written down part of their history and as the tradition of passing history down by word of mouth is dying out, what I have done is important to them.

Some things haven't changed since my grandparents' time: the beach where the John G.Paton was pulled up out of reach of storm force waves looks just the same as the photograph although the rails and the boathouse have gone. The banyan trees at the crossroads where men would meet and talk are still there with men still meeting and talking. The harbour is relatively new, where periodically a ship arrives with supplies and there are a number of resorts where visitors can stay. These have increased since we were last here and there are now some shops or buildings that sell goods when they are available. Lenakel is not a village around a central square, tight and neat, it is spread out over quite an area, scattered up the hill and along the roads leading out to the countryside. The peoples' homes are still the same, made of pandanus and grass, although some have corrugated iron roofs but I don't think their standard of cleanliness and tidiness would have met my grandfather's high standards! There is the incrongruity of mobile phones and bare feet, earthen floors and regular flights to Port Vila that we may find strange but the Tannese seem to accept it as a normal occurrance. My grandparents would still recognise Lenakel.

There is one thing that all on Tanna have in common, a love of ice-cream. Anne Harland is known locally as Ice-cream Anne as she makes delicious ice-cream and sells it at an acceptable price to anyone who wants it. At the weekends there is a steady stream of takers, grown-ups and children, arriving at Leneai Palms for their Saturday treat. Ron and Anne were able to tell us of Custom Festivals that they had seen, some like the Circumcision Ceremony where the boys are still taken into the bush for a few months to be taught the Custom ways, or Toka which is held every 5 to 10 years to celebrate the end of tribal war, cannibalism and segregation. This is celebrated over a period of three days with much feasting and for the men kava drinking. Dancing takes place; one for women called the Napen Napen which the Harlands told us they had seen, the women dancing all day and all night, another dance for men with one dance where as many as 800 men dance in an ever-decreasing circle, tighter and tighter until they burst out and race in all directions; even the women flee it is so frightening, and finally combined dancing. Grandfather would not have approved. Yet this, the Custom way, seems to sit relatively peaceably side by side with the Christian, sometimes blending, sometimes separate.

It is hard to say how long this, their way of life, will continue, it is a Third World Country and yet I got the impression that this is not an unhappy state of affairs; tourism is coming. They will reap benefits from it in that there will be more employment. The seasons won't change that much and hurricanes will always be with them, so there will be the continuing problem with the roads. Medicine would be the one thing they would need and education because, like it or not, the Western World has arrived on their doorstep.

I feel that my grandfather's principle legacy to the island is peace. There are still squabbles and skirmishes, but serious violence has gone. Healthcare and education are there and the people are managing themselves. I am convinced that my grandfather, in his time in Tanna, made a major contribution to the welfare of the people and the fact that he is still remembered with affection after a hundred years bears this out.

With all my heart, I wish the peoples of Vanuatu a happy and peaceful future.

Notes

Introduction

1. Taken from John G.Paton's Autobiography.
2. In many countries religion and tradition kept women apart and therefore to reach them, it was better to use the services of a female missionary.

Chapter 2

1. It was Frank Paton, the first missionary at Lenakel, who was on the island for six years before my grandfather, who introduced horses to the island from Norfolk Island. By all accounts the natives were terrified and didn't know what to make of them. In one instance, a native who had never seen a horse asked if the horse and rider were one or could be taken apart and another wanted my grandfather to take its hoof off – he thought it was a shoe! An interesting part of one of the Jottings that year, grandfather says, *'But there are other duties besides, though teaching, preaching and medical work are the main things. I have had a turn, for instance, at horse-breaking. First breaking a colt to the saddle and then a mare to the cart. She had not been in it for two years in consequence of a fright and a smash-up. We mended the cart and yoked her in and fought it out. Now a native is constantly carting with her.'*
2. Short form for Christian
3. Grandfather talks about Witchcraft or 'netik' as the natives called it. The ni-Vanuatu had no conception of death or sickness, they believed it was caused by sorcery. If a person became ill or died, the villagers met and picked someone to blame, the Sacred Man then obtained something that that person had touched, or a hair of his head and he was the 'disease maker'. If the person who was ill died, the villagers took revenge on the 'disease maker' even his family and so there was constant tribal warfare. Debts were long remembered too.

Chapter 3

1. I have added a note here about the French/British situation:
   When my Grandparents went to Tanna, the New Hebrides were run jointly in a rather haphazard fashion by the British and the French and towards the end of the 19th Century, the rivalry between the two of them came to a head and a compromise was reached after a bit of sabre-rattling on both sides in 1906. This was known as the Condominium, or as it was nicknamed, the Pandemonium. It was an extraordinary way to run a country, with each section of government run in tandem: two educational systems, two legal etc, including District Agents on each island and even part French, part British street names! Eventually after much unrest and confrontation the New Hebrides (Vanuatu) became independent in 1980. The time that Grandfather was there the Condominium was in existence, the tandem government did little to help the local people, basically because there was little money and the difficulties involved in trying to administer the affairs of more than eighty scattered islands proved extremely difficult and consequently the lives of the inhabitants changed little. The Missions saw to the provision of schools, medical care and basic education through the church. Vanuatu is now an independent member of the Commonwealth. (refers to letter of 3rd March)
2. James Chalmers, born in Ardrishaig in Scotland, went as a missionary with the London Mission Society to Raratonga in the Cook Is. in 1865; natives could not pronounce his name and 'Tamate' was the result. In 1877 he went to New Guinea and like John G.Paton, won the respect of the natives, helping to promote peace amongst the tribes and for the next 24 years lived and worked there. In 1884 New Guinea was annexed by the British. However, in 1901, he sailed with another missionary, Oliver Tompkins, to Aird River Point where the natives were very dangerous. They both went ashore but did not return at the appointed time and the Captain, fearing the worst, informed the Governor; when investigators returned his suspicions were confirmed; they had been cooked and eaten.

3. Beche de Mer, a seaslug found in the Pacific and much valued by the Chinese as a culinary delicacy.
4. The word used to describe the recruitment of natives for the plantations.
5. A colloquial name for the natives working on the plantations; acquired by 'blackbirding'

Chapter 4

1. The root of a shrub that was chewed by young boys and then spat into bowls; water being added before it was drunk by the native men.
2 *'May, 1861, brought with it a sorrowful and tragic event, which fell as the very shadow of doom across our path; I mean the martyrdom of the Gordons of Erromanga. Rev.G.N.Gordon was a native of Prince Edward Island, Nova Scotia, and was born in 1822. He was educated at the Free Church College, Halifax, and placed as Missionary on Erromanga in June 1857. Much troubled and opposed by the Sandalwooders, he had yet acquired the language and was making progress by inroads on Heathenism. A considerable number of young men and women embraced the Christian Faith, lived at the Mission House, and devotedly helped him and his excellent wife in all their work. But the hurricanes and the measles, already referred to, caused great mortality in Erromanga also; and the degraded Traders, who had introduced the plague, in order to save themselves from revenge, stimulated the superstitions of the Heathen and charged the Missionaries there too with causing sickness and all other calamities. The Sandalwooders hated him for fearlessly denouncing the exposing of their hideous atrocities.*

When Mr.Copeland and I placed the Native Teachers at Black Beach, Tanna, we ran across to Erromanga in the John Knox, taking a harmonium to Mrs.Gordon, just come by their order from Sydney. When it was opened out at the Mission House and Mrs.Gordon began playing on it and singing sweet hymns, the native women were in ecstasies. They at once proposed to go off to the bush and cut each a burden of long grass, to thatch the printing office which Mr.Gordon was building in order to print the Scriptures in their own tongue, if only Mrs.Gordon would play to them at night and teach them to sing. those hymns. Next day being Sabbath, we had a delightful session there, about thirty attending Church and listening eagerly. The young men and women, living at the Mission House, were being trained to become Teachers; they were reading a small book in their own language, telling them the story of Joseph; and they worked every day partly for Mrs.Gordon's health, and partly to escape the annoying and contaminating influence of the Sandalwooders on the Christian lives.

On the 20th May,1861, he was still working at the roofing of the printing office, and had sent his lads to bring each a load of the long grass to finish the thatching. Meantime, a party of Erromangans from a district called Bunk-Hill, under a chief named Lovu, had been watching him. They had been to the Mission House inquiring, and they had seen him send away his Christian lads. They then hid in the bush and sent two of their men to the Missionary to ask for calico. On a piece of wood he wrote a note to Mrs.Gordon, to give them two yards each. They asked him to go with them to the Mission House, as they needed medicine for a sick boy, and Lovu their Chief wanted to see him. He tied up in a napkin a meal of food, which had been brought to him but not eaten, and started to go with them. He requested the native Narubulet to go on before, with his companion; but they insisted upon his going in front. In crossing a streamlet, which I visited shortly afterwards, his foot slipped. A blow was aimed at him with a tomahawk which he caught. The other man struck, but his weapon was also caught. One of the tomahawks was then wrenched out of his grasp. Next moment, a blow on the spine laid the dear Missionary low, and a second on the neck almost severed the head from the body. The other Natives then rushed from their ambush and began dancing round him with frantic shoutings. Mrs.Gordon hearing the noise, came out and stood in front of the Mission House, looking in the direction of her husband's working place, and wondering what had happened. Ouben, one of the party, who had run towards the Station the moment that Mr.Gordon fell, now approached her. A merciful clump of trees hid from her eyes all that had occurred, and she said to Ouben, 'what's the cause of the noise?' He replied 'Oh nothing ! Only the boys amusing themselves' Saying 'where are the boys?' she turned round. Ouben slipped stealthily behind her, sank his tomahawk into her back and with another blow almost severed her head'

This was seen by some of the Christian natives and also vouched for by a respectable sandalwooder who saw it from a distance and helped bury the bodies. p.50 J.G.Paton Autobiography.

The horror of what the supply of guns to the natives can do can clearly be seen in grandfather's description of the terrible wounds inflicted and the conflict exacerbated by them: the traders had a lot to answer for.

Chapter 5

1. Mr. Watson was the Hon.Treasurer and Secretary of the John G.Paton Mission Fund and lived in Knock in Belfast.
2. John was Ellen Nicholson's (nee Campbell) brother.
3. The Mrs.Watt grandfather mentions is Rev.Watt's second wife. Rev. Watt served on Tanna for 42 years before retiring.
4. Great-grandfather Nicholson was on the Board of Guardians for the Workhouse in Newtownards.
5. Another name for the flower Impatians

Chapter 6

1. Associated with attitudes of that time namely, prudery and moral strictness.
2. 22 yds.

Chapter 7

1. Brother John was a ship's engineer.
2. Willie was evangelising in Belfast Docks, so it could have referred to that.
3. Nellie had just lost her two children to diptheria.

Chaper 8

1. Alexander and Chapman were missionaries on a tour from Scotland.

2. The Fekar Falls.
3. A main hospital was being built in Vila and it sounds as if grandfather had been asked to go there.
4. Heminger was the musical director with the tour missionaries.
5. Jungle Tribes Mission: the Hannas served in Southern India.

Chapter 9

1. In September the Spectator reported an accident to great grandfather; evidently a piece of metal had struck his eye and it was feared he would lose it. Two weeks later it reported the eye had been removed but great-grandfather said it would not prevent him from putting his name forward at the coming election.

Chapter 10

1. Lizzie was my Grandmother's elder sister.

Chapter 11

1. George, my Grandmother's elder brother.

Chapter 12

1. Mr.Mahaffy, Acting Resident Commissioner
2. Mr.Gillan, missionary at Uripiv, Malekula.
3. Mention is made in Grandfather's July letter that he is anxious about his father and Willie. On reading the Spectator I can see no mention of Great-grandfather on any committee so maybe at 80 plus he has decided to relax a little. There is a report in August that Willie is in Bangor recuperating from pneumonia. His brother John was a ship's engineer and with war imminent, was probably unable to visit Ireland.

Chapter 14

1. The Aniwans imitate musical instruments and natural sounds with their voices, one method being by ululation.
2. 'Inasmuch as ye have done it unto one of the least of these my brethren, ye have done it unto me.' Matthew 25 v.40.

ISBN 141209976-5
9 781412 099769